Public–Private
Partnerships

Public–Private Partnerships

Principles of Policy and Finance

E. R. Yescombe

Yescombe Consulting Ltd
London, UK
www.yescombe.com

AMSTERDAM • BOSTON • HEIDELBERG • LONDON • NEW YORK • OXFORD
PARIS • SAN DIEGO • SAN FRANCISCO • SINGAPORE • SYDNEY • TOKYO
Butterworth-Heinemann is an imprint of Elsevier

Butterworth-Heinemann is an imprint of Elsevier
30 Corporate Drive, Suite 400, Burlington, MA 01803, USA
Linacre House, Jordan Hill, Oxford, OX2 8DP, UK

First edition 2007

British Library Cataloguing in Publication Data
A catalogue record for this book is available from the British Library

Library of Congress Cataloguing in Publication Data
A catalog record for this book is available from the Library of Congress

ISBN: 978-0-7506-8054-7

For information on all Butterworth-Heinemann publications
visit our web site at http://books.elsevier.com

Typeset by Charon Tec Ltd (A Macmillan Company), Chennai, India
www.charontec.com

Printed and bound in Great Britain

07   08   09   10   11   10 9 8 7 6 5 4 3 2 1

Working together to grow
libraries in developing countries

www.elsevier.com | www.bookaid.org | www.sabre.org

ELSEVIER   BOOK AID   Sabre Foundation
                International

Contents

List of Figures   *xi*
List of Tables   *xiii*
Introduction   *xv*

Chapter 1
What are Public–Private Partnerships?   1

§1.1   **Introduction**   1
§1.2   **Public Infrastructure and the Private Sector**   1
§1.3   **Public–Private Partnerships**   2
§1.4   **Development and Structures**   4
§1.5   **PPPs and Public Infrastructure**   11
§1.6   **Types of PPP**   13

Chapter 2
PPPs—For and Against   15

§2.1   **Introduction**   15
§2.2   **New Public Management, Privatisation and PPPs**   16
§2.3   **Budgetary Benefit**   17
§2.4   **Additionality**   17
§2.5   **Financing Cost and Risk Transfer**   18
§2.6   **Risk Transfer and Value for Money**   18
§2.7   **Economies of Scale**   20
§2.8   **Whole-Life Costing and Maintenance**   21
§2.9   **Private-Sector Skills**   21
§2.10 **Public-Sector Reform**   24
§2.11 **Complexity**   26
§2.12 **Flexibility**   26
§2.13 **PPPs and Politics**   27

Chapter 3
PPPs Worldwide   29

§3.1   **Introduction**   **29**
§3.2   **Developing PPP Programmes**   **29**
§3.3   **Legal Framework**   **31**
§3.4   **United Kingdom**   **33**
§3.5   **United States**   **39**
§3.6   **Australia**   **41**
§3.7   **France**   **43**
§3.8   **Korea**   **44**
§3.9   **Spain**   **46**
§3.10 **South Africa**   **47**

Chapter 4
Cash Flow and Investment Analysis   49

§4.1   **Introduction**   **49**
§4.2   **Net Present Value/Discounted Cash Flow**   **49**
§4.3   **Internal Rate of Return**   **51**
§4.4   **Problems with DCF and IRR Calculations**   **52**
§4.5   **Uses in PPPs**   **56**

Chapter 5
The Public-Sector Investment Decision   58

§5.1   **Introduction**   **58**
§5.2   **Economic Justification**   **58**
§5.3   **Value for Money and the Public-Sector Comparator**   **62**
§5.4   **Affordability**   **67**
§5.5   **Balance-Sheet Treatment**   **68**

Chapter 6
Public-Sector Procurement and Contract Management   74

§6.1   **Introduction**   **74**
§6.2   **Project Management**   **75**
§6.3   **Procurement Procedures**   **77**
§6.4   **Other Procurement Issues**   **84**
§6.5   **Due Diligence**   **86**
§6.6   **Contract Management**   **88**
§6.7   **External Advisers**   **91**

Chapter 7
The Private-Sector Investor's Perspective   96

§7.1   Introduction   96
§7.2   The Investment Pool   96
§7.3   The Investment Decision   101
§7.4   Bidding and Project Development   107
§7.5   Joint-Venture Issues   108
§7.6   The Project Company   108
§7.7   External Advisers   111

Chapter 8
Project Finance and PPPs   113

§8.1   Introduction   113
§8.2   Development of Project Finance   114
§8.3   Features of Project Finance   115
§8.4   The Project-Finance Market   116
§8.5   Why Use Project Finance for PPPs?   120

Chapter 9
Private-Sector Financing—Sources and Procedures   124

§9.1   Introduction   124
§9.2   The Rôle of the Financial Adviser   124
§9.3   Commercial Banks   126
§9.4   Bond Issues   135
§9.5   Bank Loans v. Bonds   140
§9.6   Mezzanine Debt   142

Chapter 10
Financial Structuring   143

§10.1   Introduction   143
§10.2   The Financial Model   143
§10.3   Model Inputs and Outputs   145
§10.4   Financing Costs   150
§10.5   Debt Profile   153
§10.6   Cover Ratios   159
§10.7   Relationship between Cover Ratio, Leverage and Equity Return   166
§10.8   Accounting and Taxation Issues   167
§10.9   Recourse to the Sponsors   169

Chapter 11

Financial Hedging   171

§11.1 **Introduction**   171
§11.2 **Interest-Rate Risk**   171
§11.3 **Inflation Issues**   187

Chapter 12

Lenders' Cash-Flow Controls, Security and Enforcement   202

§12.1 **Introduction**   202
§12.2 **Control of Cash Flow**   202
§12.3 **Security**   208
§12.4 **The Rôle of Insurance**   211
§12.5 **Events of Default**   218
§12.6 **Intercreditor issues**   219

Chapter 13

Service-Fee Mechanism   223

§13.1 **Introduction**   223
§13.2 **Contract Scope**   223
§13.3 **Payment Structure**   225
§13.4 **Usage-Based Payments**   229
§13.5 **Availability-Based Payments**   236
§13.6 **Mixed Usage and Availability Payments**   241
§13.7 **Third-Party and Secondary Revenues**   241

Chapter 14

Risk Evaluation and Transfer   242

§14.1 **Introduction**   242
§14.2 **Principles of Risk Transfer**   242
§14.3 **The Risk Matrix**   245
§14.4 **Political Risks**   247
§14.5 **Site Risks**   248
§14.6 **Construction Risks**   253
§14.7 **Completion Risks**   259
§14.8 **Operation-Phase Risks**   263

Chapter 15

Changes in Circumstances and Termination   270

§15.1 **Introduction**   270
§15.2 **Compensation Events**   271

§15.3   **Relief Events**   276
§15.4   **Step-In and Substitution**   277
§15.5   **Early Termination: Default by the Project Company**   279
§15.6   **Optional Termination or Default by the Public Authority**   285
§15.7   **Early Termination: *Force Majeure***   287
§15.8   **Early Termination: Corruption**   288
§15.9   **Termination and Subcontractors**   289
§15.10 **Tax Implications of a Termination-Sum Payment**   289
§15.11 **Final Maturity, Residual-Value Risk and Hand-Back**   289

Chapter 16
Funding Competition, Debt Refinancing and Equity Sale   292

§16.1 **Introduction**   292
§16.2 **Funding Competition**   293
§16.3 **Equity Competition**   296
§16.4 **Debt Refinancing**   297
§16.5 **Equity Sale**   307

Chapter 17
Alternative Models   310

§17.1 **Introduction**   310
§17.2 **Public-Sector Procurement**   311
§17.3 **Post-Construction Take-Out**   312
§17.4 **Public-Sector Debt Funding**   313
§17.5 **Joint-Venture PPPs**   321
§17.6 **Not-for-Profit Structures**   321

Bibliography   *327*
Glossary and Abbreviations   *334*

List of Figures

Figure 1.1   Project Finance for a Power Purchase Agreement (PPA)   7
Figure 1.2   Project finance for a road Concession   9
Figure 1.3   Project finance for a PFI school project   10
Figure 5.1   Decision tree for Eurostat balance-sheet treatment   69

List of Tables

Table 1.1   Public and private provision of infrastructure   12
Table 3.1   International PPP programmes   30
Table 3.2   PFI projects, 1987–2005   36
Table 3.3   PFI projects by government department, 1987–2005   37
Table 3.4   Major U.S. PPP highway projects   40
Table 3.5   Australian PPPs   42
Table 3.6   Korean PPI projects, 1997–2005   45
Table 3.7   Major Korean PPI projects, 2003 Annual Plan   46
Table 4.1   DCF calculation   51
Table 4.2   IRR calculation   52
Table 4.3   NPV and different-sized projects   52
Table 4.4   IRR and negative/positive cash flows   53
Table 4.5   IRR and interim cash flows   54
Table 4.6   IRR and MIRR   55
Table 4.7   IRR and different project lives   56
Table 5.1   PSC calculation   66
Table 5.2   Finance-lease liabilities in U.K. public-sector debt, 2006   73
Table 6.1   Public-sector project-financing advisory mandates, 2005   93
Table 7.1   Project phases and required equity return   103
Table 8.1   Project-finance loans by sectors, 2000–5   116
Table 8.2   Project-finance lending in selected countries, 2000–5   118
Table 8.3   Benefit of leverage on investors' return   120
Table 8.4   Effect of leverage on the Service Fees   122
Table 9.1   Project-finance advisory mandates from bidders, 2005   126
Table 9.2   Major project-finance banks, 2005   127
Table 9.3   Investment-grade ratings   136
Table 9.4   Project-finance bond market by sectors, 2000–5   138
Table 9.5   Project-finance bonds by country, 2005   138
Table 9.6   Bank loans v. bonds   141

Table 10.1   Target and minimum repayments   157
Table 10.2   Effect of ADSCR on loan amount   161
Table 10.3   Cover Ratios—level principal repayments   163
Table 10.4   Cover Ratios—annuity debt service   164
Table 10.5   Relationship between Cover Ratio, leverage and Equity IRR   166
Table 11.1   Effect of interest-rate fluctuations   172
Table 11.2   Interest-rate swap   174
Table 11.3   Calculation of swap-breakage cost   175
Table 11.4   Swap breakage costs over time   175
Table 11.5   Effect of swap credit premium on breakage cost   178
Table 11.6   Bond termination costs   183
Table 11.7   Effect of inflation on project cash flow   189
Table 11.8   Effect of inflation-indexed Service Fees   191
Table 11.9   Effect of over-indexation   193
Table 11.10   Inflation-indexed v. fixed-rate loan   195
Table 11.11   Inflation-indexed loan—breakage costs   197
Table 11.12   Inflation swap   198
Table 14.1   Risk Matrix   246
Table 15.1   AVT Termination Sum calculations   286
Table 16.1   Equity competition   296
Table 16.2   Effect of refinancing   299
Table 16.3   Refinancing-Gain calculation   303
Table 16.4   Equity sale   308
Table 17.1   100% debt financing   323

Dynamic spreadsheets of some of these Tables can be downloaded from www.yescombe.com.

Introduction

Over the last decade or so, private-sector financing through public–private partnerships (PPPs) has become increasingly popular as a way of procuring and maintaining public-sector infrastructure, in sectors such as transportation (roads, bridges, tunnels, railways, ports, airports), social infrastructure (hospitals, schools, prisons, social housing), public utilities (water supply, waste water treatment, waste disposal), government offices and other accommodation, and other specialised services (such as communications networks or defence equipment).

This book reviews the general policy issues which arise for the public sector in considering whether to adopt the PPP procurement route, and the specific application of this policy approach in PPP contracts. The book also offers a systematic and integrated approach to financing PPPs within this public-policy framework. Policy and finance are inextricably entangled in PPPs, so the public sector must develop PPP policies taking account of financing constraints, and be careful to avoid entering into PPP arrangements whose financial implications are misunderstood, or not understood at all, thus undermining the benefit of the PPP. Similarly, the policy background and drivers for public-sector decisions are also often quite unclear to private-sector investors and lenders.

Structuring PPPs is complex because of the need to reconcile the aims of the large number of parties involved—on the private-sector side there are investors, lenders, and companies providing construction and operational services; on the public-sector side there are public authorities creating and implementing PPP policies as well as those actually procuring the PPP, not forgetting the general public who use the facilities that a PPP provides. Most of these parties need to have a basic understanding of policy and finance issues, and how their part of the project is linked to and affected by them.

Reflecting the author's own practical experience while sitting on both the public- and private-sector sides of the table, this book is intended to provide a guide to both general policy principles and the related financing issues that can cause the most difficulty in PPP negotiations. It serves both as a structured introduction for those who are new to the subject, whether in the academic, public-sector, investment, finance or contracting fields, and as an *aide mémoire* for those developing PPP policies and negotiating PPPs. No prior knowledge of PPPs or financing is assumed or required.

The first part of the book puts PPPs in context:

- Chapter 1 defines PPPs and reviews their place in the provision of public infrastructure as a whole.
- Chapter 2 reviews the arguments for and against PPPs, which provides a framework for the more detailed discussions of many of these issues later in the book.
- Chapter 3 surveys the development of and current policies for PPPs in a representative cross-section of countries around the world.

The next part deals with financial analysis, procurement and investment in PPPs, by both public and private sector:

- Chapter 4 provides a basic introduction to cash-flow analysis, which is at the heart of understanding the financial benefits and costs of PPPs for both public- and private-sector parties.
- Chapter 5 reviews how the public sector uses these financial concepts to make the decision to invest in public infrastructure, including PPPs.
- Chapter 6 looks at public-sector procurement and management of PPP projects.
- Chapter 7 looks at investment in PPPs from the point of view of the private sector.

Then the book deals with debt financing for PPP projects:

- Chapter 8 explains project-financing techniques, and why these are used for PPPs.
- Chapter 9 looks at the sources for project finance and procedures for raising this funding.

The next section of the book covers financial structuring for a PPP project:

- Chapter 10 explains how the different elements of the financial jigsaw are fitted together to create a financing plan.
- Chapter 11 deals with the important topic of financial hedging, and the effect of interest-rate movements and inflation on a PPP project and its funding.
- Chapter 12 looks at how lenders control and take security over a PPP project.

Then the effect of this financial structuring on the PPP's detailed contractual terms is considered:

- Chapter 13 reviews the approaches to developing payment mechanisms for PPPs.
- Chapter 14 looks at how risk assessment and transfer is dealt with in a PPP.
- Chapter 15 explains how changes in the original assumptions behind the PPP can be accommodated, as well as dealing with termination.

The final section of the book offers some variations on the themes already discussed:

- Chapter 16 looks at ways of securing a better cost of capital for PPP projects, as well as sharing the benefits of financial 'windfalls' between public and private sectors.
- Chapter 17 reviews various alternative models for PPPs, compared to the 'standard' models considered elsewhere in the book.

The selective Bibliography provides some further background reading, both about aspects of PPPs generally, and specific countries' PPP programmes. Terms used in this book which are mainly peculiar to PPPs or project finance are capitalised and defined in the Glossary, as are other financial terms. Dynamic spreadsheets which were used to construct a number of the tables in the book can be downloaded from www.yescombe.com.

Although this book is entirely self-contained, it can usefully be read in conjunction with the author's *Principles of Project Finance* (Academic Press/Elsevier, 2002), which deals in more detail with some of the topics covered only briefly here, in particular process-plant projects (such as power stations), project-finance loan negotiation, and the use of project finance in emerging markets.

Finally, it might be thought that this book concentrates too much on detailed process rather than broad policy. But in the real world it is all too easy for the potential benefits of a PPP programme to be eroded by failures of detailed implementation. Similarly, the credibility of some academic and political discussion on PPPs is eroded by a lack of understanding of how policy translates into practice. The old aphorism, quoted in *Principles of Project Finance*. 'the devil is in the detail', is equally applicable to the PPP field.

Chapter 1

What are Public–Private Partnerships?

§1.1 INTRODUCTION

This chapter examines the reasons for private involvement in public infrastructure (§1.2), defines what is meant by a PPP (§1.3), and traces their historical development and current structures (§1.4). The place of PPPs in provision of public infrastructure is considered (§1.5), and the main types of PPP are summarised (§1.6).

§1.2 PUBLIC INFRASTRUCTURE AND THE PRIVATE SECTOR

Public infrastructure can be defined as facilities which are necessary for the functioning of the economy and society. These are thus not an end in themselves, but a means of supporting a nation's economic and social activity, and include facilities which are ancillary to these functions, such as public-sector offices or accommodation. Broadly speaking, public infrastructure can be divided into:

- 'economic' infrastructure, such as transportation facilities and utility networks (for water, sewage, electricity, *etc.*), *i.e.* infrastructure considered essential for day-to-day economic activity; and
- 'social' infrastructure such as schools, hospitals, libraries, prisons, *etc.*, *i.e.* infrastructure considered essential for the structure of society.

A distinction can also be made between 'hard' infrastructure, whether economic or social, primarily involving provision of buildings or other physical facilities, and 'soft' infrastructure, involving the provision of services, either for economic infrastructure (*e.g.* street cleaning), or for social infrastructure (*e.g.* education and training, social services).

1

There is probably universal agreement that the state has to play a rôle in the provision of public infrastructure, on the grounds that:

- The private sector cannot take account of 'externalities'—*i.e.* general economic and social benefits—and therefore public-sector intervention is required (*cf.* §5.2.1).
- Without such intervention infrastructure which has to be freely available to all ('public goods') will not be built, especially where this involves networks, such as roads, or services, such as street lighting.
- Competitive provision of infrastructure may not be efficient, and a monopoly provision requires some form of public control.
- Even where competition is possible, the public sector should still provide 'merit goods', *i.e.* those that would otherwise be underprovided (such as schools, as the rich could pay for private schools but the poor would get no education).
- Infrastructure requires a high initial investment on which only a very long-term return can be expected. It may be difficult to raise private capital for this investment without some public-sector support.

It could thus be argued that infrastructure should be provided by the public sector where competitive market pricing would distort behaviour or lead to loss of socio-economic benefits. But history suggests that there are two ways for the state to do this—either by direct provision, or by facilitation of private-sector provision (whether through regulation, tax subsidy or similar incentives, or by contract). As discussed below, the use of private capital to fund economic infrastructure (*e.g.* for transportation) is of long standing. Equally, it was generally only during the 19th and 20th centuries that the state took over responsibility, mainly from religious or private charity, for the provision of much social infrastructure (*e.g.* for schools and hospitals). Indeed it may be said that private provision of a large proportion of public infrastructure was the historical norm until recently, but the definition of 'necessary' public infrastructure has clearly widened over the last couple of centuries. PPPs may therefore be considered a modern way of facilitating private provision to help meet an increased demand for public infrastructure.

§1.3 PUBLIC–PRIVATE PARTNERSHIPS

§1.3.1 MEANING

The term 'public–private partnership' appears to have originated in the United States, initially relating to joint public- and private-sector funding for educational programmes, and then in the 1950s to refer to similar funding for utilities (*cf.* §17.6.2), but came into wider use in the 1960s to refer to public–private joint ventures for urban renewal. It is also used in the United States to refer to publicly-funded provision of social services by non public-sector bodies, often from the voluntary (not-for-profit) sector, as well as public funding of private-sector research and development in fields such as technology. In the international-development field the term is used when referring to joint government, aid agency and private-sector initiatives to combat diseases such as AIDS and malaria, introduce improvements in farming methods, or promote economic development generally. Most of these can be described as 'policy-based' or 'programme-based' PPPs.

However the subject of this book is what may be called 'project-based' or 'contract-based' PPPs, a more recent development. (Although some urban-renewal PPPs are also project-specific, they do not involve the same long-term relationship.) PPPs as defined here have the following key elements:

- a long-term contract (a 'PPP Contract') between a public-sector party and a private-sector party;
- for the design, construction, financing, and operation of public infrastructure (the 'Facility') by the private-sector party;
- with payments over the life of the PPP Contract to the private-sector party for the use of the Facility, made either by the public-sector party or by the general public as users of the Facility; and
- with the Facility remaining in public-sector ownership, or reverting to public-sector ownership at the end of the PPP Contract.

In some cases, a PPP Contract may involve major upgrading of existing infrastructure rather than a 'greenfield' construction. However private-sector acquisition or management of existing public infrastructure without any major new capital investment or upgrading is not considered to be a PPP as defined here. Similarly private-sector provision of soft infrastructure, which involves no significant investment in fixed assets (and hence no need for private-sector financing), falls into the category of 'outsourcing' rather than PPPs, although obviously the boundary is not precise as soft services are often associated with hard infrastructure (cf. §13.2). Nor is a PPP a simple joint-venture investment between the public and private sectors, unless this is also linked to a PPP Contract (cf. §17.5). Also this book does not deal in detail with smaller PPPs, usually at a municipal level, in sectors such as parking garages; this smaller end of the market follows the same general principles, but is obviously less elaborate in contract form and financing (cf. §8.5.3).

The public-sector party to a PPP Contract (the 'Public Authority'—also known by a variety of other terms such as the 'Public Entity', 'Public Party', 'Government Procuring Entity', 'Institution', 'Contracting Authority' or just the 'Authority') may be a central-government department, a state or regional government, a local (municipal) authority, a public agency or any other entity which is public-sector controlled. The private-sector party is normally a special-purpose company (the 'Project Company'—also known as the 'Private Party'), created by private-sector investors specifically to undertake the PPP Contract. It should be noted that the relationship between these two parties is not a partnership in the legal sense, but is contractual, being based on the terms of the PPP Contract. 'Partnership' is largely a political slogan in this context (but cf. §6.6).

§1.3.2 PPP v. Public-Sector Procurement

A PPP is thus an alternative to procurement of the Facility by the public sector ('public-sector procurement'), using funding from tax revenues or public borrowing. In a typical public-sector procurement (known as 'design-bid-build'), the Public Authority sets out the specifications and design of the Facility, calls for bids on the basis of this detailed design, and pays for construction of the Facility by a private-sector contractor. The Public Authority has to fund the full cost of construction, including any cost overruns. Operation and maintenance of the Facility are entirely handled by the Public Authority, and the contractor takes no responsibility for the long-term performance of the Facility after the (relatively short) construction-warranty period has expired.

In a PPP, on the other hand, the Public Authority specifies its requirements in terms of 'outputs', which set out the public services which the Facility is intended to provide, but which do not specify how these are to be provided. It is then left to the private sector to design, finance, build and operate the Facility to meet these long-term output specifications. The Project Company receives payments ('Service Fees') over the life of the PPP Contract (perhaps 25 years on average) on a pre-agreed basis, which are intended to repay the financing costs and give a return to investors. The Service Fees are subject to deductions for failure to meet output specifications, and there is generally no extra allowance for cost overruns which occur during construction or in operation of the Facility.

The result of this PPP approach is that significant risks relating to:

- the costs of design and construction of the Facility, *and*
- market demand for the Facility (usage), *or*
- service provided by the Facility (including its availability for use), *and*
- the Facility's operation and maintenance costs

are transferred from the Public Authority to the Project Company.

§1.3.3 TERMINOLOGY

It should be mentioned that there are a number of alternative names for PPPs:

- Private Participation in Infrastructure (PPI), a term which seems to have been coined by the World Bank, and perhaps expresses more clearly the subject of this book; however it is little used outside the development-financing sector, except for the South Korean PPI programme;
- Private-Sector Participation (PSP), also used in the development-banking sector (however neither PPI or PSP are limited to the definition of PPPs above);
- P3, used in North America;
- Privately-Financed Projects (PFP), used in Australia;
- P-P Partnership (to avoid confusion with PPP meaning 'purchasing power parity', a method of comparing currency exchange rates to reflect the real costs of goods and services in different countries);
- Private Finance Initiative (PFI), a term originating in Britain, and now also used in Japan and Malaysia.

§1.4 DEVELOPMENT AND STRUCTURES

There are a number of different approaches to the introduction of private financing into provision of public services. Concessions have a long history (§1.4.1). Power Purchase

Agreements (§1.4.2), provided the modern contractual and financing framework for PPPs (§1.4.3)—both for Concessions (§1.4.4) and the more recent PFI Model (§1.4.5).

§1.4.1 CONCESSIONS AND FRANCHISES

Although the term PPP is a new one, the concept of using private capital to provide public facilities is very old. In 18th- and early 19th-century Britain groups of local magnates formed turnpike trusts which borrowed money from private investors to repair the roads, and repaid this debt by charging tolls. Most of London's bridges were also financed by similar bridge trusts until the mid-19th century, and similarly in the late 19th century the Brooklyn Bridge in New York was built with private-sector capital. In France, the construction of canals with private-sector capital began in the 17th century.

This type of PPP is known as a Concession: that is, a 'user pays' model in which a private-sector party (the Concessionaire) is allowed to charge the general public Service Fees for using the Facility—for example the payment of a toll for using a bridge, tunnel or road. The toll reimburses the Concessionaire for the cost of building and operating the Facility, which usually reverts to public-sector control at the end of the Concession period. Apart from roads and related facilities, Concessions were used in many countries in the 19th and early 20th centuries to construct facilities such as railways, water supply and waste-water treatment networks.

The rôle of the public sector in Concessions is to establish the framework under which the Concessionaire operates, usually under a general Concession Law or legislation specific to the particular Concession, to choose a Concessionaire, and to regulate the detailed requirements for the construction and operation of the Facility, usually through a Concession Agreement signed between the Public Authority and the Concessionaire.

A further development of Concessions is the Franchise, or to use the less-ambiguous French term, *Affermage*. A Franchise is the right to exploit an already constructed Facility, *i.e.* it is similar to a Concession but without the initial construction phase. The Franchisee (equivalent to a Concessionaire) may make a lump-sum payment to the Public Authority in return for this right. A Franchise is not considered to be a PPP as previously defined, because it does not involve the provision or upgrade of infrastructure, but only its operation. However the contractual and financial basis is similar in some respects (and hence is covered in this book). 'Farming', in its older English meaning (*e.g.* 'tax farming') means the same as the French term but has largely gone out of use in this sense. 'Lease' is also used, but this is misleading given its other meanings. In European Union terminology a Franchise is known as a 'service concession', while a Concession as defined in this book—*i.e.* involving the construction of new infrastructure—is known as a 'works concession'.

Although the use of Concessions for constructing new infrastructure faded away in many countries after the 19th century, as the rôle of the state expanded, Franchises continued to be important, *e.g.* in the French water sector. The disuse of Concessions only began to reverse at the end of the 20th century, as interest started to grow in this and other types of PPP as an alternative funding model, as discussed below. (And similarly Franchises have been revived, *e.g.* in the British rail sector.)

§1.4.2 POWER PURCHASE AGREEMENTS

The Power Purchase Agreement (PPA), developed in the United States in the 1980s, provided the template for modern PPP Contracts. (PPAs and similar process-plant offtake contracts are discussed in detail in Chapter 6 of *Principles of Project Finance.*) PPAs began after the 1978 Private Utility Regulatory Policies Act (PURPA), which encouraged the construction of cogeneration plants, whose electricity could be sold to the regulated power utilities. PPAs arrived in Europe in the early 1990s, with the privatisation of the British electricity industry; this encouraged a separation between private-sector companies involved in power generation and those involved in distribution, and the development of independent power projects to increase competition in power generation. Under a PPA, the investors are paid a 'Tariff' split between:

- an *Availability Charge* (also known as a Capacity Charge) for making their power station available to provide power to the utility: this covers the capital expenditure involved in building the power station and its fixed operating expenditure; and
- a *Usage Charge* (also known as a Variable Charge) for the marginal cost of generating power as and when required by the electricity utility: this mainly covers the cost of the fuel used to generate the electricity (*e.g.* coal or natural gas).

A key aspect of a PPA is therefore that the investors in the Project Company which builds and operates the power station do not take any risk on whether the electricity which it has the capacity to generate is actually needed: that risk remains with the utility, who pays the Availability Charge whether it uses any power or not. The Project Company is, however, responsible for the operating performance of the power station, and if for any reason it is not capable of generating the level of power committed the Availability Charge will be reduced accordingly. Thus these investors do not take usage risk, but only the risk of completing the power station to time and to budget, and thereafter operating or performance risk—unlike a Concessionaire, who is only paid if people use the Facility.

The other vital factor which enabled the PPA contract model to be developed was the financing technique known as 'project finance', which provides the high ratio of long-term debt financing required for such projects. Although such techniques had existed previously in the natural-resources sector, the project-finance structures used to fund PPAs have provided the basis for funding all types of PPPs (*cf.* Chapter 8). An important aspect of project finance is the passing of the risks mentioned above from the Project Company to Subcontractors. Figure 1.1 shows how this risk transfer fits within the main building blocks for a power-generation project. (The arrows show the direction of cash flows.) The main components in the structure are:

- a Project Company, owned by private-sector investors;
- financing for the project's capital costs through shareholder equity and project-finance debt;
- an Engineering, Procurement and Construction ('EPC') Contract, under which the Contractor agrees to deliver a completed and fully-equipped ('turnkey') power station to the required specification, at a fixed price and schedule;
- a fuel-supply contract, under which, say, coal or natural gas is provided to fuel the power station's turbines;

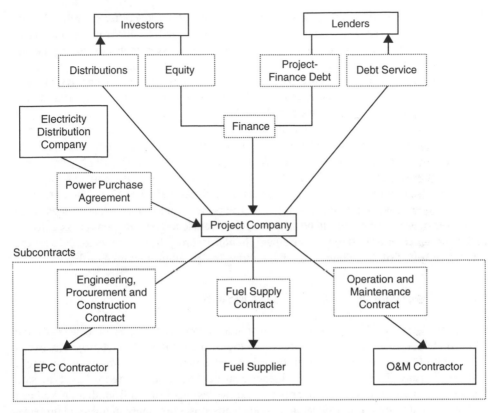

Figure 1.1   Project Finance for a Power Purchase Agreement (PPA)

- an operation and maintenance ('O&M') contract, under which an O&M contractor agrees to operate and maintain the plant on behalf of the Project Company;
- a PPA with an electricity-distribution company, with payments based on Availability and Usage Charges as discussed above;
- surplus cash flow after payment of fuel and operating costs is used, firstly, for payments of loan principal and interest ('debt service') to the lenders, and then to give a return on investment to the investors ('Distributions').

The Subcontractors have thus taken over many of the key risks, *e.g.* as to the outturn capital cost of the power station and its operating costs (other than fuel costs).

§1.4.3   BOO—BOT—BTO—DBFO

The PPA as first developed was a 'Build-Own-Operate' (BOO) contract between private-sector parties, whereby the ownership of the power station remains with its investors, but it soon became apparent that a similar structure could be used for developing public-sector projects. The concept of the 'Build-Operate-Transfer' (BOT) contract was first developed in

Turkey; this was also intended for power generation, but with the key differences that the off-taker (purchaser) of the power would be a Public Authority, the state power utility, and that at the end of the contract ownership of the power station could pass from its investors to the off-taker (usually for a nominal or no cost) and hence to the public sector.

It was but a short step from the BOT Model to the 'Build-Transfer-Operate' (BTO) contract, where ownership is transferred to the Public Authority on completion of construction, and the 'Design-Build-Finance-Operate' (DBFO) contract, under which legal ownership of the Facility remains with the Public Authority throughout the contract, with the private-sector interest in the project being based solely on the contractual rights to operate the Facility and receive revenues from the offtaker for doing so, rather than ownership of physical assets.

In developing countries BOT, BTO and DBFO contracts provided a means for cash-constrained state power utilities to fund investment in more efficient plant, without relinquishing control over either the generation of the power (since the offtaker decides when the power station is to be dispatched, *i.e.* brought into use to generate power), its delivery to the consumer, or its cost to the consumer—in other words, the private sector delivers the service on behalf of the public sector, but entirely under public-sector control.

§1.4.4 PROJECT FINANCE FOR CONCESSIONS

The modern use of project-financing techniques for Concessions, influenced by the BOT model, began with the successful financing of the Channel Tunnel project between Britain and France in 1987 (albeit in the event this was a financially-disastrous project), and the Dartford Bridge (across the Thames estuary) shortly thereafter. It has to be said that neither of these were 'typical' projects, but the lessons learned from them have been widely applied to financing Concessions since then, most commonly in toll-road projects.

Figure 1.2 shows the main contractual and financing building blocks for a road Concession. The resemblance to the 'spider diagram' above for the power project is evident, the most important difference being the source of revenues (from tolls). Here the key elements in the structure are:

- a Project Company, owned by private-sector investors;
- financing for the project's capital costs ('capex') through shareholder equity and project-finance debt;
- a Design & Build, 'D&B' Contract, under which the contractor agrees to design and construct the completed road and related works (*e.g.* toll booths) to the required specification, at a fixed price and schedule;
- an operating contract, under which a toll operation company provides services such as manning the toll booths, minor repairs, accident management, *etc.*
- a maintenance contract, under which a maintenance company provides road-maintenance services;
- a Concession Agreement (a standard name for a this type of PPP Contract) with the Public Authority, which allows the collection of tolls from road users; it does not usually involve any payment by or to the Public Authority (but *cf.* §13.3.5, §13.3.6);
- cash flow after operating costs ('opex'), *i.e.* mainly payments on the operating and maintenance contracts, being used, firstly, for debt service, and then to pay Distributions to the investors.

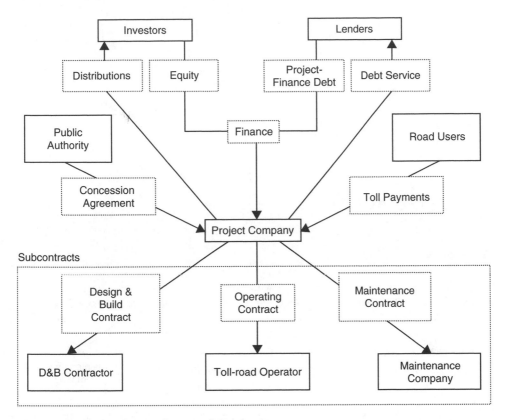

Figure 1.2   Project finance for a road Concession

§1.4.5 THE PFI MODEL

In 1992 the British government announced the Private Finance Initiative (PFI), with the aim of bringing private finance into the provision of public infrastructure (*cf.* §3.4). This really began from the rediscovery of Concessions in the 1980s, mentioned above, and the first wave of projects, in 1994, involved construction and operation of new roads. But since the scope for toll roads in Britain was limited, instead of the 'user pays' principle of a Concession, this PFI Model (as we will term it) introduced the concept of payment by the Public Authority. Initially payments from the Public Authority were still based on usage by drivers, through so-called 'Shadow Tolls', *i.e.* a fixed schedule of payments by the Public Authority per driver/km (*cf.* §13.4.5).

The next stage in the development of the 'full' PFI Model was the use of PFI contracts for the provision of public facilities where usage risk inherently cannot be transferred to the private sector, such as schools and hospitals. In these cases the structure of the contract is still based on the PPA, in that the private-sector investor is paid by the Public Authority for 'Availability', *i.e.* constructing the Facility to the required specification and making it available for the period of the PFI contract, as well as for provision of services such as maintenance, cleaning and catering.

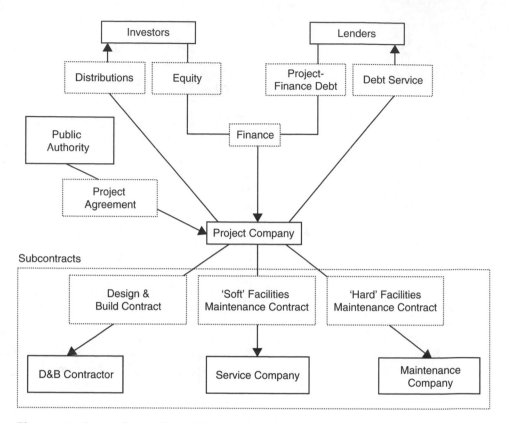

Figure 1.3   Project finance for a PFI school project

Figure 1.3 shows the main building blocks for a school project on the PFI Model. The resemblance to a PPA is evident. Here the key elements in the structure are:

- a Project Company, owned by private-sector investors;
- financing of the project's capex through shareholder equity and project-finance debt;
- a D&B Contract, under which the contractor agrees to construct the school to the required specification, at fixed price and schedule;
- a 'Soft' Facilities Maintenance ('FM') Contract, under which a Service Company provides services such as security, cleaning and catering for the school;
- a 'Hard' FM Contract, under which a maintenance company (or the original D&B contractor) provides building-maintenance services;
- a Project Agreement (a standard name for a PFI-Model contract) with the Public Authority;
- cash flow after opex—mainly payments on the FM Contracts—is used, firstly, for debt service, and then to pay Distributions to the investors.

PPPs today are therefore based on the 'rediscovery' of Concessions and the development of the PFI Model. It should be noted that in some countries only the PFI Model is called a PPP, to distinguish it from a Concession. However in this book, 'PPP' will be used for the general concepts covering both models, and 'PPP Contract' to refer both to a Concession Agreement and a Project Agreement.

§1.5 PPPS AND PUBLIC INFRASTRUCTURE

Table 1.1 provides a summary of the different ways of providing public infrastructure discussed above, and shows how PPPs lie on the spectrum from wholly public-sector projects (and risk) to wholly private-sector projects. It is important to note that:

- Ownership of the Facility has little or nothing to do with which particular PPP model is applied, and hence the Concession or PFI Model can be used whether the contractual basis is DBFO, BTO or BOT (*cf.* §1.6).
- Terminology for the various types of contract is not used consistently, but the most common usage has been followed.
- Table 1.1 does not purport to show all possible structural variations, but does set out the most important models.

The same public infrastructure may be placed at different points on this spectrum in different countries. Water supply and waste-water services show the range of possibilities in this respect:

- public-sector ownership and operation: common in many countries;
- public-sector ownership and private-sector management: this is common in France, for example, in the water sector, where water services are managed under *Affermage* contracts—the Franchisee takes over facilities which are owned by the Public Authority under a long-term management contract (typically for 10–12 years);
- PFI Model: in Turkey and China, for example, BOT/BTO contracts, transferring risk and payment to the public sector (*i.e.* with payments by a Public Authority rather than end-users), have been used for the development of new water-services projects:
- Concessions: these have also become common, especially in developing countries; here the private-sector investors build a new system, collect tariff payments from users (prices may be regulated by the Public Authority or under the Concession Agreement itself), take the demand risk, and have to meet output specifications such as water quality and availability; at the end of the Concession the works revert to the public sector;
- Privatisation (BOO): in England the state-owned water boards have been converted into private-sector regional water companies, which own the water supply and sewage networks; the public-sector involvement is though a Water Services Regulator, which monitors the service provided, fixes maximum costs for water based on a reasonable rate of return on investment, and ensures a degree of competition in water supply; a similar system can be found in Chile.

So can it be said that one type of public infrastructure is inherently more suitable for a PPP than another? There is certainly some public infrastructure which it would be generally agreed cannot be privatised, such as roads, and for which PPPs (in either the Concession or PFI Models) are therefore the only way of bringing in private finance. For other infrastructure such as water there are clearly differing views on whether privatisation or the

Table 1.1

Public and private provision of infrastructure

	Public project →		Public–Private Partnership			→ Private project
Contract Type	Public-sector procurement	Franchise (*Affermage*)	Design-Build Finance-Operate (DBFO)*	Build-Transfer-Operate (BTO)**	Build-Operate-Transfer (BOT)***	Build-Own-Operate (BOO)
Construction	Public sector(2)	Public sector(2)	Private sector	Private sector	Private sector	Private sector
Operation	Public sector(3)	Private sector	Private sector	Private sector	Private sector	Private sector
Ownership(1)	Public sector(4)	Public sector	Public sector	Private sector during construction, then public sector	Private sector during Contract, then public sector	Private sector
Who pays?	Public sector	Users	Public sector or users	Public sector or users	Public sector or users	Private-sector offtaker public sector(5), or users
Who is paid?	n/a	Private sector	Private sector	Private sector	Private sector	Private sector

* Also known as Design-Construct-Manage-Finance (DCMF) or Design-Build-Finance-Maintain (DBFM)

** Also known as Build-Transfer-Lease (BTL), Build-Lease-Operate-Transfer (BLOT) or Build-Lease-Transfer (BLT)

*** Also known as Build-Own-Operate-Transfer (BOOT)

(1) In all cases, ownership may be in the form of a joint venture between the public and private sectors (*cf.* §17.5).

(2) Public sector normally designs the Facility and engages private-sector contractors to carry out construction on its behalf (design-bid-build).

(3) Public sector may enter into service (outsourcing) contracts (for operation and maintenance) with private-sector contractors.

(4) Ownership may be through an independent publicly-owned Project Company, *i.e.* a 'Public-Public Partnership' (*cf.* §17.2.2).

(5) The BOO Contract form applies to PPPs in the minority of cases where ownership of the Facility does not revert to the Public Authority at the end of the PPP Contract (*cf.* §15.11).

PPP approach is appropriate. In other cases, such as building mobile-phone networks, there is little disagreement in most countries that this is best done on the basis of licences to the private sector, *i.e.* on a privatised basis in a competitive market rather than *via* a PPP. There is probably an irreducible core of public-sector activity which has to be provided by the state without any delegation to the private sector—private armies were used in the Middle Ages but are unlikely to be found now (although the private sector may well provide PPP-based accommodation, equipment and services to the armed forces).

§1.6 TYPES OF PPP

PPPs can be classified by the legal nature of private-sector involvement in the Facility, using expressions such as BOT, BTO, DBFO and variants on these as shown in Table 1.1, mainly reflecting the point at which legal ownership of the Facility is transferred from the Project Company to the Public Authority, or, if the Project Company is never the legal owner of the Facility, the nature of its legal interest, such as a property lease or merely a right to operate. Such distinctions are legal technicalities and do not affect the commercial and financial reality that PPP facilities are public-sector assets which cannot normally be sold off to the private sector (*cf.* §15.11).

It is more useful to classify PPPs based on the nature of the service and risk transfer inherent in the PPP Contract. On this basis PPPs can be split into two main categories—usage- and availability-based, the latter being split into three main sub-categories: accommodation, equipment, systems or networks, and process plant.

§1.6.1 USAGE-BASED

As stated above, the Concession Model, with user-paid tolls, fares or usage fees for facilities such as roads, bridges, and tunnels, as well as other transportation facilities such as ports, airports, trams and light rail networks, is the prime example of a PPP where usage risk is transferred to the private sector, and probably still the most widely-applicable type of PPP. But usage risk can also be transferred under the PFI Model, for example through the payment of Shadow Tolls, as also mentioned above; here payment is by the Public Authority, but based on usage of the Facility by drivers. There can also be a mixture of the two approaches, whereby tolls or fares are paid by users, but with public-sector subsidies.

§1.6.2 ACCOMMODATION

Accommodation-based projects are those such as hospitals, schools and prisons, where payment is generally made for making a building available for use by the Public Authority (typically in the social infrastructure field). These are the most important type of project using the PFI Model. They may also involve provision of long-term services such as cleaning, catering, maintenance, or even custodial services in a prison, as well as construction of a building, but this provision of services is secondary in importance to the construction of the building and its Availability to the Public Authority (*cf.* §13.5.2).

§1.6.3 EQUIPMENT, SYSTEMS OR NETWORKS

Equipment, systems or network-based PPPs are less common, and are all based on the PFI Model. Payments by the Public Authority in such cases are also based on a form of Availability. Examples are DBFO road projects where, instead of payment being dependent on usage, it is dependent on the road being available, Availability being judged by measures such as whether any traffic lanes are closed, the speed at which traffic is able to move on the road, the rate at which accidents or spillages are cleared from the road, and so on. Similarly payment for rail projects can be made on the basis of how well the system (*e.g.* signalling or the train sets) works rather than the volume of passengers. Projects can also involve systems like street lighting or IT (information technology), and another important sector is that of defence equipment.

§1.6.4 PROCESS PLANT

The original BOT model for power generation of course falls into this category, but (except in some parts of the Middle East) this is now quite uncommon as a PPP because of widespread privatisation of power generation and distribution. The most important types of PPP-related process plant are water and waste-water treatment plants, and waste incinerators. The key difference between these and other types of projects set out above is that they all involve a clearly-measurable process. As has already been discussed, water projects can be undertaken either under the Concession or the PFI Model, but in either case payments are primarily made for the ability to produce an end-product, treated water or waste water rather than on the actual volume processed or produced. Similarly in a waste-incineration project the Public Authority pays for the availability of a capacity to process waste, and if the plant cannot fulfil this requirement, payments will not be made. The principles in such projects are the same as those set out above for a PPA, but payments based on usage are comparatively less important; hence Availability is again the main criterion.

Chapter 2

PPPs—For and Against

§2.1 INTRODUCTION

Why has there been such a worldwide growth in interest in PPPs over the last few years? The public-sector reform movement known as 'New Public Management' provides the theoretical background for PPPs (§2.2), but in reality the main driver for growth is that PPPs avoid limitations on public-sector budgets (§2.3). However, the detailed debate on the merits and demerits of PPPs is a highly-complex one. A variety of arguments is used by governments for promoting PPP projects, but many of these are of a somewhat *ex-post* nature, *i.e.* they are used to justify a decision which has already been taken for budgetary reasons. These arguments will reappear throughout this book, but it is probably worth summarising the issues in advance. The main elements of the debate revolve around:

- whether PPPs provide 'additionality' of investment in public infrastructure (§2.4);
- the higher financing costs implicit in PPPs (§2.5);
- whether risk transfer and value for money from PPPs can be offset against higher financing costs (§2.6);
- economies of scale (§2.7);
- the benefits of whole-life costing and maintenance (§2.8);
- the value added through the use of private-sector skills (§2.9);
- PPPs as a catalyst for public-sector reform (§2.10);
- complexity (§2.11); and
- the effect of PPPs on public-sector flexibility (§2.12).

Finally the political context of this debate has to be borne in mind (§2.13).

§2.2 NEW PUBLIC MANAGEMENT, PRIVATISATION AND PPPS

PPPs must be seen within the overall context of the public-sector reform movement known as 'New Public Management' (NPM), which encourages:

- decentralisation of government;
- separating responsibility for the purchase of public services from that of their provision;
- output or performance-based measurements for public services (*cf.* §1.3.2);
- contracting-out public services to the private sector;
- privatisation of public services.

All of these increasingly blur the boundary between the public and private sectors. So while the BOT Contract and its variants provided the technical basis in the 1990s for a new generation of PPPs (*cf.* §1.4.3), the theoretical or political basis was provided by NPM.

The privatisation of public services—another British initiative—began under the Thatcher government of the 1980s, and has also spread to many other countries. The main drivers for privatisation were the NPM-based beliefs that there should be a 'roll-back of the state' with the private sector providing services where this is more efficient, especially in the utilities sector, and that the introduction of competition leads to a better service and lower cost for the citizen, as well as less waste of economic resources (especially if services are supplied free or below cost by the state). This reversed the 20th-century trend for public utilities to be provided by the state (whereas before that private-sector capital usually took the initiative, as discussed above). The subsequent British PFI programme (*cf.* §1.4.5) was aimed at extending these benefits of privatisation to core public services which could not be privatised, and the 'value for money' and other arguments discussed below (*cf.* §2.6) very much stem from this NPM way of thinking. However there are important differences between privatisation and PPPs, some of which make it difficult for a PPP to achieve the same results as a privatisation:

- The Public Authority remains directly politically accountable for a PPP-provided service, but not for a privatised service.
- The citizen will usually not be especially conscious that a PPP-based service is being provided by a private-sector company rather than the public sector, whereas this is obvious for privatised services.
- In a PPP ownership of physical assets normally remains with (or reverts to) the public sector, whereas in a privatisation they become permanently private-sector owned.
- A PPP usually involves the provision of a monopoly service, whereas a privatisation usually means the introduction of competition to provide the service.
- In a PPP the scope and cost of services is fixed by a specific contract between the private and public sectors, whereas in a privatisation they are controlled, if at all, by some form of licensing or regulation which allows for regular cost changes, or are simply left to the forces of market competition.

§2.3 BUDGETARY BENEFIT

While NPM has provided a theoretical basis for PPPs, the primary reason for their recent growth is that they do not require public-sector funding today. A PPP allows the capital cost of a public-sector Facility to be spread out over its life, rather than requiring it to be charged immediately against the public budget (*cf.* §5.5). This cost is then either (for the Concession Model) paid for by users instead of paying taxes, or (for the PFI Model) charged to the public-sector budget over the life of the PPP Contract, in either case through the payment of Service Fees. A PPP programme thus enables the public sector to break free of short-term constraints on investment in public infrastructure imposed by insufficient tax revenues and limits on public-sector borrowing. Some of the names given to PPP programmes, such as Britain's 'Private *Finance* Initiative', or the term 'innovative finance' now often used by U.S. government agencies to describe PPPs, confirm the view that PPPs are primarily about private-sector finance for public-sector investment.

This raises the question whether the budgetary constraints on infrastructure investment which create a need to go down the PPP route are appropriate, especially where these constraints are created by artificial rules such as the Maastricht Treaty limitations on budget deficits in the European Union. Using PPPs in such cases causes opponents to describe them as nothing more than 'off-balance sheet borrowing' by governments, even though they do have other merits, as discussed below. There may be an argument for changing the rules for public accounting in such cases rather than distorting the approach.

It should be noted that although PPPs are often referred to (and will be referred to below for convenience) as being 'off-balance sheet' for the public sector, the public sector does not produce a balance sheet in the same way as a private company. This expression simply means that PPPs do not show up as public-sector borrowing, nor does their original capital cost show up as expenditure in the public budget. However, in the case of the PFI Model the Service Fees are a future annual cost, and thus do have an eventual impact on the public-sector budget in much the same way as borrowing. This may eventually worsen the original constraints which led to the adoption of the PPP route in the first place, which is a particular danger where relatively small countries enter into large PFI programmes: the problem has been evident in Portugal (see Bibliography), where payments for a major and rapidly-developed PFI-Model road programme have had a significant effect on the public budget.

§2.4 ADDITIONALITY

If the initial investment in a PPP falls outside the public budget, this enables the public sector to make (or accelerate) investments in infrastructure which would not otherwise have been possible (or would have been delayed until later). Thus the realistic choice, given budgetary constraints, is generally not between a PPP and public-sector procurement of the Facility, but between a PPP and no investment at all. This 'additionality' is a frequently-used argument in favour of a PPP programme—hence government statements such as 'PPPs allow us to invest more quickly in public services', and the consequent political attraction of PPPs.

It is arguable from a macroeconomic point of view that if public investment increases, private investment decreases, and so the net result is the same whether investment is public or private, but there seems to be little evidence that PPPs 'crowd out' private-sector investment elsewhere (although they may affect the construction industry, as discussed below). Similarly, it is generally clear that PPPs are indeed undertaken in addition to other forms of public-sector investment not in substitution for it.

§2.5 FINANCING COST AND RISK TRANSFER

Private-sector finance for a PPP clearly costs more than if the project were procured in the public sector and financed with public-sector borrowing: the cost of capital for a PPP will typically be around 2–3% *p.a.* higher than that of public-sector funding, even for the PFI Model where the payment stream is still derived from the public sector.

Public-sector borrowing is cheaper because lenders to the government are not taking any significant risk with their money, whereas lenders to a PPP are obviously taking a greater risk. But a project's risks do not disappear just because the public sector is funding it—it can thus be argued that these risks are retained by the public sector and constitute a concealed cost of the project, which should be added to the lower cost of public-sector financing to make this comparable with a PPP's financing costs.

There is an alternative view that the public sector is better able to spread out risks than the private sector—hence there is a real difference between public- and private-sector risk assumption, and so the real cost of public-sector funding of a project, even taking account of risk, is actually lower than financing and managing the project by the private sector. But if this view were carried to the extreme, it would mean that the government should finance everything. And it can equally be said that companies in the private sector are owned by many individual shareholders (directly or *via* investment or pension funds) who diversify their risks by owning a wide range of shares. There is therefore not a strong case for suggesting that there are fundamental differences in the abilities of the public and private sectors to absorb risk.

But quantifying the risk transfer to a PPP (or the corresponding risk which would be retained in a public-sector procurement) is difficult, as discussed below, as is the case for other possible benefits from a PPP, also discussed below. The realistic approach is that debate about comparative financing costs assumes there is a free choice between public-sector funding and a PPP, whereas most of the time, given public-budget constraints, no such choice exists and the choice is actually between a PPP and no project. The issue then becomes whether the Facility is being procured cost-effectively as a PPP, irrespective of what might theoretically have been the outcome with public-sector procurement.

§2.6 RISK TRANSFER AND VALUE FOR MONEY

Despite this difficulty of quantification, however, risk transfer remains a key element of the value for money ('VfM') argument in favour of PPPs (*cf.* §5.3)—namely, that the risks which are transferred can be better managed by the private sector, and thus the cost of doing this will be lower than if the risks are retained by the public sector. Hence risk transfer improves VfM. In this context, VfM is not based on just what is initially cheapest, but takes account of the combination of risk transfer, whole-life cost (§2.8) and service provided by the Facility, as a basis for deciding what offers the best value. VfM arguments are of considerable political importance in gathering support for a PPP programme. The risk-transfer element of VfM is also inextricably linked with the fact that projects cannot generally be taken out of the public-sector balance sheet unless risk transfer to the private sector can be demonstrated (*cf.* §5.5).

There is no doubt that PPPs encourage the public sector to identify project risks and think about risk transfer in a way which has not been usual in conventional public-sector procurement. The way in which risk transfer works in PPP Contracts is discussed in detail in Chapter 14 and as will be seen this is a complex process, but in summary, as said above, a PPP transfers the risks of construction and either the market/usage risk or the availability/service delivery risk to the private sector. Each of the main risk categories is discussed briefly below.

§2.6.1 CONSTRUCTION RISK

Procurement of major projects by the public sector can result in large construction-cost overruns (*cf.* §5.2.3), whereas a Public Authority's payments for a PPP are fixed by contract, and therefore such overruns should not (and generally do not) occur. Thus it is clear that construction risks are transferred to the private sector in a PPP.

But the reason for this is not so much the PPP structure itself, as the fact that construction costs are fixed under a turnkey (or 'design-build') contract (*cf.* §14.6.1), in which the Project Company's (through the Construction Subcontractor) also takes design risk, i.e. the risk of any errors or omissions in the design, or other unforeseen work. Turnkey contracts do not completely eliminate the risk of cost overruns or failure to complete the Facility (*cf.* §14.6.3) but do avoid the problem, endemic in public-sector design-bid-build procurement, of initial low bids from contractors being inflated by change orders as the Public Authority develops and changes the design. However a turnkey contract's initial cost is inherently higher than a design-bid-build approach (*cf.* §14.7.1), which leaves room for cost overruns in the latter. Also there can be large increases in PPP-project costs (which may be hidden by a reduction in the scope of the project) between the time that bids are received and the final signing of the PPP Contract (*cf.* §6.3.8)—i.e. cost overruns do occur, but at a different stage in the process.

In any case, turnkey construction contracts can also be used in public-sector procurement to substantially eliminate cost overruns, provided the Public Authority can specify, negotiate and supervise these contracts effectively (*cf.* §17.2). Similarly, the combination of design and build inherent in a PPP Contract should ensure faster completion of construction, as these activities can be partly carried out in parallel instead of in sequence, but again this benefit could be secured by the Public Authority entering into a design-build contract instead of using design-bid-build.

§2.6.2 USAGE RISK

In the Concession Model, usage risk is transferred to the Concessionaire (but it may be underpinned by the Public Authority—*cf.* §13.4.3), and it may also be transferred in the PFI Model, but this may not always be cost-effective if the private sector has to charge heavily for taking on usage risk. In fact the general trend in PFI-Model projects is for usage risk to be retained by the Public Authority (*cf.* §13.4.5).

§2.6.3 AVAILABILITY AND PERFORMANCE RISKS

Although these risks may be transferred to the Project Company, their real level, once the Facility has been built, is often quite low (*cf.* §13.5).

§2.6.4 OPERATION AND MAINTENANCE COSTS

The risks of operating-cost overruns are generally transferred to the Project Company (*cf.* §14.8.5, §14.8.6); as discussed below (§2.8), this 'whole-life' approach to building and maintaining the Facility, which is fundamental to the PPP process, is one of the strongest VfM arguments for PPPs. Again, however, these risks are not always transferred in full (*cf.* §12.4.5, §15.2.5).

§2.6.5 REALITY OF RISK TRANSFER

But how real is any risk transfer? A PPP, by definition, provides an essential public service. If the private-sector investors in the PPP get it wrong they may lose their investment (*cf.* §2.9.7), but they have no obligation to put further money in to rescue the project (*cf.* §8.5.1). If the PPP fails it is quite likely that the Public Authority will incur extra costs to maintain the public service, so risk transfer will fail anyway to this extent.

Moreover, as the Public Authority's main concern is to ensure that the PPP continues to provide the contracted service, the easiest way of achieving this may be to provide extra support for the project rather than terminate the PPP Contract and then try to sort out new arrangements. Such a support process may mean that the Public Authority takes back responsibility for risks which had been transferred to the private-sector investors (*e.g.* traffic flow), thus negating the intended risk-transfer benefit of the PPP. This process has been characterised as 'privatising profits while socialising losses'. However, it would not be correct to suggest that this is what always happens if PPP projects get into trouble, so long as there are good financial incentives for the private-sector side of the table to sort the matter out (*cf.* §15.5).

It might also be argued that a Service-Fee stream which is precisely calculated to give the private sector a projected return on equity, with payments carefully structured to ensure that the net cash flow is not that seriously at risk (*cf.* §13.5), *de facto* is not that far removed from 'cost-plus' pricing. If this is a fair statement, it does suggest that risk transfer is quite limited.

§2.7 ECONOMIES OF SCALE

Because a PPP allows investment in public infrastructure to be accelerated, in some cases a project which might otherwise have been procured by the public sector in smaller parts (*e.g.* a road divided into sections) can be procured as a whole. The economies of scale in construction (*e.g.* because construction contractors do not need to start-up operations for each section separately, or in the use of specialised heavy equipment) should result in a saving in capital cost; also in some cases speeding up construction can avoid construction-cost inflation which might otherwise push up costs over a longer-term construction period.

On the other hand, a large increase in demand for construction works on PPPs can cause problems of capacity in the local construction industry, and so lead to an increase in prices, thus offsetting other benefits which might be derived from the PPP route. Significant increases in construction costs have thus been seen for British schools and hospitals, and Portuguese roads, all sectors where there have been large PPP programmes. Similarly, the size and complexity of PPP projects discourage smaller contractors from bidding, so reducing competition, which may also affect the final cost.

§2.8 WHOLE-LIFE COSTING AND MAINTENANCE

Whole-life costing is perhaps the most important element of the VfM case for PPPs. Because the same investors will be responsible both for the construction of the Facility and for its operation and service delivery, they are incentivised to design it to produce the best 'whole-life' cost—*e.g.* private-sector investors may be prepared to spend more on the initial capital cost if this will result in a greater saving in maintenance costs over the life of the PPP Contract, whereas a typical public-sector procurement approach is to go for the lowest initial capital cost. However, in cases where investment in PPP Contracts is finance-driven rather than contractor-driven, integration of the whole-life design approach may also become weaker (*cf.* §7.2.1, §7.2.3). And the case for 'bundling' construction and long-term services together is weaker in relation to Soft FM services (*cf.* §13.2).

But it is the risk-transfer argument which is more significant here. A PPP transfers the maintenance-cost risk—probably the most difficult to predict (*cf.* §14.8.6)—to the private sector. Having capital at risk ensures that the investor in and lenders to the Project Company cannot easily walk away from this risk (*cf.* §2.9.7).

It can also be said the long-term contractual nature of a PPP forces the public-sector to make provision for maintenance (through the Service Fees), without regard to short-term budget constraints which might otherwise encourage the omission of routine maintenance, and at the same time incentivises the private sector to carry out the maintenance if Service Fees are not paid (or deductions made) when maintenance standards are not met. A PPP Contract thus should ensure that the Facility is maintained to pre-determined standards throughout its life (*cf.* §15.11). However, a Public Authority could enter into a long-term contract covering design, construction and maintenance which could produce the same result (*cf.* §17.2.1).

§2.9 PRIVATE-SECTOR SKILLS

It is also argued that the involvement of the private sector in PPP brings particular benefits which are not available to public-sector procured projects.

§2.9.1 PROJECT SELECTION

Where Service Fees are dependent on demand, and assuming these are not underwritten by the Public Authority in any way (*cf.* §13.4.3), the private sector has an incentive only to back good projects, and avoid 'white elephants'.

However there is a danger that the ability to transfer some types of risks and not others distorts the decision on how to proceed with a project. For example, the risks in constructing and maintaining a new building are typically lower than those in refurbishing and maintaining an old one, so even if the latter approach may offer better VfM it is less likely to be adopted through a PPP, especially as the construction companies which are major bidders for PPP projects will be biased in favour of new building. Similarly, a road which can be funded through tolling may be preferred to an untolled alternative which produces greater economic, environmental or other benefits (*cf.* §3.10), and 'non-compete' provisions in toll road concessions may inhibit the development of the other public-sector roads (*cf.* §3.5).

§2.9.2 PROJECT MANAGEMENT

It is claimed that the private sector has greater expertise in managing complex projects, and hence delivering them on time and on budget, as well as maintaining services thereafter. This may well be the case, given that public-sector management of major projects has a fairly poor record, but PPP projects can be managed by the private sector without private-sector finance as well (*cf.* §17.2.1).

§2.9.3 SINGLE-POINT RESPONSIBILITY

A PPP Contract provides the Public Authority with a single point of responsibility for the construction and operation of the Facility, thus eliminating 'interface' problems, where each contractor blames the other for problems. Again it is possible, however, to produce a structure which could achieve this result without using private-sector financing (*cf.* §17.2.1).

§2.9.4 EFFICIENCY

The proposition here is that the private sector is fundamentally more efficient than the public sector, because the profit motive is the main incentive for efficiency. But there is a problem with this in the PPP context where the private sector is not really paid for being efficient, but for performing what is required under the PPP Contract. By 'fixing' the required level of efficiency through the performance regime of a PPP Contract (*cf.* §13.5), the Public Authority loses the opportunity to make future efficiency savings of its own over the term of the PPP Contract, unless the operating-cost element of the Service Fees is indexed at a rate below that of inflation (*cf.* §11.3.2).

This argument is much stronger when it is used in relation to privatisation of services in a competitive market, rather than in a PPP context where there is no competition once the PPP Contract has been signed, although it does at least illustrate the importance of competition when awarding PPP Contracts (*cf.* §6.3).

And although there may well be scope for improvement on how a Public Authority operates, unless careful quality controls are in place private-sector 'efficiency' may actually consist of no more than employing fewer staff at lower salaries, or other action which lowers the quality of the public service being delivered.

However this argument is not without merit: it is evident that the combination of the PPP Contract deductions and penalties for failure to perform, and controls by investors and lenders over the Project Company, should ensure that management inefficiency and other remediable performance failures are detected and dealt with swiftly, compared to public-sector procurement where such failures are more easily buried.

§2.9.5 INNOVATION

It is also argued that PPPs give private-sector bidders the opportunity to come up with a variety of different solutions, and so give the public sector the benefit of innovatory approaches, whether in design of the Facility or the method of delivering the service. This is linked to a key feature of PPPs, namely that the Public Authority usually specifies outputs rather than inputs when calling for private-sector bids—in other words the Public Authority specifies what is required, *e.g.* in terms of Facilities and service, but not how the service is to be delivered. Thus in a school project, the public sector may specify that the building must contain so many classrooms of such-and-such a size, catering facilities to feed so many pupils, and so on, rather than laying out the detailed design of the school. Service Fees are then only made if output specifications are met (*cf.* §13.5.1, §13.5.2). It is the greater flexibility of output specifications which gives bidders the opportunity to come up with innovatory solutions.

Having said this, many private-sector bidders for PPPs rely heavily on staff who originally worked in the public sector: it is difficult to believe that such staff suddenly become innovative just because they have changed jobs, so if they cannot be innovative in the public sector there is something wrong with the system rather than the people. It can indeed be argued that public-sector officials are not incentivised to innovate if this means taking more risks, but on the other hand it can also be questioned how much room for innovation there really is in many PPPs. A Public Authority which already operates similar Facilities is likely to have the best detailed knowledge of what can (and cannot) be done to make them better. This is an argument for the design of 'standard' PPP projects (such as a school building) to be specified by the Public Authority rather than using output specifications which require individual bidders for the projects to spend time and money drawing up their own designs (*cf.* §13.2). However, some care is needed here; if the Public Authority specifies inputs this may jeopardise the risk transfer—*e.g.* if the Public Authority gets the design wrong it will have to be responsible for this.

Moreover, lenders to PPP projects will generally discourage innovation if this creates additional or unknown risks from their point of view.

§2.9.6 THIRD-PARTY REVENUES

In some types of PPP, the Project Company may be able to generate additional revenues when the Facility is not fully utilised as public-sector infrastructure (*cf.* §13.7). Although the same thing could be done by a Public Authority as owner of the Facility, private-sector management skills may be more effective in this respect. Any such additional revenue may help to reduce the Service Fees and hence improve VfM for the Public Authority.

§2.9.7 CAPITAL AT RISK

Where public services are outsourced (*cf.* §1.5), if private-sector companies do not perform well they will lose the profit from this work, but (generally speaking) that is all. In a PPP the private-sector investors and lenders have capital at risk, and therefore a greater financial incentive to ensure that the service is provided as required. This is perhaps the most important long-term benefit of a PPP, since it underpins the transfer of long-term maintenance risk discussed in §2.8.

§2.9.8 THIRD-PARTY DUE DILIGENCE

The lenders' involvement in PPPs means that a third party (apart from the investors and the Public Authority) will check the project's viability (*cf.* §9.3.4), which can be beneficial to the Public Authority (*cf.* §8.5.2).

§2.9.9 PRINCIPAL-AGENT PROBLEM

In economic theory, there is a principal-agent problem where the agent who controls a business has access to more information than the principal who owns it, and this asymmetry of information can be used to give the agent an unreasonably large share of the benefits of a business. Asymmetry of information may arise in any kind of public procurement, so giving rise to potential excess profits for a private-sector supplier, but the long-term relationship inherent in a PPP gives more time for this asymmetry to develop. For example, the Public Authority may find it difficult to determine if the Project Company's proposed costs of making changes to the specifications of the Facility are reasonable (*cf.* §15.2.2).

§2.10 PUBLIC-SECTOR REFORM

A PPP programme can serve as a catalyst for wider public-sector reform in a number of different ways.

§2.10.1 TRANSPARENCY AND ACCOUNTABILITY

A PPP makes the real cost of the Facility clear—it cannot be cut into pieces and buried in the depths of public accounting. In particular it shows the whole-life cost of the Facility, including operation and maintenance, in a transparent way, and forces the public sector to make choices about how services are to be delivered and paid for. Public-sector accounting does not deal with the cost of public infrastructure in this integrated way. The result of transparency is accountability: as public-sector officials cannot hide the cost of choices, they must justify them, however uncomfortable this is.

In this connection, when comparing the costs of a PPP and public-sector procurement, it is important to ensure that like is being compared with like. Operation and maintenance costs, even in a relatively simple accommodation PPP Contract such as a school, may amount to 30% of the annual Service Fees, and up to 50% for a more complex building such as a hospital. These costs are all bundled together as part of the total cost of the PPP Contract, and it is clearly inappropriate to compare them only with the funding of the initial capital cost for a public-sector procured Facility.

However, although the costs may thus be transparent to the Public Authority, this does not necessarily mean that they are similarly transparent to the general public. Commercial confidentiality tends to be the main reason for this. But if information is not made publicly-available, over-simplified "apples and oranges" comparisons between PPPs and public sector procurement are inevitable (*cf.* §2.13), as are wider criticisms of lack of public accountability.

§2.10.2 PROCUREMENT SKILLS

The PPP process, if properly handled, develops procurement skills in the public sector. This is because public-sector requirements have to be analysed and clearly set out in advance, and once decided cannot easily be changed (at least without a cost which cannot be buried elsewhere). A major factor in the public-sector construction-cost overruns mentioned above is that the Public Authority does not specify what it wants in sufficient detail, or keeps changing its mind about what it wants during the construction phase of the project. While cost overruns are not impossible with a PPP (because the Public Authority will probably retain some construction-related risks—*cf.* §15.2.4), they are certainly less likely. Furthermore, the Public Authority has to think about the long-term service delivery, operation and maintenance of the Facility as part of the overall cost when negotiating a PPP Contract, instead of looking only at its initial capital cost. Lessons in 'joined-up thinking' learned from PPP procurements can be applied by the public sector in a much wider context. Ideally the transparency of PPP procurement would also spill over to public-sector procurement.

On the other hand, although transfers of staff from the public to the private sector are not uncommon, this does seem to take place on a relatively larger scale when a PPP programme is undertaken.

Procurement skills may also be lost because a particular Public Authority may only undertake one or two PPP projects, so once a deal is done the project team is disbanded (*cf.* §6.2). Private-sector companies are obviously able to move their teams from project to project, allowing them to accumulate experience, so creating a greater discrepancy between the public and private sectors in this respect.

§2.10.3 MANAGEMENT

A PPP allows the Public Authority to act as a regulator, and thus concentrate on service planning and performance monitoring instead getting tied up in the day-to-day delivery of the services. However, the loss of day-to-day management control of public facilities raises its own issues since the ultimate responsibility for these services still lies with the Public Authority. The flexibility issues discussed below also affect the Public Authority's ability to manage the delivery of services.

§2.10.4 'CONTESTABILITY'

If a small number of PPPs are undertaken in a particular sector (*e.g.* education), these can serve as a benchmark against which costs and service delivery in respect of the large majority of Facilities still under public-sector control can be compared, leading to improvements in public-sector procurement and service delivery as well. In fact a small number of countries (*e.g.* Norway) have undertaken PPPs primarily to test them against public-sector procurement rather than for budgetary reasons.

§2.11 COMPLEXITY

It is probably already evident to the reader that a PPP adds a substantial layer of extra complexity to the already complex task of procuring a major project. This complexity translates itself into a longer procurement period, which means that part of the additionality advantage discussed above may be eroded, and higher procurement costs, including the costs of specialised legal and financial advisers who would not be required for a public-sector procured project. PPP procurement costs can reach 5–10% of the 'hard' capital cost for a reasonably large project, and do not reduce *pro rata* for smaller projects (*cf.* §7.4). It follows from this that PPPs are not cost-effective for very small projects (unless these can be 'packaged' together). Equally, it is questionable whether PPPs are suitable for very large projects where the addition of extra complexity to the structure may make the project collapse under the weight of its own complications.

The size and complexity of PPPs inevitably limits competition from private-sector bidders, since smaller construction contractors, in particular, will not have the necessary financial resources to sustain the risks of a PPP Contract (*cf.* §14.6.2). This is another factor which will tend to increase construction costs where there is a large PPP programme.

§2.12 FLEXIBILITY

Lack of flexibility during the relatively short-term construction phase of a project has considerable merit, if, as discussed above, it ensures that the Public Authority cannot keep changing its mind about what it wants. But there are longer-term issues resulting from a Public Authority entering into a commitment which may extend for 20–30 years of operation. A PPP Contract is of a type known in legal theory as an 'incomplete contract'—*i.e.* the contract cannot provide for all possible eventualities in the future. The longer and more complex the contract the more this is the case, and therefore the more it is impossible for the Public Authority to abdicate or transfer responsibility for dealing with unforeseeable circumstances.

For, example, it is very difficult for the public sector to predict the usage requirement for some types of Facility over a long period of time—*e.g.* population changes may make a school or hospital redundant, or alternatively require it to be expanded. Similarly, there may be a change in technology which requires a significant part of the Facility to be replaced. PPP Contracts do not accommodate such events easily, and major amendment to or cancellation of a PPP Contract part-way through its life is inevitably expensive. There is a direct relationship between flexibility and VfM, albeit one that is difficult to quantify financially, and this needs to be taken into account in considering the whole-life costing of the Facility.

It follows from this that projects with a stable long-term planning horizon, such as roads or other transport facilities, fit well with the PPP approach, although even here there can be problems—*e.g.* non-compete provisions of a toll-road Concession may prevent the Public Authority from undertaking other road improvements (*cf.* §3.5). Conversely, those projects where the Public Authority cannot clearly specify and stick to its long-term requirements, or where technology is changing rapidly, are not suitable for PPPs. It was for the latter reason, *inter alia*, that the United Kingdom abandoned the use of PPPs for IT projects. (Other reasons were problems in achieving enough risk transfer to the private sector, a different cost structure—low initial costs and high continuing costs—making finance difficult, and the high failure rates for such projects.) Social infrastructure projects fall somewhere between these two positions.

However, it must be remembered that if the public sector builds a Facility, this too represents a long-term commitment, albeit buried in government accounting. If such a Facility becomes a 'stranded asset' (*i.e.* no longer viable for the purpose for which it was originally designed), it still cannot be knocked down or moved without considerable loss. It could therefore be argued that all a PPP does is make this issue transparent—but there are issues of flexibility which are peculiar to a PPP, in particular the cost of making major changes to the Facility when there is effectively a monopoly supplier in place (*cf.* §15.2.2), and the extra financial costs of terminating the PPP Contract if the Facility is no longer required (*cf.* §15.6).

§2.13 PPPS AND POLITICS

Given the public-service nature of PPPs, it is inevitable that they are subject to heavy political debate. Unless there is a strong political will on the public-sector side of the table, and the ability to communicate the case for pursuing PPPs clearly and fairly, political winds can easily blow the process off course and a PPP programme will struggle for success.

One aspect of this debate is that despite being clearly different (*cf.* §2.2), PPPs may still be regarded as a form of privatisation, which gives rise to various reasons for political opposition:

'**Private profit at the public's expense'.** It may be claimed that PPPs give private-sector investors the opportunity to make profits by providing services which could be provided by the public sector more cost-effectively. But many of the individual elements of a PPP structure, such as construction of the Facility, would have been provided by the private sector anyway. The marginal extra profit which the private sector makes from investing in a PPP project, as compared to the profits on direct public-sector procurement, is probably not great enough to sustain this argument. In any case, if the public sector does not have the budget capacity to undertake the project, this argument is based, like that of comparing costs of public- and private-sector procurement, on the false premise that there is a choice between public-sector procurement and a PPP.

However, if private-sector investors are perceived to be making 'windfall' profits, for example through high initial rates of return on investment (*cf.* §7.3.2), debt refinancing (*cf.* §16.2) or sale of their equity shareholdings (*cf.* §16.5), this certainly does weaken a PPP programme from the political point of view.

Poor operating standards. It may be argued that a Facility operated by a private company will 'sacrifice safety for profit'. But a PPP is under close supervision by the Public Authority, and safety standards should be clearly laid down in the PPP Contract: in this respect a Public Authority probably has more ability to control and supervise safety than with a privatised company.

Erosion of working conditions. It may also be claimed that a PPP erodes the working conditions of public-sector workers in cases where this work—*e.g.* in cleaning and catering—is taken over as part of the PPP. This is the one aspect of a PPP where the position is the same as that of a privatisation—in both cases public-sector workers may be taken over by a private company, and it is up to the Public Authority to ensure that private-sector investors in a PPP are not incentivised to treat the workforce unfairly, *e.g.* by concentrating on 'efficiency gains' which are only obtained by cutting the pay and numbers of staff.

Political opposition to PPPs is often quite misconceived. For example, specifications (*e.g.* the number of beds in a hospital) are a matter for the Public Authority to decide when procuring the PPP Contract, but those opposed to PPPs may claim that private investors have made such decisions. PPPs may also be disadvantaged by their greater transparency (*cf.* §2.10.1), so the costs of a PPP, including long-term operation may be wrongly compared to the initial capital cost for public-sector procurement only. Similarly the greater transparency of PPPs means that mistakes are more obvious.

On the other hand, the case made by a Public Authority for a PPP can be equally one-sided, *e.g.* with claims of large cost savings compared to public-sector procurement which cannot be proved objectively (*cf.* §5.3), or which do not compare like with like, and PPPs may be promoted for short-term political advantage.

It can thus be difficult to maintain a balanced debate on the pros and cons of a PPP programme, especially, as this chapter has made clear, because the arguments for and against PPPs are by no means black and white.

Chapter 3

PPPs Worldwide

§3.1 INTRODUCTION

As so many countries are now developing PPP programmes it would be impossible to survey worldwide activity in PPPs in detail within the scope of this book, but this chapter considers some of the general requirements for developing a PPP programme (§3.2), and its legal framework (§3.3), as well as reviewing PPP activity in a representative selection of countries:

- United Kingdom (§3.4);
- United States (§3.5);
- Australia (§3.6);
- France (§3.7);
- Korea (§3.8);
- Spain (§3.9);
- South Africa (§3.10).

An idea of international activity in PPPs can be gleaned from the (incomplete) statistics in Table 3.1 for private-sector debt raised for PPPs in countries whose programmes are currently the most active. These figures are not consistent with others in this chapter and Table 8.2, as they are derived from different databases (*cf.* the discussion in §8.4 of the problems in trying to assemble comparable international statistics in this field).

§3.2 DEVELOPING PPP PROGRAMMES

A fairly similar pattern can be seen in the way in which PPP programmes are developed in different countries. These generally begin with toll-road Concessions (or tolled road bridges or tunnels): the concept is a familiar one to most users, even if it is new to the

Table 3.1
International PPP programmes

	2003		2004		2005	
	No. PPPs	Value	No. PPPs	Value	No. PPPs	Value
United Kingdom	59	14,694	86	13,419	62	10,723
Spain	8	3,275	7	2,778	10	7,092
Italy	3	714	2	1,269	8	4,504
United States	2	927	3	2,202	5	3,304
S. Korea	3	3,010	9	9,745	4	3,179
Canada	n/a	n/a	3	746	5	3,157
Australia	4	611	9	4,648	9	2,221
France	0	0	0	0	3	1,208
Japan	5	274	15	1,473	11	675
Portugal	n/a	n/a	2	1,575	3	481
Hungary	1	251	2	1,521	n/a	n/a

Source: Dealogic (values in US$ millions)

country concerned, and the 'self-financing' nature of such projects (at least from the public-budget point of view) makes them immediately attractive. But the scope for toll projects tends to be limited, and many countries have moved or are moving to the next stage, by using the PFI Model for social infrastructure. The PPP programme then becomes much more diverse, and tends to require closer management, *e.g.* through central government PPP Units, PPP laws or standardised forms of PPP Contract, as discussed below.

The characteristics of a successful PPP programme can be summed up as:

- political will (*cf.* §2.13);
- an adequate legal framework (*cf.* §3.3);
- Facilities with significant initial capex and long-term maintenance requirements, to ensure a 'whole-life' approach is taken (*cf.* §2.8);
- projects of a suitable size, to ensure that procurement costs are not disproportionate (*cf.* §7.4);
- Facilities with clearly-definable service requirements and a stable long-term use, given the inherent lack of flexibility in a PPP Contract (*cf.* §2.12);
- a consistent and predictable flow of projects, making it worthwhile for the private sector to build up the technical, investment and financing capacities required (*cf.* §9.3.1); and
- adequate public-sector institutional capacity, both to handle the PPP programme as a whole, and to deal with individual projects.

As to the latter point, an important building block in PPP programmes is the creation of a specialised PPP Unit, usually within the National Treasury or Ministry of Finance, which provides a centre of expertise and technical support to government ministries and other Public Authorities developing PPPs. Because a much wider range of skills is required for PPPs compared to those used in direct public-sector procurement, and these skills are typically in short supply in the public sector (*cf.* §6.2), it makes sense to create a central pool. A PPP Unit therefore needs to have specialists from different areas (finance, law, engineering, planning, public policy, *etc.*), preferably with a mixture of experience in both public and private sectors. Its functions can include:

- developing the legal framework (§3.3);
- publishing guidance materials;
- training;
- developing initial pilot projects to test PPP models;
- providing continuing technical advice and support on specific projects;
- communicating lessons from *ex-ante* and *ex-post* project evaluation;
- ensuring a consistent strategy and policy approach by the public sector as a whole;
- coordinating the PPP programme and thus avoiding 'bunching' of too many projects approaching the markets at the same time; and
- coordinating public-sector 'buying power' to obtain the best terms.

It is important that the PPP Unit has a strong mandate to develop and control policy, which cuts across divisions between different branches of the public sector, and short reporting lines to senior government ministers.

In general PPP Units complement rather than substitute for the Public Authority's external professional advisers (*cf.* §6.7). However there are alternative models: in Ireland the National Development Finance Agency (NDFA) was created in 2003 (in addition to a PPP Unit in the Department of Finance which covers the scope of work set out above). One of NDFA's specific rôles is to be the exclusive financial adviser to Public Authorities (although some of this work is subcontracted to external advisers). The rationale for this is again to centralise and retain expertise within the public sector.

§3.3 LEGAL FRAMEWORK

Concessions always require a specific law relating to the project, or a 'framework' law relating to Concessions in general, to allow a private-sector company to charge and collect revenues from users for providing a public-sector service. In some countries, especially common-law countries (*i.e.* those whose legal system originates from the English common law) PFI-Model PPPs are treated as a variety of government procurement, for which no special legal arrangements are needed; in others, primarily civil-law countries (*i.e.* those whose legal system originates from the French *Code Civile*) specific PPP laws may be needed to provide a framework for this type of contract, in a similar way to Concession laws. (Civil law countries also often have separate legal frameworks and courts for public administrative law, which includes PPPs.) Thus it was necessary for France, for example, to pass a specific PPP Law to overcome legal obstacles to PFI-Model PPPs, such as:

- the requirement to conduct separate tenders for construction and long-term operation and maintenance works, rather then combining them as in a PPP;
- prohibition of deferred payments for public works (on the grounds that this was an obligation against future budgets which legally have to be agreed on an annual basis, and cannot be committed in advance);

- limitations on transfer of control of public-sector infrastructure;
- lenders' security requirements (*cf.* §12.3).

A number of countries have passed or substantially amended PPP laws (especially relating to the PFI Model) in recent years—these include Italy in 2002, Belgium (Flanders), Portugal and Spain in 2003, Brazil (at both federal and state level) and France in 2004, and Greece, South Korea, Poland and Russia in 2005. Various U.S. states have also passed or amended legislation on highway Concessions. There are clear benefits in framework legislation, whether for Concession- or PFI-Model PPPs. It provides an opportunity for the government:

- to confirm its political commitment through explicit legislation;
- to set out the rôles of the different arms of government, including control and approval of individual PPP projects;
- to provide clarity on procurement procedures;
- to set out the basis on which a Public Authority may provide support for various project risks, *e.g.* revenue guarantees;
- to provide a procedure for the Public Authority to make changes in the project's specifications, and a method of compensating the Project Company for resulting extra costs;
- to provide clarity on investors' rights if the PPP Contract is terminated early, whether because of default by the Project Company or because the Public Authority want to take the Facility back under public-sector control (*cf.* §15.5–§15.8);
- to give lenders the ability to take security over the PPP Contract (which the law might not otherwise allow), as well as 'Step-In' rights (*cf.* §15.4.2);
- if appropriate, to allow for provision of investment incentives such as special tax treatment, *etc.*

On the other hand, the contractual approach used in common-law countries has the advantage of greater flexibility to make changes in the PPP programme in the light of experience, and since many aspects of a PPP Contract are common to all projects, much can also be achieved by standardisation of PPP Contract clauses based on this experience, such as those relating to:

- requirement to complete the Facility to the agreed specification by a certain date (*cf.* §13.3.4);
- ability of the Public Authority to monitor design and construction (*cf.* §6.6.1, §6.6.3);
- obligations of the Public Authority in relation to construction (*cf.* §15.2.4);
- provisions for the Public Authority to vary the specification (*cf.* §15.2.3);
- restrictions on changes in ownership of the Project Company (*cf.* §7.2.3), or in the terms of the debt financing (*cf.* §16.4.3);
- provisions for insurance, and application of insurance proceeds to reinstatement of the Facility (*cf.* §12.4);
- provisions for the Public Authority to intervene and take over running of the Facility in case of emergency (*cf.* §15.4.1);
- long-term maintenance obligations, including provisions for return of the Facility to the Public Authority at the end of the PPP Contract (*cf.* §15.11);
- provisions for early termination of the PPP Contract, including compensation payments to the Project Company (*cf.* §15.5–§15.10).

The end result of contract standardisation may therefore be quite similar to framework legislation, and again this is beneficial in creating greater certainty for bidders and lenders, and speeding up the procurement process.

Some aspects of PPP Contracts are much more specific to the type of contract (*e.g.* Concession or PFI Model, and if the latter, the nature of the risk transfer) and the sector in which the Project Company is operating (the requirements for a road are quite different from those for a school). Thus little more than general outline legislation or a contract standard form can be drawn up for sector-specific matters such as the Service-Fee mechanism, including service requirements (*cf.* Chapter 13). However, if the pipeline of PPP projects is long enough, it is useful to draw up sector-specific contract standard forms covering such matters.

§3.4 UNITED KINGDOM

The theoretical background to the introduction of PFI in the United Kingdom has already been discussed (*cf.* §2.2). The history, growth and some current policy issues in PFI are considered below.

§3.4.1 HISTORY

In the 1980s British public policy strongly discouraged the use of private financing of public infrastructure, on the grounds that this would relax the constraint the government wanted to exercise over the public-sector budget as a whole. Private finance was largely ruled out by the 1981 'Ryrie Rules' (named after a senior Treasury official; the Rules originally applied to state companies, but were revised to deal with other public-sector investment in 1988). These required that private finance could only be used in place of public spending, not in addition to it, and also that it had to be demonstrated that there would be additional benefits from private financing which justified its higher financing cost. But it became evident that there was a need for some relaxation of this policy since these constraints meant that vital investment in public infrastructure was not taking place.

The 'substitution' part of the Ryrie Rules was abolished in 1989, and the 'Private Finance Initiative' (PFI) was launched in 1992. The PFI's purpose was to build on the private-sector financings for public infrastructure which had already taken place over the previous few years, in particular those for the Channel Tunnel between England and France (signed in 1987), the Dartford Bridge over the River Thames (also signed in 1987), and the second Severn Bridge between England and Wales (signed in 1990), all of which were Concessions. The original emphasis was on developing similar 'self-financing' projects, but there was little further development in this respect.

In 1993 a Private Finance Panel, consisting of public- and private-sector members and seconded staff, was formed to stimulate new ideas for the use of private finance for the public sector, and in 1994 all Public Authorities were required to consider whether private financing was feasible for capital projects ('universal testing'). Major government departments such as Transport, Health and Education also set up Private Finance Units (PFUs) to coordinate sector-specific expertise and project development. As a result, there were a number of further transportation projects, and the first social infrastructure projects began to be developed, all of which used the new PFI Model of payments by the Public Authority rather than through user-paid tolls (*cf.* §1.4.5).

A change of government in 1997 resulted in a restructuring of the approach to PFI, and a much more rapid development of the programme. (Rather confusingly, since then the government has used the term PPPs not only for PFI projects, but also for the introduction of private-sector ownership into state-owned businesses, *i.e.* privatisation, and for what is known as the 'Wider Markets Initiative', *i.e.* other partnership arrangements where private-sector expertise and finance are used to develop the commercial potential of government assets where these are not being used to their full capacity. Some PPP projects as defined in this book also fall outside the PFI programme, as discussed below.)

In 1997 the Treasury (Ministry of Finance) took over direct control of the PFI programme, and a Treasury Taskforce (of both public officials and private-sector staff seconded from banks, legal firms, *etc.*) was created to implement detailed procedures and guidelines, as well as working on a number of specific 'pathfinder' projects. Guidance Notes were published by the Taskforce on subjects such as accounting (*cf.* §5.5), the Public-Sector Comparator (*cf.* §5.3) and appointment of advisers (*cf.* §6.7).

The most important publication of the Treasury Taskforce was *Standardisation of PFI Contracts*, which was the first detailed policy statement of the requirements for PFI-Model PPP Contracts (it is also relevant to Concessions in some respects). This document (known as 'SoPC') has gone through two revisions (the latest in 2004—see the Bibliography for details), and a series of extra guidance notes has been added to it; it reflects market practice, as well some quite extensive negotiation with private-sector bodies representing investors, bankers and contractors. SoPC has also changed from the original broad guidance with illustrative draft legal clauses to a very specific form of PPP Contract which the public sector as a whole is obliged to follow (although individual government departments have drawn up their own sector-specific versions of SoPC). There is no doubt that SoPC—which has subsequently been used as the basis for standard PPP Contracts in a number of other countries—has been effective in helping to process the large number of individual PPP projects undertaken under the PFI programme. However, it has also become increasingly complex (*e.g.* the section on insurance was 12 pages long in 1999; a revision published in 2005 is 47 pages long)—this has led to criticism of excessive technical 'tinkering' with SoPC. Despite this standardisation, the procurement time for PFI projects remains quite slow compared to some other countries with PPP programmes (although one reason for this is the cumbersome planning process in Britain, a problem which is not specific to PPP projects).

The Treasury Taskforce was originally intended to have a limited (two-year) life, but the benefit of a permanent 'centre of expertise' to provide support to the public sector as a whole became clear. Therefore in 2000 its activities were transferred to a separate company, Partnerships UK plc (PUK). PUK is itself a PPP with both private- (51%) and public-sector (49%) shareholders, and provides technical support to the Treasury on policy issues and project-specific support to Public Authorities, as well as being involved in other non-PFI areas such as the Wider Markets Initiative. PUK only provides 'institutional support' to the public sector, and does not compete with private-sector financial or other external advisers (*cf.* §6.7). Departmental PFUs also continue to play an important rôle, as does the Public-Private Partnerships Programme (4Ps), another (wholly public-sector) centre of expertise which provides support for PPPs in the local-government sector.

At the same time as PUK took over from the Treasury Task Force in providing technical support for PFI, responsibility for PFI policy passed to a new and separate arm of the Treasury, the Office for Government Commerce (OGC), on the grounds that PFI was just another method of public-sector procurement, for which OGC was given overall responsibility. However it became clear that the political background to the PFI programme made it inappropriate for OGC to deal with PFI policy, and responsibility for this was therefore transferred back to a PFU in the Treasury in 2003. Subsequently a somewhat overlapping structure has developed, with the Treasury PFU covering policy but also sometimes dealing with technical (or *quasi*-policy) issues directly rather than *via* PUK.

The concept of a centre of expertise on PPPs for the benefit of the public sector as whole has been widely used elsewhere in the world, as discussed above, but this centre has usually been a public-sector body, rather than partly privatised as in Britain. Suggestions have been made that PUK has a conflict of interest since it has private-sector shareholders but is only supposed to act on behalf of the public sector. The argument for separation and semi-privatisation of the centre of expertise is that this may make it easier to recruit staff from a private-sector background. If the centre of expertise is staffed only by public officials it is evident that this expertise will be limited by a lack of private-sector experience, especially in investment and financing. Temporary secondment of staff from the private to the public sector is a quite common way of dealing with this problem, but this is obviously not a substitute for a permanent *cadre* of experts.

§3.4.2 GROWTH OF THE PFI PROGRAMME

Table 3.2 sets out a summary of PFI projects since 1987 (the British government has backdated PFI to 1987 for this purpose, but excluded the Channel Tunnel), listing separately the projects with a capital value of more than £100 million. As can be seen, a total of 725 projects have been signed, with a total capital value of £47.5 billion (as of mid-2006 some 500 of these were in operation). The PFI programme is thus remarkable for both volume and numbers of projects. Although some very major projects rather distort the figures, especially those relating to London Underground (see the note below Table 3.2), the large number of smaller projects is also notable.

Table 3.3 sets out the same figures arranged by sector. The PFI programme began primarily with transportation-related projects, but while these remain important, the social infrastructure areas of hospitals and education, as well as defence-related projects, now form the other main legs of PFI, with social infrastructure producing the largest number of individual projects. (Typically schools projects are on a 'group' basis, involving the construction or refurbishment of a number of schools for the same Public Authority, which means that the numbers of individual school projects are much higher than the sector total of 144). The large number of individual projects of a comparatively small average size is a notable characteristic of the PFI programme. Other countries which have large PPP programmes, such as Spain and Korea, have larger average project sizes, and hence fewer individual projects.

Table 3.2
PFI projects, 1987–2005

Year signed	No.	Value (million)	Of which: over £100 million
1987	1	£180	Dartford River Crossing (180)—N.B.: does not include the Channel Tunnel (4,900, but the outcome was around double this figure)
1988			
1989			
1990	2	£336	Second Severn Crossing (331)
1991	2	£6	
1992	5	£519	M6 Toll Road (485)—N.B.: did not begin construction until 2002
1993	1	£2	
1994	2	£11	
1995	11	£667	London Underground Northern Line Trains (409); Birmingham Metro (145)
1996	38	£1,699	A1(M) Road (128); A1-M1 Link (214); Docklands Light Railway—Lewisham Extension (202); Croydon Tramlink (205); Northern Ireland Road Services (139)—N.B.: does not include Channel Tunnel Rail Link (5,200)
1997	59	£2,474	Manchester Metrolink (160); King's College Hospital (142); Ministry of Defence helicopter training (114); Armed Forces Personnel Administration Agency (264)
1998	86	£2,769	London Underground power supply (134) and ticketing (160); hospitals in Norwich (158), Bromley (188), Lanarkshire (100), and Edinburgh (180); Dept. of Employment—IT (217); Inland Revenue offices (164); Attack Helicopter Training (165); A55 road (100)
1999	87	£2,538	Guildford waste management (103); London Underground radio network (468); hospitals in Swindon (100) and South Tees (122); Almond Valley waste water (100)
2000	105	£3,898	A13 Thames Gateway (411); Nottingham light rail (172); University College Hospital (422); Glasgow schools (225); GCHQ (330); Ministry of Defence Main Building (345); Treasury Building (141)
2001	86	£2,237	Dudley Hospital (137); Inland Revenue/Customs & Excise offices (220)
2002	71	£7,733	East London waste (102); London Underground—Jubilee, Northern & Piccadilly lines (5,484); Coventry Hospital (379); Home Office offices (197); Ministry of Defence Strategic Sealift (175)
2003	57	£14,872	Customs & Excise IT (156); East Sussex waste (145); London Underground—Bakerloo, Central & Victoria lines (4,597) & sub-surface lines (6,180); A1 Darrington—Dishforth (245); Docklands Light Railway—City Airport extension (165); hospitals in Blackburn (104) South

(Continued)

Table 3.2

(*Continued*)

Year signed	No.	Value (million)	Of which: over £100 million
2004	74	£4,021	Derbyshire (312) and Oxford (134); Northern Ireland primary schools (104); Ministry of Defence water & waste water (154); Skynet satellites (1,079) Ministry of Defence water & waste water—2nd phase (174); Portsmouth highway maintenance (121); hospitals in Barking (238) Leeds (265) and Manchester (512); Colchester army garrison (533)
2005	51	£3,567	National Roads Telecommunications Services (237); Docklands Light Railway—Woolwich extension (177); schools in Nottingham (131), Northampton (192), North Lanarkshire (138) and Renfrewshire (110); hospitals in Newcastle (238) Nottinghamshire (326) and Portsmouth (193); Oxford Radcliffe Hospital—cancer centre (123); Leeds public housing (113); Ministry of Defence 'C' vehicles (114)
Total	**725**	**£47,561**	

NB:* The figures for the cost of the 2002–3 London Underground projects take into account long-term investment over many years, much of which is not priced (costs will be fixed by an independent arbritrator), or funded: for example the 2002 project is shown above as having a capital value of £5.5 billion, but the amount of debt raised for the project was only £2 billion. Hence these figures are really not comparable with the others in Table 3.1, and rather distort the overall picture.

Source: HM Treasury—*PFI Signed Projects List*

Table 3.3

PFI projects by government department, 1987–2005

Government department	No.	Capital value (million)	
		Total	Average
Transport	51	£21,956	£431
Health	149	£6,572	£44
Defence	55	£4,570	£83
Education	144	£4,112	£29
Scotland (regional government)*	91	£2,745	£30
Work & Pensions	11	£1,341	£122
Other (below £1,000 million per department)	243	£6,355	£26
Total	**747**	**£47,561**	**£64**

* Mainly for education, health and transport projects.

Source: As for Table 3.2

A large proportion of PFI projects are in fact carried out by local authorities (municipalities, counties, *etc.*), but most of the funding for Service Fees is provided by central government. This funding is known as 'PFI Credits', and normally covers most of the capital-cost element of the Service Fees, leaving local authorities to fund the opex element from their normal revenues (on the grounds that they would have to fund these costs anyway even without new Facilities). Hence the central government controls the PFI programme, which is why projects are listed in Table 3.3 by central-government department. This high level of centralisation differs from the PPP programmes of some of the other countries discussed below, and has probably been a major factor in PFI's rapid expansion in the social infrastructure field.

However, rather confusingly, PPPs undertaken by local authorities using their normal revenues rather than relying on PFI Credits, *e.g.* in the waste-processing sector, are not counted as PFI projects and therefore do not appear in these figures. Technically speaking such projects are not subject to direct Treasury control as PFI projects are, which is a weakness as they may not benefit from central-government expertise.

Another notable feature of the British PFI programme is that the earliest projects used the Concession Model but this has now entirely disappeared. All PPP projects in recent years have used the PFI Model, and even in these cases transfer of usage risk has also largely disappeared—*i.e.* virtually all PPP Contracts are Availability-based. This differs from most of the other countries discussed in this chapter, where Concessions form a significant part, often the largest part, of the PPP programme. This is partly a consequence of the difficulty of creating new toll roads in Britain, where there is little space for road-building, and partly the result of the much wider use of PPPs for social infrastructure, where usage-based payments are difficult to apply.

While many public services have thus now come within the scope of PFI, the British Treasury has also restricted its use in some cases in the light of experience—PPPs for smaller Facilities (below £20 million of capex) and for IT projects (*cf.* §2.12) are now discouraged. Similarly, the inclusion of ancillary services (such as cleaning, catering or security) within the scope of a PPP Contract is now also discouraged (*cf.* §13.2).

§3.4.3 CURRENT POLICY

The British government maintains the position that PFI projects are not about removing Facilities from the public budget (*cf.* §2.3), but are only undertaken if there is a VfM case for doing so, and in fact approximately half of the cumulative PFI programme (*i.e.* around £23 billion) is (or will be) on the public-sector balance sheet. However, this figure includes some large projects which have ended up on the public-sector balance sheet where that does not seem to have been the original intention, in particular the £16 billion London Underground projects of 2002–3, where a high level of political controversy made lenders nervous, with the result that 95% of the debt had to be guaranteed by the public sector at a fairly late stage in the procurement process. Nevertheless while the picture on balance-sheet treatment of older projects remains somewhat confused, and further changes in treatment seem likely (*cf.* §5.5.4), new investment in PFI projects is still carried out on the assumption of off-balance sheet treatment.

PFI projects make up about 10–15% of public-sector investment, but heavily concentrated in certain sectors: *e.g.* few new schools or hospitals have been built outside the PFI programme. Given public-expenditure constraints, it is highly unlikely that most of the projects built under PFI would have been built otherwise. Taking this into account, the benefits of PFI, especially in social infrastructure, seem to be clear, although there are issues of long-term concern, *e.g.* on contract flexibility (*cf.* §2.12). The British government remains firmly committed to PFI as a method of procuring public infrastructure: as of mid 2006 there were some 200 PFI projects at various stages in the pipeline, with a capital value of some £26 billion.

§3.5 UNITED STATES

In general the private sector has always played a relatively larger part in the provision of public infrastructure in the United States than in most other countries. Utilities, for example, have been mainly developed by the private sector, without the nationalisation which took place elsewhere in the 20th century (*cf.* §1.4.1). The largest current PPP sector is water and waste water, with 15% of municipal systems being provided in this way. The private-prison sector has also grown substantially since the 1980s. Much of this consists of Franchises, whereby a Public Authority hands over operation of existing prisons to one of several specialised correctional-services companies. However, correctional-services companies also build prisons using their own resources and negotiate contracts to take prisoners on an *ad hoc* basis either with the local county or other state or federal entities, or even with entities outside the state. The argument for private prisons is focused heavily on cost-saving rather than public budgetary restrictions, but there are accusations that this cost-saving is only achieved by paying staff less or employing fewer people.

However, it has been in the transportation sector that PPPs have recently taken a higher profile. Early development of U.S. roads relied heavily on private-sector financing, and turnpike (toll) roads were common throughout the 19th century. Construction of public-sector funded toll roads and bridges was also common in the first half of the 20th century, but the use of tolls was largely superseded by direct public-sector funding with the development of the federal-funded Interstate highway system from the late 1950s. Federal funding typically provides around 80% of the cost, but the projects are carried out by individual states, which have to find the balance of the funding. Unlike most countries, in the United States public-sector funding for highways has generally come from dedicated fuel and vehicle taxes, and tolls were expressly forbidden on federal-funded roads (although they were allowed on bridges and tunnels). State funding has also come from public bond issues, which are usually tax-exempt (*i.e.* interest is not taxable) and are issued either by the state, specific Public Authorities, or publicly-controlled projects. (It is worth noting that tax-exempt bonds gave public-sector funding of infrastructure a substantial further financing-cost advantage over private-sector funding, for which tax-exempt bonds generally could not be issued, and was thus a significant factor in the slow development of the latter.) However, the growth in federal tax revenues has not kept pace with the growth in demand for highways, and as a result, from the early 1990s, various methods of private-sector involvement in highway construction were explored, especially in Virginia and California.

The federal funding framework began to change with the Intermodal Surface Transportation Act of 1991 ('ISTEA'), which allowed federal funding to be used for non-Interstate toll roads, in conjunction with state or private-sector funding. In 1995 the National Highway System Designation Act ('NHS') allowed for the creation of State Infrastructure Banks (*cf.* §17.4.2), which can leverage federal funding, *inter alia* for privately-financed projects. In 1998 the Transportation Infrastructure Finance and Innovation Act ('TIFIA') specifically encouraged the use of private-sector financing for major (US$100 million-plus) transportation projects, offering direct federal loans and guarantees covering up to 33% of project costs. The 2005 Safe, Accountable, Flexible, Efficient Transportation Equity Act: A Legacy for Users (SAFETEA-LU):

- allowed for tolling of interstate highways to fund repairs or construction of new roads;
- reduced the project size limit to US$50 million;
- allowed up to US$15 billion of tax-exempt private activity bonds ('PABs') to be issued for financing PPP projects.

Major PPP highway projects completed to date are set out in Table 3.4, from which it can be seen that despite a plethora of federal and state legislation encouraging 'innovative finance', development has been slow. (It should be noted, however, that the use of D&B Contracts for public-sector procurement of highways has grown considerably—this is included within the Federal Highway Administration's own definition of PPPs.) The first modern PPP toll-road project, the Dulles Greenway in Virginia, ran into financial problems when traffic was well below forecasts, and a major financial restructuring of the project was necessary. Similar early traffic problems were seen with Virginia's next project, the Pocahontas Parkway, and with South Carolina's Southern Connector. Reasons for this included resistance to payment of tolls, and the fact that these highways were partly built in anticipation of new economic development which did not take place as expected. California's first project, SR-91, was built to relieve congestion and was successful but had to be repurchased by the Public Authority when limitations in the Concession on competing

Table 3.4

Major U.S. PPP highway projects

Project	State	Public Authority	Start	Opened	Project cost (US$ million)
State Route 91[†]	CA	Caltrans *et al.*	1993	1995	126
State Route 125	CA	Caltrans *et al.*	2000	2007	722
Route 3 North[††]	MA	Mass. Highways	1999	2006	385
Southern Connector[††]	SC	S. Carolina DOT	1998	2001	217
Dulles Greenway*	VA	Virginia DOT	1993	1995	338
I-895 Pocahontas Parkway[††]	VA	Virginia DOT	1998	2002	377

All the above projects are toll highways except for Route 3 North, where the State makes lease payments.
[†] Concession repurchased by Public Authority, 2002.
[††] Owned by not-for-profit corporations (*cf.* §17.6.2); Pocahontas Parkway sold to private-sector investors, 2006.
* Substantial financial reconstruction in 1999; in 2005 refinanced again, concession extended in return for construction of further lanes and connectors, and sold to new investors.

roads proved too restrictive (*cf.* §2.9.1, §14.8.2). The first major private-sector project under TIFIA, California's SR-125, ran into severe delays in construction because of planning issues.

However the market was transformed from 2004 onwards by the 'sale' of fixed-term Franchises (*cf.* §1.4.1) in 'brownfield' toll roads, *i.e.* toll roads had already been built, and were in public-sector ownership. Buyers get a Franchise to operate the road and collect revenues for a fixed term, and the price paid by private-sector investors is thus the present value of these future revenues (less opex). Such sales are not PPPs as defined in this book, because they do not involve investment in significant new infrastructure (although there are continuing maintenance obligations); the purpose of the sale is to generate funds for the general public-sector budget. In terms of ownership, contracting and financial structure, however, the position is the same as for a newly-completed PPP Facility. The first such Franchise sale was that of the Chicago Skyway by the City of Chicago for US$1.8 billion (a price well over the original expectation) in 2004. The Dulles Greenway was sold to new investors (who will fund some major upgrades) in 2005, as was the Pocahontas Parkway (still facing traffic problems) in 2006, and Indiana Toll Road was franchised for US$3.8 billion in 2006. Much larger Franchise sales, such as the Illinois Tollway, said to be worth US$15 billion, have also been contemplated.

This activity has generated interest in major new 'greenfield' Concession toll-road projects: *e.g.* in 2006 Oregon signed a development agreement with private-sector investors on three toll-road projects (the investors become the state's preferred partner, and will expend some US$20 million of development financing, which they will recoup if the projects proceed), and Florida was working on several toll roads, the largest being the 110-mile Heartland Parkway, estimated to cost US$3 billion. Concessions are likely to form a large proportion of the Trans-Texas Corridor, a new road and rail network estimated to cost up to US$180 billion, and potentially the world's largest PPP programme; in 2005 the state signed a development agreement with private-sector investors relating to TTC-35, covering some 600 miles from Dallas/Fort Worth to the Mexican border, and in 2006 agreement was reached to build the state's first privately-financed highway, SH-130 near Austin, at a cost of $1.3 billion.

§3.6 AUSTRALIA

As a federal country like the United States, Australia's PPP projects are primarily run by the states rather than the Commonwealth (albeit with some central funding). This activity has been mainly concentrated in two states, New South Wales and Victoria, and in terms of volume is primarily based on toll roads, but Victoria has also developed PFI-Model social-infrastructure projects which are likely to become a model for other parts of the country. Table 3.5 summarises Australian PPPs up to 2005.

Although Sydney Harbour Bridge (opened 1932) was funded with tolls as a public-sector project, tolls were not widely used in Australia until private-sector toll-road projects began with the Sydney Harbour Tunnel in 1988. Early toll-road projects transferred little traffic risk to the private sector, and in fact the M4 and M5 motorways were subsequently converted from Concessions to usage-based PFI-Model projects, to the benefit of the original investors. (This is a not-uncommon course of events with Concession roads, caused by the Public Authority having to integrate the road with the rest of the network, especially in urban motorways.) Later toll roads have transferred traffic risk more fully to the private

Table 3.5
Australian PPPs

State/Sector	Project	Year	Cost*
Commonwealth			
Defence	Defence HQ	2006	300
New South Wales			
Education	Axiom Education	2002	100
Health	Hawkesbury Hospital	1996	47
Justice	Long Bay	2006	130
Leisure, *etc.*	Stadium Australia (Telstra Stadium)	1996	513
Leisure, *etc.*	Sydney SuperDome	1997	190
Rail	Sydney Airport Rail Link (stations)	1996	200
Road	Sydney Harbour Tunnel	1986	750
Road	M4 Motorway	1988	246
Road	M5 Motorway	1991	295
Road	M2 Motorway	1994	552
Road	M1–Eastern Distributor	2000	700
Road	M7 Westlink (Western Sydney Orbital)	2002	1,500
Road	Cross City Tunnel	2002	680
Road	Lane Cove Tunnel	2003	1,100
Water	Prospect Water Filtration Plant	1993	264
Water	Macarthur Water Treatment Plant	1995	124
	Total New South Wales		**7,391**
Queensland			
Education	Brisbane Southbank Institute	2005	250
Rail	Brisbane Airport Rail Link	1998	223
South Australia			
Water	Riverland water (10 Water Filtration Plants)	1999	115
Water	Victor Harbour	2004	20
Victoria			
Emergency services	Mobile Data Network	2003	140
Emergency services	Emergency Alerting System	2004	100
Emergency services	Metropolitan Mobile Radio	2004	120
Health	Casey Community Hospital	2004	90
Health	Royal Women's Hospital	2005	364
Justice	Victoria County Court	2002	140
Leisure, *etc.*	Docklands Film and Television Studios	2002	70
Leisure, *etc.*	Royal Melbourne Showgrounds	2004	146
Prison	Victorian Correctional Facilities	2004	275
Rail	Southern Cross Station	2000	700
Road	Melbourne CityLink	1996	1,780
Road	Eastlink (Mitcham-Frankston Freeway)	2004	2,600
Water	Echuca/Rochester Wastewater Treatment	2004	40
	Total Victoria		**6,565**
	Total Australia		**14,864**

* NPV cost in A$ millions; A$1.00 ≈ US$0.75.
Sources: Australian Council for Infrastructure Development; Partnerships Victoria

sector (although some, such as the Sydney Cross City Tunnel, have run into problems as a result (*cf.* §14.8.1)). Australian toll roads are typically urban motorways with a high construction cost and sophisticated operation, and the scale of this programme has been such that it has formed a base from which Australian investors have been able to play an active rôle in the later development of toll roads elsewhere in the world, *e.g.* in the United States.

Victoria's Department of Treasury and Finance set up the 'Partnerships Victoria' unit in 2000 as a centre of expertise within the Department. Social infrastructure projects under the Partnerships Victoria banner, using the PFI Model, began with the Victoria Country Court project in 2002. Since then, although the total volume of PPP investments in Victoria has been similar to that in New South Wales, the nature of the projects has been more varied as can be seen in Table 3.5. Partnerships Victoria has produced a comprehensive suite of guidance documents for PPPs (see Bibliography), which have largely been adopted as a standard by the other states.

There is little central coordination for PPPs as the Commonwealth only covers defence (where some PPPs are planned) and foreign affairs, so Victoria launched a National PPP Forum in 2004, 'to reduce bid costs, increase the level of consistency across jurisdictions and to share lessons learned to increase skills and knowledge in the public sector', with membership from all the states and the Commonwealth government. As of 2006 some A$10 billion of further PPP projects were in the pipeline for Australia as a whole.

§3.7 FRANCE

France has a long history of Concessions for public infrastructure, dating back to the *Canal du Midi* from the Atlantic to the Mediterranean in the mid-17th century. During the 19th century and the first half of the 20th centuries municipal PPPs in the water and sewage sectors became commonplace, and this led to a general framework, widely adopted in civil-law countries, for the provision of services such as waste management and urban transport. Similarly utilities such as rail and electricity were developed in Concession frameworks. After World War II many of these utilities reverted to the state, and much new infrastructure such as motorways was built through structures which—at that time—kept the investment off the public-sector balance sheet, by making use of publicly-owned companies with implicit government support, but which charged tolls to users (*cf.* §17.2.2).

Concessions are one form of a contract for *délégation de gestion du service public* ('delegation of operation of a public service'); the other main form is *Affermage* (*i.e.* Franchises), which involves operation and maintenance being carried out under a contract with the Public Authority, with the private-sector investors taking demand risk and having to meet performance targets, but with funding for construction the Facility by the Public Authority, which also retains ownership. An *Affermage* contract can also come into play at the end of a Concession, to allow continued operation of a Facility by the private sector (*cf.* §15.11). The water sector uses *Affermage* contracts extensively.

France began adoption of PFI-Model structures for social infrastructure from 2002, with sector-specific legislation covering health and prisons. A €1.3 billion prison PPP programme and a €1.4 billion hospital programme is now under way. General PPP legislation was passed in 2004. New Concessions are also being undertaken in the road sector, and Franchises to take over operation of state-owned toll motorways have also been sold.

§3.8 KOREA

§3.8.1 BACKGROUND

The rapid export-based industrialisation and economic growth of South Korea up to the early 1990s was not accompanied by adequate investment in public infrastructure (which is known in Korea as Social Overhead Capital (SOC)). The Private Capital Inducement Act of 1994 was the country's first attempt at bringing private-sector investment to help fill this gap through the use of Concessions, but limited progress was made because too much risk was left with the private sector. Seven projects (primarily roads) began, but were then over-taken by the Asian financial crisis of 1997 and subsequent controls imposed on the Korean economy by the International Monetary Fund (IMF).

In 1999 the process in effect began again with the Private Participation in Infrastructure Act, which continues (with amendments) to provide the basis for the current PPI pro-gramme. At the same time as the PPI Act, regulations to improve transparency of the pro-curement process were introduced with World Bank technical assistance. The result of the PPI Act has been a sustained programme of Concessions, with substantial levels of locally-sourced investment and debt, even though the PPI Act was initially aimed at securing foreign investment. The Act requires the government to set out an annual PPI Plan, which specifies the expected level of private investment for each project in the Plan—the purpose of this is to ensure a coordinated national approach to PPI. The PPI Act also encourages 'unsolicited projects', *i.e.* PPI projects which did not form part of the Plan, but are pro-posed by the private sector (*cf.* §6.4.7).

A key aspect in the growth of the PPI programme has been the Minimum Revenue Guarantee ('MRG'). As originally enacted, this provided for public-sector guarantees of up to 90% of the projected revenues of the Facility (80% in the case of unsolicited pro-jects). The PPI Amendment Act of 2005 changed this to a sliding scale of 75% for the first 5 years, 65% for the next 5, and zero thereafter, restricted to solicited projects only. Moreover a 'floor' was introduced for the MRG in future projects: if a Facility does not reach 50% of its projected revenues, no MRG payments are due. There is also a 'cap', whereby the Public Authority gets revenues above 110–140% of projections.

The PPI Act also provided compensation for foreign exchange losses in excess of 20% (in line with the objective of encouraging foreign investment in PPI projects), and allowed the Public Authority to take an equity share of up to 50% while allowing all dividends to be paid to the private-sector investors. There are also provisions for public-sector sub-sidies, subsidised loans and tax exemptions.

Larger projects—defined as those whose cost exceeds Won 200 billion ($\approx$US\$200 mil-lion), or with government support over Won 30 billion ($\approx$US\$30 million)—which make up about one-third of the total, are controlled by the Ministry of Planning & Budget, while smaller ones are controlled by local governments.

The 1999 PPI Act also established the Private Infrastructure Investment Center of Korea ('PICKO') as a 'one-stop' centre of expertise, to provide policy support, appraise and develop new projects, assist in bid evaluation and negotiation of Concession Agreements, and provide education and training in PPI. PICKO was originally an agency of the Ministry of Communication & Transport ('MOCT'), then the Ministry of Planning & Budget, but—now renamed Public and Private Infrastructure Investment Management Center ('PIMAC')—it is now part of the Korea Development Institute, a research institute which reports to the Korean President. The purpose of the move seems to have been to isolate PIMAC more clearly from political influence, to enable it to take a more objective approach.

Other key changes to PPI programme in the 2005 Amendment Act were the introduction of a VfM test (cf. §5.3), projects using the PFI Model (known in Korea as Build-Transfer-Lease ('BTL'), and provisions to encourage the growth of infrastructure investment funds (cf. §7.2.1) and for sharing of Refinancing Gains between the public and private sector (cf. §16.4.5).

§3.8.2 GROWTH OF THE PPI PROGRAMME

Table 3.6 sets out a summary of approved PPI projects by year since 1997. As can be seen, the overall scale of the PPI programme is comparable to the British PFI programme (setting aside London Underground), but the number of individual projects is far smaller, i.e. average project size is far larger. This reflects the fact that the projects to date have been mainly for major transport infrastructure. Examples of current major PPI projects (from the 2003 Annual Plan) are set out in Table 3.7.

While transportation Concessions thus remain a major part of the PPI programme, following the 2005 PPI Act amendments the Korean government began PFI-Model social-infrastructure projects, e.g. for schools, and other accommodation projects, especially for the Army, as well as other new sectors such as waste treatment. At the end of 2005, 86 such BTL projects had been announced, with a total value of Won 3.8 trillion (≈US$3.8 billion). PPI projects now make up about 15% of the total investment in SOC, a proportion which has grown over recent years. The overall proportion of investment in public infrastructure though PPPs (PPI and BTL) should therefore increase still further.

Debt financing of PPI projects was originally from a combination of the state-owned Korea Development Bank and foreign banks (for larger projects, where sufficient funding

Table 3.6

Korean PPI projects, 1997–2005

Year	Projects approved	Investment (US$ billion)
1997	14	5.5
1998	7	4.8
1999	11	0.6
2000	13	2.1
2001	19	5.8
2002	12	2.7
2003	16	4.8
2004	14	5.4
2005	12	6.3
Total	**118**	**38.0**

Source: Korea Development Institute

Table 3.7
Major Korean PPI projects, 2003 Annual Plan

Project	Total Cost (US$ million)	Public-Sector Funding		Private-sector Funding
Seoul-Chuncheon Expressway	1,535	492	(MOCT)	1,043
Seoul Beltway	1,104	338	(MOCT)	766
New Bundang Subway, Seoul	1,615	800	(MOCT)	815
Seoul Subway Line No. 9	1,900	1,239	(Seoul Metropolitan Govt.)	680
Uijongbu Light Rail Transit (LRT)	313	125	(MOCT/Uijongbu City)	188
Yongin Light Rail Transit (LRT)	488	195	(MOCT/Yongin City)	293
Puchon Light Rail Transit (LRT)	341	136	(MOCT/Puchon City)	205
Jeonju Light Rail Transit (LRT)	308	154		154

could not be raised domestically). Korean commercial banks and some other non-banking sources such as insurance companies now also play a major rôle in the market. Foreign investors are also beginning to appear in the market.

Debt financing for PPI projects is supported by the Korea Infrastructure Credit Guarantee Fund ('KICGF'), also set up under the 1994 PPI Act. KICGF receives its funding from government, MRG fees, its own guarantee fees and bank loans, and provides guarantees for revenues or debt in PPI projects, subject to a limit of Won 200 billion ($\approx$ US$200 million) per project. Although KICGF covers project revenues or debt service as a whole there is no reason why toll revenues should not be received, and KICGF thus *de facto* assures beneficiaries of the MRG that funds will actually be available to make payments if they fall due (*cf.* §14.8.3). In the 10 years to 2005, KICGF had guaranteed 65 projects, with accumulated guarantees of Won 3,442 billion ($\approx$ US$ 3.4 billion).

There has been criticism of some aspects of the PPI programme—in particular a lack of competition in a market dominated by the 5 big Korean construction companies, and bid-evaluation criteria which concentrate too much on a 'public works' view, *e.g.* putting too much weight on how the Facility is to be built. It also appears that the MRG encouraged projects to be built without adequate analysis of usage risks (*cf.* §13.4.3), and as a result some large claims have been made on MRGs. (The changes to the MRG in 2005 reflect this experience.) However, it has to be said that without the MRG the PPI programme could never have developed on the scale which has been achieved to date, and even if some public subsidy of Concessions has resulted this is not unreasonable in macroeconomic terms (*cf.* §5.2.1).

§3.9 SPAIN

Spanish toll-road Concessions began in the 19th century, when tolled bridges and railways were also developed by private investors. A programme of private-sector motorway development (the first in Europe) began in 1967 and by 1976 15 Concessions covering 1,500 km had been signed. Several of these turned out not to be financially viable and were bought out by the state, but others ran for the full Concession term (typically 30 years) and have now reverted to the public sector. In more recent years budgetary constraints have led to a large-scale growth in new Concessions. 22 PPP road Concessions with a value of more than €6 billion were signed between 1998 and 2003. The 1972 Concession Law was primarily intended for roads, but was superseded in 2003 by a new law which covers all types of PPP, including the PFI Model. PPPs now account for around 20% of Spain's infrastructure investment.

Because of the highly-devolved nature of government in Spain, there is little central direction on PPPs—each autonomous regional government works out its own policies, and there is no particular national centre of expertise.

The procurement process is fast and low in cost; typically Spanish projects are said to incur bidding costs one-tenth of those for a British PFI project, and to be procured in a substantially shorter time (shorter time and lower cost are certainly connected). An important factor in this respect is the amount of preparation undertaken in advance by the public sector, including preliminary design, planning and environmental-impact assessment, and prior consultation with the market before launching PPP tenders.

Spanish PPPs are dominated by major construction contractors, and financial investors (cf. §7.2.1) do not play a significant part in the Spanish market, other than domestic banks which are closely linked to contractors. Therefore Spain is de facto a market closed to foreign competition and investment, although Spanish contractors would claim they compete fiercely between themselves.

As with Australia, the high level of activity in the toll-road sector has given Spanish contractor/investors a base for development of similar business in overseas markets.

§3.10 SOUTH AFRICA

South Africa has developed a varied PPP programme, and offers an interesting example of what can be achieved in a developing country, albeit one with a sophisticated finance and investment sector, which has been a key factor in the growth of the programme. PPPs provide an important means of accelerating the necessary investment in economic and social infrastructure in South Africa.

PPPs began in the mid-1990s on an entirely ad hoc basis—the National Roads Agency, which already tolled parts of the major national roads, developed Concession structures to overcome budgetary constraints on upgrading parts of this network. The first of these projects, in 1996, related to a R2.6 billion PPP (US$1 ≈ R7) on the N4 toll road which provides a connection between South Africa and the port of Maputo in Mozambique. Although privately financed, the debt on this transaction was guaranteed by the governments of South Africa and Mozambique. (There were also South African-supported PPPs for the development of Maputo port, and a connecting railway.) This was followed by a R3 billion PPP for the upgrading and tolling of part of the N3 (between Pretoria/Johannesburg and Durban), on which the private-sector investors and lenders take the full traffic risk.

The next stage of PPP development related to prisons: bids were called for 11 prison PPP projects, but it became apparent that costs had been substantially underestimated, and finally only two contracts were signed in 2000, for prisons at Bloemfontein and Louis Trichardt. This led to a more orderly approach to PPPs: these are now regulated by the National Treasury, which has established a PPP Unit, whose approval to proceed is required at three stages:

- after preparation feasibility study;
- before procurement documentation; and
- before signing final documentation.

A standard form of PPP Contract (based heavily on the British SoPC) was issued in 2004, after consultations with private-sector investors and lenders.

The first substantial project concluded under Treasury regulation was Inkosi Albert Luthuli Hospital (R4.5 billion) in 2001; there have been a number of subsequent projects, but relatively small scale other than for government offices and IT. Development of PPPs at the local/municipal level has also been slow, despite the establishment in 1998 of the Municipal Infrastructure Investment Unit (MIIU), a body with similar aims to 4Ps in the United Kingdom. Nonetheless the general pipeline of new projects has grown, and the PPP programme will take a major step forward with the R20 billion (US$3.5 billion) Gautrain project, for a rapid rail link between Johannesburg, its Airport and Pretoria, signed in 2006. However this project has been criticised for being out of scale with other investment in public transport in South Africa, and one that will primarily benefit the well-off; this illustrates the point that investments in infrastructure may be made because they are attractive as PPPs, and not necessarily those that would be given the highest priority were public-sector funding freely available (*cf.* §2.9.1).

Chapter 4

Cash Flow and Investment Analysis

§4.1 INTRODUCTION

As a large part of this book deals with the financial aspects of PPPs and their effect on policy issues, it is necessary for the reader to have a basic understanding of certain key concepts used in financial analysis, which will be used hereafter. A PPP deals with cash flows over long periods of time, and the value of money is affected by the time that this money is received or paid. It is evident that a dollar today is worth more than a dollar in a year's time, but is a dollar today worth more than two dollars in a year's time? Two inter-linked types of calculation are normally used to make this decision:

- a discounted cash flow (DCF) calculation, which gives a value today, or 'net present value' (NPV), for a future cash flow (§4.2); and
- an internal rate of return (IRR) calculation, which determines of the overall rate of return on an investment based on its future cash flow (§4.3)

Although both of these methods of calculation have some problems (§4.4), they are widely used in PPP projects in a variety of contexts (§4.5).

§4.2 NET PRESENT VALUE/DISCOUNTED CASH FLOW

The NPV is the value today of a sum of money due in the future, discounted at the cost of money, *i.e.* a relevant interest rate. The formula for an NPV calculation is:

$$PV = \frac{FV}{(1 + i)^n},$$

where PV = present value, *i.e.* the 'money of today',
      FV = future value, *i.e.* the 'money of the future',
        i = the interest or discount rate, and
        n = the number of periods (*e.g.* annual, semi-annual, *etc.*, with the discount rate adjusted accordingly).

Thus if the discount rate is 10% *p.a.*, and a sum of 1000 is due in a year's time, the present value (NPV) of that sum is:

$$\frac{1000}{(1+0.10)},$$

or 909.1. To turn the calculation the other way round, if 909.1 is invested for a year at 10%, 1000 (*i.e.* 909.1 × 1.10) will be repaid at the end of the year. Similarly the NPV of a sum of 1000 due in two years' time, at a discount rate of 10% *p.a.* calculated semi-annually (*i.e.* 5% per half year) is:

$$\frac{1000}{(1+0.05)^4},$$

or 822.7.

    A DCF calculation is the NPV of a series of future cash sums. It is calculated as:

$$\sum \frac{FV^n}{{}^n(1+i)^n},$$

i.e. the sum (Σ) of the net cash flow for each future period (usually semi-annually in PPP calculations), each period's cash flow being discounted to its NPV as set out above. Typically a DCF calculation offsets the NPV of the costs of investment in a project against the NPV of the stream of future revenues which the project produces. Although DCF calculations can easily be done using the relevant spreadsheet software function, it is important to understand the underlying formulae and calculations as a way of checking the final result.

    The discount rate used for DCF calculations is a combination of two factors:

- the general time value of money (*i.e.* related to financial market interest rates); and
- a premium for the particular risks involved in the investment.

The choice of discount rate is obviously crucial in determining the present value of a project's cash flow, and hence the value of the project as an investment: the higher the rate the lower the NPV, and *vice versa*. The discount rate is often used as a 'hurdle rate', meaning that if the NPV is positive using this rate the investment is acceptable, whereas if it is negative the return is too low and therefore the investment is not acceptable.

    The use of DCF calculations can be illustrated by the two contrasting investment cash flows set out in Table 4.1. Both have an initial investment of 1000, and cash flows over 5 years of 1350, producing a surplus (net of the initial investment) of 350. The cash flow for each annual period has been discounted to its NPV at 10% *p.a.* Year 0 is the first day of the project, when the investment is made (the investment being shown as a negative figure in the cash flow); the remaining cash flows are received at annual intervals thereafter.

Table 4.1

DCF calculation

| (a) | (b) | Investment A | | Investment B | |
| | | (c) | | (d) | |
Year	Discount factor $[(1 + 0.1)^{(a)}]$	Cash flow	NPV $[(c) \div (b)]$	Cash flow	NPV $[(d) \div (b)]$
0	1.0000	−1,000	−1,000	−1,000	−1,000
1	1.1000	340	309	200	182
2	1.2100	305	252	235	194
3	1.3310	270	203	270	203
4	1.4641	235	161	305	208
5	1.6105	200	124	340	211
Total		350	49	350	−2

It will be seen that although the undiscounted cash flows produce the same net result over the 5-year period, the NPV of Investment A is 49 (*i.e.* discounted cash flows from years 1–5 of 1049, less the original investment of 1000), whereas that of Investment B is –2. Investment A is thus the better project. These differences in the DCF calculations illustrate the importance to investors of the timing of cash flows.

If the same cash flows are discounted at 5% *p.a.* the NPV of Investment A is 184 and that of Investment B 154: so changing the hurdle rate does not affect the decision that Investment A is the better one, but it also clearly turns Investment B from a doubtful into an attractive investment. Were Investment B the only choice, changing the hurdle rate from 10% to 5% would affect the decision whether to go ahead with it or not, which illustrates the importance of the choice of discount rate.

A DCF calculation also provides a means of valuing an investment which is already held. If a PPP Contract is expected to provide a stream of net revenues of, say, 1,000 a year for the next 20 years, the value of this business is determined by discounting this stream of revenues to an NPV. The choice of discount rate again makes a substantial difference to the result: if this stream is discounted at 15% *p.a.* its value today is 6,259, but if discounted at 8% *p.a.* its value is 9,818. As will be seen, investors have different views about the value of a stream of future revenues, and so will use different discount rates—thus the same PPP project may have a different value for different investors.

§4.3 INTERNAL RATE OF RETURN

The IRR measures the return on the investment over its life. It is the discount rate at which the NPV of the cash flow is zero. Thus, using the examples in Table 4.1, as set out in Table 4.2, the IRR of Investment A is 12.08% and Investment B is 9.94%, so again showing that Investment A is the better of the two; the calculation can be checked by discounting the

Table 4.2
IRR calculation

End Year	Investment A		Investment B	
	Cash flow	NPV @ 12.08%	Cash flow	NPV @ 9.94%
0	−1,000	−1,000	−1,000	−1,000
1	340	303	200	182
2	305	243	235	194
3	270	192	270	203
4	235	149	305	209
5	200	113	340	212
Total	350	0	350	0

two cash flows at these respective rates. Again a minimum IRR can be used as a hurdle rate, so if the investor has an IRR hurdle rate of say 12%, Investment A will be acceptable but Investment B will not.

§4.4 PROBLEMS WITH DCF AND IRR CALCULATIONS

Some caution must be exercised with DCF and IRR calculations, as both have defects or weaknesses which need to be understood.

§4.4.1 NPV AND DIFFERENT-SIZED PROJECTS

When comparing two different projects, account has to be taken of their relative sizes. This is illustrated in Table 4.3.

Investment D has a higher NPV than Investment C, but this is merely because of its larger size. As is apparent from the IRR calculation, Investment C is the better investment; the incremental 1000 invested in Investment D compared to Investment C gives a much poorer return.

Table 4.3
NPV and different-sized projects

	Investment C	Investment D
(a) Original investment	−1000	−2000
(b) Cash flow 1 year later	1400	2600
NPV @ 10%	273	364
IRR	40%	30%
Cost–benefit analysis		
(c) NPV of benefits [= NPV of (b)]	1273	2364
(d) NPV of costs [= (a)]	1000	2000
Cost–benefit ratio [(c) ÷ (d)]	1.27:1	1.18:1

To better compare these investments, the NPV comparison can be expanded with a cost–benefit analysis, as shown in the second half of Table 4.3. This suggests that Investment C gives a better return in relation to the amount of the investment, a point confirmed by the IRR calculation. The approach here is that any project with a cost–benefit ratio over 1 is a sound one, but the project with the highest cost–benefit ratio is the one which should be chosen. On the other hand, if availability of funding is not a problem, and there is no other use for the funds, it could be argued that Investment D is still better because it produces a higher absolute net benefit.

§4.4.2 IRR AND POSITIVE/NEGATIVE CASH FLOWS

IRR calculations are not suitable where a cash flow flips between negative and positive and back again in different periods (*e.g.* where an investment takes place in phases, with revenues building up between each phase of investment, or where there is a final cost to an investment, such as cleaning up a quarry after it is exhausted), as the same calculation may then give more than one different answer. This is illustrated by Table 4.4, in which it can be seen that the same cash flow, in which amounts are negative at the beginning, then positive in period 1, then negative in period 2, can be discounted at both 10% and 20% to produce an NPV of zero, *i.e.* the IRR can be either 10% or 20%.

It should be noted that standard spread-sheet software will probably only give one of these answers, with no indication it is not the only possible one.

Table 4.4

IRR and negative/positive cash flows

Period	Cash flow	10% discount rate		20% discount rate	
		Discount factor	NPV	Discount factor	NPV
0	−50,000	1.00000	−50,000	1.00000	−50,000
1	115,000	0.90909	104,545	0.83333	95,833
2	−66,000	0.82644	−54,545	0.69444	−45,833
Total NPV			0		0

§4.4.3 IRR AND CASH REINVESTMENT

A more general problem with IRR is the assumption in the calculation on what happens to interim cash flows. This is illustrated by Table 4.5.

It is evident that Investment E gives a better return, and the DCF calculation supports this, but the IRRs of the two investments are the same. This is because the standard IRR calculation assumes that cash taken out of the project is reinvested at the IRR rate until the end of the calculation period. Thus, as shown in the last column of Table 4.5, if the Investment F cash flow in years 1–4 is reinvested at 15% *p.a.* compounded, the total

Table 4.5

IRR and interim cash flows

Year	Investment E	Investment F	
	Cash flow	Cash flow	Annual cash flow reinvested @ 15% to year 5
0	−1,000	−1,000	
1	0	298	522
2	0	298	454
3	0	298	395
4	0	298	343
5	2,011	298	298
Total	1,011	492	2,011
NPV @ 12%	141	74	
IRR	15%	15%	

amounts to 2,011 at the end of year 5, the same as Investment E. Clearly some account should be taken of Investment F generating cash more quickly, but the assumption that this cash can be reinvested at 15% is not correct unless this is the investor's cost of capital (*cf.* §7.3.1), and so may double-count the return on another investment at that rate. The effect of an IRR calculation can be clearly seen in Table 4.5: it over-values early cash flow—the longer the cash flow period, the more the IRR is exaggerated by using a high reinvestment rate—and conversely undervalues cash flows further into the future. This is of particular relevance to PPP projects, which have very long cash flows.

There are two ways of dealing with this type of distortion:

Modified IRR (MIRR). The MIRR calculation assumes a lower reinvestment rate (*e.g.* the investor's cost of capital, as assumed for the discount rate in a DCF calculation, instead of the IRR rate) for cash taken out of the project. This is a better representation of the real world. If we take the examples in Table 4.5, but the reinvestment rate is taken as 12% (*i.e.* the cost of capital used for the DCF calculation) as shown in Table 4.6, the MIRR of Investment F is 13.6%, while that of Investment E of course remains at 15% (as there is no interim cash flow to invest). This then makes it clear that Investment E is the better one. Surprisingly, the use of MIRR by investors is not widespread.

Payback period. An alternative (or at least supplementary) approach is to ignore the reinvestment issue in looking at IRR calculations but require that any investment also has a maximum payback period (*i.e.* the length of time that it takes to recover the original cash investment). This to a certain extent balances the exaggerating effect of IRR calculations on longer term cash flows, but it is a crude measure—in particular it does not take account of returns after the end of the payback period. Nonetheless, it may still provide a useful check. Thus besides requiring a minimum IRR level, a maximum payback period of not more than a certain number of years may be required as one

Table 4.6

IRR and MIRR

Year	Investment E Cash flow	Investment F Cash flow	Investment F Annual cash flow reinvested @ 12% to year 5
0	−1,000	−1,000	−1,000
1	0	298	469
2	0	298	419
3	0	298	374
4	0	298	334
5	2,011	298	298
Total	**1,011**	**492**	**105**
NPV @ 12%	141	74	
IRR	**15.0%**	**15.0%**	
MIRR	**15.0%**		**13.6%**

of the criteria for making a new investment. The payback period for Investment E in the above Table is 3–4 years, and that for Investment F is the full 5 years.

§4.4.4 IRR AND DIFFERENT PROJECT LIVES

Another consequence of the over-valuation of early cash flow in the IRR calculation is that projects with different lives cannot be compared using their IRRs. This is illustrated by Table 4.7, which shows the cash flow from two projects which have identical IRRs—but it is evident, and confirmed by the DCF calculation, that the longer Investment J is better than the shorter Investment G.

§4.4.5 SINGLE DISCOUNT RATE

The use of a single discount rate or IRR to assess investments suggests that the risks involved in a PPP project are the same throughout its life. In reality of course this is not the case (*cf.* §7.3.2).

§4.4.6 CASH INVESTMENT V. RISK

DCF and IRR calculations are based only on investment of cash: they take no account of the risk involved in making a commitment to invest cash in the future (*cf.* §7.3.4), nor of the need (and hence the cost) of setting aside resources to make this future investment (*cf.* §5.2.2). This is of particular relevance in PPPs, where construction and hence investment may take place over several years, or where there may be investments of cash in later stages of a project.

Table 4.7

IRR and different project lives

Year	Investment G	Investment J
0	−1000	−1000
1	200	145
2	200	145
3	200	145
4	200	145
5	200	145
6	200	145
7	200	145
8	200	145
9		145
10		145
11		145
12		145
13		145
14		145
15		145
IRR	**11.8%**	**11.8%**
NPV @ 10%	67	105

§4.5 USES IN PPPs

DCF and IRR calculations are used in a variety of different ways by the different parties to a PPP project. The following just summarises these, and provides cross-references to the context in which they are used elsewhere in this book. However, one general point should be made—all these calculations involve estimates of future cash flows, and the calculations are thus only as good as the data used for these estimates. Financial models (*cf.* §10.2) often work to a spurious level of accuracy down to fine decimal points—such calculations may be correct arithmetically, but have limited use since the underlying data cannot be that accurate.

§4.5.1 BY THE PUBLIC SECTOR

A DCF calculation may be used:

- when deciding whether to proceed with the procurement of a project (*cf.* §5.2.3)—an Economic Rate of Return calculation (a form of IRR) may also be used in this case (*cf.* §5.2.4);
- in a Public-Sector Comparator (*cf.* §5.3);
- to evaluate bids for a PPP project (*cf.* §6.3.6).

§4.5.2 By Investors

The Project IRR—*i.e.* the IRR of the cash flow before debt service or equity returns—may be used to assess the general financial viability of a project without taking account of its financial structure (*cf.* §7.3.1).

However the main measure for investors is the Equity IRR—*i.e.* the IRR of the equity cash flow (distributions) *versus* the original equity investment (*cf.* §7.3.2). This is commonly used as a hurdle rate for investments—*i.e.* in order for an investment to be justified the Equity IRR must be x% or above.

§4.5.3 In PPP Contracts

The Equity IRR may be used to calculate:

- the initial Service Fees (*cf.* §10.7);
- revisions to Service Fees, or compensation for changes in circumstances during the life of the PPP Contract in some cases (*cf.* §15.2);
- Refinancing-Gain calculations (*cf.* §16.4.6); and
- compensation to investors for early termination of the PPP Contract, for which a DCF calculation may also be used (§15.6);

and the Project IRR may be used to calculate the payment due on termination for a default by the Project Company (*cf.* §15.5).

§4.5.4 By Lenders

Lenders use the Project IRR to calculate their Loan-Life Cover Ratio (*cf.* §10.6.3).

Chapter 5

The Public-Sector Investment Decision

§5.1 INTRODUCTION

This chapter reviews how the Public Authority decides to invest in new public infrastructure, and whether doing so *via* a PPP is the right approach. There are various measures which a Public Authority may use to determine if an investment in new public infrastructure is economically justifiable (§5.2). These measures do not of themselves point in the direction of either public-sector procurement or a PPP. Additional factors need to be taken into account to make this decision:

- VfM (§5.3);
- Affordability (§5.4); and
- balance-sheet treatment (§5.5).

Of course since the demand for funding for public-sector projects is almost infinite, and resources are limited (even with the help of a PPP programme), the decision to proceed with a project is based on other factors beside the financial measures set out here.

§5.2 ECONOMIC JUSTIFICATION

When deciding if an investment is economically justifiable, a Public Authority:

- identifies the benefits and costs of the project, including its indirect effects (§5.2.1);
- prepares a cost–benefit analysis (§5.2.2), a key element of which is the discount rate to be applied to future benefits and costs (§5.2.3);
- or calculates the economic return of the project (§5.2.4).

§5.2.1 EXTERNALITIES

Apart from simple long-term financial benefits from a new Facility compared to continu-ing the existing one (*e.g.* on maintenance costs, or because the new Facility replaces several older ones), or other benefits which can be priced (*e.g.* the saving on driving time from a new road), an initial evaluation of a public-sector project also has to take account of (and place a valuation on) its wider economic or social benefits or costs ('externalities', also known as 'external economies or diseconomies'). Externalities, which will be positive where they provide a benefit and negative where there is a cost, may include:

- economic development—*e.g.* increases in land values and general economic activity;
- effects on safety or public health—*e.g.* reductions in accident deaths once a new road has been built;
- environmental impact—*e.g.* increases or decreases in noise or air pollution (*cf.* §14.5.4).

It is worth noting that externalities cannot easily be included in the costs paid by Concession users, which is why there is a case for public-sector subsidy in such cases (*cf.* §13.4.3). Within the European Union, any such support is only allowed if it does not constitute 'State Aid' (other than certain specific exceptions, such as support for underdeveloped regions, or to promote a major project of common European interest). If it is found to con-stitute State Aid any subsidies must be refunded, and the enforceability of guarantees may be uncertain. The European Commission reviewed State Aid for PPPs in the context of the London Underground PPPs in 2002 (see Bibliography). The general conclusion, which illustrates the principle that the public sector should pay for externalities, was that '. . . when these types of infrastructure arrangements are concluded after the observance of an open, transparent and non-discriminatory [procurement] procedure, it is, in principle, presumed that the level of any public sector support can be regarded as representing the market price for the execution of a project. This conclusion should lead to the assumption that, in prin-ciple, no State Aid is involved.'

§5.2.2 COST–BENEFIT ANALYSIS

The benefits and the net externalities should be compared with the Facility's costs; funding of these costs—whether from taxation, public-sector borrowing or a PPP—is irrelevant in this context, since economic benefits should be independent of this. The Public Authority has to use either a DCF or an IRR calculation for this purpose, to allow for the different timing of these costs and benefits. Using a DCF calculation, the benefit of a public-sector project can be assessed as:

- the NPV of project benefits, plus
- the NPV of positive externalities

and the costs can be assessed as:

- the NPV of project costs, plus
- the NPV of negative externalities.

The NPV of these figures is calculated using the public-sector discount rate ('PSDR'), discussed below. As with any investment, if the total NPV is positive the investment can be justified. However, as discussed in §4.4.1, the difficulty with a simple DCF approach is that if a choice of projects is being evaluated, the more expensive project may be favoured by the DCF approach, and therefore a cost–benefit analysis is needed. If benefits cannot easily be measured, which may be the case with social infrastructure, then costs alone of different solutions would have to be compared—this is known as a 'cost-effectiveness analysis'.

There is a further issue with using DCF calculations to make public-sector investment decisions—the effect of discounting costs a long way in the future (*e.g.* the decommissioning costs for a nuclear power station, or the cost of repurchasing land). If, say, a project involves a cost for the public sector of $1 million in 30 years' time, discounting this at 6% gives a cost in today's terms of $174,110, which may be considered small in relation to the NPV of the project as a whole. But in 30 years' time the $1 million will still have to be found, unless $174,000 is set aside today and saved up with interest for 30 years, which does not happen. Thus the generation of today places an undervalued burden on the future by using a DCF calculation to make investment decisions where there are large-scale costs towards the end of the project. Moreover the higher the discount rate the more the effect of such costs is disregarded.

§5.2.3 PUBLIC-SECTOR DISCOUNT RATE

The question of what rate should be taken as the PSDR is difficult to resolve, and the approach varies widely from country to country. It is important not to make the discount rate too high, as the effect of this may be to undervalue benefits which may only be available some considerable time in the future, and hence to discourage long-term thinking in public-sector investment. A public-sector investment typically involves an initial negative investment cost followed by years of benefits—hence the lower the PSDR the more attractive the investment will seem. There is surprisingly little international consensus on how to determine the PSDR.

One approach is to use a public-sector 'risk-free' rate, and then add an adjustment to this rate to reflect project risk, which can be done through:

- a generic risk adjustment to the rate for all public-sector projects (typically used where no comparison has to be made with private-sector projects); or
- a standard risk adjustment to the rate for all projects in a particular sector (as in Norway)—thus for a road project which has high risk of construction-cost overruns and uncertainty of long-term usage requirements, a high PSDR would be used; or
- a rate adjustment for a project which reflects its particular risk (*e.g.* as in Ireland and the Netherlands).

The argument for a generic PSDR is that the public sector is spreading risks over many projects, so it is the average risk rather than the worst-case or project-specific risk which has to be taken into account. However this means that high-risk projects, which should be less favoured than low-risk projects, will in fact be treated the same way. There is a strong case for accepting that there is no 'right' answer to the level of the PSDR, and therefore the best thing to do is to use a range of different discount rates, and see whether an overall pattern emerges from doing so.

But there is also a problem with any discount rate, as construction costs occur early on, so even using a high discount rate will not adjust these by very much to reflect the risk of cost overruns. Therefore an alternative approach is to use the risk-free rate for all public-sector investment, but adjust the projected outcomes which are being discounted to reflect risk—thus in the road case, the project cost, operating expenses and usage projections would be adjusted to reflect the risk that the outcome would not be as projected (*cf.* more detailed comments on this in §5.3). As projections of costs and benefits are uncertain, it again makes sense to use a range of different risk scenarios when discounting at the risk-free rate, and make a judgement from this spectrum of results. There may be some merit in using a risk-adjusted rate and a risk-free rate with separate risk adjustments to see if they come up with different answers, and if so why, but this is not generally done.

Studies were carried out in Britain in 2002 and 2004 (see Bibliography) to try to establish a reasonable range of 'optimism bias' as a basis for adjusting projected public-sector project outcomes for risk—*i.e.* the risk that the public sector is usually over-optimistic about outcomes, and thus, *e.g.* there are substantial cost overruns compared to the original projections (*cf.* §2.6.1). (One reason for this 'optimism', other than poor project management skills, is that when public-sector investment is constrained, public officials—whose careers benefit from completing projects, and are not necessarily penalised if project costs overrun—have an incentive to understate likely costs to get their projects approved.) The wide range of results—reflected in the British Treasury's current allowable ranges for optimism bias on capex for new (standard construction) buildings of between 2% and 24%, and for roads of between 15% and 32%—illustrates how much uncertainty there is in this area. (Such figures do not of course take into account the possibility of the Public Authority eliminating cost overruns *via* a turnkey D&B Contract instead of the conventional design-bid-build approach to public-sector procurement (*cf.* §2.6).)

A further issue needs consideration here—what is the 'risk-free' rate which should be used as a base for any of these calculations? There are several answers to this, each of which is used in various countries:

- the current market rate for government bonds (as in Ireland, the Netherlands and the United States); or
- a fixed rate based on the historical average for government bonds; or
- the 'social time preference rate' (STPR), *i.e.* the rate which private investors expect to receive for foregoing present consumption in favour of future consumption (assuming this is a risk-free transaction).

The STPR and the long-term historical average government bond rate should be similar, but the problem with using either a fixed historical rate or a fixed STPR is that these may get seriously out of line with current market rates, which distorts the results, especially where market-based financing comes into the picture as it does with PPPs. Again there is little international consensus on the correct approach here. Thus in the United Kingdom the risk-free PDSR was reduced from 6% real (*i.e.* without including the effect of inflation) to 3.5% in 2003, which was the government's calculation of the STPR. Since that time interest rates have dropped considerably and even the 3.5% real rate is currently well over the returns investors expect for a risk-free investment, and the government's own cost of borrowing.

The arbitrary nature of a fixed PSDR is illustrated by changes made by the Norwegian government in 2005. Until then, the PSDR was 3.5% plus a sector-based risk mark-up in the range 0.5%–4.5%. 4.5% was applied to road projects, considered to represent a high risk, making a total discount rate of 8%. Sweden, on the other hand, used a total rate of 3%. This meant that a particular bridge between Sweden and Norway was economically justified for Sweden but not for Norway, even though most of its users were Norwegian. In 2005 Norway changed the PSDR to 2% plus a general risk-mark-up of 2%. An article on this change in *Nordic Road and Transport Research* (see Bibliography) was entitled (presumably with tongue in cheek) 'Norwegian Road Projects are now Profitable—the Government Reduces the Discount Rate'.

§5.2.4 ECONOMIC RATE OF RETURN

The alternative to a DCF-based calculation is to use the 'economic rate of return' (ERR), *i.e.* an IRR calculation which uses the same economic data. This may be contrasted with the 'financial rate of return' (FIRR), *i.e.* the direct cash-flow return from the project. In the ERR calculation, the investment has to pass an IRR hurdle rate similar to the PSDR to be justifiable. But again, as has been seen above, an IRR calculation has its defects in this respect—in particular the undervaluation of benefits received in the long term. This measure too must therefore be treated with care, and ideally adjusted by changing the reinvestment rate to the PDSR *via* a MIRR calculation to better reflect reality. Moreover choosing the hurdle rate and dealing with risk adjustment is as difficult as doing so with a DCF calculation.

§5.3 VALUE FOR MONEY AND THE PUBLIC-SECTOR COMPARATOR

Having decided that a new Facility is economically justified, how can a Public Authority decide whether the PPP route is the right one? This question has two aspects:

- Does a PPP offer good VfM compared to public-sector procurement?
- Is the project being procured as a PPP in a way which offers good VfM?

A Public-Sector Comparator (PSC—also known as a Public-Sector Benchmark (PSB)) is an attempt to answer the first of these questions. ('Lease-purchase analysis', as required by the Office of Management and Budget, is the nearest U.S. equivalent to a PSC.)

A PSC is an assumption of what the NPV cost (sometimes known as the net present cost (NPC)) of the project would have been had it been acquired through a conventional public-sector procurement, which is then compared with the NPV cost of the PPP. The latter may also be estimated, or it may be known if bids have been received for it. If the PPP's NPV cost is lower than the PSC, the PPP can be justified. (This is not the same as the economic cost–benefit analysis discussed above—here only the two sets of project costs are being compared.) Even if payments are not made by the Public Authority, as in the case of a Concession, the user charges represent revenue foregone by the public sector, and hence the analysis is the same as for a PFI-Model Facility.

But a PSC raises a number of difficult issues—in particular:

- how comparable costs are to be produced (§5.3.1);
- what discount rate is to be used to make these costs comparable in NPV terms (§5.3.2);
- how adjustments are to be made for risk transfer and other differences between the two types of procurement (§5.3.3), including tax (§5.3.4).

In the final analysis, it is not easy to produce a PSC which will stand up to detailed scrutiny, and it is better to concentrate on other ways of ensuring VfM.

§5.3.1 COST COMPARISON

It is difficult to compare a PSC's costs with those for a PPP, whether based on initial estimates or actual bids. It obviously cannot be assumed that these costs would be the same for each. Because risks are being transferred to the private sector under the PPP, the PPP's costs will increase to compensate for this. For example, if a Construction Subcontractor for a PPP project has to take on extra, the construction price itself will be increased to allow for this risk (*cf.* §14.7.1), so the same construction cost cannot therefore be used in the PSC, where this extra risk will not apply. Similarly, if there is scope for the private-sector innovation which should be a benefit of a PPP (*cf.* §2.9), by definition this cannot be predicted in advance and included in the Public Authority's initial evaluation comparing the PPP to the PSC.

As to opex, FM Subcontractors will also charge more where risks are transferred to them under the PPP. Also in a PPP a Public Authority will incur additional costs in procurement, negotiation and later supervision of the Project Company which would not be required if its own officers were running the Facility.

§5.3.2 DISCOUNT RATE

Obviously the discount rate which is used for this calculation also greatly affects the result—should this be the same for the PSC and the PPP (including bid evaluation—*cf.* §6.3.6)? Suppose the PSDR is 6% (including an allowance for inflation), compared to a cost of capital (*cf.* §7.3.1) for a typical PPP project of, say, 8%. If the difference between the two represents a valuation of the risk transfer to the private sector, it would be logical to use the 6% PSDR for the PSC and 8% for the PPP to compare the two—assuming a perfect risk transfer the result should be exactly the same, but this is of course a big assumption. (Tax payments by the PPP also distort the position.) Different public- and private-sector discount rates also raise issues, *e.g.* when valuing a Franchise sale (*cf.* §13.3.6). And there are other problems with this approach:

- It seems inherently odd to use a higher discount rate when discounting a PPP's costs, as the higher the discount rate the more a risky project will be favoured. Clearly the Public Authority is taking a greater risk with public-sector procurement than with a PPP, which is an argument for discounting the costs of the latter at a higher rather than a lower rate.

- The nature of the cash flows being discounted is quite different: the PSC costs consist of a high level of initial capex and a lower level of long-term opex, whereas the costs of a PPP consist of higher long-term Service Fees only, with no initial cost. The NPV cost of a PPP is thus much more dependent on the discount rate than the NPV cost of a PSC. As discussed above, where a project is capital-intensive, as with a PPP, discount rates alone cannot properly allow for the initial capex-related risks.

Alternative approaches therefore reflect those used for the economic justification discussed above (again there is little international consensus), namely:

- to use a single generic, sector or project-specific discount rate which is applied to both the PPP and the PSC, without adjusting the latter for risk transfer (this may or may not be the same as the PSDR—*i.e.* a different rate may be used than that for the original economic justification, which does not consider how the Facility is to be procured or funded); or
- to use the same risk-free discount rate for both PPP and PSC, and adjust the latter's cash flows for risk as discussed below (as in Britain); or
- use a discount rate reflecting the private-sector cost of capital for both PPP and PSC, and again adjust the latter for risk (as in Australia (Victoria)).

Whatever the discount rate, so long as it is below the Project Company's own cost of capital (*cf.* §7.3.1) a PPP will be inherently more expensive in financing terms and hence risk-transfer (and tax) adjustments are likely to be required in the PSC to demonstrate VfM—the lower the PPP discount rate, the greater the adjustments required. Therefore the Australian approach above is more favourable to PPPs than the British one.

§5.3.3 RISK-TRANSFER ADJUSTMENTS

If, therefore, the PSC is to be adjusted for risk transfer, the PSC calculation will then consist of:

- the unadjusted NPV of the PSC, *i.e.* that based on cash-flow projections without taking account of risks retained by the Public Authority; plus
- the NPV of risks transferred to the Project Company under the PPP, which would otherwise be retained by the Public Authority and so should be included in the PSC costs; plus
- the NPV of risks retained by the Public Authority; plus
- an adjustment to take account of the different tax positions of the PSC and PPP (see below).

There is an obvious relationship with the decision on balance-sheet treatment for a PPP, which as discussed below may also be decided by the level of risk transfer. The approach to calculating the risk-transfer adjustments (which are the same as 'optimism bias', mentioned above) is the mirror image of that for deciding balance-sheet treatment, *i.e.* it looks mainly at the risks transferred to the private sector rather than those retained by the public sector, by:

- identifying all relevant risks transferred to the private sector (in summary, these will relate to capex, usage, opex and macroeconomic risks—*cf.* Table 14.1);
- assigning a range of likely costs for each risk, had it been retained by the Public Authority (taking account of the optimism bias discussed above);
- assigning percentage probabilities of occurrence for each risk;
- multiplying the cost impact by the probability to arrive a value for the risk;
- identifying the probable timing of each risk event;
- calculating the NPV of the risk value based on this timing; and
- adding the result to the PSC, as these risks are retained by the Public Authority in a public-sector procurement.

The process can be carried out in reverse to assess the value of risks retained by the Public Authority, but this is generally less important as the same risks would probably be retained by the Public Authority under a PPP, and so the result will be same for either route.

Another area of risk transfer in the reverse direction, namely that of the inherent lack of flexibility in a PPP leading to increased costs for the Public Authority (*cf.* §2.12), is seldom taken into account in a PSC. It is true that this effect is difficult to quantify (though perhaps not much more so than the other risk-transfer calculations), but it is a major issue and should not be ignored.

The PSC should be based on a range of outcomes varying with the probabilities of the risks, rather than one simple NPV amount for the risk transfer—there will be no 'right' answer, and there is inevitably a high degree of judgement or subjectivity in this process, as seen from the large range of possible adjustments for optimism bias, discussed above, which could be applied here. Furthermore it is arguable whether weighting of risks in this way properly reflects the real world. (Lenders do not take this approach when considering their risk analysis—*cf.* §10.3.6/14.2.)

Moreover, if the real choice is between a PPP and no project, not a PPP and public-sector procurement, the Public Authority and its advisers will be under strong pressure to manipulate the results to 'prove' that the PSC cost is higher than the PPP cost by making large risk adjustments. This pressure, combined with the subjectivity of the process (however much it is buried in a welter of probability analysis), fundamentally undermines the credibility of PSCs which use this risk-adjustment approach, despite the logic of the theory behind them.

§5.3.4 Tax Revenues

Calculation of the adjustment for the different tax position of a PPP should theoretically be a more straightforward process, as this results primarily from the marginal tax on the project's net revenues. If the Public Authority is not a tax-raising body it may not receive any direct benefit from this extra tax flow into central or local government, but nonetheless from the point of view of the economy as a whole it is reasonable to take this benefit into account. However, theory and reality of tax payments have a tendency to deviate from each other, being very dependent on the structure of the Project Company's ownership and how it and its investors deal with their tax affairs. For example, use of shareholder subordinated debt instead of equity can almost eliminate tax payments by the Project Company (*cf.* §7.3.3). It is therefore very difficult to generalise about the extra tax benefit to be received from PPPs, or even to compare one bidder accurately with another in this respect.

§5.3.5 CREDIBILITY OF A PSC

When a risk-adjusted PSC is published, either by the Public Authority or by a government audit office, the end result may look something like Table 5.1. The NPV of the Service Fees will usually be higher than the NPV of the cost of public-sector procurement because of the higher cost of finance. Detailed justifications for the PSC adjustments which counterbalance this are seldom published, so the calculation has to be taken on trust. Hence published risk-adjusted PSCs are seldom very convincing, but, as discussed above, PSCs which are not risk-adjusted do not work well either, and in either case the choice of discount rate(s) for the PSC and PPP evaluation makes a big difference to the answer.

Should the PSC be disclosed to bidders? Practice on this is varied: some countries take the view that it should not be disclosed because it may lead bidders to treat the PSC as a target price instead of submitting their best bids; on the other hand others take the view that disclosing the PSC will ensure that bidders understand the requirements of the bid correctly.

Logically, the NPV cost of the PPP should be recalculated regularly throughout the procurement process and compared with the PSC, to ensure that the PPP maintains its advantage over PSC. The PSC itself should only be changed if there are significant changes in the scope or nature of the project, or if it is apparent that cost or risk elements have to be re-priced (although the latter is obviously open to manipulation to produce the 'right' result once more). This was the approach in the United Kingdom until 2004, and remains the case in some other countries which use PSCs, such as Australia and the Netherlands; it has some benefit, as late-stage use of the PSC can be an instrument for negotiating with bidders to push their prices down.

But reality dictates that it is not possible to reverse course towards the end of a lengthy period of procurement based on a calculation which is merely theoretical in nature, and so

Table 5.1
PSC calculation

	PSC	PPP
NPV of cost of public-sector procurement (including capex and opex)	900	
NPV of Service Fees		1,000
NPV of risk adjustments	90	
NPV of additional tax	45	
Risk-adjusted NPV cost	**1,035**	**1,000**

if a PSC is to be used at all, it is best used at the initial stages of procurement when it could possibly affect the decision. This approach is now taken in the United Kingdom. However this means that the PSC and PPP figures are both based on initial cost estimates, not bids, which makes them even more difficult to prove; in particular optimism-bias adjustments only against the PSC become very questionable because there is also often substantial optimism bias in the early stages of procuring a PPP, so that the final Service Fees may be much higher (or the scope of the Facility lower) than expected at the initial planning stage (*cf.* §6.3.8).

If there is no PSC (because the Public Authority has recognised that a PPP is the only way that the Facility can be procured), or if the PSC is a 'one-time' calculation at an early stage of procurement, how can the Public Authority ensure that a PPP procurement is giving the best available VfM? The simple answer to this is that VfM is best produced through competitive tension between bidders, and therefore the procurement process must be such as to maintain this tension for a long as possible, as discussed in Chapter 6.

§5.4 AFFORDABILITY

While VfM is important for the Public Authority, an equally relevant question is that of 'Affordability', *i.e.* whether it can actually afford to pay the Service Fees (in the PFI Model), as the Public Authority will probably have a set budget for the project, within which it has to work. Equally, in the Concession Model, the Facility has to be affordable for users. It may be simplest just to set an Affordability limit for the first year of operation, assuming that Service Fees are level thereafter (*cf.* §13.3.2), and measure bids against this, but some care needs to be taken where Service Fees are indexed against inflation to ensure there is no mismatch with the Public Authority's own resources in later years (*cf.* §11.3.5).

The first step to ensure that this Affordability limit is not breached is for the Public Authority to take advice on costs (*cf.* §6.7.3), financing (*cf.* §6.7.1), and usage (*cf.* §13.4.1) where this is relevant, to form the basis for a realistic 'shadow' financial model which demonstrates that the Service Fees should be affordable before the procurement process begins (*cf.* §10.2).

If, despite this, bids come in over expectation and the budget cannot be increased, the Public Authority will have to redesign the project in some way, *e.g.* by reducing its scope, to reduce its PPP payments to an affordable level. There are two things to bear in mind in this situation:

- If the bids are found not to be affordable, a Preferred Bidder should not be appointed until there has been a further round of bidding on a reduced project scope. Entering into negotiations with a Preferred Bidder without a defined project scope is certain to lose VfM (*cf.* §6.3.8).
- The Service Fees should not be manipulated so that they are abnormally low at the beginning of the PPP Contract, as a way of making the PPP 'affordable' to begin with, and then rise steeply later on (*cf.* §13.3.2). This is a particular temptation when Affordability is primarily measured by taking the Service Fee during the first full year of operation as a baseline.

As with the PSC, a Public Authority has to consider whether it is better to let bidders know what the Affordability limit is from the start, so that unrealistic bids are not submitted, but with the danger that the bidders treat this as a target price instead of offering the best bid. Alternatively, late-stage disclosure of Affordability can be used as a way of negotiating with bidders to bring their final prices down.

§5.5 BALANCE-SHEET TREATMENT

If it is clear that the choice is between a project which is outside the public-sector budget (at least in relation to its initial capex), and no project at all, which as discussed above is the usual motive for going down the PPP path, then there needs to be a method for deciding whether or not a project is 'on-balance sheet' for the Public Authority and hence the public sector as a whole.

It is clearly not an ideal approach for Governments to set their own public-accounting rules for PPPs, and there are international efforts to create consistency in this respect, based on the United Nations *System of National Accounts* ('SNA') last updated in 1993 (see Bibliography). The International Monetary Fund (IMF) has a 'Task Force on the Harmonization of the Public Sector Accounting', which covers, *inter alia*, the topic of 'Government/Public Sector/Private Sector Delineation' (see Bibliography). Within the European Union, Eurostat, the Statistical Office of the European Communities, provides the European Union with statistics from EU member countries on a harmonised basis, and as part of this process has to decide what should and should not be included within the figures for public-sector budgets. Eurostat's rules on government accounting which are based on SNA, are therefore a useful starting point in considering balance-sheet treatment for PPPs. (Figure 5.1 sets out the overall Eurostat approach in the form of a decision tree.)

§5.5.1 CONCESSIONS

In relation to Concessions, Eurostat's approach is quite straightforward: so long as less than 50% of the project's revenues are derived from public-sector payments (by subsidy or otherwise—*cf.* §13.4.3), the Facility concerned will be outside the public budget. But questions soon arise with this simple approach:

Public-sector guarantees. What if a financial or revenue guarantee, as opposed to funding or revenue support payments, is provided by the public sector? In this case the risk of such a guarantee being called upon has to be assessed, and it will only be counted against the public budget if it is likely to be called on for payment, and this would take public-sector support over 50%. This can obviously lead to some highly subjective views about what might happen, years into the future.

Public Concessionaires. What if the Project Company is publicly owned? Eurostat rules allow its assets to remain off the public-sector balance sheet if it is a 'market unit', *i.e.* is a publicly-owned entity which is already operating on an arm's length basis

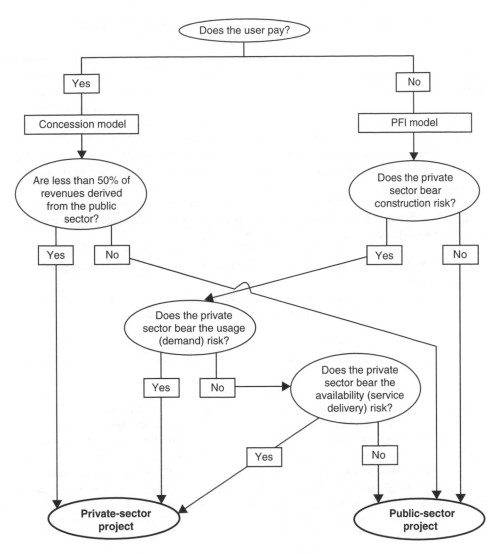

Figure 5.1   Decision tree for Eurostat balance-sheet treatment

from the state, follows the same rules in respect of subsidies or guarantees as a privately-owned company, and was not specifically set up for the sake of the particular project. This obviously leaves a lot of room for using 'public–public partnerships' (*cf.* §17.2.2).

50% of what? Eurostat takes a 'form over substance' approach when considering the 50% rule, so it is possible for a government to subsidise different parts of a system (*e.g.* a railway line and its trains) through different private-sector companies (one for the track and one for the trains) such that on a consolidated basis the subsidy exceeds 50%, but not when considered company by company.

§5.5.2 PFI MODEL—FINANCE LEASES AND OPERATING LEASES

Balance-sheet treatment of the PFI Model is more complex. A PFI-Model PPP Contract has obvious similarities with a lease (*cf.* §8.4.2). A lease involves payment for the use of an asset. If a car is hired for a day or two, it is obvious that the car belongs to the car-leasing company and should therefore be on its balance sheet. But if an aircraft is leased by an airline for 15 years, with the payments over that time substantially covering its capital and financing costs, this is evidently the same thing as a loan to buy the aircraft, and should therefore be on the balance sheet of the airline lessee not the financing lessor. Accounting standards for leasing therefore generally look at the extent to which the risks of ownership are transferred to the lessee (the user of the asset), *i.e.* a distinction is made between legal ownership (which remains with the lessor) and 'economic ownership', which reflects the reality of the situation. So if there are fixed lease payments and little substantial residual risk is left with the lessor, *e.g.*:

- if the NPV of the lease payments covers most of the cost of the asset—say 90% or more; and
- the term of the lease covers most of the useful life of the asset—say above 75%; and
- the lessee has the right to acquire the asset for a nominal sum;

the lessee is clearly the economic owner. This position is known as a 'finance lease' and will usually be treated in the same way as a loan, and thus transfer to the lessee's balance sheet. The amount to be shown on the balance is sheet is typically the NPV of the future lease payments, discounted at the effective lease interest rate.

On the other hand, if the lessor is the economic (as well as legal) owner, this is known as an 'operating lease' and the asset remains on the lessor's balance sheet. The short-term car rental mentioned above comes into this category. An operating lease may include the provision of other services—*e.g.* an operating 'wet lease' of an aircraft can include provision of not only the aircraft but also its flight crew, cabin staff and maintenance services.

Most PFI-Model structures do not involve residual risk (*cf.* §15.11), which suggests that the element of the Service Fees covering the capital cost of the project should be treated like an on-balance sheet finance lease to the Public Authority (especially if the Public Authority is also the legal owner of the Facility). The argument for not doing this is that in a PFI-Model contract other economic-ownership risks are taken by the Project Company, and it is thus similar to an operating lease; but as the discussion below will show, this is a very grey area. It is probably questionable whether a black-and-white decision—on or off the public-sector balance sheet—is appropriate, since it is clear that a PPP involves complex gradations of risk transfer. There is an argument for a more sophisticated approach which reflects this and would divide the balance-sheet recording between public and private sector.

However, where a project is still in the construction phase, it is generally accepted that public accounting does not require the Facility to be included in the public-sector balance sheet during this time, even if it might be considered a finance lease and placed on the public-sector balance sheet thereafter. Hence some variants of PPP structures just cover the construction phase, with the Facility reverting to public-sector control thereafter (*cf.* §17.3).

§5.5.3 The PFI Model—The Eurostat Approach

The Eurostat approach is based on the level of risk transfer—for a PFI-Model Facility to be off the public-sector balance sheet Eurostat requires a transfer to the private sector of (a) construction risk, and (b) either Availability risk (*i.e.* operating/service risk), or demand (usage) risk—which is of course the definition of a PPP adopted in this book (*cf.* §1.3). But the dividing line cannot be drawn as clearly as this statement might suggest. The problem is that transferring risk is not a simple issue which can be covered under such broad headings, as illustrated by the fuller discussion of risk transfer in Chapter 14, and in fact Eurostat states that the Public Authority must transfer 'most' (not 'all') of the risks involved, *e.g.*:

- If the Public Authority funds a substantial part of the construction cost, and does so irrespective of the progress of construction, this is likely to mean that the Public Authority is really taking the construction risk (*cf.* §13.3.5, §14.5.9).
- If the Public Authority has the right to deduct payments for poor performance, like any commercial client, this is likely to mean that the operating and service risk has been transferred to the Project Company, even if these deductions form a relatively small part of the Service Fees (*cf.* §13.5.2).
- If the Public Authority provides a guarantee (either of revenues or of the Project Company's debt), the same rule applies as for Concessions: if it is 'not likely' the guarantee will be called, this will not of itself affect the balance-sheet treatment.
- Eurostat rules on public-sector ownership of the Project Company are the same as for Concessions, so it is possible for an established public-sector company to enter into a PFI-Model PPP which is off the public-sector balance sheet, but not where it is a Project Company just set up to finance a specific Facility.

These uncertain boundaries for off-balance sheet treatment give rise to a danger of 'financial engineering' a structure for purely public-sector balance-sheet reasons—this is likely to be poor VfM for the Public Authority, since it will probably involve artificial risk transfer of some kind, whereby the private sector is paid for a risk it is not actually assuming. There must also be an implication—which adds further pressure to the process of measuring risk—that if a Facility remains on-balance sheet for the public sector, the level of risk transfer has not been adequate, and hence the PPP does not offer good VfM for the public sector (*cf.* §5.3.3).

§5.5.4 The PFI Model—The British Approach

The British Treasury has developed a more detailed approach to the public-sector balance-sheet treatment of the PFI Model, based on the British FRS5 accounting standard for private-sector companies (which remain consistent with the later and broader Eurostat rules discussed above). This takes a 'substance over form' approach (*i.e.* the balance-sheet status cannot be passed by mechanical tests; the commercial reality of the transaction has to be taken into account). There are three stages to the balance-sheet decision:

Separability. The question to be asked here is whether the Service Fees under the PPP Contract can be divided into a 'lease'-type payment covering the project's capex, and a service payment covering the opex. This would be the case if the payments were clearly divided into a part which covers the capex (similar to the Availability Charge in the case of a PPA (*cf.* §1.4.2) and another part which covers the opex. If so the capex element would be on the public-sector balance sheet (unless there is a significant transfer of residual risk (*cf.* §15.11)). Therefore although, as will be seen below, the payments by the Public Authority are built up from both capex and opex elements, once the initial level of the payments has been calculated it should not vary on this basis thereafter if the Facility is to remain off the public-sector balance sheet. This is the reason that the term 'Unitary Charge' (or 'Unitary Payment') was devised in the United Kingdom for the Service Fees under a PFI-Model PPP Contract, emphasising the point that the Service Fees are not separable into their different elements. Having said this, as will be seen below (*cf.* §12.4.8, 15.2.5), in reality the Service Fees may vary with individual cost items.

Risk transfer Assuming that the Public Authority's payments are not separable, the next question is whether there has been a substantial transfer of risk to the private sector, or have significant risks been retained by the Public Authority, for example:

- Does the Public Authority repay the project's debt if it goes into default (*cf.* §15.5.1)?
- Is there such a high level of debt that lenders must be taking no risks?
- Does the Public Authority decide how the PFI Contract is to be fulfilled (since presumably it would then be taking the risk if it is not fulfilled)? This obviously reinforces the requirement that a PPP should be based on output specifications (*cf.* §1.3.2, §2.2).

If the answer to any of these questions is 'yes', the project will probably be on the public-sector balance sheet.

Quantitative risk analysis. Inevitably there will be some risks retained by the Public Authority (*cf.* §15.2.4); these should be quantified and discounted to an NPV. If this NPV is 'substantial' in relation to the NPV of project costs as a whole, or to risks assumed by the Project Company it is reasonable to assume that adequate risk transfer has not taken place to get the Facility off the public-sector balance sheet. This means that, for example, usage risk for a school has to be quantified and shown not be substantial, where this risk is retained by the Public Authority.

Since this approach looks at the substance of the transaction rather than its formal structure, it has to involve questions of judgement, *e.g.* in 'valuing' risk transfer. This means that the final decision on balance-sheet treatment is not always obvious, relies heavily on accountants' opinions, and is actually as subjective as the similar process in preparing a PSC, discussed above.

Perhaps not surprisingly, the actual balance-sheet treatment of PFI projects in Britain is confusing, and different government auditing bodies have taken different views on the matter. Central-government accommodation projects, prisons, roads (*cf.* §13.4.5), *etc.*, have been placed on-balance sheet after further review of risk transfer; however hospitals in England (but not in Scotland) are off-balance sheet as are most local-government projects. PFI projects classified as finance leases and so included in public-sector debt in 2006 are shown in Table 5.2; these are considerably smaller in total than the £23 billion of PFI

Table 5.2
Finance-lease liabilities in U.K. public-sector debt, 2006

Public Authority	Projects	Finance Amount (£ million)
Department for Transport	Shadow-Toll roads ($\times$11)	973
Transport for London	London Underground ($\times$3)	858
Ministry of Defence	Accommodation & equipment ($\times$13)	658
Home Office	Prisons ($\times$12)	378
Foreign Office	Government Communications HQ	310
HM Treasury	Office	152
HM Revenue & Customs	Office	187
Scottish Executive	Hospitals ($\times$3)	207
n/a	Channel Tunnel Rail Link	220
Other		208
Total		**4,151**

Source: Office for National Statistics (see Bibliography)

projects said to be on-balance sheet at that time (*cf.* §3.4.3), firstly because, as discussed above, where PFI projects are shown as public-sector debt, this only occurs after completion of construction, and secondly because the amount shown is the finance lease amount, *i.e.* the NPV of only the capital element of the Service Fees. (The London Underground projects also inflate the £23 billion figure considerably—see the note to Table 3.2.) The original intention seems to have been that all PFI projects should be off-balance sheet, but at some point during the procurement process (when it was too late to change the procurement strategy), or thereafter, the view changed. If an increasing proportion of projects finds its way onto the public-sector balance sheet, the prospects for further growth in the PFI programme appear limited, since the same construction-period balance-sheet benefits and at least some long-term transfer of maintenance risks can be achieved by other less financially-complex means (*cf.* §17.2.1, §17.3). A reduction in central-government projects is already evident.

However, discussion on balance-sheet treatment is only relevant in countries where restraints on public-infrastructure investment arise from artificial constraints, such as the Maastricht Treaty limits on public budgets in the European Union. In other countries, such as South Africa, the issue is not artificial—there is a clear budgetary limit on the government's ability to provide funding for infrastructure, and private-sector funding through PPPs therefore offers the only way of accelerating this provision.

Chapter 6

Public-Sector Procurement and Contract Management

§6.1 INTRODUCTION

This chapter considers procurement and management of a PPP project from the point of view of a Public Authority (sometimes known in this context as the 'Promoter' of the project). The following chapter follows the same process from the point of view of investors, and later chapters consider the lenders' viewpoint.

The life of a PPP project can be divided into four phases:

Initial feasibility. This is the period during which the Public Authority considers whether direct public-sector procurement or indirect procurement through a PPP is the appropriate route, and decides in principle to proceed with the project on a PPP basis, as discussed in the previous Chapter. The presentation of the project, taking all these factors into account, for political approval within the Public Authority (or to regional or central government) is known as the 'Business Case', which is often publicly available. The Public Authority needs to set up a project-management structure to manage the process thereafter (§6.2).

Procurement phase. The period during which:

- bids are requested and received, and a bidder is chosen (§6.3–§6.4);
- a special-purpose Project Company (*cf.* §7.6) is formed, in whose name the PPP Contract and the various Subcontracts for construction, service delivery/operation, *etc.* (all of which are known collectively as the 'Project Contracts') are negotiated (*cf.* §6.5.2);
- the Public Authority's due-diligence process is completed (§6.5);
- the investors' equity investment (see Chapter 7) and the lenders' funding (see Chapter 9) are put in place.

It should be noted that 'public procurement' is used in this context to mean the process whereby a Public Authority enters into a contract with a private-sector supplier, to be distinguished from 'public-sector procurement', which is used to mean direct procurement by the Public Authority instead of *via* a PPP (cf. §1.3.2).

The end of the public-procurement phase is known as 'Financial Close' (or the 'Effective Date'), *i.e.* the point at which all the inter-linked conditions precedent for the Project Contracts and the funding are met (§6.5.4), and construction of the Facility can begin.

Construction phase. Once a project has reached Financial Close, the Public Authority's relationship with the Project Company (and through the Project Company with the investors, lenders, and Subcontractors) is one of contract management (§6.6).

During the construction phase the project's debt and equity investment are drawn down, and these funds are used to build the Facility—the end of this process, when the Facility is formally accepted as being available for use as specified in the PPP Contract (*cf.* §6.6.6), is known as the Service Availability Date (or the Service Commencement Date).

Operation phase. The period during which the Facility provides the services required by the PPP Contract and produces cash flow to pay the lenders' debt service, and the investors' equity return. The Public Authority's contract management rôle continues.

Throughout these processes, the Public Authority uses the services of specialised external advisers (§6.7).

§6.2 PROJECT MANAGEMENT

The procurement process can be very demanding for the Public Authority, which may have limited experience of procuring major projects, and even less with PPPs, since such projects are typically scattered across a variety of different public-sector bodies within a country. If this is the case, it does not make economic sense for the Public Authority to maintain staff with procurement skills, so once a deal has been done the project team will be disbanded. PPP procurement seldom forms part of the regular career path for a civil servant, and it is often difficult for expertise gained in a PPP by one Public Authority to be transferred to others. So although it can be argued that PPPs improve public-sector procurement skills (*cf.* §2.10), in reality the experience may be wasted. The importance of public-sector centres of expertise (*cf.* §3.2) is therefore evident.

This is not a book about project management, but some of the organisational issues for a Public Authority taking a PPP project through procurement and negotiation to Financial Close are considered briefly below.

§6.2.1 PROJECT TEAM AND GOVERNANCE

A full-time project director is needed—this is not a job which can be combined easily with other official work. The project director should be able to draw in expertise from the Public

Authority's other departments, *e.g.* technical, finance and legal, to put together the procurement team. As discussed below (§6.7), external advisers will provide support, but should not be put in the position of running the project because of a vacuum within the Public Authority's project team.

If the government has set up a central or departmental PPP Unit, someone from this unit may be available to provide further support. Ireland took this a step further in 2005 by extending the functions of the National Development Finance Agency (*cf.* §3.2) from pure advisory work to running procurements on behalf of the Public Authority in newer sectors of the PPP market—which *de facto* is what PPP Units tend to end up doing anyway.

The project director is likely to report to an *ad hoc* project board or steering committee, which may include senior officers from the Public Authority, and possibly politicians as well, depending on the Public Authority's general organisation. The project board will agree the overall plan for procurement and the parameters for negotiation, and monitor progress against targets. One of the most regular criticisms of public-sector procurement of PPPs is a lack of clarity about the decision chain: it is obviously important for the project director to have authority to negotiate matters of detail with the private-sector side of the table, rather than constantly having to refer back to the project board, although the final PPP Contract will probably require formal approval from the Public Authority's political masters, and perhaps also other government departments.

The project director will need to ensure that political support for the PPP is not lost (*cf.* §2.11): part of this rôle is likely to involve liaison with 'stakeholders', *i.e.* potential users of the Facility such as parents and teachers in a new school. If important stakeholder groups are not properly involved this is likely to mean either that outright opposition to the project develops, or that late and expensive alterations have to be made to the plans when stakeholders start raising objections.

§6.2.2 PROJECT REVIEW

It is also helpful for there to be some form of independent review procedure as the project reaches each key stage, preferably by a regional or central government committee which can take full advantage of wider PPP experience, including in other economic sectors. This can take place (through reviewing successive revisions of the Business Case) at the time of:

- the initial decision to use the PPP route (*cf.* Chapter 5);
- formal approaches to the private sector for bids (*cf.* §6.3.4);
- bid evaluation (*cf.* §6.3.6);
- just prior to Financial Close, to reconfirm that the final result of the process still appears to offer VfM for the Public Authority.

An independent *ex-post* audit of the procurement procedure for transparency and fairness, and to confirm VfM and that the original policy objectives have been met, is also valuable, not least to summarise lessons for the future. Similarly, continuing audit and evaluation is important once a Facility is in operation, to review whether the original objectives (*e.g.* as to costs, service and risk transfer) have been met, and whether there have been other unexpected outcomes, so that the benefit of this experience can also be used in future.

§6.3 PROCUREMENT PROCEDURES

Procurement procedure may be considered no more than a technical matter of little general importance, but actually it is at the core of the PPP process. The major argument in favour of using PPPs is that they can create savings in cost compared to publicly funded projects (*cf.* §2.6), but a badly run procurement can all too easily destroy any potential for such a saving. Only effective competition—*i.e.* an efficient procurement procedure—can generate VfM for the Public Authority.

A competitive public-procurement process is a legal requirement in most countries where services are being provided to the public (as in a Concession), or a public contract is involved (as in the PFI Model), and it is generally also required if funding or guarantees are being provided by multilateral banks, such as the European Investment Bank (*cf.* §17.4.4). In such cases the bidding process has to follow a specific procurement procedure. The framework for public-procurement procedures is provided by the *Agreement on Government Procurement* (GPA), administered by the World Trade Organisation (WTO), to which most developed countries are parties. This was first signed in 1979, and last amended in 1994. Important detailed rules based on these provisions are those contained in the European Union (EU) public-procurement regulations, which have been developed to deal with PPPs in a variety of countries with differing approaches and legal frameworks.

§6.3.1 THE BIDDING PROCESS

The WTO GPA allows for three types of public procurement:

'Open' procedure. This procedure allows anyone to bid.
'Selective' procedure. This procedure allows the Public Authority to reduce the number of prospective bidders through a pre-qualification procedure (*cf.* §6.3.3).
'Limited' procedure. Under this procedure the Public Authority approaches prospective bidders directly rather than calling for tenders (with or without pre-qualification).

The limited procedure is unlikely to be appropriate for a PPP, and is therefore not considered further in this context. Using EU procurement procedures as an example of how the GPA is implemented, until 2006, EU law allowed for three types of bid procedure:

Open procedure. As under the GPA—not normally used for PPPs.
Restricted Procedure. Under this procedure, following pre-qualification, the requirements of the bid may be discussed with bidders, and then tender documents are issued. Further clarifications may be made thereafter, but once bids are received that is the end of the process: the decision is made on the basis of the bids, and there should be no further negotiation with bidders, who are expected to sign the PPP Contract on the basis set out in their bids. This approach is mainly used for Concessions, *e.g.* in Italy and Spain, and provides a relatively quick and hence potentially lower-cost procedure for bidders. It is also considered preferable in countries (not just in Europe) where there is concern about any kind of post-bid discussion being open to suggestions of corruption.

Negotiated Procedure. The Negotiated Procedure is intended for complex contracts
where bidders may provide different solutions for the service concerned, and the
basis for bidding the overall pricing cannot be easily specified in advance, so requiring further discussion after bids are received. Such 'clarification' should not however
result in fundamental changes to the basis of the original bid, and also implies that
detailed negotiations take place with all bidders. (This procedure broadly reflects the
GPA rules, which also allow for negotiations.)

De facto, however, the scope of the Negotiated Procedure has been expanded well beyond
'clarification', especially in the British PFI programme, and other countries' PPP programmes
where PFI has been used as a model (*e.g.* Portugal). In such cases, the Public Authority
chooses a 'Preferred Bidder' (also known as 'Preferred Proponent'), often after going through a
multi-stage bidding procedure—*e.g.* three bidders may put in initial proposals, and then after
further negotiations two of them are chosen to submit their 'best and final offer' ('BAFO');
there may be a further stage where bidders submit their 'LAFO' ('last and final offer').
Further detailed and often quite lengthy negotiations then take place with the Preferred Bidder
before final award of the PPP Contract. This procedure has changed little in Britain, despite the
fact that PFI-Model projects such as schools have become increasingly 'commoditised', making
the argument that the project is so complex that it needs a special procedure rather weak.

To better accommodate the British procedure, and because in a number of European countries with strict domestic laws on public procurement, there were concerns on whether the
Negotiated Procedure was sufficiently open and transparent, the EU introduced a new procedure in 2006:

Competitive Dialogue. Under this procedure, following pre-qualification the Public
Authority discusses the form of PPP Contract and the technical specifications of the
project with the pre-qualified bidders. Tender documents are then issued. The Public
Authority can then enter into further discussions with bidders on any issues that they
may raise on the contract, which may result in revisions to the project requirements,
before the bidders finally present their bids. There is still provision for 'clarifications'
of bids after they are presented.

In summary, therefore, there is a major divide in PPP procurement practice between what
may be described as the 'bid envelope' procedure—*i.e.* one where bidders are primarily
bidding a price (and perhaps a design), with little or no contract negotiation taking place
with the Public Authority after the bid has taken place—and the 'Preferred Bidder' procedure,
where such negotiation does take place. There is normally a substantial difference in time
and cost between the bid envelope and Preferred Bidder approaches. And, as discussed in
§6.3.8, a bidding procedure which allows for negotiation, of whatever kind, after submission
of the bids, is very difficult to control.

§6.3.2 MARKET SOUNDINGS

Whatever the formal procurement procedure, the Public Authority needs to take some
initial steps to confirm that its own view of the basic viability of its PPP project is shared

by major private-sector participants in the market. This is normally undertaken by making preliminary market soundings, explaining the concept behind the project. Clearly the Public Authority needs to ensure that no party is given an advantage through having been involved in these soundings, and in some cases the best way to do this may be to hold an open public meeting.

In parallel with this, as discussed above (*cf.* §6.2.1), stakeholders need to be kept fully involved.

§6.3.3 PRE-QUALIFICATION

A 'Request for Qualifications' (RFQ) or call for 'Expressions of Interest' (EoI) from prospective bidders is usually the first formal stage in the bidding process for a public-sector contract. The project is advertised in official publications—in Europe this means the *Official Journal of the European Union* (known as 'OJEU'; formerly the *Official Journal of the European Communities* or 'OJEC')—and the financial and trade press. Interested bidding groups are provided with a summary of the project and its requirements (insofar as these can be specified in advance of proposals), and they are invited to set out their qualifications to undertake the project, demonstrating:

- technical capacity to carry out the project (either directly or *via* specified major Subcontractors);
- experience and performance with similar projects;
- financial capacity to carry out the project (*cf.* §14.6.2).

Bidders who do not meet minimum criteria at this stage are then excluded, and the other bidders invited to bid. Pre-qualification decisions may be fairly subjective, where the criteria for pre-qualification are themselves subjective judgements.

Pre-qualification may go a stage further by drawing up a initial short-list of bidders (typically three or four), if the relevant procurement rules allow this (World Bank procurement rules, for example, do not). This procedure is desirable because if there are too many bidders for the project the chances of winning the bid may be too small to make it worth the prospective bidders' while to spend the considerable time and cost involved in preparing and submitting a bid. Of course, fewer bidders also make managing the whole process easier.

§6.3.4 TENDER DOCUMENTS

There are a variety of names for the tender document package, depending on the nature of the bidding procedure:

- Restricted Procedure—Invitation to Tender (ITT), Invitation to Bid (ITB) or Request for Proposals (RFP);
- Negotiated Procedure—Invitation to Negotiate (ITN), or Project Brief;
- Competitive Dialogue—Invitation to Competitive Dialogue (ICD).

The basic content of all these tender documents is the same; it is mainly the dialogue with bidders and procedures before and after they are issued, as discussed above, which differ. The tender documents are accompanied with an information package which sets out, *e.g.*:

- general legislative and policy background;
- project *raison d'être*;
- service requirements;
- support to be provided by the Public Authority, either financial (*cf.* §13.4.3), or, *e.g.* through building a connecting road (*cf.* §14.5.7);
- data on the market, *e.g.* traffic flows, for PPPs where usage risk is being transferred to the private sector;
- a draft PPP Contract, including risk-transfer provisions, performance specifications and proposed pricing formula (*cf.* §3.3);
- programme for site visits, bid meetings, and procedure for clarifications;
- the form of bid required;
- bid deadline;
- bid-evaluation criteria (*cf.* §6.3.6);
- overall project timetable.

The bidder's response to the tender is likely to be required to cover issues (insofar as these have not been clarified in advance) such as:

- technology and design;
- construction programme;
- service standards and delivery;
- details of Subcontracts and Subcontractors;
- management structures for both the construction and service delivery/operation phases;
- quality- and safety-assurance procedures;
- commercial viability (*e.g.* traffic or demand projections for a Concession);
- insurance coverage;
- project costs (*cf.* §10.2);
- financing strategy and structure (*cf.* §9.3.3);
- qualifications or proposed amendments to the proposed draft PPP Contract;
- proposals for the Service Fees.

§6.3.5 COMMUNICATION WITH BIDDERS

Whatever the bid procedure, the same information should be made available to all bidders, *e.g.* by:

- holding bidder meetings and site visits which all attend, which can be helpful to flush out any major issues which bidders may have with the project; and
- copying written answers to questions or issues raised by one bidder to all of them, without indicating who asked the original question.

Bidders should be given a specific point of contact within the Public Authority, and should not be allowed to make contacts elsewhere in the organisation.

Discussions with bidders may lead to modifications in the bid requirements: in such cases the bid schedule may have to be delayed to give bidders enough time to deal with these modifications. On the other hand, bidder confidentiality has to be respected, *e.g.* where there may be several different solutions to executing the project.

§6.3.6 BID EVALUATION

A method is needed to compare the bids with each other, and bidders need to understand clearly what they have to do to produce the best bid. There are various approaches for comparing the bids:

Price comparison. If the bids can be submitted on virtually identical bases then the final decision may be a question of simply comparing the Service Fees, although it may be necessary to discount the amounts payable in future to an NPV to compare like with like. The choice of a discount rate for this purpose will obviously affect the result(*cf.* §5.3.2).

Adjustments may still have to be made to a simple comparison, however, for the cost of exceptions to the proposed terms of the PPP Contract or other differences in risk transfer, or bids that are considered to be over-ambitious in their projections of performance or financing plans.

This approach may be workable for a well-controlled Restricted Bid procedure for a process plant or, say, a road Concession, where all other issues have been clarified before the bid, but is unlikely to be the only basis for a decision in a project with a more complex payment structure such as a PFI-Model accommodation project (*cf.* §13.5). Furthermore, even when considering cost alone, which appears simple in principle, one of the most difficult aspects of PPP bid evaluation is the trade-off between cost and long-term flexibility, especially where a low initial cost is produced by financing structuring (*cf.* §11.3.4).

Contract term. An alternative approach, especially for Concessions, is to fix the Service Fees and then ask bidders to bid for whatever term of PPP Contract they require—obviously the shortest bid wins (*cf.* §13.3.1). Variants on this approach are to leave the term open-ended, and terminate the PPP Contract when:

- the rate of return required by bidders is achieved—here the lowest required rate of return wins the bid; or
- the NPV of revenues required by bidders has been reached—here the bidder with the lowest required NPV of revenues wins the bid (*cf.* §13.4.4).

But all these approaches raise similar issues to a simple price comparison.

Level of subsidy. Some tenders are not based on the basis of the price to be charged for the service, but the level of subsidy to be provided by the public-sector. This approach is relevant if the bid relates to a Concession where it is known that Service Fees will not produce sufficient revenue to cover the funding required for the project (*cf.* §13.4.3). Conversely, bids may include payments by the bidders instead of to them (*cf.* §13.3.6).

'Most economically advantageous' bid. A more complex system is based on 'scoring' different aspects of the bid—giving points for design, speed of completion, reliability, quality of service, risk assumption by the bidder (*i.e.* transfer of risk away from the public sector) and any other characteristics that are important to the Public Authority as well as the price, thus identifying the bid that is the 'most economically advantageous' to the project. The weight to be given to different factors should be set out in the ITT/ITN; there must inevitably be an element of subjectivity, both in how these factors are weighted against each other, and how different aspects of the same factors are compared when these are non-financial. Weightings are obviously quite project-specific: *e.g.* if bidders are likely to rely on the same design or technology solutions, Service-Fee cost might be weighted 70%, but if there is much scope for innovative solutions, technical proposals might be weighted 70%.

The prequalification process should have already eliminated bidders for whom there are questions about financial capacity, technology, or ability to do undertake the project, so further fundamental qualitative comparisons of this nature should be limited in scope. However, the overall financing plan for the project does need to be examined (*cf.* §6.5.3), and bids must be submitted using common financial assumptions where this is appropriate (*e.g.* as to base interest and inflation rates—see Chapter 11). Similarly, the detailed feasibility of the construction and operation arrangements, including Subcontracts needs to be reviewed (*cf.* §6.5.2).

§6.3.7 COMMERCIAL VIABILITY

When evaluating bids it is always worth stepping back and considering whether the bidders' proposals make commercial sense—*i.e.* if the bid is accepted, would the Facility be provided on viable terms for all parties—investors, Subcontractors, the Public Authority and end-users? Contracts that give a disproportionate advantage to one side are vulnerable as an aggrieved party will obviously make use of any flaw in the contract to get out of an unduly onerous obligation.

If a bidder's pricing is much lower than the Public Authority's original estimates (*cf.* §10.2), this suggests that the bidder or a Subcontractor has made a mistake somewhere. The Public Authority may take the view that pricing mistakes are the bidder's problem, but the primary objective of the PPP is to deliver a public service, and it is highly likely this delivery will be jeopardised if the Project Company or its Subcontractor cannot earn enough to make the work worthwhile. If the Project Company fails to perform as required, the Public Authority can terminate the PPP Contract (*cf.* §15.5), but this is likely to result in extra costs to sort the situation out, and unlikely to result in the service being provided in the way originally expected.

§6.3.8 POST-BID NEGOTIATION

Negotiations post-bid—*i.e.* after the Public Authority has appointed a Preferred Bidder—should not happen in the Restricted Bid procedure, and are undesirable, even if permitted, in the Negotiated procedure. Such negotiations can sometimes drag on for long periods of time. The reasons for these delays (and the need for negotiations in the first place) include:

- lack of adequate preparation by the Public Authority before launching the bid process, often linked to political pressure to be seen to be moving the project forward; this results in incomplete project specification or PPP Contract drafting, so forcing the Public Authority into substantial renegotiation of the bid under the guise of 'clarification';
- even worse, the Public Authority changing its mind about the requirements after the bid process has begun, perhaps because of Affordability problems;
- poor programme management by the Public Authority and a failure to drive the project forward;
- tripartite negotiations with the lenders, if their commitment to provide funding has not been secured before the bid is presented (*cf.* §9.3.3);
- environmental, planning or other site-related issues which were not dealt with before the bids are submitted (*cf.* §14.5);
- issues arising from the due-diligence process on the part of the Public Authority (*cf.* §6.5), the lenders (*cf.* §9.3.4) or other parties such as Subcontractors.

Any significant delay between appointment of a Preferred Bidder and Financial Close almost inevitably leads to rises in project costs, and hence in the Service Fees. The Construction Subcontract price will be based on starting work by a certain date, and will be subject to inflation indexing, or open to complete revision, if this date is not achieved. Worse than this, the issues set out above may be used as a hook to increase other aspects of the PPP Contract pricing or to change risk transfer for the benefit of the Preferred Bidder (a process known as 'deal creep'), even though substantial changes to the final bid terms could be open to legal challenge by losing bidders (*cf.* §6.4.6).

It is a fairly simple rule that the longer the post-bid negotiation period the worse the Public Authority's position becomes. Without any competitive tension between bidders, the Preferred Bidder effectively becomes a monopoly supplier (even if theoretically the Public Authority could go back to the other bidders this is seldom workable in practice, not least because the losing bidding team will have been redeployed elsewhere by their employers). The Public Authority, which by then will be heavily and publicly committed to the project, cannot easily walk away and start again without causing major political problems. The claim that PPP projects do not involve cost overruns (*cf.* §2.6.1) becomes dubious if deal creep causes increases in cost (or reductions in project scope, which come to the same thing) between appointment of the Preferred Bidder and final signature of the PPP Contract. Time and care spent on preparation before beginning the bidding process is seldom wasted. Therefore there is a lot to be said for using the Restricted Bid procedure, which relies on this preparation and should avoid deal creep after the bids.

It is also true to say that even though long negotiations may thus be beneficial to private-sector bidders, a lengthy and complex procurement process is of concern to them because of the accumulated bid costs which they have at risk (*cf.* §7.4).

§6.3.9 BID AWARD

Fairness and transparency in the bidding process are essential; if bidders do not understand or trust the process, or do not believe there is a genuine competition in which they have a good prospect of winning, it is evident that the best results will not be achieved. Thus, a full and detailed record should be kept of the bid comparisons, and why a particular bidder was chosen (indeed this is often a legal requirement). It is a common procedure for the losing bidder to be given a briefing on why the winner was chosen in preference.

§6.4 OTHER PROCUREMENT ISSUES

§6.4.1 FUNDING COMMITMENTS

See §9.3.3 for a discussion of the extent to which bids should be accompanied by funding commitments from lenders, and §9.3.4 for lenders' own due diligence.

§6.4.2 NONCONFORMING BIDS

It may be beneficial not to be too prescriptive about the bid requirements, since bidders may then come up with solutions for providing the Facility which, although not previously considered, may actually be better for the Public Authority. This links to the 'private-sector innovation' argument for PPPs (*cf.* §2.9.5).

A standard procedure is that bidders must make at least one bid that conforms to the requirements of the ITT/ITN, but they may also offer alternative ('variant') bids that do not conform (perhaps within pre-defined parameters). The Public Authority then has the option to choose such a nonconforming bid if it offers a better solution.

§6.4.3 BID CONSORTIUM CHANGES

After a particular bidding consortium has been pre-qualified, one of its members may not wish to proceed, and the consortium may wish to introduce a new member, perhaps a bidder in a consortium that previously did not pre-qualify. Other bidders may object to this, but it may be preferable not to exclude changes of this kind completely and to leave some discretion on the matter (*e.g.* if the new member can demonstrate it is as well qualified as the one it is succeeding, and would not have caused the consortium to be ruled out at the pre-qualification stage). An alternative approach is to allow changes in the consortium only after the winning bid has been selected. However in some countries (*e.g.* Germany) changes in bidding consortia are simply not allowed.

Obviously no bidder should be allowed to participate in more than one consortium at the same time, as this could lead to leakages of information or collusion between consortia.

§6.4.4 Bonding

Bidders are sometimes required to provide bid bonds from their bankers, as security for their proceeding with the bid once it has been made. The bond is released when the contract documentation is signed, or when construction of the project begins. The amount of the bond may be quite significant in absolute terms (*e.g.* 1–2% of the project value). This helps to deal with the problem of 'deliverability'—*i.e.* presentation of an aggressive bid which cannot be financed, or where the bidders hope to improve their position once they are the Preferred Bidder.

§6.4.5 Payment of Bid Costs

The corollary of bonding for bidders is an agreement by the Public Authority conducting the bid that if the process is cancelled at any stage bidders should be compensated for the costs they have incurred, perhaps up to a certain limit. Losing bidders may even be given some compensation for their costs in any case, to encourage competition in a complex project, or to help secure funding commitments with their bids (*cf.* §9.3.3).

§6.4.6 Challenges

Failure to follow procurement laws may lay the award of the PPP Contract open to legal attack; this may be a problem only for the Public Authority if the legal remedy is financial compensation, but it may also be possible for the PPP Contract to be declared invalid, which clearly has serious consequences for the private-sector side and the project itself.

§6.4.7 Unsolicited Proposals

An issue which cuts across standard procurement procedures is that of unsolicited proposals for PPP projects—*i.e.* a private-sector consortium proposes a PPP rather than responds to a public-sector request for proposals. If private-sector innovation is a merit of PPPs (*cf.* §2.9.5) then such proposals should be encouraged if they really consist of new ideas, but if the Public Authority just picks up the ideas and then calls for open bids in the same way as described above there is obviously no incentive for a private-sector party to make the unsolicited proposal in the first place. There is thus a difficult balance, for if, on the other hand, too much preference is given to the original proposer there will be no competing bids and the pricing can easily become excessive.

A procedure which tries to strike a balance is for the details of the unsolicited proposal to be published by the Public Authority, inviting other competing proposals on a similar basis to the unsolicited bid. If a competing proposal is considered more economically advantageous, the unsolicited bidder will have a right to match its terms and be awarded the PPP Contract, or the original proposer may be given an extra weighting in the evaluation criteria (for example under the Korean PPI Law an extra weighting of up to 10% can be given in bid evaluations). However, the incentive for competitive bidding is still less than ideal in such cases, and hence unsolicited proposals have to be treated with considerable caution. Under the Korean PPI Law unsolicited proposals can only relate to Concessions, not PFI-Model projects, presumably on the grounds that the latter will not require any direct public-sector funding.

§6.5 DUE DILIGENCE

The Public Authority needs to go through a due-diligence process—*i.e.* a detailed review of contracts to ensure that they appear 'fit for purpose' and able to provide what is needed for the PPP project to be successful, and also that terms do not indirectly create onerous obligations for the Public Authority—with respect to design (§6.5.1), the Subcontracts (§6.5.2), financing documents (§6.5.3) and insurance arrangements (*cf.* §6.7.4), prior to Financial Close (§6.5.4).

This process should ideally be completed at the bid evaluation stage, but it may, at least partly, slip beyond that, *i.e.* after a Preferred Bidder has been appointed (*cf.* §6.3.8). A parallel process is carried out by the lenders (*cf.* §9.3.4), and by other parties such as Subcontractors.

§6.5.1 PROJECT DESIGN

Design proposals submitted at the bid stage are typically conceptual in nature and are more often than not substantially modified during negotiations. Even then detailed design is usually finalised after Financial Close. Design is thus a process where due diligence continues after Financial Close, as discussed in more detail in §6.6.1.

§6.5.2 SUBCONTRACTS

At the time of pre-qualification the Project Company's main Subcontractors—*e.g.* for construction, operation, maintenance or services—should have been approved by the Public Authority from the point of view of both financial and technical capacity. These issues should therefore not need to be reopened unless there is a significant change since they were reviewed. But it is still necessary to review:

- the detailed costing and planning for these contracts to ensure that they appear to be capable of delivering the requirements of the PPP Contract; and
- their detailed terms to ensure that there is nothing in them obviously incompatible with the Project Company's own obligations under the PPP Contract. For example, the levels of delay liquidated damages in the Subcontracts (and the bonding for this) should be adequate in relation to the Project Company's liabilities to the Public Authority for delay in completing the Facility (*cf.* §13.3.4).

The Public Authority may wish to be able to take over the Subcontracts if it steps in to take control of the Facility or the PPP Contract is terminated for default by the Project Company (*cf.* §15.4.1): if so such provisions will need to be 'entrenched', although they will have to take second place to the lenders' security interests. In addition, the Public Authority will need to ensure that in cases where provisions of the Subcontracts may have a direct effect on its liabilities (*e.g.* relating to payments on termination of the PPP Contract—*cf.* §15.9) these are acceptable and also cannot be changed without the Public Authority's consent.

However, this does not imply that the Public Authority should 'sign off' on these Subcontracts, and hence take the risk of any incompatibility between them and the PPP Contract requirements.

§6.5.3 FINANCING

The purist view would be that the bidder is responsible for financing and therefore the Public Authority need not concern itself with the matter. In reality, the Public Authority will find it hard to keep the finance at arm's length, as the lenders' own due-diligence process (*cf.* §9.3.4) may throw up issues which the lenders may wish to negotiate with the Public Authority directly. This is something best avoided (although this can be difficult), as it is likely to mean that bidders get 'two bites at the cherry', *i.e.* what they cannot win in their own negotiation with the Public Authority can be reopened and renegotiated by the lenders on their behalf.

Nevertheless, various aspects of the financing should be reviewed by the Public Authority from its own due-diligence point of view. It is no use appointing a Preferred Bidder who does not have a realistic financing plan, and therefore the Public Authority needs to assess this plan in reasonable detail to ensure that it is both deliverable in the short term, and provides a stable long-term basis for the Project Company's operations. The Public Authority also needs to understand the implications of the financing structure for the PPP Contract as a whole, both as to the payment structure (*cf.* §13.2) and long-term flexibility and the cost of early termination of the PPP Contract (*cf.* §15.5–§15.10), taking any financial hedging into account (*cf.* Chapter 11). Lenders' views on risk transfer (*cf.* §14.2) have to be taken into account. Attention will need to be paid to the lenders' security requirements, including Reserve Accounts (*cf.* §12.2.4). It is clearly in the Public Authority's interests to make suggestions for any improvement to the financing plan in the early stages of negotiations, if this is possible, to be fed through as a reduction in the Service Fees; and if there is a Funding Competition (*cf.* §16.2), the Public Authority's involvement will be substantial.

Of course this is why the Public Authority needs its own financial adviser (*cf.* §6.7.1).

§6.5.4 FINANCIAL CLOSE

The formal legal requirements which have to be fulfilled to reach Financial Close usually consist of a very long list of documents, which if not managed effectively may seriously delay the start of construction. The Preferred Bidder will need the support of the Public Authority to manage this process, for example by gathering and checking off as much of this condition-precedent documentation as possible in advance of the signing of the PPP Contracts and the financing documentation, to ensure the minimum delay before Financial Close. Checking off conditions precedent before signing the financing documentation also ensures that there are no unexpected surprises, *e.g.* from issues raised by lenders after the loan has been signed.

The Financial Close conditions are often circular in nature—*e.g.* the PPP Contract does not become effective until the funding is available for drawing, and the funding does not become available until the PPP Contract is effective—and so Financial Close is a simultaneous exercise in which all the parties to the PPP project structure are involved.

There can also be an interim 'Commercial Close' (also known as 'Contractual Close'), when the Project Contracts have been signed but are still subject to the completion of the financing or the satisfaction of other Financial Close conditions, often so the politicians can say the deal has been done. But this takes the pressure off the process and it is better to avoid this limbo stage if possible.

§6.6 CONTRACT MANAGEMENT

The Public Authority's contract management team takes over after Financial Close. It is obviously preferable for there to be the maximum continuity with the project-management team discussed above (*cf.* §6.2.1), and if contract managers are not actually part of the project-management team, they should still be involved in the detailed final stages of negotiating the PPP Contract.

An important aspect of the delivery of the PPP project to the contract-management team is a project manual, which should be drawn up by the project-management team and sets out the key terms of the PPP Contract, and particular points to watch out for.

In an ideal world, once the PPP Contract has been signed, both parties can just put it in the drawer and concentrate on getting the job done, but matters are seldom as simple as this. However it is true to say that a cooperative relationship (not a one-sided one which uses 'partnership' as a façade for commercial gain) is the best way to ensure long-term success for a PPP.

§6.6.1 PROJECT DESIGN

Detailed design (and engineering, where relevant) of the Facility after Financial Close is normally the responsibility of the Project Company (*cf.* §6.5.1, but *cf.* further comments on design in §14.7.3). Although the basic design will have been set out in the PPP Contract (perhaps based on an outline design from the Public Authority), much of the detailed work may not be undertaken until after Financial Close. If the Public Authority has specified the output required (*cf.* §2.9.5), the Project Company must take the risk that the detailed design will not fulfil this requirement.

This does not mean that the Public Authority will pay no attention to the Project Company's design development (or, more commonly, design development by the Construction

Subcontractor): it is not in the Public Authority's interests for the Project Company to develop a design which fails to provide the service required under the PPP Contract. It is therefore quite normal for the Public Authority to have a right to review and comment on detailed designs, but this would not normally involve the Authority in approving or 'signing off' the designs, either in stages or as a whole, as it would mean the risk of a design error being transferred back to the Public Authority. The review process may be taken a stage further, giving the Public Authority the right to raise objections to the design if it considers it not to be in accordance with the PPP Contract specification: if the parties cannot agree at this stage independent arbitration will be required.

The Public Authority should also be given flexibility to require small design changes which do not significantly affect costs or the ability to provide the service.

§6.6.2 SUBCONTRACTORS

It is difficult for a Public Authority used to procuring its own requirements to step back and allow the Project Company to do so on its behalf, but an essential element of a PPP is that the Project Company is fully responsible for its Subcontractors, which means that the Public Authority generally cannot interfere in this relationship. Communications with Subcontractors should therefore only be *via* the Project Company, and follow the same principles as set out above on design issues.

Having said this, however, at the time of pre-qualification the main Subcontractors will have been approved, from the point of view of both financial and technical capacity, and the Public Authority may reasonably claim to exercise some control if the Project Company plans to bring in different Subcontractors (*cf.* §13.5.3). Therefore it is normal to include a right of reasonable approval by the Public Authority of replacement Subcontractors, based on such technical and financial criteria.

The Public Authority will generally not have any control over changes to the terms of the Subcontracts except where:

- they are linked to changes in the PPP Contract itself (*cf.* §15.2.3); or
- they relate to agreed provisions which have a direct effect on the Public Authority's own risks or liabilities (*cf.* §6.5.2);

but again some comfort can be taken from the lenders' much wider controls over such changes as part of their security package (*cf.* §12.3.1), their interests in this respect being virtually identical with the Public Authority's.

§6.6.3 CONSTRUCTION SUPERVISION

The position on construction supervision is much the same as on design: while the Public Authority should not 'approve' any aspect of the construction stages, it will want to check what is being done, and point out any aspects which seem to be deviating from the PPP Contract requirements.

§6.6.4 FINANCING

Lenders need to continue to monitor and control the activities of the Project Company to ensure that the basis on which they originally assessed the project's risks is not undermined. This may also leave the investor with much less independent management of the project than would be the case with a corporate financing. (The controls imposed by lenders are discussed in Chapter 12.)

Once the financing is signed up the Public Authority has no formal or regular relationship with the lenders. (The Direct Agreement—*cf.* §12.3.3—is a document which only comes into action in a crisis.) Nonetheless the lenders share many of the same aims: it is in their interests for the Project Company to meet the requirements of the PPP Contract in full, and they also want to hear if the Public Authority has issues with this. Therefore an informal continuing dialogue with the lenders as the project gets under way is beneficial both to them and the Public Authority.

§6.6.5 INTERIM SERVICES

Some projects, especially involving refurbishment of an existing Facility, or an extension to it, may involve the private-sector investors taking over an existing Facility and providing services from it immediately after Financial Close, while construction of the new Facility proceeds. In such cases the operation-phase regime discussed below will also come into place immediately on a *pro rata* basis.

§6.6.6 ACCEPTANCE

Formal acceptance of the Facility by the Public Authority at the end of the construction phase triggers the Service Availability Date. The conditions for acceptance are obviously very project-specific, but at a minimum include receipt of all necessary permits to operate the Facility, and an inspection of the Facility and confirmation that it appears to be able to deliver the services (*cf.* §14.7). Where equipment or engineering is involved, there will be acceptance trials to ensure these function correctly (*cf.* §14.7.4). As with design approval, acceptance does not imply that the Public Authority takes on responsibility for whether or not the Facility can meet the service requirements under the PPP Contract: it is merely the trigger for the Service Availability Date. Acceptance may also be certified independently by a Checker.

In some types of project acceptance may be in stages—*e.g.* separate sections of a road may be opened to traffic as they are complete, or a building project may also be completed in stages. Acceptance may be on the basis that there are still minor rectifications to be completed which do not seriously affect the service delivery (*cf.* §14.7).

Failure to pass acceptance conditions may cause a delay in completion for which the Public Authority can claim liquidated damages (*cf.* §13.3.4), and in any case Service Fees should not normally be paid until acceptance is complete (*cf.* §13.3.3), although where acceptance is in stages *pro rata* payments may again be appropriate.

§6.6.7 OPERATION PHASE

The rôle of the contract-management team once the PPP is operating is to monitor the service provision and maintenance of the Facility, ensuring that the contractual penalties and deductions are made as appropriate (*cf.* §13.5). Good reporting systems and liaison with the Project Company are necessary, to give early warning of any problems. There may be some reluctance to insist on a strict interpretation of the PPP Contract penalties or deductions during the start-up of operations (say the first 6–12 months), but enforcement is probably the best way to ensure that the Project Company quickly does whatever is needed to sort out 'teething' problems.

§6.6.8 HAND-BACK

Issues which arise towards the end of the PPP Contract's life are discussed in §15.11.

§6.7 EXTERNAL ADVISERS

The Public Authority will probably use external advisers throughout the project preparation, bidding, due-diligence and (to a lesser extent) contract-management phases discussed above (unless these functions are provided by a central-government body—*cf.* §3.2). The costs of these advisers—along with those of the bidders (*cf.* §7.7) and the lenders (*cf.* §9.3.4) can make up a significant part of the initial project costs, and while they are usually necessary to give the Public Authority objective advice, a wider commercial perspective and the benefit of experience in similar projects, they also need to be well-managed. Broadly speaking, the rôle of the Public Authority's advisers is to provide support in:

- carrying out the initial feasibility review of the PPP;
- preparing the bidding package;
- evaluating bids;
- negotiating with bidders;
- supervision of the Project Company, especially during the construction phase of the PPP project.

But advisers must advise, not run the project, or costs will never be kept under control. Unfortunately it is quite common for the Public Authority's own staffing to be seriously under-resourced, and far too much reliance placed on the advisers (*e.g.* advisers may be left to make policy decisions on the Public Authority's behalf). If there is no command and control from within the Public Authority this is usually a recipe for a PPP project to drift on much more slowly and expensively (in advisory costs at least) than necessary (*cf.* §6.2.1). Centres of expertise within the public sector (*cf.* §3.2) can help to support the Public Authority's officers in this respect, especially where the particular Public Authority—as is commonly the case—only undertakes one or two PPPs, so there is little opportunity for expertise to be developed by its own officers.

Advisers should generally be selected on a competitive basis, and should demonstrate that they have the skills relevant to the scope of their work. For example, a legal adviser who is experienced in public administrative law but has never worked on a privately-financed PPP project will be of little use. Advisers should not be allowed to learn about PPPs at the expense of the Public Authority. A pre-qualification process, including references from other Public Authorities for whom other work has been carried out, is therefore important.

Moreover, appointment of a 'big-name' adviser will not be efficient and effective if the advisory work is then delegated to a junior member of staff—therefore when advisers are appointed, the Public Authority must ensure that named individuals with appropriate experience are committed to working on the project, rather than the adviser's senior director turning up to make the initial presentation and then never being seen again until the signing dinner.

Typical external advisers are:

- financial (§6.7.1);
- legal (§6.7.2);
- technical (§6.7.3); and
- insurance (§6.7.4).

In all these cases a method of payment for services needs to be agreed which keeps the Public Authority's development costs under control (§6.7.5). It need hardly be said that lowest cost should certainly not be the sole criterion for selecting advisers (although a high cost is no guarantee of quality either).

§6.7.1 FINANCIAL ADVISER

The financial adviser's scope of activities may include advice or assistance with:

- initial feasibility and structuring of the PPP, including advice on its financeability;
- risk analysis and balance-sheet treatment (*cf.* §5.5);
- preparation of the initial VfM appraisal and any PSC (*cf.* §5.3);
- initial soundings in the PPP market;
- preparation of bid documentation;
- financial evaluation of the bids;
- specialised advice, *e.g.* on taxation;
- negotiation with bidders.

Financial-advisory services can be provided to the public sector by the same banks which also advise bidders in the private sector (*cf.* §9.2), but the most active players in this market are the major firms of accountants. This can be seen from Table 6.1, which lists the main advisory mandates for public-sector clients in the project-financing market in 2005. (It should be noted that PPPs form a large part but not all of this work and that this table relates to mandates, not completed transactions, some of which may never be completed.)

Why do banks feature so little on this list? As discussed in §9.3.1, project-financing work is people-intensive, and financial-advisory work even more so as it requires more resources

Table 6.1

Public-sector project-financing advisory mandates, 2005

Firm	Category	No. of mandates
Ernst & Young	Accountants	77
PricewaterhouseCoopers	Accountants	59
Grant Thornton	Accountants	25
KPMG	Accountants	19
State Bank of India	Bank	8
Dexia	Bank	4
HSBC	Bank	4
Lazard	Investment bank	4
National Bank of Greece	Bank	4
Standard Chartered Bank	Bank	4
TASC	Corporate-finance consultants	4
Others (3 or less mandates)		24
	Total	**236**

Source: *Project Finance International* (Issue 329, 25 January 2006)

for a longer period of time. This is unattractive to banks because they have a limited number of people available, whereas accountants work on a different staffing model. In general, banks prefer to lend money rather than acting as pure financial advisers (*cf.* §9.3.2). Public-sector advisory work is also inherently less attractive because the public sector tends to pay less, and there is less repeat business than from private-sector bidders who are pursuing world-wide PPP business.

However, accountants' staff are predominantly trained as accountants and not financial advisers; also accounting firms rely on a very broad-based pyramid of staff, so although they have more staff available for this work than banks, they are predominantly relatively junior staff. This means that there may be a lack of financial creativity in the advice given to the Public Authority, and also that the financial advisory 'firepower' on the public-sector side of the table may match up rather poorly with the support which lenders offer to the bidders.

As a result of the relative lack of competition in this field, some project-management firms, whose normal rôle is discussed below, have added financial advice to their overall service, either by subcontracting this work to smaller advisory boutiques, or recruiting their own staff for this purpose. (The list in Table 6.1 is probably incomplete in this respect. It also has no figures from one of the 'big four' firms of accountants, Deloitte & Touche.)

§6.7.2 LEGAL ADVISER

The Public Authority will normally have an in-house legal department, but handling of the work for a PPP will probably be beyond its capacity and experience. However the legal department should be closely involved in the process, and in particular should manage and control the work to be undertaken by external legal advisers. External legal advisers' scope of work may include advice on:

- general legislative background (for a new PPP programme);
- drafting the PPP Contract, making use of standard forms, where these exist (*cf.* §3.3), and the experience of PPP Contracts in other countries;
- advice on other specialised legal aspects of the project such as site-related issues (*cf.* §14.5), staff transfers (*cf.* §2.13) and tax (if not covered by the financial adviser);
- preparing bid documentation, and ensuring that the bidding procedure fits with relevant procurement legislation (*cf.* §6.3.1);
- negotiation with bidders; and
- handling the formal legal procedures and documentation.

The competition for legal advisory services to the public-sector for a PPP is probably greater than that for financial advisory services, and although law firms also work on a pyramid structure, this is less broad at the base than accountants. International law firms, especially the London-based ones, have played a major rôle in developing PPP programme documentation around the world.

§6.7.3 TECHNICAL ADVISER

The scope of the technical adviser's work can be wider or narrower, depending on the Public Authority's in-house ability to take on rôles such as project management; the work may therefore include different aspects of the PPP project such as:

- general project-management services throughout the procurement process;
- preparation of construction costs and assumptions to be used for the initial feasibility review;
- support in drafting output specifications and risk analysis for the PPP Contract;
- structuring the technical aspects of the bid documentation;
- evaluating the technical aspects of bids;
- negotiation of technical aspects of bids;
- design review;
- construction supervision.

In projects with transfer of usage risk to the bidders, *e.g.* a Concession, the technical adviser will prepare the initial traffic or other usage studies. As discussed above, the technical adviser's rôle may even be extended into financial advisory work.

This work is generally undertaken by construction or services companies using their own experience in previous PPP projects, or by project-management firms. Depending on the scope of the work, parts of it such as traffic studies may be subcontracted. Alternatively the Public Authority may split the work among two or more advisers.

Design review and construction supervision may be carried out by an independent Checker (also known as the Certifier, Contract Administrator or *Maître d'Œuvre*). The Checker's rôle is to be impartial between the Project Company and the Public Authority, and in due course to certify that the completed Facility meets the initial output specifications. Costs are paid by the Project Company, but the appointment is a joint one with the Public Authority. Employment of a Checker should not relieve the Project Company of its own obligations under the PPP Contract to meet output specifications.

§6.7.4 INSURANCE ADVISER

Insurance advice in the PPP context is provided by specialist advisory departments of major insurance brokers. Similar but separate advisers are appointed by the Project Company (*cf.* §7.7) and lenders (*cf.* §9.3.4). The rôle is a minor but important one, since the Public Authority's interests in the project insurances have to be properly protected (*cf.* §12.4.1).

§6.7.5 ADVISORY COSTS

While the first criterion for choosing an external adviser is certainly expertise, not cost, the Public Authority has to plan and control advisers' costs carefully or they will soon become a cash haemorrhage. A clear and detailed brief should be agreed for the work, ideally split into stages such as initial feasibility, bid preparation, bid evaluation, and negotiation. Payment may be split to match these stages.

Payment may be on a simple hourly-rate basis, but there is merit in considering other alternatives to limit the cost risk. *e.g.*:

- a fixed fee or cap for each stage of the work; or
- regressive fee arrangements, whereby the more the work the lower the hourly rates; or
- payment of part of the fee on a success basis.

Fixed fees or capped fees are likely only to apply for a period of time, after which time-based fees will resume: this means that if the timetable is unrealistic, fixed or capped fees are of limited value. Care needs to be taken in negotiating success fees, so that the adviser is not given a perverse incentive to close the deal to earn the fee even if this is not in the Public Authority's best interests; on the other hand a pure hourly-rate basis creates a reverse incentive to spin out discussions. Fees based on a percentage of project costs, rather than fixed amounts, are also best avoided.

Particular care needs to be taken to control legal costs if the legal advisers are paid for the time they spend working rather than by a fixed fee: their time needs to be used effectively. For example, lawyers should not be used as an expensive secretarial service, *i.e.* hosting and writing notes on meetings discussing commercial issues, rather than just being told the result of this meeting. However, this is not to say that lawyers should always be kept away from commercial issues, as their experience in other PPPs may be useful in this respect.

Chapter 7

The Private-Sector Investor's Perspective

§7.1 INTRODUCTION

Having thus considered how the Public Authority goes through the process of developing and signing up to a PPP Contract, this chapter considers the parallel process on the part of the private-sector investors, *i.e.*:

- the investment 'pool' for PPP projects (§7.2);
- the financial basis for the investment decision (§7.3);
- bidding and project development (§7.4);
- joint-venture issues (§7.5);
- formation and management of the Project Company (§7.6);
- the use of external advisers (§7.7).

§7.2 THE INVESTMENT POOL

§7.2.1 SPONSORS AND OTHER PRIMARY INVESTORS

In order to obtain debt financing for the Project Company, its investors have to offer priority payment to the lenders, out of the Project Company's cash flow, thus accepting that they will only receive any return on their investment after the lenders have been satisfied (*cf.* §12.2.3). Therefore, investors assume the highest financial risk, but at the same time they receive the highest return from the Project Company (*pro rata* to the money they have at risk) if all goes according to plan.

Investors in Project Companies are usually very limited in number: no more than two or three is quite common, as this makes the complex arrangements for developing and controlling a PPP project easier to coordinate. The key investors are the ones who are responsible for bidding for, developing and managing the project, known as the Sponsors. Even though the Project Company's debt will probably be non-recourse, *i.e.* have no guarantees from the Sponsors (*cf.* §10.9), their involvement is important. Both the Public Authority and the lenders have to consider whether the Sponsors of the project are appropriate parties, taking into account such factors as:

- Do the Sponsors have experience in the sector concerned and, hence, the ability to provide any technical support required by the project? (This experience may be divided between several Sponsors with different backgrounds.)
- Have the Sponsors worked together successfully before?
- Do the Sponsors have the financial ability (although not the obligation) to support the Project Company if it runs into difficulty?
- Do the Sponsors have a reasonable amount of equity invested in the Project Company, which gives them an incentive to provide support to protect their investment if it gets into difficulty?
- Do the Sponsors have arm's-length contractual arrangements with the Project Company (where they act as Subcontractors, *e.g.* for construction of the Facility)?
- Is there a reasonable return on the Sponsors' investment? (If the return is low—*e.g.* because there are high Subcontract prices—there may be little incentive for the Sponsors to continue their involvement with the Project Company.)
- Do any of the Sponsors have a clear interest in the long-term success of the project, or is their interest limited to the construction phase only?

Typical Sponsors for PPP projects can be divided into two main categories:

- 'operational' investors—*i.e.* companies for whom investment is part of a strategy for securing other business as Subcontractors to the Project Company;
- 'financial' investors—*i.e.* entities only interested in the investment and not in ancillary business as Subcontractors; these may be banks or specialised PPP investment funds.

To look at these in more detail:

Subcontractors. PPPs offer a way of expanding business (or compensating for loss of other public-sector business which may now be procured as a PPP) for both construction and service or maintenance contractors, who will sign Subcontracts with the Project Company. The return on the investment in the Project Company thus becomes part of their overall return along with the profit on the subcontracting work they undertake.

There are inherent conflicts of interest in Subcontractors acting as investors in the Project Company, when it comes to dealing with issues arising on the Subcontracts, although it could also be argued that equity investment means that a Subcontractor is more committed to the success of a project. Subcontractors with a substantial equity involvement usually keep a separation between this investment and the contractual relationship with the Project Company, to ensure their own decisions are made in a balanced way.

There is also a more fundamental conflict arising from the fact that each Subcontractor may only be interested in a limited phase or aspect of the PPP Contract; thus the Construction Subcontractor may have little long-term interest in the project after it is built, and will often prefer to dispose of the investment in the Project Company at that time. However, some construction contractors have transformed themselves into long-term investors in infrastructure projects. If a construction contractor can be re-rated by the stock market as an infrastructure investor this is likely to add considerable value to its shares, as its revenues will then be considered by the market to be long-term in nature, instead of continually vulnerable to the short-term fluctuations of the construction industry.

Companies with long-term maintenance or other operating Subcontracts, on the other hand, should normally maintain their investment while they have this contractual relationship with the Project Company.

Support from potential Subcontractors is essential for the development of a PPP programme, and there are some countries (*e.g.* Spain) where most PPP investment is undertaken only by Subcontractors (or closely-associated financial institutions). But in general PPPs are now a worldwide business, and so although local contractors and other investors may have some advantage, they may also benefit from teaming up with international contractors and financial investors who can bring PPP structuring expertise to the table.

Banks. It is a natural step for banks to move from acting as lenders (for which see Chapter 9) to investors in PPP projects. An equity investment may be a relatively small addition to the funding they have already committed to the project, and while the risks are higher they are similar in nature to the risks which are also assessed before providing the debt financing (for which see Chapter 14).

Again there are potential conflicts of interest between these investment and lending rôles (although some banks will only act as lenders or investors, not both, depending on their overall business model).

PPP funds. PPP equity-investment funds are set up by banks and other financial institutions, leveraging on their own expertise and experience in the PPP markets. Investment in a PPP fund can offer a fairly secure low-risk return over a long period of time. This is especially attractive to life-insurance companies and pension funds, which have similar long-term liabilities. However, they tend not to be well-equipped to evaluate and monitor PPP investments (since they form a small part of their total portfolios), and therefore usually take up such investments through PPP funds run by investment banks and other specialised financial institutions. But it will only be worth developing such PPP funds where there is a steady flow of new business in an active PPP programme, and therefore they are to be found primarily in the more mature and financially sophisticated PPP markets such as Britain and Australia.

Financial facilitators. PPP Sponsors are typically a mixture of subcontractors and financial investors, but another recent development in some PPP markets is the growth of 'financial facilitators' (known in Australia as the 'ABN Model', after the investment bank which introduced it there). These are usually investment banks, PPP funds or similar institutions, which completely control the bidding process, as the only real

Sponsor, providing or placing both equity and debt, and bringing in Subcontractors as and when required. If the Sponsors of the project are primarily financial investors, whose interest is in financial rather than physical engineering, this has a number of possible consequences:

- A significant part of the return earned by such financial facilitators may come from arrangement or advisory fees which are paid out of the financing (as part of the development costs), rather than out of the long-term operating cash flow of the project, thus encouraging a riskier approach to structuring the financing (although Subcontractor Sponsors may also be paid development fees—*cf.* §7.3.2).
- On the other hand, financial facilitators perform an independent 'due diligence' rôle and have an incentive to get the best possible terms out of Subcontractors, whereas Sponsor Subcontractors obviously have a conflict of interest in this respect, however well-controlled, as discussed above.
- If a bid is put together by a financial facilitator, with major Subcontractors in a secondary rôle, this may raise questions about the whole-life integration of the design and construction, and so weaken one of the arguments in favour of PPPs (*cf.* §2.8).
- Paradoxically, a heavy reliance on financial facilitators may result in a higher cost of equity than would otherwise be the case (*cf.* §7.3.2).

Although some investors will only get involved with PPPs in their own country, there is an increasingly large international pool of PPP investment. Public Authorities have to bear in mind that their particular project may be the only one in the country, but may have to compete for investment with other PPP projects going on elsewhere in the world.

§7.2.2 SECONDARY INVESTORS

Some of the Sponsors' business models may depend on selling off their investment shortly after the project has been completed and has demonstrated that it is producing net revenues as expected. Even where the investment is long-term in intention, investors who have built up a portfolio of PPP investments may choose to sell off parts of the portfolio from time to time, as a way of establishing its overall value. Once a PPP programme is established therefore, there is likely to be a reasonably active secondary market, into which other new investors may enter, *e.g.*:

- A contractor building up its infrastructure investment portfolio may purchase investments from an existing Subcontractor.
- A 'secondary' PPP investment fund may purchase the 'primary' PPP fund's investment. Primary PPP funds invest in the project from the beginning, as discussed above, and therefore usually form part of the bidding consortium. They aim at a higher target return because of the higher risk inherent in the bidding and construction phases of a project (*cf.* §7.3.2). Secondary funds usually purchase their investments from primary investors (both funds and other parties such as contractors) once the project is complete, and risks have reduced, offering a correspondingly lower return.

- An insurance company may purchase a portfolio of PPP secondary investments instead of investing *via* a secondary fund.

§7.2.3 RESTRICTIONS ON SHARE TRANSFERS

The Sponsors are often required by both the Public Authority and the lenders to retain their investment until construction of the project is complete, since they are both relying heavily on the ability of the Sponsors to manage the completion of what is usually the most risky phase of a project. Where particular technical skills are required for long-term operation, relevant Subcontractor Sponsors may be required to maintain their shareholdings for longer periods.

Subject to these controls, a secondary market in PPP investments, as described above, creates liquidity in the primary market which is valuable to a continuing PPP programme because it enables primary investors to recycle their capital back into new projects. Also, from the public-sector point of view, although there is some security in a committed long-term ownership of the project, liquidity in primary investments will tend to increase their value, and thus make the cost of investment lower in future (although there are anomalies in the PPP market in this respect—*cf.* §7.3.2). Conversely, if excessive restrictions on investment transfers are put in place, this will reduce the value of these investments in the secondary market, and thus tend to push up the primary-market pricing, which feeds through to the Service Fees in future bids. It also makes the PPP sector less attractive to investors, and so may reduce bid competition. Moreover in practice it is very difficult to restrain transfers of the benefits of ownership, even if legal title to shares is retained by the original Sponsors (*cf.* §16.5).

The Public Authority should therefore only exercise any control over transfers of ownership:

- during the construction phase, to ensure that the original Sponsors are not just bidding to take a quick profit turn, but have a real financial commitment to get the PPP up and running; typically this may mean a restriction on transfers for up to two years from completion of construction;
- where this could reasonably have an effect on the long-term service provision: this is a difficult area—even if a Subcontractor sells its shareholding in the Project Company, it will still have to carry out the contractual obligations, but may have less financial incentive to do so without capital at risk (*cf.* §2.9.7); similarly the argument for whole-life costing and maintenance risk transfer (*cf.* §2.8) may be weakened if the project is put together by a financial facilitator who intends to sell out early;
- where there are issues of national security, *e.g.* in a PPP for defence equipment;
- in the case of a limited number of 'reputation' objections—*e.g.* it may be reasonable to bar companies in the tobacco or pornography business from being shareholders in a school PPP, however remote their ability to have any influence on the school in such respects through the PPP.

Lenders will generally allow share transfers to take place without requiring their permission from a reasonable period (again a year or so) after completion of construction.

It should also be noted that similar issues arise with debt refinancing, since this usually has the effect of reducing the investor's capital at risk in the project (*cf.* §16.2).

§7.3 THE INVESTMENT DECISION

§7.3.1 COST OF CAPITAL

In deciding whether to invest in a new project, an investor has to consider whether the investment provides an adequate return. The baseline against which this is measured is normally the investor's own cost of capital. For a company the weighted average cost of capital ('WACC') is used, *i.e.* the weighted average of the costs of its own equity and debt funding. A simplified WACC calculation would be:

$$WACC = \left(\frac{E}{E + D} \times Re \right) + \left(\frac{D}{E + D} \times Rd \times (1 - T\%) \right)$$

where E = market value of company's equity,
      D = company's outstanding debt,
     Re = return on equity, expressed as a rate of return,
     Rd = return on debt, *i.e.* the cost of borrowing expressed as a rate of interest, and
    T% = effective tax rate (as debt is tax-deductible)—a more sophisticated calculation might distinguish between initial tax benefits on investment, and later tax charges.

While 'Rd' (the cost of debt), is quite easy to measure, 'Re' (the cost of equity) is more complex. This measurement has to take into account both the general risk premium applied to any company compared to a risk-free investment in government debt, and the particular risk premium which the stock market attributes to the company's own business. The calculation (known as the Capital Asset Pricing Model (CAPM)) is thus:

$$Re = Rf + \beta\ (Rm\text{---}Rf)$$

where Rf = the risk-free rate, *i.e.* the cost of government debt,
    Rm = the market-risk premium, *i.e.* the average rate of return which investors expect from investing in the equity market, and
  β (beta) = the risk premium for the particular company's business compared to the market as a whole; if the company is considered to have the same risk as the market as a whole, β = 1.

Thus if a company is financed 50% by equity whose cost (Re) has been calculated as 15% *p.a.* using the CAPM, and 50% by debt costing 6% (Rd), with a tax rate of 30%, the calculation would be:

$$WACC = \left(\frac{50}{100} \times 15\% \right) + \left(\frac{50}{100} \times 6\% \times (1 - 30\%) \right) = 9.6\%$$

The WACC, used as a discount rate to discount future pre-financing cash flows expected from the company's business, will produce a NPV calculation of the current value of the company. Since the WACC is thus the overall required return on the company's business, pre-financing cash flows from new investments must at least match this rate of return to preserve the company's value.

In corporate-finance theory, changes in a company's leverage (*i.e.* the ratio between equity and debt, also known as 'gearing') do not change its WACC (if the risk inherent in the business has not changed); so if the leverage increases (*e.g.* debt goes above 50% in the example above), the relative costs of Re (*i.e.* the CAPM calculation) and Rd will adjust such that WACC remains at 9.6% (but *cf.* §8.5.1).

The above might suggest that the WACC in a separate Project Company should equal the investor's own WACC, but this is not the case: the Project Company's own WACC has to be taken into account. This may differ from that of its investors because of:

- the different risk profile of the Project Company and its investors' other businesses; only business with the same overall risk should have the same WACC;
- different investors themselves have different WACCs;
- substantial changes in leverage over the project's life (high to begin with and low at the end), so there is no consistent weighting of equity and debt, unlike the assumption in the WACC model;
- the tax position of the Project Company is likely to be quite different from that of its investors, and also to change substantially over time (*cf.* §10.8.1).

But there also typically seems to be a difference between many PPP Project Companies' theoretically-expected WACCs, and their actual WACCs (and hence the level of Service Fees are higher than they should be), revolving around the β which should be applied to the CAPM. One might expect the β for a PPP project to be the same as a utility, which may have a β of about 0.5, *i.e.* half the average risk of the market as a whole (unless it can be argued that it should be higher for a PPP because there are extra risks in construction and operation). In fact the β required by PPP investors is usually significantly higher than this, as discussed further below.

Looking at this another way, as the WACC calculation is based on the market value of the equity investment, if once a bidder has won a bid, the value of the equity invested is immediately higher than the equity invested, this suggests that the bidder is not paying full value for the investment, or that it is over-priced from the Public Authority's point of view.

WACC may not be an appropriate measure for a Project Company. An alternative measure of the cost of capital for PPP projects is the Project IRR. This is calculated as the IRR on the original investment derived from the projected net operating cash-flow (before financing costs) over the project life, and hence is equal to the weighted return on the equity and debt. The Project IRR for a PPP Project Company is not the same as its WACC, because WACC is a snapshot at the beginning of the project (which assumes it continues indefinitely in the same constant state), whereas Project IRR is based on a projection over the project life (and hence allows for changing leverage and the finite nature of the project). Project IRR thus gives a more accurate view of the expected cost of capital over the life of a typical PPP project.

It should also be noted that both the WACC and the Project IRR represent not only the return on the capex for the Facility but also the profit on the continuing services (or the return on continuing risks, such as maintenance). This cannot be compared with a 'pure' funding of the capex (*cf.* §2.10). From the Public Authority's point of view, the Project IRR thus represents the overall return which the private sector is getting for providing the Facility *and* associated services.

§7.3.2 EQUITY IRR

Setting theory aside, the standard approach which bidders use for pricing PPP projects is to determine the leverage and cost of debt, and then to apply their required equity return to the balance of the funding (*cf.* §10.7). The equity return in PPP projects is calculated using the Equity IRR. This is the IRR of the cash flow derived from:

- the initial investment in the Project Company's share capital;
- the dividends on this capital over the life of the project; and
- any residual value (*e.g.* from sale of project land at the end of the PPP Contract).

The Equity IRR required by investors varies depending on when they come into the project. Investors come in to projects at different stages, and with different investment strategies (*cf.* §7.2). A PPP project has both an inherent project risk, and various different levels of risk during successive phases of the project, and investors price their required return depending when they come into the project. This is illustrated by Table 7.1, which looks at how an equity investor coming in at different stages might build up the Equity IRR target, taking these factors into account:

Table 7.1

Project phases and required equity return

Phase	Risk-free Rate	Project Risk	Phase Risk	Equity IRR
Construction	6%	2–4%	4%*	12–14%
Ramp-up**	6%	2–4%	2%	10–12%
Long-term operation	6%	2–4%	—	8–10%

* This includes an allowance for not winning a proportion of projects bid, and therefore having to make up the bid costs of the failed bids from the equity return on a successful bid.
** Relates to a traffic project, and the length of time it takes to build up to a stable traffic base after the Facility has been completed; a similar phase would apply to any Facility where there is a distinct start-up phase.

The risk-free rate is the bidder's own WACC. The project risk is the risk which applies throughout the project life, given the nature of the project: thus a road Concession with high traffic risk would be at the top end of this scale, and an accommodation project with no usage risk at the low end. The phase risk is the risk relating to the point at which the investor comes into the project.

So, roughly speaking, the nominal Equity IRR (*i.e.* without deducting the effect of inflation—see §11.3.1) primary-market bidders currently expect on PPP projects in markets such as Australia, Canada, Britain and the United States—*i.e.* those easily open to general international competition from equity investors—is in the range 12–14%. Required returns do gradually decline as a PPP programme develops, the project risks are better understood by investors, and the investment pool becomes deeper, but PPP equity returns are still generally higher than those returns provided by investing in utilities, suggesting that there is an anomaly. Moreover, these returns do not take account of the potential benifits from debt refinancing (*cf.* §16.4) or equity sale to the secondary market (*cf.* §16.5).

For example, in Australia (Victoria), the theoretical CAPM for PPP projects has to be calculated because it is used as the discount rate when evaluating PPPs against each other and against the PSC (*cf.* §5.2.3). This approach assumes no leverage, and hence that the CAPM rate is the same as the WACC, which is perhaps dubious (*cf.* §8.5.1), but does not affect the point here. For this purpose, the market-risk premium has been calculated by Partnerships Victoria as 6% real (*i.e.* excluding inflation) and the CAPM β for PPP projects (other than those involving usage risk) has been calculated at 0.3–0.5%. Taking the latter at 0.5%, the CAPM rate for a PPP project should be:

- risk-free rate 3% (being the government bond rate), plus
- risk premium 3% (6% market-risk premium $\times$ 0.5 β), plus
- inflation 2.25% (the assumption used in the Victoria calculations),

making a total return of 8.38% (*cf.* §11.3.1 for the inflation adjustment in this calculation). This is obviously well below the actual Equity IRR of 12–14% mentioned above as being typical for such projects.

The reasons for this discrepancy between theory and reality may include:

- the need to take account of the costs of losing bids—if a bidder wins one deal in three this one deal must pay for the bid costs on the other two;
- the use of standard hurdle rates for investments by corporate investors which do not take account of the lower long-term risk of a PPP investment, with a secure income stream, compared to investors' other business where there is much greater uncertainty— *e.g.* in Table 7.1, which applies this approach, it is not correct to assume that the 'risk-free' corporate WACC is a base to which a project-specific return should be added, as the corporate WACC already has an allowance for risk;
- competition from other high-yield investments in the private equity (venture-capital) field, especially relevant where a significant part of the equity investment comes from financial investors or financial facilitators (*cf.* §7.2.1)—although it is certainly questionable whether it is appropriate to measure the relatively low risk of equity investment in a PPP (even during the construction phase) against the high risk of a venture-capital fund;
- the effect of combining high leverage and the lenders' loan-cover requirements, which effectively dictates the equity return (*cf.* §10.7).

However, the effect should not be exaggerated: in a project with 90% debt at a cost of say 6% and the 8.48% CAPM rate calculated as above, the WACC (and hence ultimate financing cost to the Public Authority) is 6.25% (ignoring tax), compared to 6.90% if the CAPM rate is increased to 15%. A study on PFI rates of return carried out for the British Treasury in 2002 (see Bibliography) similarly concluded that the WACC was about 0.7% too high. The problem here is partly political: 15% may be seen as an excessive rate of return on equity investment for a low risk, thus undermining the PPP programme (*cf.* §2.13).

As can be seen from Table 7.1, if the project develops successfully, the Equity IRR required by new investors declines as it passes through the various project stages. Thus a Sponsor developing a project who brings in another investor to commit the balance of the equity at Financial Close (*i.e.* the end of the bid phase) expects to be compensated for having assumed the highest risk. This can be achieved:

- by requiring the new investor to pay a premium for its shares (a higher price per share than that paid by the original Sponsor); or
- crediting the original Sponsor with a notional high rate of interest on cash already spent on the project, and including this when allocating shares based on the amount invested; or
- allowing the original Sponsor to charge the Project Company a 'development fee', which is usually payable at Financial Close: obviously any such fee has to be partly financed by the lenders as part of the Project Company's costs, and therefore cannot be at a level which upsets its long-term financial viability, or leaves the original Sponsor with little incentive to support the project thereafter.

All of these methods increase the original investor's Equity IRR at the expense of the new investors, but the first method can offer the Public Authority a way of alleviating the problem of high initial equity returns (*cf.* §16.3).

Once the Facility has been completed and is operating normally, the Equity IRR requirement drops further, to a level more comparable with utilities. This enables the original Sponsor to sell out at a profit. A primary equity fund, for example, will probably wish to earn a high return (say 25%) for its investors over a relatively short period of time (*e.g.* 3–4 years), because it will probably be competing with private equity funds, whereas a contractor with a long-term business interest may accept a lower return over a longer period of time, or a secondary equity fund will have investors who are also content with a lower risk and lower return over a longer period of time. Thus the primary equity fund's requirements can be accommodated by allowing the sale of its investment after completion of the Facility (*cf.* §16.5).

§7.3.3 SHAREHOLDER EQUITY AND SUBORDINATED DEBT

Investors in PPP Project Companies often provide subordinated debt (*i.e.* debt which is only paid when third-party 'senior' lenders such as banks have been paid what they are due) instead of investing only in the share capital of the Project Company. Shareholders' subordinated debt is used instead of share capital (at least to some extent) for several reasons:

- It is more tax-efficient if subordinated-debt interest payments by the Project Company are tax-deductible (provided 'thin capitalisation' or other tax provisions do not treat shareholder-provided subordinated loans as equity for tax purposes rather than as debt).
- It eliminates the 'dividend trap' problem (*cf.* §10.8.3).
- It is easier to return funds to investors by prepaying a shareholder subordinated loan rather than repaying equity shares if a refinancing takes place and the senior debt is increased (*cf.* §16.2), or in the later years of the project when the investors may wish to have their equity investment gradually paid back.

From the point of view of the Public Authority or the lenders, it makes little difference how the 'equity' is made up, *i.e.* the split between share capital and subordinated debt: it is only necessary to ensure that:

- The investors' funding, in whatever form, is fully committed to the project (and thus cannot be withdrawn or cancelled half-way through the construction phase if it has not already been spent by then).
- Investors have a long-term interest in the project derived from earning their return—whether by dividends or subordinated debt service—over the full life of the PPP Contract (and, *e.g.* not skewed towards the early years of the PPP Contract).
- Investors do not get any extra rights at the lenders' expense as a result of funding through subordinated debt instead of share capital (*cf.* §12.6.5).

A Public Authority may feel that it should specify that bidders should invest at least *x*% as share capital (and not subordinated debt) in the Project Company—a common provision in rules on foreign investment in developing countries. But the result may be to force bidders to use a less efficient shareholding structure, and hence offer a less attractive pricing for the PPP Contract.

When calculating their return, investors who also provide subordinated debt will normally amalgamate the two, *i.e.* the cash flow from both types of investment is added together and a 'Blended Equity IRR' calculated on this basis. ('Equity IRR' hereafter is intended to mean the total equity return calculation, *i.e.* the Blended Equity IRR where this is relevant.)

Blended Equity IRR calculations are normally done using the Project Company's cash flows as paid out to the investors. (The combination of dividend payments on shares and debt service on shareholder subordinated debt is known as 'Distributions'.) The calculations will thus take account of any tax payable by the Project Company; a separate calculation may take account of tax payable by investors on the receipts from the Project Company, but this is normally internal in nature, as each investor's tax position is likely to be different.

The Equity IRR may also be used to fix the Service Fees at Financial Close (*cf.* §11.2.13), after changes in the PPP Contract (*cf.* §15.2.1), and to calculate the termination payment (*cf.* §15.5.4).

§7.3.4 Equity Commitment v. Investment Returns

The use of Equity IRR calculations as the main measure for investors' returns leads to some strange distortions of behaviour. Lenders often require investors to invest their money into the project first (rather than, say, *pro rata*, with the debt). The earlier the investment is paid in—given that the rest of the cash flow from the project does not change—the lower the investor's Equity IRR. This therefore leads investors to find ways of giving a commitment to make the investment, in a way that satisfies lenders, but which does not require their IRR calculation to run from day one of the project, *e.g.*:

- providing an on-demand bank guarantee for the equity, and then paying-in the equity in cash towards the end of the construction period (when the debt has been fully used), or

- arranging an 'Equity Bridge' loan: this is a loan, usually provided by the lenders to the Project Company and guaranteed by the Sponsors *pro rata* to their shareholding, which is drawn in lieu of the equity; it is repaid by a committed equity subscription at the end of the construction period. The cost of the loan is relatively low as it represents a corporate risk on the Sponsors rather than a risk on the Project Company, thanks to the guarantee.

Neither of these two structures makes the slightest difference to the Sponsors' actual risk: whether they invest the equity on day one, or commit to do so in future, the risk is exactly the same. A proper assessment on the part of investors would take account of the commitment rather than the cash investment, *e.g.* by notionally charging the project the investor's cost of funds less a redeposit rate during the period when the investment is undrawn.

However there are categories of investor who do not usually use such structures—*e.g.* a PPP fund, as the fund will have collected cash investments and would not want to have the cash lying idle during the construction period, because this would reduce the fund's IRR even more than subscribing the cash up-front.

So long as a simple IRR approach is taken by investors whatever the timing of their investment, the Public Authority should of course try to encourage the use of an equity guarantee or bridge, as this will help to reduce the Service Fees, because this reduces the cost of capital during the construction period, and hence the eventual Service Fees.

§7.4 BIDDING AND PROJECT DEVELOPMENT

Successful PPP project management requires a systematic and well-organised approach to carrying out a complex series of interrelated tasks. The Sponsors' bidding and project-development team will need a mixture of disciplines, depending on the nature of the project:

- design and construction;
- service delivery/operation;
- legal, covering site acquisition, planning, project and loan documentation;
- accounting and tax;
- financial modelling;
- financial structuring.

As the bidding and development process (to Financial Close) on all projects runs into months, and on some projects into years, Sponsors should not underestimate the scale of costs involved. High costs are unavoidable, with the Sponsor's own development staff working for long periods of time on one project. The costs of external advisers (*cf.* §7.7) have to be added to this. There are also limited economies of scale—large projects also tend to be more complex in structure, so the bidding and development costs also grow in proportion, although it is probably true to say that if a project is too small the bid costs will not reduce and so will become out of proportion with the size of the project.

Bid costs alone can reach a significant proportion (5–10%) of the project cost, and clearly if there are three bidders each may have a two in three chance of losing these costs. Regular participants in bidding for PPP Contracts therefore have to judge carefully which projects they want to bid for, and ensure they have adequate cost-control systems.

§7.5 JOINT-VENTURE ISSUES

As has been seen, the investment in the Project Company is usually split between several Sponsors (*cf*. §7.2.1). Developing a project through a joint venture adds a further layer of complexity to the process: one partner may have a good understanding of PPPs and related financing issues while the other does not; corporate cultural differences become more acute under the heat of third-party negotiations (*e.g.* with the Public Authority or the lenders), or negotiations may be undertaken before all intra-partnership issues have been clearly resolved. Indeed it is not unknown for the development of a PPP project to be held up, not because the Public Authority or the lenders raise problems, but because the Sponsors have not agreed on key issues among themselves. If a bid is to be credible in front of a Public Authority, the bidders must speak with one voice, and resolve any differences behind the scenes.

Sponsors bidding for and developing a PPP project together usually sign a Project Development Agreement, which covers matters such as:

- the scope and structure of the project;
- exclusivity and confidentiality commitments;
- equity allocation;
- project-management rôles and responsibilities;
- an agreed programme for feasibility studies, appointment of advisers, negotiations with Subcontractors and other potential parties to the Project Contracts, and approaches to other prospective investors and lenders;
- rules for decision making;
- arrangements for funding of bidding and development costs, or the crediting of these costs against each Sponsor's allocation of equity (taking account of both the amount of the costs and the timing of when they were incurred);
- provisions for 'reserved rôles' (if any)—*e.g.* if one of the Sponsors is to be appointed as a Subcontractor without being subject to third-party competition;
- arrangements for withdrawal, or transfer of a Sponsor's interest.

Major decisions on the project have to be taken unanimously, because if the project develops in a direction not acceptable to one partner, that partner will not wish to keep funding it. Lesser issues—such as appointment of an adviser—may be taken on a majority-vote basis. If a Sponsor wishes to withdraw, the other Sponsors usually have a right to purchase its share. The Development Agreement may be superseded by a Shareholder Agreement when the Project Company has been set up and takes over responsibility for the project (*cf*. §7.6.2).

There are particular issues where the Public Authority itself is a joint-venture investor (*cf*. §17.5).

§7.6 THE PROJECT COMPANY

§7.6.1 STRUCTURE

The Project Company lies at the centre of all the contractual and financial relationships in a PPP project. Where project finance (*cf*. Chapter 8) is being used, these relationships have to be contained inside a separate 'box', known as a Special Purpose Vehicle ('SPV'; the term Special Purpose Entity ('SPE') is also used), *i.e.* the Project Company as an SPV cannot carry out any other business that is not part of the project. The reasons for using an SPV include:

- It ensures that there is no recourse to the Sponsors, by isolating the project in a separate legal entity.
- It also ensures that the business of the Project Company is not affected by problems with any unrelated businesses.

Since the Project Company should have no assets or liabilities except those directly related to the project, a new company should be formed specifically to carry out the PPP project rather than reusing an existing one that may have accrued liabilities. The corporate form of borrower (*i.e.* a Project Company) is generally preferred by lenders for security and control reasons (*cf.* §12.3.2).

The Project Company may not always be directly owned by the Sponsors; the Sponsors may use a holding company for this purpose, *e.g.* because:

- lenders require this for security reasons (*cf.* §12.3.2);
- there is some tax benefit from doing so—for example the holding company may be incorporated in a favourable jurisdiction (*e.g.* to ensure that withholding tax is not deducted from Distributions before they flow on to the investors).

In some PPP projects a form other than that of a limited company is used. This is usually a partnership, with the Sponsors as limited partners, so their liability remains limited in the same way as if they were shareholders in a limited company. Reasons for this include:

- 'tax transparency', *i.e.* enabling the income of the project to be taxed directly at the level of the Sponsors, or tax depreciation on its capex to be deducted directly against Sponsors' other income, rather than in the Project Company, which may be more tax-efficient;
- different tax positions of the Sponsors: an obvious example being a Joint-Venture PPP (*cf.* §17.5), where the Public Authority, as an investor, is not subject to tax—it may be considered preferable for tax not to be 'lost' at the Project Company level, *i.e.* for the Public Authority's share of the income, which would otherwise be tax-free, to be taxed; similarly a PPP fund may be taxed differently to a corporate investor;
- if lenders' Cover Ratios are based on post-tax cash flow, eliminating tax from the SPV's cash flow increases the cash flow which the lenders will take into account in their calculations, and hence increases the amount which can be borrowed against this cash flow (*cf.* §10.6.6).

§7.6.2 SHAREHOLDER AGREEMENT

If there is more than one Sponsor, at or before Financial Close, once the Project Company has been set up and is responsible for managing the implementation of the PPP project, the Project Development Agreement previously signed by the Sponsors (*cf.* §7.5) is normally superseded by a Shareholder Agreement (although it is possible to have one agreement for both phases of the project). The Shareholder Agreement covers issues such as:

- subscriptions to equity and shareholder subordinated debt;
- board representation;
- governance issues such as conflicts of interest (*e.g.* if a Subcontractor is a Sponsor, participation in voting on issues relating to the relevant Subcontract is not allowed, although the Subcontractor's director may be allowed to participate in board discussion on the subject);
- appointment and authority of management;
- budgeting;
- policy on Distributions (*cf.* §7.3.3);
- voting of shares at company meetings;
- sale of shares by Sponsors, usually with a first refusal (pre-emption) right being given to the other Sponsors.

Some of these provisions may be included in the Project Company's corporate articles rather than a separate Shareholder Agreement. The Sponsors may also have a separate agreement with the Project Company to pay in their agreed levels of equity or subordinated debt (if this is not paid in at Financial Close—*cf.* §7.3.4); if so, this agreement is assigned to the lenders as part of their security.

50:50 joint ventures are not uncommon in the PPP field, and they give rise to obvious problems in decision making. In cases with more Sponsors, it may still not be possible to get a consensus where a minority partner can block a vote on major issues. Arbitration or other legal procedures are seldom a way forward in this context. Clearly, if there is a deadlock one partner will have to buy out the other, for which a suitable process has to be established—typically whichever partner offers the highest price can buy out the other.

§7.6.3 MANAGEMENT AND OPERATIONS

The Project Company is often formed at a late stage in the project-development process, because it normally has no function to perform until the Project Contracts and financing are in place. Sponsors may even sign some of the Project Contacts to begin with (*e.g.* for construction) and transfer them in due course to the Project Company. However, even if the Project Company comes into formal existence late in the development process, as mentioned previously (*cf.* §7.2.1) arm's-length arrangements need to be in place from an early stage for negotiating any Subcontracts which it is going to sign with its Sponsors.

Similarly, the Project Company may not have a formal organisation and management structure until a late stage, as the Sponsors' staff will be doing the project-development work. There is, however, only a limited overlap between the skills needed at this development stage and those needed once the Project Company is set up and the project itself is under way, and arrangements must be made to ensure there is a smooth transition between the two phases of the project.

Project management after Financial Close may be undertaken by a combination of the Project Company's own staff and Subcontractors. There are various models for this: at one

extreme the Project Company may have no permanent staff at all: all its key functions—
i.e. construction, operation and maintenance—are subcontracted out, and supervision of
these Subcontracts, as well as corporate functions such as accounting, are carried out by
third parties such as project-management companies and accounting firms. The only 'permanent presence' that the Project Company has in this model is the board of directors. This
is a not untypical structure for a low-risk accommodation project. At the other extreme, the
Project Company may only contract out the construction of the Facility and retain all other
aspects of the project in-house. This approach is often used in Concessions.

While there is obviously merit—both financial and operational—in subcontracting project
functions to experienced organisations, it is generally preferable for the Project Company
to have a minimum level of staff, which probably consists of a general manager (reporting
to the board) and one or two assistants. This gives a clear point of contact for the Public
Authority, and a 'public face' for the Project Company—*e.g.* it may be required to meet with
user groups such as the parents' association in a school project. Furthermore, it is important
to have an independent person dedicated to supervising Subcontractors regularly, rather
than having to juggle this with other work. The Public Authority should consider during
bid evaluation whether the plans for long-term management of the Project Company will be
adequate for providing the quality of service required—*e.g.* whether there is a single point
of contact with responsibility for the total relationship under the PPP Contract.

§7.7 EXTERNAL ADVISERS

Various external advisers are used by the Sponsors during the bidding and project-
development processes. They can play a valuable rôle since they will probably have had
greater experience in a variety of projects than the Sponsors' in-house staff; if a Sponsor is
not developing a continuous pipeline of projects, employing people with the necessary
expertise just to work on one project may be difficult. Using advisers with a good record
of working in successful projects also gives the project credibility with lenders. In addition
to these Sponsors' advisers, the Public Authority has its own advisers (*cf.* §7.7) and lenders
use a parallel set of advisers as part of their due-diligence process (*cf.* §9.3.4), but the largest
part of the advisory work is likely to be done by the Sponsors' advisers.

Advisers may be prepared to work on a 'contingency' basis during the bidding stage, on
the understanding that they will be engaged (at an enhanced rate) if the bid is successful.
Thereafter, the options for fee-payment structures are similar to those available to the
Public Authority (*cf.* §6.7.5).

External advisers working for Sponsors may include:

Legal adviser. Legal advisers have to deal not only with the Project Contracts, but also
with how these interact with project-finance requirements, as well as being familiar
with project-finance documentation. This work tends to be concentrated in a small
pool of major law firms who have built up the necessary mixture of expertise.

Owner's Engineer. The Project Company may not need third-party technical advisers at all if this function can be carried out by one of its shareholders. However, if one
major shareholder is the Construction Subcontractor, other shareholders may wish to

ensure that their work is checked and supervised on behalf of shareholders as a whole, although of course there is also checking by the Public Authority (*cf.* §6.7.3) and the lenders (*cf.* §9.3.4) which may be adequate for this purpose.

Planning and environmental consultant. If the Public Authority has not already obtained planning permission for the project the Sponsor may have to take on advisers to deal with this process (*cf.* §14.5.3), albeit with support from the Public Authority. Separate advice may be required on environmental issues (*cf.* §14.5.4).

Market consultant. Market-risk advisers are required for a Concession, or PFI-Model project involving usage risk, *e.g.* traffic consultants (*cf.* §14.8.1). The expertise of these advisers, and the degree of their involvement in the project, may be significant factors in obtaining initial lender support for a bid even though the lenders will have their own advisers in due course.

Accountants. Accountants are often retained to advise on the accounting and tax aspects of the project (*cf.* §10.8), both for the Project Company itself and for the Sponsors.

Insurance adviser. For the rôle of the insurance broker, *cf.* §12.4.1.

Financial adviser. For the rôle of the financial adviser, *cf.* §9.2.

Chapter 8

Project Finance and PPPs

§8.1 INTRODUCTION

The recent growth of PPPs is closely linked to the financing technique known as 'project finance', itself a relatively recent development. An understanding of project-finance techniques and their application in PPPs is therefore necessary when considering policy-related financing issues in PPPs.

Project finance is a method of raising long-term debt financing for major projects. It is a form of 'financial engineering', based on lending against the cash flow generated by the project, and depends on a detailed evaluation of a project's construction, operating and revenue risks, and their allocation between investors, lenders, and other parties through contractual and other arrangements. As such, it is well-suited to financing PPP projects. 'Project finance' is not the same thing as 'financing projects', because projects may be financed in many different ways—it is evident that a project could be financed by public-sector debt using public-sector procurement instead of a PPP; alternative approaches to financing PPP projects are discussed in Chapter 17.

This chapter therefore provides a general background on project finance:

- its development (§8.2);
- key features (§8.3);
- the scale of the project-finance market and its links to related forms of financing (§8.4);
- why project finance is used for PPPs (§8.5).

Chapter 9 looks in detail at sources for project finance, and subsequent chapters at financial structuring.

§8.2 DEVELOPMENT OF PROJECT FINANCE

The growth in project finance is linked to some of the same factors which have led to the growth in PPPs. Some successive waves of development in project-financing techniques and coverage can be identified:

- Finance for natural resources projects (mining, oil and gas), from which modern project finance techniques are derived, developed first in the Texas oil fields in the 1930s; this approach was first used in Europe for development of North Sea oil fields in the 1970s, and has seen a new boom with commodity price rises over the last few years.
- Finance for independent power projects (IPPs) in the electricity sector (primarily for power generation) using BOO/BOT structures developed in the 1980s as discussed in §1.4.2. Linked to this is the more recent growth in the use of gas for power generation, which has led to project financing of gas pipelines and liquefied natural gas (LNG) receiving terminals (*i.e.* gas delivery as opposed to gas production).
- Finance for public infrastructure (*i.e.* PPPs) was revived with the Channel Tunnel project and thereafter with the creation of the British PFI programme from the early 1990's (*cf.* §1.4.5).
- Finance for mobile-telephone networks was also a large part of the market from the mid-1990s until the build-out of most of these networks was complete in the early 2000s.

So the three main legs on which project finance stands today are the natural resources, energy and infrastructure sectors.

Other changes in financing techniques, developed in the early 1970s, which helped the evolution of project finance included:

- long-term commercial bank lending to corporate customers—previously commercial banks only lent on a short-term basis, to match their deposits (*cf.* §11.2);
- the use of export credits for financing major projects, albeit the risk in such cases is substantially borne by host governments rather than the private sector, and insured by government export-credit agencies (see Chapter 11 of *Principles of Project Finance*);
- shipping finance, where banks make loans to pay for construction of large vessels, on the security of long-term charters—*i.e.* construction lending against a contractual cash flow, with the borrower being a separate special-purpose company owning the ship, in a way very similar to later project-finance structures;
- property (real estate) finance, again involving loans for construction secured against long-term cash-flow (rental) projections;
- tax-based financial leasing, which accustomed banks to complex cash-flows (*cf.* §8.4.2).

The final vital element in the development of project finance was the creation (in the mid-1980s) of spreadsheet software, without which project financing would be practically impossible.

§8.3 FEATURES OF PROJECT FINANCE

Project-finance structures differ between various industry sectors and from deal to deal: there is no such thing as 'standard' project finance, since each deal has its own unique characteristics. But there are common principles underlying the project-finance approach. Some typical characteristics of project finance are the following:

- It is provided for a 'ring-fenced' project (*i.e.* one which is legally and economically self-contained), carried out through an SPV (*cf.* §7.6.1).
- It is usually raised for a new project rather than an established business (except for sales of Franchises; also project-finance loans may be refinanced).
- There is a high ratio of debt to equity ('leverage' or 'gearing')—roughly speaking project finance debt may fund 70–95% of a project's capex.
- There are no guarantees from the investors in the Project Company ('non-recourse' finance), or only limited guarantees ('limited-recourse' financing), for the project-finance debt.
- Lenders rely on the future cash flow of the project for payment of their interest and loan repayments ('debt service'), rather than the value of its assets or analysis of historical financial results.
- Therefore the Project Contracts are the main security for lenders; the Project Company's physical assets are likely to be worth much less than the debt if they are sold off after a default on the financing.
- Therefore lenders exercise a close control over the activities of the Project Company to ensure the value of these Project Contracts is not jeopardised, *e.g.* by performance failures.
- The project has a finite life, based on such factors as the length of the contracts or licences, or the reserves of natural resources.
- Therefore the project finance debt must be fully repaid by the end of this life.

Hence project finance differs from a corporate loan, which:

- is primarily lent against asset values in a company's balance sheet, and projections extrapolating from its past cash flow and profit record;
- assumes that the company will remain in business for an indefinite period and so can keep renewing ('rolling over') its loans;
- has access to the whole cash flow from the spread of the borrower's business as security, instead of the limited cash flow from a specific project—thus even if an individual project fails, corporate lenders can still reasonably expect to be repaid;
- can use buildings and equipment as security;
- generally leaves the management of the company to run the business as they see fit, so long as this does not have significant adverse financial consequences.

Project finance is made up of a number of 'building blocks'. One set of blocks relates to the funding for the Project Company, which has two elements:

- equity, provided by investors in the Project Company (*cf.* Chapter 7);
- project finance-based debt, provided by one or more groups of lenders to the Project Company.

The project-finance debt has first call on the Project Company's net operating cash flow—it is thus 'senior' to other claims, especially that of the investors (equity shareholders). The investors' return is therefore at a higher risk because it is more dependent on the success of the project—hence investors' returns are higher than lenders'.

The other major building blocks relate to the Project Contracts entered into by the Project Company—namely the PPP Contract, and Subcontracts for construction, operation and maintenance of the Facility. These are the means by which risks are transferred from the Project Company to the other parties (*cf.* Chapter 14), and form the most important part of the lenders' security package. Of course, none of these structures or contractual relationships is unique to project finance. However, the relative importance of these matters, and the way in which they are linked together, is a key factor in a project-financed PPP.

The close resemblance between the use of project finance for a power-generation project, as described in §1.4.2, and its subsequent development in different types of PPP, can be seen from the structural diagrams in Chapter 1 for a PPA (Figure 1.1), a Concession (Figure 1.2) and a PFI-Model PPP (Figure 1.3).

§8.4 THE PROJECT-FINANCE MARKET

§8.4.1 SCALE OF THE MARKET

Table 8.1 sets out the overall scale of the world project-finance market (for both bank loans and bond issues—*cf.* Chapter 9), from which the division into the three legs of infrastructure, energy and natural resources, as well as the decline in telecommunications-related financing mentioned above, are evident. Infrastructure, of which PPPs form the largest component, has shown continued and steady growth in business volume. The recent years of commodity-price boom have meant that the natural resources sector (which includes oil and gas as well as mining), which had been declining in the 1990s, is now expanding again. The power industry suffered badly from events in the United States and elsewhere following the Enron *débâcle*, but has since revived.

Table 8.1
Project-finance loans by sectors, 2000–5

(US$ millions)	2000	2001	2002	2003	2004	2005
Infrastructure	18,393	21,003	27,056	32,873	44,736	55,246
Power	56,512	64,528	24,517	36,417	46,633	51,683
Natural Resources	16,518	18,859	15,778	23,039	40,948	44,254
Telecoms	36,735	25,445	7,286	5,849	7,341	10,193
Other	3,538	3,646	1,324	3,543	5,428	4,241
Total	**131,696**	**133,481**	**75,961**	**101,721**	**145,086**	**165,617**

Source: *Project Finance International*, issues 233, 257, 281, 305, 329 (data summarised)

These 'market' statistics have to be treated with some care:

- Financial institutions draw the boundaries between project finance and other types of lending based on convenience rather than theory, taking into account that skills used by loan officers in project finance may also be used in similar types of financing. Many deal with project finance as part of their structured-finance operations (§8.4.2). As a result, project-finance market statistics may be affected by inclusion or exclusion of large deals on the borderline between project finance and other types of structured finance.
- The figures do not distinguish between new projects and projects which have become established and are then refinanced (*cf.* §16.2), or financing acquisitions of infrastructure projects such as toll-road Franchises (*cf.* §3.5).
- The statistics are based on figures provided by financial institutions to database companies, and hence do not necessarily include projects funded by development banks or other public-sector sources of finance, or projects where commercial-bank debt is not a major component of the funding (*cf.* §17.3.2).
- Not all private-sector financial institutions active in PPPs provide statistics either.
- Conversely, the financial institutions which do supply the figures have an interest in making the market, and their own involvement, look as large as possible.
- The figures from different financial databases differ quite widely (*cf.* Table 3.1 and the individual country statistics in Chapter 3), again because of issues of reporting and classification.
- Specifically in relation to PPPs, lender figures relate to the amount of debt raised, whereas figures produced by the public sector relate to the 'cost' of the project, which may mean either the capex (including equity investment), or the NPV of the Service Fees.

Nonetheless, the year-to-year figures give a fair picture of overall trends in the project-finance market.

Table 8.2 sets out the key geographical areas of activity in project financing. As can be seen, the most important areas of growth in recent years have been in Europe and the Middle East—the latter has been mainly due to the boom in oil, gas and petrochemicals, but PPPs have played a substantial part in the growth of the European project-finance market. In the Asia-Pacific region the most important countries in the PPP field have been Australia and South Korea. (PPP activity in these and other countries is discussed in Chapter 3.) The U.S. figures reflect the decline in the power sector post-Enron. It is also worth remarking that project finance to developing countries is highly concentrated in the power, natural resources and telecoms areas, rather than infrastructure of a PPP nature—*i.e.* private-sector project finance for PPPs is predominantly a product for developed countries.

§8.4.2 PROJECT FINANCE AND STRUCTURED FINANCE

The broad term 'structured finance', covers any kind of finance where an SPV has to be created to raise the funding, with its debt structured to fit the cash flow, unlike corporate loans, which are made to a borrower already in business, as discussed above. Various types

Table 8.2
Project-finance lending in selected countries, 2000–5

(US$ millions)	2000	2001	2002	2003	2004	2005
Americas						
Brazil	10,092	5,611	1,788	5,112	4,715	3,061
Canada	3,015	622	505	538	1,575	2,488
Chile	3,236	5,442	1,490	718	3,198	3,452
Mexico	3,984	4,412	4,422	5,186	9,094	3,675
U.S.A.	44,886	47,588	13,233	15,448	23,587	25,581
Asia-Pacific						
Australia	5,099	4,459	8,948	6,511	13,129	9,745
China	0	0	3,842	3,930	2,787	759
India	129	114	1,016	122	1,187	3,123
Japan	131	2,265	498	1,629	3,720	2,205
Malaysia	0	1,709	2,368	1,983	3,233	2,935
South Korea	718	1,415	1,141	2,732	6,341	4,575
Taiwan	0	222	613	76	4,968	216
Thailand	1,718	536	1,436	1,496	2,010	1,444
Europe						
France	49	360	721	136	201	1,997
Germany	12,806	4,978	401	492	705	2,006
Hungary	500	125	226	596	1,640	1,413
Italy	5,602	13,787	7,952	12,406	3,795	9,824
Netherlands	300	1,176	1,527	769	92	1,159
Portugal	1,537	1,643	1,249	870	2,606	2,995
Spain	567	6,371	1,410	8,167	5,602	16,147
U.K.	13,988	6,329	10,579	14,485	17,692	21,594
Middle East & Africa						
Azerbaijan	0	0	0	0	1,600	780
Kazakhstan	0	0	0	60	1,100	75
Bahrain	0	0	255	1,350	1,925	153
Egypt	0	651	0	950	1,853	2,183
Oman	513	2,030	677	908	1,608	5,671
Qatar	0	1,132	300	1,295	6,778	16,326
Saudi Arabia	852	2,176	280	820	3,726	2,466
UAE	1,096	1,638	0	1,855	1,933	2,367
Nigeria	0	0	1,000	879	1,650	1,702
South Africa	127	718	333	318	261	600

Source: *Project Finance International*, as for Table 8.1

of structured finance overlap with project finance to a certain extent, and also compete with it for resources within the financial institution concerned (*cf.* §9.3.1).

   Asset finance. This is based on lending against the value of assets easily saleable in the open market *e.g.* aircraft or real-estate (property) financing, whereas project finance lending is against the cash flow produced by the asset, which may have little open-market value.

Receivables financing. This is based on lending against the established cash flow of a business and involves transferring a cash-flow stream to an SPV similar to a Project Company (but normally off the balance sheet of the true beneficiary of the cash flow). This cash flow may be derived from the general business (*e.g.* a hotel chain) or specific contracts which give rise to this cash flow (*e.g.* consumer loans, sales contracts, *etc.*). The SPV then borrows against this cash flow, without any significant recourse or guarantee to the owners of the original business, who are thus able to raise funding off-balance sheet, as well as reducing their own business risks.

The key difference from project finance is that the latter is based on a projection of cash flow from a project yet to be established. However, the sale of a Franchise for an already-constructed road is a form of receivables finance, even though it may be classified by the parties concerned as project financing.

Securitisation. If receivables financing is procured by raising funds in the bond market (*cf.* §9.4), it is known as securitisation of receivables. There have also been a few securitisations of receivables due from banks' project-finance loan books, but so far this has not been a significant feature in the market. PPP projects are quite suitable for securitisation because of their low risk, and further growth in this sector can be expected. Such securitisations can take two forms—a transfer of the loans from the bank to an SPV, to provide a pool of security for bond-holders ('real' securitisation), or a 'synthetic' securitisation, where the risk is transferred but the loans remain on the bank's balance sheet (albeit with a low or nil capital requirement for the bank, because of the risk transfer), funded by a bond issue.

Leveraged buyout (LBO) or management buyout (MBO) financing. This highly-leveraged financing provides for the acquisition of an existing business by portfolio investors (LBO) or its own management (MBO). It is usually based on a mixture of the cash flow of the business and the value of its assets. It does not normally involve finance for construction of a new project, nor does this type of financing use contracts as security as does project finance.

Acquisition finance. Probably the largest sector in structured finance, acquisition finance enables company A to acquire company B using highly-leveraged debt. In that sense it is similar to LBO and MBO financing, but based on the combined business of the two companies. The risks and returns on these sectors are higher than those for PPPs, but as the funding sources overlap they have tended to drag up pricing for PPP projects (*cf.* §7.3.2).

Leasing. Leasing is a form of asset finance in which ownership of the asset financed remains with the lessor (*i.e.* lender), with the lessee (*i.e.* borrower) paying for the right to use it (*cf.* §5.5.2). A major motive for leasing in the past was that it enabled tax benefits from large capital investments to be transferred to the lessor, and fed back to the lessee *via* lower lease payments than would have been made under an equivalent loan (*cf.* §8.2). These tax benefits have been substantially eroded in most countries over recent years, and leasing finance is now seldom used in the PPP field, especially as many PPPs involve substantial investment in buildings or civil works (such as for a road), which generally do not receive as favourable tax treatment as investing in equipment.

§8.5 WHY USE PROJECT FINANCE FOR PPPS?

Like PPPs, project finance is complex, slow and has a high up-front cost. Adding the two together obviously makes these problems worse. It also severely restricts the ability of the owners of a project to manage it freely. Nonetheless, there are good reasons why project-financing is commonly used for PPP projects, since it has benefits both for the private-sector investors in such projects and for the Public Authority.

§8.5.1 BENEFITS FOR INVESTORS

There are a number of reasons why investors use project financing for PPP projects.

High leverage. As has been seen, investors in PPPs typically require a hurdle-rate Equity IRR which—despite corporate-finance theory—looks more at the risk of the project than its funding structure (*cf.* §7.3.2). It follows arithmetically from this that the higher the leverage the easier it is to earn a high level of equity return, taking advantage of debt being cheaper than equity, and the fact that in a project-finance transaction higher leverage does not imply proportionately higher risk for lenders, and hence although the cost of debt goes up this is not in proportion to the increase in leverage.

Table 8.3 sets out a very simplified example of the benefit of leverage on an investor's return. Both the low-leverage and high-leverage columns relate to the same investment of 1,000, which produces revenue of 75 *p.a.* If it is financed with 50% debt, as in the low-leverage column (a typical level of debt for a good corporate credit) the return on equity is 10%. On the other hand, if it is financed with 90% (project finance-style) leverage, the return on the (reduced level) of equity is 21%, despite an increase in the cost of the debt (reflecting the higher risk for lenders).

But it must be emphasised that this example is highly simplified, and as will be seen below, leverage is dictated largely by the lenders' requirements for a cash-flow cushion, which in turn may actually dictate the equity return on the project (*cf.* §10.7).

Table 8.3
Benefit of leverage on investors' return

		Low leverage	High leverage
Project cost		1,000	1,000
(a) Debt		500	900
(b) Equity		500	100
(c) Revenue from project (*p.a.*)		75	75
(d) Interest rate on debt (*p.a.*)		5%	6%
(e) Interest payable	[(a) × (d)]	25	54
(f) Profit	[(c) − (e)]	50	21
Return on equity	[(f) ÷ (b)]	10%	21%

Another important factor encouraging a high level of debt in Project Companies is that it is generally more difficult to raise equity than to raise debt, and makes the project more complex to manage (especially during the bidding and development phases) if the result of having to raise more equity is that more investors have to be brought in. Moreover if more investors have to be brought in, this means that the original Sponsors may lose control of the project.

Risk spreading and limitation. Project finance is a structure under which groups of investors can easily work together, thus easily enabling the risk of the investment to be divided up.

Moreover, an investor in a project raising funds through project finance does not normally guarantee the repayment of the debt—the risk is therefore limited to the amount of the equity investment only, and the investor's business as a whole is not usually at risk from failure of the specific project, *i.e.* there is limited 'risk contamination' between the project and the rest of the investor's business. In effect, in return for a relatively small fee (its equity share), a Sponsor has established an 'option price' at which it may retain the investment if successful or walk away if its failure could otherwise have a high impact on its other business.

It is also worth noting that one of the highest areas of risk for a PPP project is the expenditure on bidding, and so forming a partnership at the bidding stage obviously reduces this risk too.

Unequal partnerships/combining skills. Thanks to high leverage, the relatively small amount of equity required for a major PPP project where project finance is used enables parties with different financial strengths to work together. It would be quite normal for example, for the investors in a PFI-Model school project to consist of a financial investor (say a large bank), a construction company, and an FM company, whose balance-sheet strengths would probably be very different, but with each bringing particular skills to this partnership. This aspect of a project-finance structure also makes it easy for the Public Authority to be brought in as a shareholder in the case of a Joint-Venture PPP.

Long-term finance. Project-finance loans typically have a longer term than corporate loans. Long-term financing is necessary if the assets financed normally have a high capex, which cannot be recovered over a short term without pushing up the cost that must be charged for the project's end-product. So loans for PPP projects may run for 20–30 years, compared to a normal corporate loan of perhaps 5–7 years.

Paradoxically, a longer-term loan may reduce the risk of default during a PPP project's early years of operation, when the cash flow may be most uncertain, by reducing the level of cash flow required for annual debt-service payments.

Borrowing capacity. Non-recourse finance raised by a Project Company affiliate is not normally counted against corporate-credit lines. It may thus increase an investor's overall borrowing capacity, and hence the ability to undertake several major projects simultaneously. Similarly, a company's credit rating is less likely to be downgraded if its risks on project investments are limited through a project-finance structure, again enabling it to invest in more projects.

Off-balance sheet. If the investor has to raise the debt and then inject it into the project, this will clearly appear on the investor's balance sheet. A project-finance structure may allow the investor to keep the debt off the consolidated balance sheet, but usually only if the investor is a minority shareholder in the project—which may be achieved if the project is owned with other partners.

Keeping debt off the balance sheet is sometimes seen as beneficial to a company's position in the financial markets, but a company's shareholders and lenders should normally take account of risks involved in any off-balance-sheet activities, which are generally revealed in notes to the published accounts even if they are not included in the balance sheet figures; so project finance is not usually undertaken purely to keep debt off the investors' balance sheets.

However there is another related benefit, which is that investment in a project through an unconsolidated affiliated company is useful during the construction phase of a project, when it is a 'dead weight' on the rest of a company's business, because it requires a high capital investment in the balance sheet which is producing no revenue.

Also a project-finance structure enables Subcontractors to make a clearer separation between their contracting and investment activities (*cf.* §7.2.1).

§8.5.2 BENEFITS FOR THE PUBLIC AUTHORITY

Equally, encouraging investors to use project finance for PPP projects may bring benefits to the Public Authority, and to the overall PPP programme in the country concerned.

Lower cost. The higher leverage inherent in a project-finance structure helps to ensure the lowest cost to the Public Authority. This can be illustrated by doing the calculation in Table 8.3 in reverse: suppose the investor in the project requires a return of at least 15%, then, as Table 8.4 shows, to produce this revenue of 100 *p.a.* is required using low-leverage finance, but only 69 using high-leverage finance, and hence the Service Fees reduce accordingly. (But as with Table 8.3, it must be emphasised that this example is highly simplified.)

So if the Public Authority wishes to achieve the lowest long-term cost for the project, and is able to influence how it is financed, this suggests that the use of project finance should be encouraged, *e.g.* for example, by agreeing to sign an PPP Contract which fits project-finance requirements as to risk transfer between public and private sector.

Table 8.4
Effect of leverage on the Service Fees

		Low leverage	High leverage
Project cost		1,000	1,000
(a) Debt		500	900
(b) Equity		500	100
(c) Return on equity required	[(b) × 15%]	75	15
(d) Interest rate on debt (*p.a.*)		5%	6%
(e) Interest payment	[(a) × (d)]	25	54
Revenue required	[(c) + (e)]	100	69

Increased competition. For the reasons set out above, project finance enables investors to undertake more projects by increasing their financial capacity, the effect of which should be to create a more competitive market for projects, to the benefit of the Public Authority.

Rôle of lenders. The Public Authority may benefit from the independent due diligence and control of the project exercised by the lenders (*cf.* §9.3.4), who will want to ensure that the project is viable, and that all obligations to the Public Authority can be safely fulfilled. Project-finance techniques are based on risk allocation, and so this due diligence fits well with the overall philosophy of risk transfer which is one of the arguments for PPPs (*cf.* §2.6). The involvement of third parties, especially lenders and their advisers, in a PPP structure should therefore mean that a rigorous review of the risk transfer is carried out, and any weaknesses exposed, before the Public Authority has made a commitment to go ahead. However, it must be borne in mind that lenders will always want to ensure that project risks are taken primarily by Subcontractors or the Public Authority rather than the Project Company (*cf.* §14.2), and so their objectives are not the same as those of the Public Authority. Moreover lenders are frequently used as proxies by Sponsors to re-open PPP Contract negotiations—*i.e.* if they are on anybody's side it is the Sponsors rather than the Public Authority.

In addition, once a PPP Contract has been signed, project-finance lenders exercise continuing controls on the activities of the Project Company (*cf.* Chapter 12), thus helping to ensure that the requirements of the PPP Contract are fulfilled.

Transparency. As project financing is self-contained (*i.e.* it deals only with the assets and liabilities, costs and revenues of the particular project), the true costs of the service can more easily be measured and monitored. This fits well with the need for transparency in a PPP (*cf.* §2.10).

§8.5.3 CORPORATE FINANCE

While project finance provides the commonest method of financing PPPs, there are many cases where a corporate-finance approach—in which the funding for the project is provided from the investor's own balance-sheet resources, *i.e.* as a corporate loan—is a suitable alternative. In this case, the investor's available cash and credit lines are used to pay for the project, or if necessary new credit lines or even new equity capital are raised to finance the project's cost. Provided it can be supported by the investor's balance sheet and earnings record, a corporate-finance loan to finance a project is normally fairly simple, quick, and cheap to arrange. In a corporate-finance structure for PPPs, the Project Company is usually a wholly-owned subsidiary of the investor, or the investor may enter directly into a Project Agreement with the Public Authority.

Clearly both the cost of finance and ancillary costs will be lower in this case than in a project-financed transaction. This may translate into a lower cost for the Public Authority, depending on the overall level of the investor's cost of capital. But this approach is obviously dependent on the investor having the necessary balance-sheet and financial capacity, and is therefore typically used for smaller PPPs, or ones in which the level of capital investment, as opposed to long-term service provision, is lower.

Chapter 9

Private-Sector Financing—
Sources and Procedures

§9.1 INTRODUCTION

This chapter reviews the main private-sector financing sources for PPP projects (assuming finance on a project-finance basis). The use of public-sector funding for PPPs is discussed in Chapter 17.

One of the first steps a bidder for a PPP Contract normally takes to secure financing is to engage a financial adviser, with experience in project finance and PPPs (§9.2). Private-sector project-finance debt is provided from two main sources—commercial banks (§9.3) and bond investors (§9.4). Commercial banks provide long-term loans to project companies; bond holders—typically long-term investors such as insurance companies and pension funds—purchase long-term bonds (tradable debt instruments) issued by project companies. ('Lender' is used in this book to mean either a bank lender or a bond investor.) Although the legal structures, procedures and markets are different, the criteria under which debt is raised in each of these markets are much the same, but they each have advantages and disadvantages (§9.5). Mezzanine debt (third-party subordinated debt) can also play a limited rôle in financing PPP projects (§9.6).

§9.2 THE RÔLE OF THE FINANCIAL ADVISER

Unless the Sponsors are experienced in PPP project development, problems are highly likely to be caused by negotiation (or even signature) of PPP Contract arrangements that are later found to be unacceptable to the project-finance market. Therefore bidders for PPP projects—even those with in-house project finance expertise—usually make use of external financial advice to make sure that they are on the right track as they bid on and develop the project. The financial adviser obviously needs to have a good record of achieving success-ful financing on similar PPP projects. Bidders also need to ensure that the individual actu-ally doing the work has this experience, rather than just relying on the general reputation and record of the financial adviser.

The financial adviser for a PPP project has a wider-ranging rôle than would be the case for a corporate loan (where the work would be centred around financial structuring). One of the most common errors during project development is for the Sponsors to agree on a Project Contract that is commercially sound, but not acceptable from a project finance point of view—for example, the PPP Contract may leave too much risk with the Project Company instead of passing risks down to the Subcontractors, perhaps because the Public Authority has tried to pass too much risk to the private-sector side of the table (*cf.* §14.2)—and so the financial adviser must anticipate all the issues that might arise during the lenders' due-diligence process (*cf.* §9.3.4), ensuring they are addressed in the Project Contracts or elsewhere.

The terms of the financial adviser's engagement are set out in an advisory agreement, usually signed with the Sponsors. (The Sponsors may transfer the advisory agreement to the Project Company in the latter stages of the project-development process.) The financial adviser's scope of work under an advisory agreement may include:

- assisting in preparing a financial model for the project;
- advising on sources of debt and likely financing terms;
- advising on the optimum financial structure for the project;
- advising on the financing implications of Project Contracts;
- assisting in bid preparation;
- assisting in negotiations with the Public Authority;
- preparing an information memorandum to present the project to the financial markets;
- advising on selection of commercial-bank lenders or placement of bonds;
- assisting in negotiation of financing documentation.

As has been seen (*cf.* §6.7.1), the public sector relies mainly on large accounting firms for financial advice on PPP projects. Major international banks (or domestic banks in partic-ular markets) do provide advisory services to bidders for PPP projects, though usually in conjunction with lending, as discussed in §9.3.2. Financial advice is also provided to bidders by investment banks (*i.e.* banks that arrange finance but that do not normally lend money themselves), specialist project-finance advisory firms or individual advisers. Table 9.1 sets out the leading advisers to bidders for projects in general (not just PPP projects, although these probably constitute a large part of the total), and may be contrasted with the similar figures in Table 6.1. As can be seen there are still two firms of accountants at the top, but in general financial advisory mandates for bidders are less concentrated with account-ants than those from the public sector.

Financial advisers are usually paid by a combination of fixed or time-based retainer fees, and a success fee on conclusion of the financing. Major out-of-pocket costs, such as travel, are also paid by the Sponsors. These costs are charged on to the Project Company in due course as part of the development costs. However, as is the case with other advisers, they often work for the Sponsors during the bid phase on a contingency basis, *i.e.* they only start to earn fees when their client has been appointed as Preferred Bidder, or perhaps not until Financial Close.

Table 9.1
Project-finance advisory mandates from bidders, 2005

Firm	Category	No. of Mandates
PricewaterhouseCoopers	Accountants	36
Ernst & Young	Accountants	33
Royal Bank of Canada	Bank	28
Macquarie	Investment bank	14
CIT Group	Asset finance	12
Dexia	Bank	11
Investec	Investment bank	10
Société Générale	Bank	9
Banco Espirito Santo	Bank	7
ING Bank	Bank	7
IXIS (Groupe Caisse d'Epargne)	Bank	7
Others (6 or less mandates)		54
	Total	**236**

Source: *Project Finance International* (Issue 329, 25 January 2006).

These financial-advisory services may be essential to the successful development of the project, but they are necessarily expensive (costing around 1% of the capex on an average-sized project). Costs may be reduced by using smaller advisory boutiques or individual consultants, but less experienced Sponsors may feel uneasy about not using a 'big name' adviser. There is also always some risk that the financial adviser—however well qualified—thinks a project is financeable but the lending market does not agree.

§9.3 COMMERCIAL BANKS

Commercial banks are the most important source for project finance for PPPs: in 2005 they provided US$140 billion, or some 85% of the total project-finance funding shown in Table 8.1 (although it should be noted that some of this was not new money, but refinancing old loans on better terms, as mentioned above).

§9.3.1 MAJOR PROJECT-FINANCE BANKS

Within the international project-finance market there is a fluctuating 'inner circle' of perhaps 20–30 international banks which play a key role in putting together major trans-actions wherever these are located. However, where a country has a strong PPP programme, local banks not otherwise extensively involved in project finance also typically play leading rôles in PPP project financing. Table 9.2, which sets out the 'top 20' project-finance banks in 2005, illustrates this mixture.

Table 9.2

Major project-finance banks, 2005

		Total underwriting (US$ million)	No. projects	Average underwriting (US$ million)
Royal Bank of Scotland	U.K.	8,891	54	165
BNP Paribas	France	7,648	48	159
Société Générale	France	7,214	37	195
Calyon	France	6,912	59	117
Mizuho Financial	Japan	5,530	38	146
Caja Madrid	Spain	3,859	16	241
Bank of Tokyo-Mitsubishi	Japan	3,633	44	83
Westdeutsche Landesbank	Germany	3,620	36	101
Dexia	Belgium	3,545	31	114
Royal Bank of Canada	Canada	3,512	11	319
HSBC Bank	U.K.	3,624	28	129
Barclays Bank	U.K.	3,074	20	154
ING	Netherlands	2,862	28	102
Sumitomo Mitsui Banking Corp.	Japan	2,815	34	83
Hypovereinsbank	Germany	2,802	27	104
Standard Chartered	U.K.	2,734	18	152
Citigroup	U.S.A.	2,635	21	125
ABN Amro	Netherlands	2,630	21	125
Banco Bilbao Viscaya Argentaria	Spain	2,619	28	94
Credit Suisse First Boston	Switzerland	2,589	10	259
Others (180 banks)		57,555		
	Total	**140,303**	**513**	**273**

Source: as for Table 9.1.

Most international commercial banks have specialist departments that work on putting project finance deals together. There are three main approaches to organising such departments:

Project finance department. The longest-standing approach is to have a department purely specialising in project finance transactions. Larger departments are divided into industry teams, covering the main project-finance sectors such as energy, infrastructure (including PPPs), and natural resources. Concentrating all the project-finance expertise in one department ensures an efficient use of resources and good cross-fertilisation, using experience of project finance for different industries; however, it may not offer clients the best range of services. But probably only a minority of banks now maintain this structure.

Structured finance department. As mentioned in §8.4.2, the divisions between project finance and other types of structured finance are quite blurred, and therefore nowadays project finance often forms part of a larger structured-finance department. This approach may offer a more sophisticated range of products, but there is some danger that project finance may not fit easily into the operation since other structured-finance business is based on a much shorter time horizon.

Industry-based departments. Another approach is to combine all financing for a particular industry sector (*e.g.* electricity, oil and gas/mining, or construction/infrastructure/PPPs) in one department; if this industry makes regular use of project finance, project finance experts form part of the team. This provides one-stop services to the bank's clients in that particular industry, but obviously may diminish cross-fertilisation between project finance experience in different industries.

It has to be said that banks do not always pursue consistent policies towards project-finance business. Some major banks such as Bank of America, Deutsche Bank and UBS, which formerly were very successful in project finance, have closed these activities down. Citibank, which was number one in the market with $6.4 billion of underwriting in 2004, dropped back in 2005 as shown in Table 9.2 as a result of stepping away from the market. The problem with project finance from the perspective of such banks is that the process is much slower and more people-intensive than other structured-finance activities, and the revenues are also unpredictable (in the sense that one large project will push up fee income in one quarter, but the income cannot be sustained in the next quarter). Having said this, *Project Finance International* statistics show that the number of bank underwriters active in the project-finance market increased from 105 in 2000 to 200 in 2005, indicating that the disappearance of some of the traditional market leaders has had no real effect on the ability of the market to expand (and *cf.* §14.2 for the effect of the 'Basel II' capital requirements).

Therefore so long as a country's PPP programme offers a steady and reliable stream of business this should ensure that commercial banks are prepared to make the staffing and balance-sheet commitments which are needed to ensure that there is enough market competition for this programme to get financing on the best terms.

§9.3.2 LEAD ARRANGERS AND FINANCIAL ADVISERS

The normal approach to arranging a project-finance loan is to appoint one or more banks as Lead Arranger(s), who will ultimately underwrite the debt and place it in the market. (Other terms are used for this rôle, such as Lead Manager.) As with a financial adviser, experience of lending to similar PPP projects is a key factor in selecting a Lead Arranger; a wider banking relationship with one or more of the Sponsors is often another element in the decision. Lead Arrangers' fees are predominately based on a successful conclusion of the financing, although there may be a small retainer, and other out-of-pocket costs, such as travel, are usually covered by the Sponsors.

One of the first questions Sponsors have to consider on the financing side is when the Lead Arrangers should be brought into the transaction. Ideally, to ensure the maximum competition between banks on the financing terms, the whole of the project package should be finalised (including all the Project Contracts) and a number of banks then invited to bid in a competition to underwrite and provide the loan—which may actually be required by the

Public Authority (*cf.* §16.2). This implies either that the Sponsors make use of a financial adviser to put this package together, or do it themselves if they have the experience.

An alternative approach is to agree with a bank at an early stage of the project development process that it will act both as financial adviser and Lead Arranger. This should reduce the cost of the combined financial advisory and banking underwriting fees, and also ensure that the advice given is based on what the bank is itself willing to do, and therefore that the project should be financeable. Moreover, many of the major banks in the market are not interested in 'pure' financial advisory work, which is even more unpredictable in income, and consumes much more staff time in relation to this income, than being a Lead Arranger— such banks are therefore only interested in doing advisory work if it is combined with being the Lead Arranger.

If this procedure is used a mandate letter is normally signed between the Sponsors and the Lead Arranger, which provides for services similar to those of the financial adviser set out above, but also expresses the bank's intention—subject to due diligence, credit clearance, and agreement on detailed terms—to underwrite the debt required; some indication of pricing and other debt terms may also be given, although this may be difficult at an early stage of the transaction. This mandate letter does not impose a legal obligation on the bank to underwrite or lend money for the project—it is merely a statement of intent, albeit a serious one (since if the deal is not signed the bank will have done a lot of work for little if any fee). The obvious problem with this approach is that the bank is not in a competitive position (even if there may have originally been some kind of bidding process for the mandate), and therefore the Sponsors will probably not get the most aggressive final terms for the financing. However, this may be a reasonable price to pay for the saving on advisory fees, greater efficiency of the process and greater certainty of obtaining finance that this method affords. Clearly the general relationship between the Sponsors and the banks concerned may also affect this decision. Some competition can also be retained by appointing at least two banks as joint lead arrangers, with each committed to underwrite all of the financing if necessary. If one bank steps too far out of line it will be dropped and the other will take up the slack. However, this cannot be done for small projects.

In major projects, both a financial adviser and Lead Arranger(s) may be appointed separately at an early stage to provide more balanced advice, although obviously this adds to bid costs.

§9.3.3 COMMITMENT LETTERS AND LETTERS OF INTENT

If a Public Authority wants a fully-committed bid, on which there will be no further negotiation (*cf.* §6.3.8), it may require the financing to be committed at the time of the bid. This means that banks have to complete their due-diligence process (*cf.* §9.3.4), put together a detailed financing package (*cf.* Chapter 10), obtain credit approvals, and perhaps even have agreed loan documentation with the bidders, for the bidders to demonstrate that the financing can be provided and thus the project can begin without delay. The disadvantage of this approach is that a full underwriting commitment by banks will involve fee payments (*cf.* §10.4.3) and substantial legal and other advisory costs, and bidders may be unwilling to pay for all this with no certainty that they will win the bid, in which case it is not uncommon for losing bidders' costs to be covered up to an agreed level by the Public Authority (*cf.* §6.4.5). But there is no strong reason for the Public Authority to require full commitments with each bid, unless there is something novel about the structure or risk of the PPP, and hence some doubt about the terms on which it may be financeable.

Therefore the normal approach is for banks to provide letters of intent (or letters of interest) to Sponsors to support their bids for a PPP project. These are usually short— perhaps 2 pages long—and

- confirm the bank's basic interest in getting involved in the project, based on a review of the draft Project Contracts (on which they may have taken legal advice);
- set out outline terms and commitment levels for their share of the financing;
- confirm that the bank sees no reason not to be able to achieve Financial Close on the schedule required by the Public Authority, but
- state that the letter is not a legal commitment on the bank's part, and is subject, *inter alia*, to full due diligence and final credit approval.

If the letter requires the Sponsors to deal exclusively with the bank concerned, this may become to a Lead Arranger's mandate letter as described above. Alternatively, the Sponsors may collect a number of such letters from different banks. Letters of this nature provide initial reassurance to the Sponsors that their planned bid is reasonably realistic, and to the Public Authority that the required finance can be delivered. Although banks treat such 'support letters' seriously, they should not be regarded as a real commitment on the banks' part. Many banks issue these letters without going through any internal credit-approval procedure. They are often used by banks to ensure they keep their foot in the door of the project, and therefore should not be interpreted too strongly.

If a separate financial adviser is used, the adviser normally also provides a support letter for the bid, confirming that in their view the project can be successfully financed.

§9.3.4 LENDERS' DUE DILIGENCE

A Project Company, unlike a corporate borrower, has no business record to serve as the basis for a lending decision. Therefore lenders have to be confident that they will be repaid, especially taking account of the additional risk from the high level of debt inherent in a project-finance transaction. This means that they need to have a high degree of confidence that:

- The project can be completed on time and on budget.
- Revenues and opex can be predicted with reasonable certainty.
- There will be enough net cash flow from the project's operation to cover their debt service adequately; project economics also need to be robust enough to cover any temporary problems that may arise.

So the lenders need to evaluate the terms of the Project Contracts insofar as these provide a basis for its construction costs and operating cash flow, and quantify the risks inherent in the project, with particular care. As the Project Company has a limited ability to absorb risk (because of its high leverage) lenders need to ensure that project risks are allocated to other appropriate parties, or, where this is not possible, mitigated in other ways (*cf.* §14.2). This due-diligence process may cause slow and frustrating progress for a PPP project, especially if it leads lenders to get involved—directly or indirectly—in the negotiation of the Project Contracts (*cf.* §6.3.8), but it is an unavoidable aspect of raising project-finance debt. Finance can thus become a critical-path item.

To help with this due diligence, the Lead Arrangers—like the Public Authority (*cf.* §6.7) and the Sponsors (*cf.* §7.7)—employ external advisers (at the Sponsors' or Project Company's expense):

Legal advisers. Lawyers will be required both to prepare loan and security documentation, and to review the Project Contracts. Their own and the lenders' legal costs are one of the main categories of bidding and development costs for the Sponsors, which ultimately feed through to the Service Fees as they become part of the total capex (*cf.* §10.3.2), although it is generally the Sponsors who are risk if these costs exceed the levels assumed in their bid. It is preferable for legal work to be done on a fixed-fee basis (*cf.* §6.7.5), but if this is not possible costs need to be carefully controlled. If their lawyers are working on time-based fees the lenders—who normally receive fixed fees—have every incentive to try to shift due-diligence work onto them to get a better return on the time of their staff involved in the project. Typical examples of this are the use of lawyers to act as secretaries of meetings that are primarily discussing commercial or financial (rather than legal) issues, or to draw up the term sheet (*cf.* §9.3.5). The Sponsors must therefore agree to the lenders' legal advisers' scope of work and carefully supervise the time spent.

Technical Adviser ('T/A'). A consultant (a surveying or engineering company) will be needed to advise the lenders on:

- the cost and feasibility of the construction;
- FM costs and the maintenance cycle;
- other opex (where relevant);
- the technical aspects of the Project Contracts.

Market-risk adviser. In the case of a Concession, or a PFI-Model Contract which transfers usage risk, an adviser will be required to review this risk, *e.g.* by modelling or reviewing models for traffic flows and tolls (*cf.* §14.8.1).

Insurance adviser. The major international insurance brokers all have departments which specialise in advising lenders to major projects, insurance being an important part of the lenders' security (*cf.* §12.4).

Financial model auditor. The rôle played by the financial model, and the Model Auditor, in project development and due diligence is discussed in Chapter 10.

Throughout the due-diligence process, the financial advisers or Lead Arrangers are likely to play an active rôle in any further negotiation (or renegotiation) of the Project Contracts, to ensure that financing implications of these contracts are taken into account. Any changes in the Project Contracts that are good for the Sponsors are generally good for lenders too, and so the banks are also frequently used by Sponsors to improve their commercial position in any negotiations with the Public Authority.

This whole due-diligence and control process can be of value to the Public Authority, despite the extra work and cost it may create, as it helps to 'validate' the project and ensure its long-term viability (*cf.* §2.9.8). However the Public Authority must also conduct its own due diligence on the financing structure and terms (*cf.* §6.5.3, *cf.* §8.5.2).

§9.3.5 TERM SHEET, UNDERWRITING AND DOCUMENTATION

As the financing structure develops a term sheet is drawn up, setting out in summary form the basis on which the finance will be provided (as discussed in detail in Chapter 10). This can develop into quite an elaborate document, especially if the bank lawyers are involved in drawing it up, which can add substantially to the Sponsors' legal costs. It is preferable for term-sheet discussions to concentrate on commercial rather than legal issues, although the dividing line may be difficult to draw.

A term sheet may be drafted by the financial adviser as a basis for requesting financing bids from prospective Lead Arrangers, or at a later stage by the Lead Arrangers to crystallise their commitment to the financing.

The final term sheet provides the basis for the Lead Arrangers to complete their internal credit proposals and obtain the necessary approvals to go ahead with the loan. The work of a bank's project finance team, and the consequent proposal for a loan, is normally reviewed by a separate credit department, and it may be presented to a formal credit committee for approval. Banks must have a well-organised interface between the credit team and the project-finance team, especially where a bank is acting as a Lead Arranger: it may take a long time to develop a PPP project, and if the loan is turned down at the end of that process on credit grounds, this obviously has serious consequences for both the Sponsors and the Public Authority (and does not help the bank's project-finance business very much). On the other hand, the bank cannot obtain full credit approval at the beginning of the development process, because the structure of the transaction will probably not be sufficiently finalised. The Sponsors and the Public Authority therefore need to have confidence that a Lead Arranger has the experience and credibility to manage this internal-review process.

After obtaining their credit approval, Lead Arranger(s) may 'underwrite' the debt, usually by signing the agreed term sheet. The term sheet provides for a final date by which documentation should be signed, as banks usually have to reapply for internal credit approval if their loan is not signed within a reasonable period. This signature of a term sheet is still normally no more than a moral obligation, as the commitment by the banks is usually subject to further detailed due diligence on the Project Contracts and agreement on financing and security documentation. Bank technical or other advisers may also still have due-diligence work to do. Nonetheless, a term sheet is treated seriously, and banks normally only withdraw from an underwriting if there is a major change of circumstances, either in relation to the project itself, the country in which it is situated, or the market in general.

The next phase in the financing is the negotiation of financing documentation, typical terms for which are discussed below; when this is signed the Sponsors finally have obtained committed financing for the Project Company. Even at this stage, the banks may not actually provide the funding, as there are numerous conditions precedent that have to be fulfilled before the project reaches Financial Close (*cf.* §6.5.4), and a drawing can be made.

It is evident from this description that arranging project finance is not a quick process. If the project is presented to potential Lead Arrangers as a completed package, with all the Project Contracts in place, it is likely to take a minimum of 3 months before signature of the loan documentation by the Lead Arrangers. But there is clearly a lengthy process to go through before such a package can be completed, and issues may well arise during banks' due diligence that further slow down the matter. Finance is therefore usually an important critical-path item, and it is not uncommon for banks to work for a year or more on the financing side of a major PPP project.

§9.3.6 SYNDICATION

For larger loans, the Lead Arrangers may wish to reduce their loan exposure by placing part of the financing with other banks in the market, while retaining arranging and under-writing fees. There are many banks participating in the project finance market at the next level down as sub-underwriters or participants in syndicated loans. Some of these participate in domestic lending in their own countries, others in syndications of a wider range of loans around the world originally arranged and underwritten by the larger players in the market.

The Lead Arrangers prepare an information package to facilitate this loan-sale process (which is known as 'syndication'), at the heart of which is an information memorandum. This may be based on a Preliminary Information Memorandum ('PIM') originally prepared by the Sponsors or their financial adviser to present the project to prospective Lead Arrangers, and will probably also import a lot of information from the ITT/ITN prepared by the Public Authority. The information memorandum (usually around 100 pages long) provides a detailed summary of the transaction, including:

- a summary overview of the project, its general background, and *raison d'être*;
- the Project Company, its ownership, organisation and management;
- financial and other information on Sponsors, including their experience in similar projects and the nature of their involvement in and support for the current project;
- similar information on the parties to the Project Contracts;
- technical description of the construction and O&M of the project;
- where relevant, information relevant to usage of the Facility, *e.g.* historic and projected traffic flows;
- summary of the PPP Contract and other Project Contracts;
- project costs and financing plan;
- risk analysis (*cf.* §14.3)
- financial analysis, including the Base Case financial model (*cf.* §10.3.8) and sensitivity analyses (*cf.* §10.3.6)
- a detailed term sheet for the financing (*cf.* §9.3.5).

In other words, the information memorandum provides a synopsis of the structure of the project and the whole due-diligence process, which speeds up the credit analysis by prospective participant banks. (If well-organised and written, it also provides the Project Company's staff and the Public Authority with a useful long-term reference manual on the project and its financing.) The information memorandum is accompanied by supplementary reports and information:

- a copy of the financial model, with the Model Auditor's report (*cf.* §10.3.7);
- the T/A's report (*cf.* §9.3.4), summarising their due-diligence review;
- if relevant, the T/A's report on usage-risk aspects of the project and its revenue projections;
- the legal advisers may provide a summary of legal aspects of the project;
- a report on insurances from the insurance adviser;
- annual reports or other information on the various parties to the project.

The Sponsors and the Project Company are actively involved in the production of the information memorandum, which is normally subject to their approval and confirmation of its accuracy; the Public Authority may also review the draft.

A formal presentation is often made to prospective participant banks by Lead Arrangers, the Sponsors and other relevant project parties, which may include the Public Authority, sometimes through a 'road show' in different financial centres. Prospective participant banks are usually given 3–4 weeks to absorb this information and come to a decision whether to participate in the financing. They are generally given the documentation to review after they have taken this decision in principle to participate, and may sign up for the financing 2–3 weeks after receiving this.

The Project Company does not usually take any direct risk on whether the syndication is successful or not; by then the loan should have been signed and thus underwritten by the Lead Arrangers. Public Authorities and Sponsors should resist delay tactics by Lead Arrangers who try to avoid signing the financing documentation until after they have syndicated the loan and thus eliminated their underwriting risk. Similarly, syndication should not be of concern to the Public Authority. (In some cases 'market flex' provisions give bank underwriters some flexibility to increase their loan pricing, for a large loan before syndication, to reflect changes in the loan markets, but this is not common in the PPP project-finance market.)

Participant banks may also transfer part or all of their loans to other banks at any time during the life of the loan. This is important as part of their portfolio management—commercial banks are not naturally lenders for the 20 years or more of financing required for a PPP project, since their deposits are mainly short-term in nature (*cf.* §11.2), and portfolio liquidity is therefore important.

The Public Authority should not control either the syndication process or subsequent transfers by banks to other lenders, since a change in lenders should have no effect on the services provided under the PPP Contract (unless, *e.g.* the involvement of certain classes of lender such as banks lending from other countries, raises issues such as withholding tax on interest payments). Any such restrictions will reduce the liquidity of the bank loan, which has an associated cost. Of course, new lenders must assume any obligations to the Public Authority which exist under the Direct Agreement (*cf.* §12.3.3), e.g. as to confidentiality.

§9.3.7 AGENCY OPERATION

Once the financing documentation has been signed, one of the Lead Arrangers acts as agent for the bank syndicate as a whole: this agent bank acts as a channel between the Project

Company (and the Public Authority if necessary) and the banks, as otherwise the Project Company could find it is spending an excessive amount of time communicating with individual banks. The agent bank:

- collects the funds from the syndicate when drawings are made and passes these on to the Project Company;
- holds the project security on behalf of the lenders (this function may be carried out by a separate security trustee, acting on the instructions of the agent bank);
- calculates loan interest payments and principal repayments;
- receives payments from the Project Company and passes these on to the individual syndicate banks;
- gathers information about the progress of the project, in liaison with the lenders' advisers, and distributes this to the syndicate at regular intervals;
- monitors the Project Company's compliance with the requirements of the financing documentation and provides information on this to the syndicate banks;
- arranges meetings and site visits as necessary for the Project Company and the Sponsors to make more formal presentations to the syndicate banks on the project's progress;
- organises discussions with and voting by the syndicate if the Project Company needs to obtain an amendment or waiver of some term of the financing;
- takes enforcement action against the Project Company or the security after a default.

The agent bank seldom has any discretion to make decisions about the project finance (for example, as to placing the Project Company in default), but acts as directed by a defined majority of the banks. Requiring collective voting by the banks in this way ensures that one rogue bank cannot hold the rest of the syndicate (and the Project Company) for ransom.

§9.4 BOND ISSUES

A bond issued by a Project Company is similar to a loan from the Project Company's point of view. As the borrower—known as the 'issuer' in this context—the Project Company agrees to repay to the bond holder the amount of the bond plus interest on fixed future instalment dates. A 'bond' in this context has nothing to do with 'bonding' or 'bonds' issued as security, *e.g.* when making a bid (*cf.* §6.4.4). Bonds may also be referred to as 'securities', 'notes' or 'debentures'. Bonds are often held by bond-investment funds, with a similar client base to PPP equity funds (*cf.* §7.2.1).

Buyers of project-finance bonds are investors who require a good long-term return on their investment without taking equity risks, in particular insurance companies and pension funds. The key difference between loans and bonds is that bonds are tradable instruments and therefore have at least a theoretical liquidity, which loans do not. This difference is not as great as it at first appears, because many PPP bonds are sold on a private-placement basis (*cf.* §9.4.2), to investors who do not intend to trade them in the market, whereas loans are in fact traded on an *ad hoc* basis between banks. However, the Project Company and the Public Authority will have less knowledge of, and potential contact with, bond holders than with bank lenders.

§9.4.1 DUE DILIGENCE

Investors in bonds generally do not get directly involved in the due-diligence process to the extent that banks do, and rely more on the project's investment bank and a rating agency to carry out this work. An investment bank (*i.e.* a bank that arranges and underwrites financing but does not normally provide the financing itself, except on a temporary basis) is appointed as Lead Arranger for the bond issue, and assists in structuring the project in a similar way to a financial adviser on a bank loan (*cf.* §9.2). The investment bank then makes a presentation on the project to a credit-rating agency (the leaders in the field as far as project-finance bonds are concerned are Standard & Poor's and Moody's Investors Services), which assigns the bond a credit rating based on its independent review of the risks of the project, including legal documentation and independent advisers' reports (using external advisers in a similar way to banks—*cf.* §9.3.4). This review considers the same risk issues as a commercial bank would do. As project-finance bonds will form a very small part of a bond investor's portfolio, it is more cost-effective to rely on the rating as the main basis for the credit decision, rather than have to employ staff to undertake the kind of detailed due diligence undertaken by banks.

Gradations of credit ratings by Standard & Poor's and Moody's from the prime credit level of AAA/Aaa down to the minimum 'investment grade' rating of BBB-/Baa3 (below which many bond investors will not—and in some cases legally cannot—purchase a bond issue) are listed in Table 9.3. Most PPP-project ratings are at the lower end of this range. (Below the investment-grade level the ratings continue from BB+/Ba1, *etc.*) Some bank loans are also rated by the ratings agencies, to assist in a wider syndication, and because some institutional investors are beginning to participate in bank syndicated loans. However, this is not a widespread practice in the project-finance market. From the borrower's point of view, the disadvantage of dealing with credit through a rating agency, as compared to negotiating with a bank lender, is that the former is not under the same competitive pressure to do the deal. This can mean that the bond has to be issued on less aggressive terms than might be the case if banks were competing for the business, or Sponsors may be forced to provide extra security or other credit support (*cf.* §10.9).

Table 9.3
Investment-grade ratings

Standard & Poor's	Moody's
AAA	Aaa
AA+	Aa1
AA	Aa2
AA−	Aa3
A+	A1
A	A2
A−	A3
BBB+	Baa1
BBB	Baa2
BBB−	Baa3

Having obtained the rating, the investment bank prepares a preliminary bond prospectus that covers similar ground to an information memorandum for a bank syndication (*cf.* §9.3.6), although in less detail. The work done by the investment bank and the rating agency reduces the need for due diligence by bond investors—provided the bond rating fits the bond investor's maximum risk profile, such investors can just decide to buy it without having to do a lot of work.

§9.4.2 BOND PLACEMENT

After any necessary preliminary testing of the market (which may include a road show of presentations to investors), the investment bank issues the final bond prospectus and underwrites the bond issue through a subscription agreement. The coupon (interest rate) and other key conditions of the bond are fixed based on the market at the time of underwriting, and the bond proceeds are paid over to the Project Company a few days later. The investment bank places (or resells) the bonds with investors, and may also maintain a liquid market by trading in the bond. As can be seen, the timing of this process means that the underwriting does not take place until the underwriter already knows that there are buyers for the bonds, and the price at which they can be sold: thus unlike a bank underwriter (*cf.* §9.3.5), the bond underwriter takes little if any market risk.

The pricing for project-finance bonds may be based on a margin over government bonds of a comparable maturity—this is a combination of two separate elements, a specific credit margin for the bond based mainly on its rating, and a market premium reflecting the overall supply and demand for corporate bonds. It is preferable, where possible, for pricing to be fixed in advance, especially for private placements, at a margin over the interest-rate swap rate (*i.e.* the rate at which banks can obtain fixed-rate funding—*cf.* §11.2.2), which fixes the project-specific credit pricing, leaving only the underlying market pricing to be fixed at the time of placement.

Bonds may either be public issues (*i.e.* quoted on a stock exchange and—at least theoretically—quite widely traded), or private placements, which are not quoted and are sold to a limited number of large investors who typically hold them throughout their life. It is possible for a private placement to take place without the intervention of an investment bank (*i.e.* the Sponsors can deal directly with investors, as they can deal direct with banks, without the use of a financial adviser), although this seldom occurs.

Paying agents (also known as fiscal agents) and trustees are appointed for the bond issue, with similar rôles to that of an agent bank for a loan (*cf.* §9.3.7). The paying agent pays over the proceeds of the bond to the borrower and collects payments due to the bond investors. The bond trustee holds the security on behalf of the investors, and calls meetings of bond holders to vote on waivers or amendments of the bond terms.

§9.4.3 THE PROJECT-FINANCE BOND MARKET

As Table 9.4 illustrates, the market for project finance bonds is far smaller in scale than that for bank loans, and has shown little overall growth in recent years.

Table 9.4

Project-finance bond market by sectors, 2000–5

(US$ millions)	2000	2001	2002	2003	2004	2005
Infrastructure	3,394	2,430	6,591	11,931	11,082	8,779
Natural resources	3,285	3,813	2,632	7,023	6,061	10,795
Power	11,920	17,273	4,315	12,346	11,376	7,261
Telecoms	2,036	1,487		864		
Other	176		250		128	
	20,811	**25,003**	**13,788**	**32,164**	**28,647**	**26,835**

Source: as for Table 8.1.

The market is also heavily concentrated in certain countries, as illustrated by Table 9.5.

The U.S. market for project-finance bond issues is by far the largest. This reflects the combination of reluctance by American banks to lend for long terms (because they can make money on short-term consumer and commercial lending), and the high demand for bonds from institutional investors, especially pension funds. The project-finance bond market is based on rule 144a, adopted by the Securities and Exchange Commission ('SEC') in 1990. A private placement of a bond issue does not have to go through the SEC's lengthy full registration procedure, but cannot be sold on to another party for two years. This lack of liquidity is generally not acceptable to U.S. bond investors. However, Rule 144a allows secondary trading (*i.e.* reselling) of private placements of debt securities, provided sales are to qualified institutional buyers ('QIBs') with a portfolio of at least US$100 million in securities. Rule 144a bonds are therefore sold by the Project Company to an investment bank, which then resells them to QIBs. Thus Rule 144a provides an efficient and effective way of raising project finance in the world's largest bond market, and it is the main basis on which project-finance bonds are issued in that market, whether they are limited private placements

Table 9.5

Project-finance bonds by country, 2005

(US$ millions)	2005
United States	12,582
United Kingdom	4,669
Mexico	3,000
Malaysia	2,278
Qatar	2,250
Canada	1,093
Australia	841
El Salvador	75
Peru	50
	26,835

Source: as for Table 8.1.

or more widely-traded issues, although they have to be relatively large in size—at least US$100–200 million. Rule 144a US$ project-finance bonds are the only important source of cross-border (international) project-finance bond financing, primarily for projects in the Americas, *e.g.* in Mexico, but are also placed for projects elsewhere from time to time, such as the issues for Qatar shown in Table 9.5. It is also worth noting that a large proportion of the project-finance bonds issued in the U.S. relate to acquisitions of projects (such as toll-road Franchises), or refinancings, rather than 'greenfield' projects.

The non-US$ bond market is concentrated in a few locations. This partly reflects the fact that European and Asian banks are more aggressive lenders to the project-finance market, and tend to have closer relationships with major project Sponsors, and partly that the investor market is also much smaller. In Europe, the British (£ sterling) market is the most important for project-finance bonds, with PFI projects using most of the market capacity, both in public and private placements. The minimum size for public placements is around £100 million; smaller amounts can be raised through private placements. Bonds are typically used for large projects (£150 million and above), where there may be more limited bank liquidity, and also for refinancing. There are similar markets in Australia and Canada for infrastructure-related bonds.

Malaysia has been one of the main markets for 'Sukuk' bonds. Technically such bonds do not charge interest, but rely on the underlying business of the borrower, which is a structure which fits well with PPP financing. The bonds are intended for Islamic investors, but are held quite widely by non-Islamic investors too. Their use has now spread from Malaysia to other parts of the world, *e.g.* the Middle East, and it can be expected that Sukuk bonds will play an increasing rôle in PPP financing.

Inflation-indexed bonds, where interest and principal repayments are linked to inflation, are discussed in §11.3.6.

§9.4.4 MONOLINE INSURANCE

'Monoline' insurance companies insure against default by a bond issuer: this structure was originally used to insure municipal bonds in the United States; the insurance companies active in this field are primarily U.S.-based. Bonds insured in this way are known as 'wrapped' bonds. Theoretically, the bond investors need to pay little attention to the background or risks of the project itself and can rely on the credit rating of the insurance company 'wrapper' (usually AAA). The wrapper has to go through its own due-diligence process, and projects generally have to secure a 'shadow' investment-grade rating (BBB or above) in their own right to obtain wrapped cover, as monoline insurers have to convince the ratings agencies that their portfolio has a reasonable spread of risk while meeting minimum credit standards.

This structure may offer benefits of greater certainty, speed, and flexibility, and savings in cost if the wrapper is willing to take a lower return for the credit risk than direct investors— the latter being the usual motive for wrapped bonds in the PPP market. It also ensures a greater demand and hence liquidity for the bonds, which should also be reflected in the bond pricing. However, the market pricing for wrapped bonds does not fully reflect the AAA credit status of the monoline insurers, reflecting a degree of caution amongst bond investors about the value of such cover. Insurance is primarily about spreading predictable risks amongst a wide range of insured persons, rather than very specific financial guarantees of this nature,

and there is something anomalous about two types of financial institutions—insurance companies and banks—changing different rates for taking the same kind of risk. The wrapping
fee may be about 0.3% *p.a.*, compared to a bank credit margin over double this figure
(*cf.* §10.4.1), which suggests that one of the two must have got the pricing wrong.

According to the *Project Finance International* market database (see Table 8.1 for references), in 2005 there were 4 monoline insurers active in the project bond market, who
collectively wrapped 16% of the project-finance bonds issued in the market. (This compares
with 44% of the market in 2003—two of the major insurers have dropped out of the 2005
statistics.) Each monoline insurer reinsures a large part of its risk with other insurance companies in this market. A significant proportion of the PPP-project bond financing in the
United Kingdom has been on a wrapped basis—all the 2005 wrapped bonds related to PFI
projects except for one large U.S. issue (a refinancing of the Chicago Skyway Franchise
acquisition—*cf.* §3.5).

A further refinement on monoline insurance—albeit little used in PPPs to date—is the
'double wrap', where the Public Authority guarantees the obligations of the monoline insurer.
This involves little risk for the Public Authority given the double security of the monoline
insurer and the underlying project, but further reduces the cost of finance and hence the
level of the Service Fees.

§9.5 BANK LOANS *v.* BONDS

The key factors which are likely to affect a Project Company's decision whether to use
commercial-bank or bond financing (in a market where bond financing is available) are:

- *Size*: Bonds can only be used for larger projects, as investors want the bond issue to
  be sufficiently large for the issue to have market liquidity. For very large (say more
  than US$250 million) projects there may be more limited bank liquidity and so bonds
  may be more suitable.
- *Cost*: Bonds have tended to have a lower cost than equivalent bank loans, partly
  because there is a wider investor base; however the cost advantage for bonds in these
  markets now seems to depend mainly on monoline insurers taking the credit risk at a
  lower cost than banks (see above).
- *Term*: Bonds have always been used to provide very long-term finance, whereas until
  the mid-1990s it was unusual for a bank project-finance loans (or any other loans)
  to be for longer than 20 years. It remains the case that for very long term loans (say
  30 years or more) bonds will be more competitive.

There are a number of other more detailed or technical pros and cons between loans and
bonds, summarised in Table 9.6.

Because of some of the uncertainties about the final availability or terms of bond financing, Sponsors may arrange a bank loan as an 'insurance policy' in case the bond issue falls
through, or put together a bank loan with the intention of refinancing it rapidly with a bond.
Obviously this involves extra costs.

In general, bonds are suitable for 'standard' projects. They are also especially suitable if
a project is being refinanced after it has been built and has operated successfully for a period.

Table 9.6
Bank loans *v.* bonds

Bank loans	Bonds
Banks can be involved in and effectively (though not legally) committed to the project from an early stage	Bond investors only come in at a very late stage, and may be more affected by short-term market sentiment
Although banks do not formally commit to loan terms (including credit margin) in advance, they are more likely to stand by the terms they offer at an early stage (unless market-flex provisions apply)	The terms for the bond and the market appetite for it are only finally known at a late stage in the process, when the underwriting takes place
The Sponsors' corporate-banking lines may be used up in project-finance loans (but *cf.* §8.5.1)	Bonds bring a different investor base, thus avoiding the need to tie up bank credit lines
Project Contracts kept confidential, in a loan syndicated to a restricted number of banks	The terms of Project Contracts may have to be published in a public rating report (*cf.* §9.4.1) or bond prospectus: this may not be acceptable to the Sponsors for reasons of commercial confidentiality
Generally only offer fixed rates of interest through hedging arrangements (*cf.* §11.2.2)	Fixed rates of interest
Interest-rate pricing is based on open-market quotations (but *cf.* §11.2.8)	Interest-rate pricing is a 'block box' (*cf.* §9.4.2), although the likely outcome can be monitored by watching the prices of comparable bonds already issued
Inflation-indexed loans generally not available or only available through hedging arrangements (*cf.* §11.3.9)	In some markets can be issued on an inflation-indexed basis (*cf.* §11.3.6)
Funds from the loan drawn only when needed	Funds from the bond have to be drawn all at once, and then redeposited until required to pay for capex—there is likely to be a loss of interest (known as 'negative arbitrage') caused by the redeposit rate being lower than the coupon on the bond (*cf.* §11.2.11)
Banks can offer flexible loan repayment schedules (*cf.* §10.5.5), and short-term working capital loans	Bond loan repayment schedules are inflexible and cannot offer short-term funding
Banks exercise control over all changes to Project Contracts, and impose tight controls on the Project Company	Bond investors only control matters that significantly affect their cash flow cover or security, and Events of Default leading to accelerated repayment of the financing are more limited in bond issues
Decisions on waivers and amendments to loan terms are taken on a case-by-case basis by banks; this is more flexible, especially during the construction phase	Bond investors cannot easily take complex decisions (because of the wide spread and number of investors), and so rely mainly on mechanical tests such as Cover Ratios (*cf.* §10.6); this may be less flexible if amendments to these ratios are required (although bond holders may allow any parallel bank lenders to take decisions on their behalves)

(Continued)

Table 9.6

(*Continued*)

Bank loans	Bonds
Banks tightly control the addition of any new debt, and are unlikely to agree the basis for this in advance	It is may be easier to add new debt (*e.g.* for a project expansion) to bond financing as bond investors will agree the terms for this in advance through 'variation bonds' (*cf.* §15.2.1)
Low penalties for prepayment (*e.g.* because the debt can be refinanced on more favourable terms)	High penalties for prepayment (*cf.* §11.2.12)
It is easier to negotiate with banks if the project gets into difficulty	If the project gets into serious trouble it can be difficult to have a direct dialogue with bond holders, who are more passive in nature than a bank syndicate; banks are often wary of lending in partnership with bond holders for this reason
If a project gets into difficulty, negotiations with banks should remain private	Negotiations with bond holders may be publicised

Conversely, the greater flexibility of bank loans tends to make them more suitable for the construction and early operation phases of a project, projects where there are likely to be changes in the Public Authority's requirements, more complex projects, or projects in more difficult markets. However, the distinction between the two is becoming blurred, as investment funds and some other categories of non-bank investor may buy into both bank loans and bonds.

§9.6 MEZZANINE DEBT

Mezzanine debt is subordinated debt provided by third parties rather than the investors in the Project Company (*cf.* §7.3.3). These may include non-bank investors, such as insurance companies or specialised funds.

Mezzanine debt may be used in cases where either there is a gap between the amount that Senior Lenders (*i.e.* the lenders with the highest priority in security and repayment) are willing to provide and the total debt requirements of the project, or in lieu of part of the equity to produce more a more competitive bid, as the pricing of mezzanine debt lies between that for senior debt and that for equity. Mezzanine debt may also be provided by institutional investors as part of a debt package including bond financing.

Bringing third-party debt into the financing package obviously creates greater issues of repayment priority and control over the project between the different levels of lenders than when subordinated debt is provided by shareholders (*cf.* §12.6.4).

Although mezzanine debt is common in other forms of structured finance, it has not been widely used in project finance, probably because the relatively high levels of leverage leave little space for it: it is thus more common in the Concession Model where leverage is typically lower.

Chapter 10

Financial Structuring

§10.1 INTRODUCTION

This chapter deals with the process by which bidders and their lenders structure the financing for a PPP project. The Service Fees (*cf.* Chapter 13) are the final output of this process, since these have to cover the Project Company's financing and operating costs and provide a return on the bidders' equity investment.

A financial model is used to make the required calculations for the bid, and at various other phases of the project (§10.2); although this book is not intended to cover financial modelling in depth, the key inputs and outputs for the financial model are reviewed (§10.3), including the financing costs (§10.4). The model has to work within the constraints of:

- the Public Authority's requirements for the PPP Contract term and Service-Fee profile (*cf.* §13.2);
- lenders' requirements for the term and payment profile of their debt (§10.5);
- lenders' Cover Ratio requirements (§10.6);
- investors' Equity IRR requirements (*cf.* §7.3.2);
- and the complex interplay between all of these (§10.7).

The financial model covers of the whole of the Project Company's operations, not just the Facility itself, and thus takes into account tax and accounting issues that may affect the final cash flow of the Project Company (§10.8).

§10.2 THE FINANCIAL MODEL

A financial model is used in different ways during the bidding and development phase of a PPP project:

- initial feasibility from the Public Authority's point of view: a 'shadow' financial model will be produced by the Public Authority's financial adviser, which will attempt to predict the bidder's costs, financing structure and other assumptions (in Australia this is called the Private Financing Predictor ('PFP')), and hence whether the outcome in terms of Service Fees is likely to be acceptable from the public-sector point of view;

- structuring the bidders' financing and reviewing the benefits of different financial terms and arrangements;
- calculation of the Service Fees required to cover capex, opex, debt service and the investors' return as a basis for the bid;
- as part of the lenders' due-diligence process;
- fixing the Service Fees where these depend on interest rates at Financial Close (*cf.* §11.12.13).

After Financial Close the model continues to be used:

- as a basis for lenders to review the changing long-term prospects for the project and thus their continuing risk exposure;
- to price variations and compensation payments in the PPP Contract (*cf.* §15.2.1);
- to calculate any Refinancing Gain to be shared between the Public Authority and the Project Company (*cf.* §16.4.6);
- as a budgeting tool for the Project Company.

However, given that the original objective of the model has changed, it will require some adaptation to undertake these tasks, especially the last.

As there are three parties involved—the Public Authority, the Sponsors and the lenders—there could theoretically be three parallel financial models, but this is seldom the case. The more usual course is for the Public Authority's financial adviser and the lenders to review the model prepared by the Preferred Bidder (or the latter's financial adviser), calibrate it against the Public Authority's shadow financial model to ensure that the results are the same (given the same assumptions), and then use the bidders' model thereafter, in the ways listed above. Alternatively, there is some merit in the Public Authority providing a template financial model to be used, with suitable adaptation, by all bidders, to make comparison of bids easier.

It may be asked why the Public Authority should have access in this way to the Preferred Bidder's financial model—isn't the data in this model commercially confidential? But this is unlikely to be the case because:

- The Public Authority needs to be able to check whether the bid is financially viable, and can thus deliver the initial investment in the PPP project and its long-term service requirements (*cf.* §6.5.3).
- If the financial model is used to calculate the Service Fees at Financial Close (*cf.* §11.12.13) it obviously has to be agreed by both parties.
- There has to be an agreed Base Case (*cf.* §10.3.8), because should compensation be required later (*cf.* §15.2.1, §15.6) it has to be measured against the outcome in the PPP Contract which both parties originally agreed was reasonable.

Therefore transparency between the parties on model assumptions and calculations is the better practice.

§10.3 MODEL INPUTS AND OUTPUTS

It is not the intention to discuss modelling techniques in any depth here. But it is necessary to have a basic understanding of what goes into and comes out of a financial model for a PPP, and how this output is used.

The model's initial purpose is to calculate the Service Fees, based on various 'building blocks' of inputs. The basis for the inputs must be clearly documented; the standard way of doing this is for an 'assumptions book' to be compiled. This takes each line of the financial model and sets out the source for the input (or the calculation based on these inputs) in that line, with copies of the documentation to back this up.

§10.3.1 MACROECONOMIC ASSUMPTIONS

Background assumptions are needed for interest rates and inflation (*cf.* Chapter 11). The Public Authority should ensure, at the bidding stage, that the same assumptions are used by all bidders if changes in these would affect the Service Fees (*cf.* §11.12.13).

§10.3.2 CAPITAL EXPENDITURE

The capex budget for the project takes into account costs incurred during the bidding, development and construction phases of the project, *i.e.* both 'hard' construction costs and the 'soft' costs for financing, advisory fees and administration. The main items here are likely to include:

Bidding and development costs. These are the main pre-Financial Close costs, *i.e.* the Sponsors' own staff costs and those of external advisers (*cf.* §7.7), including lenders' advisers (*cf.* §9.3.4). There is often a time gap between when the total capex budget is agreed with the lenders and Financial Close, and during that time there is a risk that legal and similar costs which are not fixed may mount up more than budgeted. If they are not treated as part of the initial equity investment, such development costs are normally reimbursed to the Sponsors at Financial Close, but if they are finally above budget by that time, lenders may require reimbursement of the excess to be deferred until the end of the construction period, at which time reimbursement may be allowed if sufficient funds are then available.

Development fees. Project economics may allow one or more Sponsors to take out an initial fee from the Project Company for developing the project, and thus cover their up-front costs and perhaps make a profit on these (*cf.* §7.3.2). This figure may fluctuate (or be eliminated entirely) as the financial evaluation of the project develops.

Project Company costs. These include costs after Financial Close such as:

- staff and administration; some administration costs such as accounting may be subcontracted (*cf.* §7.6.3); office and equipment;

- continuing external advisory costs, *e.g.* for construction supervision;
- construction-phase insurance (*cf.* §12.4.2).

Apart from insurance premiums, the amounts should be relatively small in the context of the overall capex budget if most of the Project Company's activities have been contracted out to FM Subcontractors.

Construction Subcontract price. As discussed in §14.6.1, the Construction Subcontract, which will obviously form the largest part of the capex, should normally be on a fixed-price 'turnkey' basis, with payments made *pro rata* to the progress of construction. Taxes such as Valued Added Tax (VAT) on this price (and any other costs) will also need to be taken into account if they cannot be recovered before the end of the construction period.

Working capital. The working capital is the amount of money required to cover the time difference between payment of the Project Company's opex and receipt of revenues in cash. In effect it is the short-term (usually 30–60 day) cash-flow cycle of the project, which cannot be calculated directly in a financial model that runs for six-monthly periods during the operating phase of the project. It is thus the initial costs that the Project Company has to incur until it receives its first revenues. These costs are unlikely to be substantial for the Project Company as long as its Subcontractors are paid on a cycle which matches its revenue cycle. The most significant initial cost may be payment of the first operating-phase insurance premium (as these premiums are normally paid annually in advance).

Reserve Accounts. Reserve Accounts (*cf.* §12.2.4) are normally funded as part of the capex rather than from operating cash flow, as this improves the investors' Equity IRR. (If they are funded as part of the capex this means that most of the funding will come from the lenders, whereas if they are funded out of cash flow this effectively means that all of the funding is provided by the investors, who have to give up Distributions to do this, hence reducing their Equity IRR.)

Interest during construction ('IDC') and funding drawdown. Project costs as set out above then give rise to a requirement for the total funding (in debt and equity) required for the project. However there is a circularity about this calculation (*i.e.* the answer changes the inputs), because:

- IDC, which is funded by further drawings on the funding sources (*cf.* §11.2), itself needs to be included in the total funding requirement;
- the funding split between debt and equity is determined by the ability of the operating cash flows to support that debt.

This means that various iterations of the calculations are required to get the right balance of debt and equity.

Contingency. Finally, an overall contingency may be added to the project cost to allow for unexpected events (*cf.* §10.5.9).

All of these costs need to be reviewed carefully to ensure there is no risk of cost overruns (*cf.* §14.6).

§10.3.3 OPERATING AND MAINTENANCE COSTS

The next block of modelling deals with the operation phase. Opex (and any payments to and from Reserve Accounts) is deducted from projected revenues to calculate the cash flow available for debt service ('CADS'). Opex, which is typically smaller than the debt service for a PPP project with a heavy initial investment in infrastructure and a consequent high level of debt, would include:

- the Project Company's own direct costs (*cf.* §7.6.3);
- Subcontract payments;
- insurance (*cf.* §12.4.3);
- taxation (*cf.* §10.8.2).

Maintenance costs are likely to form the largest part of the operating costs, whether incurred *via* Subcontractors or by the Project Company, and can be difficult to predict if this cost risk has not been subcontracted (*cf.* §14.8.6). Typically maintenance costs can be split into several categories, although the dividing lines between them (and hence the scope of any Subcontract) is not a fixed one. In the case of a building these categories may be:

Soft FM. This could include items such as cleaning, security, and catering. If such services form part of the PPP Contract (*cf.* §13.2), they are typically provided under a Soft FM Subcontract, with the costs fixed to the extent that they are fixed under this Subcontract (*cf.* §11.3.13).

Hard FM. This is the routine maintenance for the building. This would include matters such as servicing and maintaining the heating, toilets and other utility systems, painting, replacing broken windows or light bulbs, *etc.*, maintaining paving, repairs to the roof, and so on. This is typically provided under a Hard FM Subcontract.

Lifecycle costs. These costs relate to aspects of the Facility which require renewal or replacement on a regular cycle; for example the boilers in a building may need to be replaced after so many years. Again these costs may be included within the scope of the Hard FM Subcontract, but it probably more common for this to be on a 'cost-plus' basis, *i.e.* leaving the real risk with the Project Company.

In the case of a road, maintenance requirements may consist of:

Routine Maintenance. This might cover such matters as repairing potholes or cracks, clearing any obstructions, cleaning drainage and signs, and maintaining grass verges, often *via* a Maintenance Subcontract.

Major Maintenance. There is normally a cycle whereby the skimmed surface of the road is resealed say every five years, the road is resurfaced every 10–12 years, and the underlying concrete layer strengthened or renewed every 18–20 years. The costs get greater for each of these procedures, and are difficult to estimate because they are so far ahead (and timing is very dependent on usage levels). The further ahead these costs are, the less likely it is that a Maintenance Subcontract will apply. Similarly, major maintenance is often a significant cost item for process plant (*e.g.* a waste incinerator may have be shut down for a major maintenance every 3–5 years or so).

§10.3.4 REVENUES

There are natural caps on the level of Service Fees which can be fed into the financial structure at the time of bidding, insofar as the Project Company's revenues are derived from Service Fees:

- In the case of a Concession, projected demand and 'willingness to pay' will determine the levels of usage and the rates to be charged for tolls, *etc.* (*cf.* §13.4).
- In the case of a PFI-Model project, the Public Authority's VfM (*cf.* §5.3) and Affordability (*cf.* §5.4) requirements have to be taken into account.

Subject to these overall constraints, there is again some circularity about calculating the minimum required Service Fees as these have to be sufficient to pay debt service and provide the investors' return, *i.e.* there is a requirement for a certain level of CADS. There is thus a logical sequence in arriving at the level of Service Fees to bid—these need to be sufficient to:

- cover opex, *and*
- fit within the 'envelope' of the Public Authority's requirements, *and*
- meet lender debt-service and other requirements, *and*
- give the investors their required rate of return.

Having established the first of these requirements as above, the interplay between the latter three requirements is quite complex, as discussed in §10.7.

§10.3.5 MODEL OUTPUTS

The model outputs are a series of calculations:

- capex;
- drawdown of equity;
- drawdown of debt;
- Service Fees;
- other operating revenues (*cf.* §13.7);
- opex;
- interest calculations;
- tax;
- debt repayments;
- profit and loss account (income statement);
- balance sheet;
- cash flow (source and use of funds);
- lenders' Cover Ratios (*cf.* §10.6);
- investors' returns;
- the NPV of these payments, to enable the Public Authority to compare bids (*cf.* §6.3.6).

A summary sheet usually sets out the key results on one page.

§10.3.6 SENSITIVITIES

The financial model also needs to be sufficiently flexible to allow both investors and lenders to calculate a series of 'sensitivities' (also known as 'cases') showing the effects of variations in the key input assumptions. Such sensitivities may include calculating the effect on Cover Ratios and the Equity IRR of:

- construction-cost overrun;
- delay in completion (say for 6 months);
- deductions or penalties for failure to meet Availability or service requirements (*cf.* §13.5);
- reduced usage of the project (where the Project Company assumes usage risk);
- higher opex and maintenance costs;
- higher interest rates (where these are not fixed—*cf.* §11.2);
- changes in inflation (*cf.* §11.3.3).

In summary, the sensitivities look at the financial effect of the commercial- and financial-risk aspects of the project not working out as originally expected. Lenders also usually run a 'combined downside case' to check the effects of several adverse things happening at once (*e.g.* 3 months' delay in completion, a 10% drop in usage (if relevant), and 10% increase in opex). This calculation of several different adverse events happening at once is also called 'scenario analysis' (*cf.* §14.2).

§10.3.7 MODEL AUDIT

Lenders usually require the model to be audited by a Model Auditor, a service provided by specialist departments within major firms of accountants, or by specialised financial-modelling companies. The functions of the Model Auditor are to confirm that:

- the model properly reflects the Project Contracts and other stated assumptions (*e.g.* as to the rate of inflation);
- accounting and taxation calculations are correct;
- the model has the ability to calculate a reasonable range of sensitivities, as discussed above.

The Public Authority should also be a beneficiary of this audit if its own financial advisers do not audit and certify the model (which it is preferable they should do, because of the various ways in which it may be used—*cf.* §10.2).

§10.3.8 THE BASE CASE

Once the Public Authority, Sponsors and lenders agree that the financial model's structure and calculation formulae reflect the project and the Project Contracts correctly, the basic input assumptions are settled, and the financial structure and terms discussed below are agreed to and also incorporated in the model, the final run of the model—which is known as the 'Base Case' (or 'Banking Case')—usually takes place at or just before Financial Close:

- to enable the lenders to check that, using fully up-to-date assumptions, and the final versions of the Project Contracts, the project still provides them with adequate coverage for their loan;
- in some cases, to fix the level of the Service Fees to reflect interest rates at Financial Close (*cf.* §11.2.13).

§10.4 FINANCING COSTS

Apart from the lenders' advisers' fees (*cf.* §9.3.4), the main financing costs payable by the Project Company for commercial-bank loans are:

- the lenders' own cost of funds in the wholesale money market, most probably on a 'floating-rate' basis, and costs relating to financial hedging, if any (*cf.* Chapter 11);
- the lenders' credit margin (§10.4.1);
- a cost-of-capital charge, and other additional costs (§10.4.2);
- advisory, arranging and underwriting fees (§10.4.3);
- commitment fees (§10.4.4);
- agency and security trustee fees (§10.4.5).

The pricing for bonds is similar to this (§10.4.6).

§10.4.1 CREDIT MARGIN

Project-finance loans for PPP projects typically have credit margins in the range of 0.75%–1.5% over the lenders' cost of funds (*cf.* §11.2). The top end of this range would relate to high-risk projects such as Concession roads, whereas the bottom end would relate to low-risk projects such as PFI-Model accommodation projects. Pricing is usually higher until completion of construction, reflecting the higher risk of this stage of the project, then drops down, and then may gradually climb back again over time. Thus an accommodation project with a loan covering a 2-year construction and 25-year operation period might have a credit margin of 1% for years 1–2, 0.85% for years 3–5, and 1% thereafter. The increase in the margin is partly intended to encourage refinancing (*cf.* §16.4).

§10.4.2 ADDITIONAL COSTS

Bank lenders are also exposed to the possibility of additional funding costs, which would erode their credit margin, arising from:

Liquidity or capital costs. Banks may face an increased requirement from their central bank for liquidity reserves against long-term lending, or for increased capital to support such lending; these are known as minimum liquidity requirements ('MLRs'), or minimum liquid asset requirements ('MLAs'). If these costs are of any significance (usually the effect is minimal), they are borne by the borrower.

Banks may also be required to raise the ratio of capital which they have to hold against different classes of asset (as a protection for their depositors). The cost of their loans would have to be increased to preserve their return on capital. Capital requirements for project-finance loans have been a matter of great debate in the context of the introduction of the 'Basel II' capital requirements (*cf.* §9.4.4, §14.2).

Taxes. In the minority of cases where loans are made from outside the Project Company's country, lenders may not be able to offset withholding taxes on interest payments from the Project Company against their other tax liabilities—but apart from such cases lenders should not be able to charge any of their tax liabilities onto the Project Company.

Where withholding taxes do apply, the Project Company usually has to 'gross up' its interest payments (*i.e.* increase them by an amount sufficient to produce the amount of net interest payment to the lenders after deduction of tax). A lender may agree that if it can offset this amount of tax against its other tax liabilities in due course, the withholding will be refunded to the borrower. However, lenders are not prepared to get into debates about how they manage their tax affairs, and therefore any refund relies entirely on a lender's good faith.

Market disruption. The Project Company also takes the risk, where the bank funding is on a short-term floating-rate basis, that the banks may not be able to roll over their funding due to disruption in the market—this could mean changing the market-interest pricing basis, or if the banks cannot fund at all, prepaying the loan. If one or two banks get into trouble because of their own rather than general market problems, these provisions do not apply.

These provisions are not peculiar to the project-finance market, but should only be increased to cover the banks actually affected, not the whole syndicate. In practice, these provisions (other than those relating to liquidity costs and withholding tax) have not had to be applied in recent years.

§10.4.3 FEES

Arranging and underwriting fees charged by Lead Arrangers are derived from several factors:

- the size and complexity of the financing;
- the time and work involved in structuring the financing;
- the risk that a success-based fee may not be earned because the project does not go ahead;
- the bank's overall return targets for work of this kind (bearing competitive pressure in mind), taking into account both the fees earned and the return on the loan balance that it keeps on its own books;
- the length of time the underwriting bank has to carry the syndication risk (where the loan is being syndicated)—for a variety of reasons there can often be a considerable time lag between the signing of loan documentation and hence underwriting, and syndication to other participating banks in the project-finance market;

- the proportion of the fee that has to be re-allowed to sub-underwriting or participating banks to induce them to join the syndication (which is itself a function of the time the participating bank has to spend on reviewing it, the overall return the market requires for the risk, taking credit margin and fees together into account, and perhaps competition from other transactions in the market at the same time).

As a rough rule of thumb, the arranging and underwriting fees will be around 1%. If the arranging bank is also acting as financial adviser this may increase the fees by around 0.5%, although this does not always apply.

§10.4.4 COMMITMENT FEES

Commitment fees are paid on the available but undrawn portion of the debt during the construction period (*i.e.* so long as drawings may be made on the loan). As most project-finance loans are drawn very slowly (during, say, a 2–3 year construction period) banks need the commitment fee to give them a reasonable rate of return on their risk during the construction of the project when they are not earning the full loan margin. Commitment fees are usually around half of the credit margin in project-finance loans.

§10.4.5 AGENCY FEES

Finally there are the agency fees payable to the agent bank or security trustee (*cf.* §9.3.7). The time that a bank has to spend on agency work can be quite considerable, and it is in the Project Company's interests to ensure that a reasonable annual agency fee covers this work adequately, but this should be based on a fair assessment of costs, not a major source of extra profit for the agent.

§10.4.6 BONDS AND OTHER FIXED-RATE FINANCE

The pricing of bonds, *i.e.* their interest-rate coupon, is based on that for government bonds of a similar maturity. However, most bonds have 'bullet' repayments, *i.e.* the principal is repaid in one amount at the final maturity date. Project-finance bonds have to be repaid over the whole life of the financing term, and hence the pricing for such bonds is based on the market price for bonds with a final maturity equal to the average life of the project-finance bond. The same pricing principles apply where lenders are providing fixed-rate loans.

The pricing premium over the government-bond rate—known as the 'issue spread'—is based on a combination of the bond's credit rating, and the general supply and demand in the market. Thus, when placing a new bond, it should be possible to see what a reasonable pricing for it should be, by comparing it with the pricing of other bonds with a similar credit rating and average life/maturity already being traded in the market. The issue spread is often fixed only at the time of placing the bond, although it may be possible to negotiate a cap in advance (*cf.* §9.4.2). Overall pricing in most bond markets is however likely to end up being broadly similar to that in the banking markets.

Fees for bonds are a combination of a financial-advisory fee and an underwriting fee. Financial-advisory fees are comparable to those for bank loans—indeed at the beginning of the financial-advisory process it may not be clear whether a bank or bond financing offers the best option, so the financial adviser may have to consider both as part of the advisory work. Bond-underwriting fees tend to vary between domestic bond markets, and are affected by the degree of competition for underwriting mandates. In some markets there are effectively fee cartels which tends to keep fees relatively high, and to charge the same percentage fee however large the bond issue, but in general competition breaks down this approach. Given the very limited level of risk in a bond underwriting—as has been seen above, bonds are not underwritten until the underwriter is already confident they can be sold, as the sale takes place very shortly after the underwriting—there is no reason for fees over 0.5% of the amount of the bond. Commitment fees do not apply to bonds, as they are drawn immediately, and trustee fees are similar to bank agency fees. As with bank loans, other due-diligence costs, including the costs of the rating agency, are payable by the Project Company.

If the bond is covered by monoline insurance, the insurer's fee (technically an insurance premium) is typically around half that charged as a credit margin by banks (*cf.* §9.4.4). Ideally the monolines like to charge the whole of their fee as an up-front payment, *i.e.* the NPV of the future stream of fee payments, but it is clearly preferable for them to be paid over time like the bank credit margin, and again competition should ensure this is the case.

§10.5 DEBT PROFILE

§10.5.1 DEBT TERM

While project-finance loans in general have long repayment terms—say 15–20 years—most PPP project cash flows require debt service to be spread out over 20 years or more to match the natural life of the project, and produce an affordable cost for the Public Authority (*cf.* §13.3.1). PPP projects offer a high level of certainty of long-term cash flow, and therefore provide a good basis for such long-term loans. Typically when a new PPP market opens up loan terms are shorter, and lengthen as lenders become used to the risks involved.

Another factor which determines the length of a loan is the lenders' Cover Ratio requirements (*cf.* §10.6)—the shorter the loan the higher the debt-service payments, and so the worse the Cover Ratios become; so from this point of view, paradoxically, the longer a loan the safer it appears.

But the 'long-term' nature of a loan to a PPP project may be misleading. Most commercial banks' deposits are short-term in nature, so lending long-term leaves them with a mismatch—despite this they are prepared to make long-term loans for PPP projects because a large proportion of PPP loans are refinanced after the end of the construction period (*cf.* §16.4).

In developing countries, there may be no commercial lenders willing to provide long-term loans; so in a country such as Brazil, where banks can earn a high return from short-term lending, there would no good reason for them to divert funds to long-term loans, whether for PPP projects or anything else. In such cases, other sources of finance will have to be found (*cf.* §17.4.2).

§10.5.2 REPAYMENT PROFILE

Loan repayments usually begin around 6 months after the construction of the Facility is complete, and are usually made at 6-monthly intervals. (In the case of a project with usage risk, an initial ramp-up period may be allowed for, with lower debt service while the usage is building up.) The standard bond-market practice is for a bond to be repaid in full on its final maturity date (although a sinking fund may be built up to repay the whole amount of the bond on its final maturity rather than making repayments in instalments, but this obviously adds to the financing cost, especially over a long period of time). However, project-finance bonds are generally amortised (repaid) in a similar way to loans.

If the Service Fees are to be kept level, as discussed in §13.3.2, the debt service has to be level as well. But if a loan of 1000 is paid back over 10 years in equal annual instalments of 100, at an interest rate of say 5%, the debt-service payments will not be level. At the end of year 1 there will a payment of 150, being 100 of principal and 50 of interest on the 1000 loan outstanding over the first year, while at the end of year 10 there will be a payment of 105, with an interest payment of 5 on the final loan balance of 100. This is not a viable approach (*cf.* Table 10.3).

Therefore debt service has to be based on an 'annuity' schedule. In the example above, the annual debt-service payment required to pay the loan off and cover interest over its 10-year period is 129.5, *i.e.* in between the debt service of 150 in year 1 and 105 in year 10 produced by the 'straight-line' repayment schedule above. An annuity calculation is set out in Table 10.4 below, where it will be seen that another reason for requiring annuity repayments is that straight-line repayments give rise to problems with lenders' Cover Ratios.

Having said this, it is unlikely that a precise annuity repayment schedule will work for the Project Company, given the Public Authority's requirement that the Service Fees resulting from this should also be level. This is because there will most probably be other fluctuations in the cash flow, and the loan payment schedule will need to be 'sculpted' to smooth these out (a complex modelling process) and so maintain the PPP payments level. These include:

- the maintenance schedule, if this is cyclical in nature;
- taxation payments: a typical Project Company does not pay tax in its early years of operation because of a high level of write-off of project costs against its tax liability; there is then a sudden drop in cash flow when tax payments begin;
- the effect of inflation, which can be very significant (*cf.* §11.3.4).

Predictable temporary cash-flow swings such as major maintenance or a large tax payment can be smoothed out by the establishment of Reserve Accounts (*i.e.* accumulating cash in advance from the cash flow—*cf.* §12.2.4) to maintain constant Cover Ratios, but it is not efficient from the investors' point of view to have cash tied up in the Project Company unnecessarily, and, as far as possible, debt sculpting is a preferable way of dealing with this.

But the Project Company cannot expect *carte blanche* to make repayments whenever it chooses within the overall debt term. Net cash flow from the project after debt service can be paid as Distributions to the investors in the Project Company. Lenders want to see investors having a long-term incentive to manage the business well, and will not be comfortable with debt repayments being pushed towards the back end of the project cash flow if this implies that the investors are getting higher than appropriate payments at the front end.

§10.5.3 AVERAGE LIFE

Apart from the overall term of the loan, lenders also look at the repayment schedule to assess how rapidly their risk reduces over the term. There is obviously a considerable difference in risk between a loan of 1000 repaid in 100 instalments over 10 years, and a loan of 1000 repaid in one bullet instalment at the end of 10 years. This is measured by looking at the loan's average life, which is used by lenders as a check to ensure that the repayment schedule is not overextended, in a similar way to the payback-period calculation by investors (*cf.* §4.4.3). The average life of a loan is thus the average number of years that the principal is outstanding. This can be calculated in a variety of ways:

- simply looking at the period of time until half the loan has been repaid; thus if a loan of 4 is repaid over 4 years in annual instalments of 1, the average life would be 2 years, because at that point half the loan has been repaid; or
- weighting the loan principal outstanding for each year, by adding these together, and then dividing by the original loan amount; thus for the same loan the average life on this basis would be 2½ years ([4 + 3 + 2 + 1] ÷ 4);
- weighting the repayments, by multiplying each instalment by the number of years outstanding, and dividing by the loan amount; for the same loan this calculation would be [((1 × 1) + (1 × 2) + (1 × 3) + (1 × 4)) ÷ 4] which of course produces the same result.

A weighting calculation is more appropriate because it takes account of the repayment schedule. Suppose the loan of 4 was repaid as 2 at the end of year 2, and 2 at the end of year 4: the simple calculation would still give this an average life of 2 years, the same as with 4 annual repayments of 1, but the weighted calculation would give an average life of 3 years [((2 × 2) + (2 × 4)) ÷ 4], so making it clear that it has a longer weighted average life than the loan repaid by equal annual instalments.

However, this calculation is made more complex in a project-finance context, as project-finance loans are drawn down over a period of time, during the project's construction phase—in such a case how long is each drawing outstanding, and how can this be averaged? There is no simple answer to this, but probably the commonest approach is to add the whole drawdown period into the calculation of the average life of the repayment period, the argument for this being that the lenders are on risk for the whole of their loan during the drawdown period. Thus if the loan of 4, with annual repayments of 1, were drawn down over 2 years and then repaid in equal instalments over the following 4, its weighted average life would be 4½ years (2 years' drawdown plus the 2½ years' average life for the repayment as calculated above).

Lenders may have an average-life limitation as part of their overall credit policy towards PPP loans, and so if a bidder wants to offer a longer total term for the PPP Contract it may be necessary for investors' Distributions to be slowed down, and debt service speeded up, to maintain the required average life.

§10.5.4 The Cash-Flow 'Tail'

Another factor which determines the length of the debt financing is the requirement which lenders have for a cash-flow Tail, that is, the period between the scheduled final repayment of the debt and the end of the PPP contract, during which the Service Fees continue. This builds in a safety margin, so that if the project gets into temporary difficulties, or cash flow is a bit below expectation, there may still be enough cash flow left to ensure the debt is paid off, albeit later than expected.

The greater the inherent revenue risk in the project, the longer the Tail period that will be required. So for an accommodation project in an established market, where the lenders' risk is relatively small, it may be possible to negotiate a Tail period as short as six months. On the other hand, a road Concession project with a high level of traffic risk may require a Tail of some years. The longer the Tail period:

- the higher the Service Fees will have to be (because the debt is being repaid over a shorter period within the overall 'envelope' of the PPP Contract term), and
- the more the receipt of Distributions will be pushed to the back of the cash flow, making them less valuable in Equity IRR terms (*cf.* §4.4.4).

Therefore bidders will want to keep the Tail period as short as possible, and the Public Authority should also not enter into PPP Contracts which are going to require long Tail periods (*cf.* §13.3.1), as this is financially inefficient (and liable to lead to later windfall gains on refinancing the debt if the market becomes more favourable—*cf.* §16.4.8).

§10.5.5 Flexible Repayment

Projects where there is usage risk may often face an initial problem in meeting the required usage levels because the ramp-up is slower than anticipated. To provide the Project Company with some room to manoeuvre in this respect, lenders may agree to build some flexibility into the repayment structure.

Two repayment schedules are agreed to: one is the level that the lenders actually wish to achieve if the project operates as expected (*i.e.* the 'target' repayments), and one is the minimum level of repayment required to avoid a default by the Project Company under the loan. If the Project Company has cash flow available, it must make a repayment sufficient to bring the loan outstanding down to the target schedule, but if not, it must at least achieve the minimum schedule. For example, if the target loan repayments for a 1000 10-year loan are (for the sake of simplicity) 20 equal semi-annual instalments, the target and minimum schedules could be calculated as in Table 10.1. As can be seen, the two schedules differ by one loan repayment (50) to begin with, this loan repayment being spread over the remaining 19 payments in the minimum schedule. The loan outstanding in each schedule becomes closer and closer as time goes on so that final repayment is achieved at the same time on both schedules; thus at the end of the first six months the whole repayment due at that time can be deferred, while only 2.6 of the penultimate repayment can be deferred. This gives the Project Company the maximum room to manoeuvre at the beginning of the project's operation, when usage problems are likely to be at their greatest.

Table 10.1

Target and minimum repayments

Repayment No.	Target repayments		Minimum repayments		Difference
	Repayment	Loan outstanding	Repayment	Loan outstanding	
0		1,000		1,000.0	0.0
1	50	950	–	1,000.0	50.0
2	50	900	52.6	947.4	47.4
3	50	850	52.6	894.7	44.7
4	50	800	52.6	842.1	42.1
5	50	750	52.6	789.5	39.5
... etc.					
18	50	100	52.6	105.3	5.3
19	50	50	52.6	52.6	2.6
20	50	0	52.6	0.0	0.0

§10.5.6 BALLOON REPAYMENTS

It is possible for a 25-year PPP Contract to be financed with 15-year debt. However, unless a large element of the debt is left as a 'balloon'—*i.e.* repayable at the end of the 15 years, on the assumption that it will be refinanced at that point—the debt-service payments will be too high in relation to the level of Service Fees which the Public Authority is trying to achieve (*cf.* §10.5.1). Thus a balloon-repayment structure may involve debt-service payments profiled for 14 years at the same level as a for a 25-year loan, with the balance of the loan outstanding repayable at the end of the 15-year period. So, using the repayment schedule set out in Table 10.4, a 7-year 1,000 loan would have annual debt-service payments of 73, and a balloon principal repayment at the end of 7 years of 766.

The risks in a balloon-repayment structure are:

- The Project Company may not be able to obtain replacement funding—the risk of this is probably quite limited: either, by the time the funding is needed, the Project Company's business will be well-established and able to service the replacement debt, in which case it should not be difficult to find a lender, or things are going badly, in which case a longer-maturity loan would be in difficulty if not default by then anyway.
- It leaves the Project Company exposed to interest-rate risk (*cf.* §11.2.7) after the initial loan term—this is the main objection to a balloon structure, which explains why it is not widely used.

However, in markets where lenders are reluctant to lend for the total term required to make the project viable, a balloon structure is the best way of bridging this financing gap. Taking this further, in the United States banks provide short-term construction loans, which are refinanced by long-term 'permanent' loans, or bond issues, on completion. The initial loan is usually arranged to mature 2–3 years after completion of construction (making it what is known as a 'mini-perm') to allow flexibility of timing for the refinancing. In a mini-perm, any principal repayments after completion of construction are based on a long-term debt-service schedule, but cut off after 3–5 years, so giving rise to a balloon repayment of the balance of the loan. Some 85% of project financings in the United States in 2000 were structured as 3–5 year mini-perms. Mini-perms of 7–9 years (from signing) are typically used for road Concession financings in Spain.

In fact from the point of view of long-term flexibility of PPP Contracts, there is merit in a greater use of mini-perms, reflecting the reality that loans are often refinanced anyway (*cf.* §16.4), although this is only viable where banks are happy that there is no significant refinancing risk and the project can accommodate the risk of higher market interest rates at the time of the refinancing. This is easier if the initial leverage is in the 70–80% range rather than 90%, and also if there is a significant Tail at the end of the PPP Contract, giving extra room for manoeuvre—which implies that a mini-perm is easier for a Concession-model PPP where these conditions are more likely to apply.

§10.5.7 CASH SWEEP

Where a balloon-payment structure is used, this may be linked with a 'Cash Sweep' in the latter years of the loan, which requires some or all of the cash flow which would otherwise have been distributed to investors (*cf.* §12.2.3) to be used for debt prepayment instead (or placed in a Reserve Account to secure the debt). The purpose of this is to 'encourage' refinancing of the debt well before the final balloon repayment date.

A Cash Sweep may also be useful for debt structuring in other circumstances:

- Where there is uncertainty about the growth of future revenues, which could apply in a Concession, or a PFI-Model project with usage risk transferred to the Project Company. In such projects, after an agreed level of Distributions to the investors, the balance of the cash flow is used to prepay the debt or split between prepayment and a further distribution to the investors. Thus if the project performs according to the agreed Base Case, the investors will receive the Base Case return, but cash flow from the project above this level is split between investors and debt repayment. In this way surplus cash generated in good times is used to reduce debt and so provide a buffer against a downturn.
- Where costs have to be incurred a long time in the future, and are too substantial to be covered by setting aside spare cash in a Reserve Account (*cf.* §12.2.4). For example, an additional traffic lane may have to be built for a road Concession once traffic has reached a certain level after, say, 15 years, and the cost of this is to be covered by tolls over the following 15 years. The initial loan may run for 20–25 years (*i.e.* past the date when additional funding may be needed). It is likely to be very difficult to fix the costs of the major works 15 years in advance, and raising debt that would not be used for 15 years is virtually impossible (and uneconomic). The solution may be a Cash-Sweep arrangement beginning several years before the date for the new works, to build up cash for the new works, but also to encourage the investors to refinance the loan and raise the additional debt required when it becomes feasible nearer that time.
- Where lenders are concerned about the Tail risk. In such cases, several years before the Tail begins, some or all of the cash flow after debt service is not distributed to the investors, but is used for debt prepayment, or placed in a Reserve Account.

§10.5.8 DEBT ACCRETION

However in the case of very long (50 year-plus) Concessions, where bond rather than bank financing would be used (*cf.* §9.5), 'capital accretion bonds' may be used. Under this structure drawdown of debt can continue, and hence the loan amount increase, after completion of construction, rather than the lenders requiring repayments to begin from that point. Subject to the performance of the project, this is done by capitalising part of the interest on the bond and adding this to the principal amount, such that the peak loan balance occurs after 15–20 years, and the bond is then repaid thereafter. This reflects the slow but steady long-term growth in traffic or other usage which should be expected in such a project. In effect debt accretion is an advance commitment by the lenders to refinance the loan if the project meets expectations (*cf.* §16.4), and gives the flexibility of a mini-perm or balloon repayment structure while removing a large part of their risks. The same result can be produced through an accretion swap (*cf.* §11.2.10).

§10.5.9 CONTINGENT FUNDING

Although the likelihood of capex cost overruns should be limited (*cf.* §14.6), a prudent lender would generally require the Project Company to have some contingent funding in hand to meet unexpected events. The simplest way of doing this is to add a contingency to the capex budget—if it is not needed, the undrawn funding for this can be cancelled. More formally, additional 'standby' equity and debt can be provided separately, In this case the contingency funding, if required, is drawn after the Base Case equity and debt is fully drawn.

§10.6 COVER RATIOS

Financial ratios are a basis for all kinds of medium and long-term corporate lending—the normal measures are:

- liquidity ratio (also known as the 'current ratio'), *i.e.* short-term assets (primarily cash and debtors) divided by short-term liabilities (*e.g.* trade creditors and debt due within one year); lenders may require a liquidity ratio of, say, 1.5x;
- interest cover, *i.e.* earnings before interest, depreciation and amortisation (EBITDA—a simple proxy for the company's cash flow), divided by the interest payable, during the relevant period; lenders will seek to ensure that at all times they have an interest-Cover Ratio of, say, 2x; and
- leverage, *i.e.* the ratio of debt to equity; lenders will seek to ensure that the borrower's debt is not more than, say, 50% of its equity; this can also be expressed as a 'loan-to-value' ratio, *i.e.* the ratio of the loan to the value of the company's assets in general, or the particular assets given to the lender as security.

These measures are not appropriate for a PPP project financing, because:

- The short-term liquidity of a Project Company is assured by the creation of Reserve Accounts.
- The project has a finite life, during which all its debt must be repaid; as discussed above (*cf.* §8.3) a corporate borrower will always have some outstanding debt and therefore an interest-cover ratio which only looks at the ability to pay interest, but does not assess the ability to repay debt, is inadequate.
- A leverage ratio is based on the assumption that the assets of the borrowing company will be worth a proportion at least of their book value if the company is wound-up, and hence the leverage ratio is an indication of the safety margin for lenders, as it is the excess of liabilities, excluding equity, over assets; however, as discussed above, such a residual value cannot be assumed for a Project Company's physical assets, as its value is based primarily on its Project Contracts (in particular to PPP Contract).

Having said this, however:

- As discussed below (*cf.* §10.6.3), the Loan-Life Cover Ratio is in fact a form of loan-to-value ratio in a project-finance context.
- The lenders to a Project Company will expect the Sponsors to have a 'reasonable' amount of equity at risk: 100% debt financing, even if theoretically possible using the Cover-Ratio approach set out below, would not normally be acceptable (but *cf.* §17.6.1).
- A debt-to-equity ratio may have to be used during the construction phase to keep the Sponsors' and banks' exposures in parallel, *e.g.* where Sponsor equity is being paid in *pro rata* with bank debt drawings, or at the end of the construction phase (*cf.* §7.3.4).

Thus the amount of debt which can be raised by a Project Company (and hence the split in funding between debt and equity, *i.e.* the leverage) is primarily determined by its projected ability to pay its debt service, with a comfortable margin of safety; this margin is of course the same as the Distributions to investors. To assess this safety margin, lenders calculate Cover Ratios, which measure cash flow against debt service, assessed both on a period-to-period basis, and over the life of the project, namely:

- Annual Debt-Service Cover Ratio ('ADSCR') (§10.6.2);
- Loan-Life Cover Ratio ('LLCR') (§10.6.3);
- Project-Life Cover Ratio ('PLCR') (§10.6.4).

Taken together, these determine the maximum loan amount (§10.6.5), although it should be noted that are various issues arising on precisely how the calculations are done (§10.6.6).

§10.6.1 Cash Flow Available for Debt Service (CADS)

The basis for all these ratio calculations is the CADS, *i.e.* operating revenues less operating expenses—taking account of any transfers to the Maintenance Reserve Account or similar Reserve Accounts covering anything other than debt service (*cf.* §12.2.3), and ignoring any non-cash items such as depreciation. This may look similar to the EBITDA measure above, but should be based strictly on cash flow rather than accounting results. Thus income or expenditures accrued but not actually paid during the period being measured should be excluded, as should, *e.g.* tax accruals where the tax is not actually payable until a later period.

§10.6.2 ANNUAL DEBT-SERVICE COVER RATIO

The ADSCR assesses the Project Company's ability to service its debt from its annual cash flow, and is calculated as CADS divided by debt service. Thus if CADS for the year is 120, interest payments are 55, and loan repayments are 45, the ADSCR would be 1.2:1 (120 ÷ (55 + 45)).

The ADSCR is usually calculated semi-annually, on a rolling annual basis. The ratio can obviously only be calculated when the project has been in operation for a year, although because it may affect the ability to pay Distributions (*cf.* §12.2.5), it may be calculated for the previous 6 months only for the first period after the project begins operation. The debt-service figures are adjusted for the effects of any financial hedging (*cf.* Chapter 11). The ADSCR is the primary determinant of the maximum loan which can be raised against the project, as illustrated by Table 10.2. The assumption here is that there is £1,000 *p.a.* of cash flow after opex, with a 25-year debt term. Assuming the lenders have an ADSCR requirement of 1.30x, the maximum debt service allowable is 769 (1,000 ÷ 1.30), which means that the maximum amount of debt which can be raised is 9,833—*i.e.* an annual payment of 769 is required to pay interest at 6% and repay a loan of 9,833 on an annuity basis over 25 years. However, if the cover ratio is reduced to 1.15x, the amount of debt which can be raised goes up to 11,116.

In their Base Case projections the lenders structure both the amount and the repayment schedule of their loan such that projected ADSCR for each period throughout the term of the loan does not fall below their required minimum at any time. The minimum ADSCR requirement, which thus effectively determines the maximum loan, is a function of the risk inherent in the project from the lender's point of view—the greater the uncertainty of the

Table 10.2
Effect of ADSCR on loan amount

		25 years	25 years
	Debt term	25 years	25 years
	Interest rate	6%	6%
[a]	Project cash flow (pre-debt service) *p.a.*	1,000	1,000
[b]	ADSCR requirement	**1.30**	**1.15**
	Maximum annual debt service ([a] ÷ [b])	769	870
	Amount of debt which can be raised (annuity repayment)	**9,833**	**11,116**

cash flow, the higher the risk, and hence the higher the Cover-Ratio requirement. In the PPP sector, the highest-risk category of projects is that involving usage risk, on which a minimum ADSCR in the range 1.5–2.0x may be required, depending on the perceived level of risk (or certainty of the cash flows). The lowest-risk category is that of accommodation projects, where the minimum ADSCR may be in the range 1.15–1.20x.

The actual ADSCRs are reviewed (and projections may be recalculated) once the project is in operation (*cf.* §12.2.5).

§10.6.3 LOAN-LIFE COVER RATIO

The LLCR is based on a similar calculation, but taken over the whole term of the loan, *i.e.*

- projected CADS for the life of the loan, discounted to its NPV at the same interest rate as that assumed for the debt (again taking account of any financial hedging); *divided by*
- debt outstanding on the calculation date.

Since the 'value' of a Project Company is effectively the NPV of its future revenues, it could be said that the LLCR is a kind of loan-to-value ratio.

LLCR is a useful measure for the initial assessment of a Project Company's ability to service its debt over its whole term, but clearly it is not so useful if there are likely to be significant cash flow fluctuations from year to year. ADSCR is thus a more significant measure of a Project Company's ability to service its debt as it falls due.

The minimum initial LLCR requirement in lenders' Base Case projections for 'standard' projects is typically around 10% higher than the figures shown above for minimum ADSCR.

Apart from the initial LLCR on project completion, the LLCR may be recalculated throughout the project life, comparing the projected operating cash flow for the remainder of the loan term with the remaining loan outstanding on the calculation date, as part of the lenders' continuing controls, in a similar way to the continuing use of the ADSCR, although this is of dubious value for a PPP (*cf.* §12.2.5).

§10.6.4 PROJECT-LIFE COVER RATIO

Another point that lenders check is whether the Project Company has capacity to make repayments after the original final maturity of the debt, within the Tail period of the PPP Contract (*cf.* §10.5.4), in case there have been difficulties in repaying all of the debt in time.

The value to lenders of the Tail can be calculated using the PLCR; here projected CADS for the whole life of the project (not just the term of the debt as for the LLCR) is discounted to its NPV, and this figure is divided by the debt outstanding. Obviously the PLCR will be higher than the LLCR; lenders may wish to see it around 15–20% higher than the minimum ADSCR.

§10.6.5 Cover-Ratio Calculations

Table 10.3 sets out typical cover-ratio calculations for a PPP project, but where the debt is repaid in equal instalments of principal. It will be seen that in order to achieve the required 15% Equity IRR the investors need to ensure a CADS of 95 *per annum* (which when added to opex, produces the Service Fees). However, this will not satisfy the lenders' cover-ratio requirements, because even though the average ADSCR is 1.50x, the initial

Table 10.3
Cover Ratios—level principal repayments

Assumptions:

Project cost	1,000
Debt:equity ratio	90:10
PPP Contract term	25 years
Loan term	23 years, paid in equal annual principal instalments
Interest rate	6% *p.a.*
Required Equity IRR	15%

Year:	0	1	2	3	20	21	22	23	24	25	Total
(a) CADS		95	95	95	95	95	95	95	95	95	2,375
Lenders' viewpoint:											
(b) Loan repayments		39	39	39	39	39	39	39			900
(c) Interest payments		54	52	49	9	7	5	2			648
(d) Total debt service [(b) + (c)]		93	91	88	49	46	44	41			1,548
(e) Year-end loan outstanding	*900*	*861*	*822*	*783*	*117*	*78*	*39*	*0*			
ADSCR [(a) ÷ (d)]		1.02	1.05	1.07	1.96	2.06	2.17	2.29			
Average ADSCR		1.50	1.52	1.54	2.12	2.17	2.23				
LLCR [(NPV (a)*) ÷ (e)]	1.30	1.33	1.36	1.39	2.16	2.23	2.29				
Average LLCR	1.73	1.75	1.77	1.79	2.23	2.26					
PLCR [(NPV (a)) ÷ (e)]	1.35										
Average life of loan	12 years										
Investors' viewpoint:											
Equity investment:	−100										
Distributions [(a) − (d)]		2	4	7	46	49	51	54	95	95	827
IRR	*15%*										
Payback period	*c. 9 years*										

* to year 23.

ADSCR is only 1.02x, and it must be remembered that the lenders look at the minimum ADSCR as a primary basis for the loan. The LLCR, on the other hand, is reasonably satisfactory at 1.30x. (The table also shows variations of the simple form of ADSCR or LLCR calculations which may be used by some lenders, such as the average ADSCR or LLCR. It is doubtful if these add any real value for lenders, and they just make modelling more complex.) The problem here is that the debt service is not on an annuity basis, and changing to this makes a fundamental difference to the results.

As shown in Table 10.4, if the same assumptions are used, but the loan is repaid on a level-annuity basis, the CADS can be reduced to 88, while giving the lenders a regular ADSCR of 1.20x, and preserving the investors' Equity IRR of 15%. In fact this calculation produces the unlikely result—in the real world—that both ADSCR and LLCR ratios are identical throughout the life of the loan; in reality—as discussed above—this is difficult to

Table 10.4
Cover Ratios—annuity debt service

Assumptions:
As for Table 10.3, except that loan is repaid on an annuity basis

Year:	0	1	2	3	20	21	22	23	24	25	Total
(a) CADS		88	88	88	88	88	88	88	88	88	2,200
Lenders' viewpoint:											
(b) Loan repayments		19	20	22	58	61	65	69			900
(c) Interest payments		54	53	52	15	12	8	4			782
(d) Total debt service [(b) + (c)]		73	73	73	73	73	73	73	73		1,682
(e) Year-end loan outstanding	900	881	861	839	196	134	69	0			
ADSCR [(a) ÷ (d)]		1.20	1.20	1.20	1.20	1.20	1.20	1.20			
Average ADSCR		1.20	1.20	1.20	1.20	1.20	1.20				
LLCR [(NPV (a)*) ÷ (e)]	1.20	1.20	1.20	1.20	1.20	1.20	1.20				
Average LLCR	1.20	1.20	1.20	1.20	1.20	1.20					
PLCR [(NPV (a)) ÷ (e)]	1.25										
Average life of loan	14 years										
Investors' viewpoint:											
Equity investment:	−100										
Distributions [(a) − (d)]		15	15	15	15	15	15	15	88	88	518
Equity IRR	15%										
Payback period	c. 7 years										

* to year 23.

achieve quite so precisely. However, it is clear that even if the Public Authority did not have a requirement to keep the Service Fees level (*cf.* §13.3.2), bidders would in any case always try to use an annuity-payment structure for the debt rather than level principal payments, to provide the most competitive level of Service Fees.

§10.6.6 OTHER ISSUES WITH COVER-RATIO CALCULATIONS

There are some issues which may arise on the mechanics of Cover-Ratio calculations:

Treatment of cash balances. The Project Company may have cash balances in Reserve Accounts (*cf.* §12.2.4): since both the ADSCR and the LLCR measure the ability to repay debt, and cash balances can also be used for this purpose, should these be taken into the calculation? In respect of the ADSCR, the answer is that they should not—this ratio measures the ability to pay debt on a year-to-year basis, and if the cash balance is used to improve the ratio in year 1, it is then no longer available in year 2. In the case of the LLCR it is reasonable to take into account cash in a Reserve Account intended to cover debt service, as it is part of the total picture of resources available for debt service over the project life. The Project Company may argue that balances on other Reserve Accounts such as for maintenance should also be deducted in the LLCR calculation for the same reason; lenders may, however, point out that this cash is not intended for debt reduction.

There are two ways of bringing these balances into the LLCR calculations—add them to the CADS NPV, or deduct them from the debt balance. The latter produces a higher Cover Ratio, but the former is probably the commoner project-finance market practice.

Payments to and from Reserve Accounts. In calculating the ADSCR and LLCR, payments to Reserve Accounts other than for debt service are treated as a deduction from the operating cash flow in the period concerned, and drawings from such accounts (*e.g.* to pay maintenance costs) are added back to the cash flow (and hence offset the actual expenditure). Payments to and from any Reserve Account for debt service are ignored in the ADSCR calculation (which is intended to show the Project Company's ability to service its debt on a regular basis without using reserves).

Interest earned on Reserve Accounts is normally added to the operating income when calculating Cover Ratios, unless the balance of the Reserve Account concerned is below the minimum required (which would mean that the interest earned cannot be taken out of the Reserve Account).

Taxation. Strictly speaking, CADS does not include taxation payable by the Project Company, because tax is calculated after interest payments. Nonetheless, it is a fairly common practice to deduct projected tax payments (when paid in cash) from cash flow to arrive at CADS. Thus using a limited-partnership structure for the Project Company (*cf.* §7.6.1), where there is no tax in the financial model, can be advantageous for investors if lenders do not increase their cover-ratio requirements to compensate for this.

§10.7 RELATIONSHIP BETWEEN COVER RATIO, LEVERAGE AND EQUITY RETURN

There is a complex interplay between leverage (the debt:equity ratio), Cover-Ratio requirements, the cost of the debt and its repayment schedule, and the investors' required return—a bidder needs to balance all these factors to offer the most competitive level of Service Fees. This is illustrated by Table 10.5.

There are five scenarios in the table:

- Case 1 has a project cost of 1,000, with the lenders being willing to fund 95% of this cost so long as they have an ADSCR of 1.2x. Debt is provided over 26 years, on an annuity repayment basis, at a rate of 6% *p.a.* This produces an annual debt-service payment of 73. Investors require an Equity IRR of 15%, which produces an annual distribution of 8. Thus the total Service Fees to cover both debt service and equity return (ignoring the further payments to cover opex) amount to 81 (73 + 8). But these payments are insufficient to provide the lenders with a 1.2x ADSCR, for which 88 (73 × 1.2) is required. The Cover Ratio thus sets a natural limit on what can be borrowed by the Project Company.
- Case 2 gets the figures back into equilibrium. By reducing the leverage to 91% the annual debt service is reduced to 70, and then the required Service Fees of 84 (70 + 14) are sufficient to give the lenders a Cover Ratio of 1.2x (70 × 1.2).
- Case 3 supposes that the lenders are willing to reduce the Cover Ratio from 1.20x to 1.15x. This means that leverage can be increased to 93%, and Service Fees are reduced to 82. (To achieve the same result by keeping the Cover Ratio at 1.20x, and reducing the cost of the debt, the debt interest rate would have to be reduced from

Table 10.5
Relationship between Cover Ratio, leverage and Equity IRR

	Case 1	Case 2	Case 3	Case 4	Case 5
Project cost	1,000	1,000	1,000	1,000	1,000
Debt:equity ratio (leverage)	95:5	91:9	93:7	91:9	70:30
Minimum ADSCR required	1.20x	1.20x	1.15x	1.20x	1.20x
Debt interest rate	6.0%	6.0%	6.0%	6.0%	5.8%
Investors' required Equity IRR	15.0%	15.0%	15.0%	9.0%	9.0%
Debt term (years)	26	26	26	26	26
Annual payments					
Annual debt service (annuity repayment)	73	70	72	70	53
Investors' required annual return	8	14	11	9	30
Service Fees to cover debt service + return*	81	**84**	**82**	79	**83**
Actual ADSCR	1.11x	1.20x	1.15	1.13	1.57
Service Fees required for Cover Ratio*	**88**	84	82	**84**	63

* net of amounts to cover opex.

6% to 5.8%, which shows that reducing the Cover Ratio is an alternative to reducing the cost of the debt.)

- Case 4 supposes that the bidders want to make their bid more competitive by reducing the required Equity IRR from 15% to 9%. This would produce annual debt-service and equity return payments of 79 (70 + 9), but in fact it does not lead to a lower level of Service Fees, as these have to be maintained at the previous figure of 84 *p.a.* in order to provide the lenders' Cover Ratio. So it can be seen that the combination of Cover Ratio and leverage also effectively dictates the investors' return.
- Case 5 puts this position back into equilibrium: this can only be achieved by reducing the leverage from 91% to 70%. Note that the cost of debt is slightly lower because of the high (1.57x) Cover Ratio now being offered to lenders. This restructuring produces similar Service Fees to Case 2. As discussed in §8.5.1, it does not necessarily follow that investors in a Project Company would accept reductions in the equity return proportional to this lower leverage, although there are some countries (such as Spain) where the Case 5 structure and equity returns can be seen, especially in the Concession sector where lenders require higher Cover Ratios anyway because of the usage risk.

Of course all these calculations are highly simplified, to illustrate the principles involved, and they do not take account of:

- the LLCR requirement (*cf.* §10.6.3);
- tax (see below);
- inflation (*cf.* §11.3);
- the effect of any Tail on the Equity IRR (*cf.* §10.5.4).

§10.8 ACCOUNTING AND TAXATION ISSUES

Although a financial model for a PPP project financing is concerned with cash flows rather than accounting results, it is usually necessary to add accounting calculations—*i.e.* profit and loss accounts (income statements) and balance sheets for each calculation period—to the model, because:

- The accounting results are important to the Sponsors, who will not wish to report an accounting loss from investment in a Project Company affiliate.
- Tax payments are based on accounting results rather than cash flow (*cf.* §10.8.1–§10.8.2).
- The accounting results affect the Project Company's ability to pay dividends, and could affect its ability to keep trading (*cf.* §10.8.3).
- Adding a balance sheet is a good way of checking for errors in the financial model: if the balance sheet docs not balance, there is a mistake somewhere.

§10.8.1 TAX CALCULATIONS

The main differences between cash flow and accounting results in a financial model for a PPP Project Company relate to the calculation and payment of corporate taxes on the

Project Company's income. (This is assuming it is a tax-paying entity rather than a partnership, or not subject to tax for other reasons.)

A PPP project involves the Project Company a high initial capex. If the Project Company had to charge off the costs of the project as they were incurred, the result would be an enormous loss in the construction phase of the project, followed by enormous profits in the operating phase. This obviously does not represent the real situation of the project. In most countries, the project's capex is capitalised (*i.e.* added to the asset side of the balance sheet). As discussed above (*cf.* §10.3.2), capex includes not only the construction (or 'hard') cost, but also the 'soft' costs incurred until the project is in operation (*i.e.* bidding, development and financing costs, payments to advisers, *etc.*). The total of these costs is then written off (depreciated) over the life of the asset, and it is these write-off amounts which are charged against tax. The write-off may be increased in the early years of the project by an acceleration of the tax-depreciation allowances. In some countries (*e.g.* the United States and United Kingdom) depreciation may be dealt with in different ways for accounting and tax purposes: for accounting purposes the project asset is depreciated over its useful life, thus spreading the cost of the asset against the earnings it generates and increasing the reported profits in the early years of the project, whereas for tax purposes accelerated depreciation is used. The difference between the two is taken directly to (or later deducted from) a tax reserve on the liability side of the balance sheet. In other countries (*e.g.* France and Germany), the accounting and tax depreciation must be the same.

Alternatively, the Project Company's investment in the project may be treated as a financial claim under the PPP Contract, and depreciated so as to produce a level income over the life of the PPP Contract (a system known as 'contract debtor' accounting in the United Kingdom).

§10.8.2 TAX PAYMENTS

Any of these methods of calculating tax is likely to produce tax payments which are not in proportion to CADS for the relevant period. A common pattern is that the Project Company pays little corporate tax in its early years, because of a high level of write-off of its investment against tax, but makes higher tax payments in the later years of the project. Since the rest of the opex is likely to remain reasonably constant (subject to inflation), this makes the process of producing level Service Fees (*cf.* §13.3.2) that much more complex. It may mean, for example, that debt repayment probably cannot follow a simple annuity schedule, but has to be somewhat weighted towards the latter periods of the project. Moreover, a sudden 'blip' in the cash flow can be caused by the Project Company having to start making tax payments once it has written off its initial tax losses; if tax is included in CADS for the purpose of lenders' cover-ratio calculations (*cf.* §10.6.6) this is likely to be the point at which the ADSCR is lowest, and hence may determine how much debt can be raised (*cf.* §10.6.2).

The timing of tax payments also has to be taken into account in the financial modelling. Again systems vary from country to country—in some cases corporate taxes are paid in the year following the relevant tax year, while in others payments are made on account during the year, and adjusted thereafter based on the final taxable income for that year.

§10.8.3 THE DIVIDEND TRAP

Another reason that accounting projections are required in a financial model, is to ensure that the Project Company is legally able to pay dividends on its shares when the model shows there is sufficient cash flow to do so. The Project Company may make accounting losses in its early years because of a higher level of depreciation of its assets (while the revenues remain constant over the whole term of the PPP Contract, unless adjusted for inflation—*cf.* §11.3), but still be generating a positive cash flow after debt-service payments. A company generally cannot pay a dividend to its shareholders if there is a negative balance on its profit and loss account, *i.e.* if accumulated accounting losses (plus past dividends) are greater than accumulated accounting profits. This is a function of the difference between tax depreciation and debt principal repayment; if the former is much greater than the latter a negative profit balance develops, which disappears as the situation is reversed. (It is clearly less of an issue in countries where the accounting depreciation does not have to mirror the tax depreciation.) The structure of the investment in the Project Company therefore has to be adjusted to take account of this 'dividend trap', which can be done by:

- making part of this investment in subordinated debt rather than equity share capital (*cf.* §7.3.3); the financial model is used to check that this structure should work properly by reviewing the accounting results over the life of the project;
- making temporary loans to its own shareholders of surplus cash flow which cannot be distributed, to be repaid from later dividends; this is likely to have complex tax implications, and would therefore only be used if a subordinated-loan structure did not work for some reason.

On the other hand, if the Project Company has a relatively small proportion of equity, with a large proportion of the equity investment funded with shareholder-provided subordinated debt, there is a danger that accumulated accounting losses in the early years of operation may be greater than the book amount of the equity. If a company has a 'negative equity' it may have to go through a court-approved capital restructuring, or cease trading. Again, therefore, the financial model is used to ensure that the mix of funding provided by the investors should not create this problem.

§10.9 RECOURSE TO THE SPONSORS

The only financial obligation that Sponsors have in all PPP project financings is to subscribe their equity share in the Project Company (*i.e.* the lenders provide a loan to the Project Company with no guarantee of repayment from the Sponsors—thus the loan is non-recourse to the Sponsors).

The Public Authority may feel uneasy about contracting with a Project Company which has no track record and no significant assets beyond the PPP Contract itself, and so want to request some form of completion guarantee or performance bonding from either the Sponsors or the Subcontractors. This is usually impossible for the Project Company to provide, especially as the lenders will want first claim on any security of this type. The Public

Authority has to rely primarily on its own due diligence on the Sponsors, and the quality and financial strength of the Subcontractors, combined with the considerable financial incentives under the PPP Contract (and its financial penalties for failure). The nature of a project-finance structure makes it much easier for a detailed due diligence to be undertaken, because all that is required for this is isolated in the Project Company.

However, while in principle Sponsors do not provide loan guarantees to the Project Company's lenders either, limited guarantees may sometimes be provided to lenders to cover a risk that proves to be unacceptable. Examples of such limited-recourse guarantees are:

- *underwriting site acquisition* (*cf.* §14.5.1) or disposal (*cf.* §14.5.9);
- *contingent equity commitment*: the Sponsors agree to inject a specific additional amount as equity into the Project Company to meet specified cash-flow requirements;
- *cost-overrun guarantee*: the Sponsors agree to inject additional equity up to a certain limit to cover any cost overruns during construction (or operating cost overruns);
- *completion guarantee*: the Sponsors undertake to inject extra funding if necessary to ensure that construction of the project is completed by a certain date, thus taking on the risk that more funding for construction or initial debt service may be required; this can also be cast in the more vague form of taking responsibility for completion, thus leaving lenders to prove what loss they have suffered if completion is late;
- *financial completion guarantee*: the Sponsors provide a guarantee not only that the project will be physically completed, but that it will achieve a minimum level of operating revenues or cash flow, and so make up any debt shortfall caused by a cash-flow deficit;
- *buy-down commitment*: the Sponsors guarantee that minimum Cover Ratios will be achieved on completion; if this is not the case the Sponsors pay down the loan until the required Cover Ratios are met;
- *performance guarantee*: the Sponsors agree to provide additional funding for debt service if the cash flow is reduced by the project not operating to a minimum performance standard;
- *claw-back guarantee*: the Sponsors agree to make up any deficiency in the Project Company's cash flow for debt service, to the extent they have received Distributions;
- *interest guarantee*: the Sponsors agree to pay the interest on the loan if the Project Company cannot do so—in practical terms this is very close to a full guarantee of the loan; if it is not paid back the Sponsors will have to keep paying interest indefinitely;
- *cash-deficiency guarantee*: the Sponsors agree to make up any debt service that cannot be paid because of a lack of cash in the Project Company—this is, of course, virtually a full financial guarantee;
- *shortfall guarantee*: a guarantee to pay any sums remaining due to lenders after termination of the loan and realisation of other security.

But it should be emphasised that Sponsor support in any of these ways is the exception rather than the rule.

Chapter 11

Financial Hedging

§11.1 INTRODUCTION

This chapter covers the two main macroeconomic issues in the financial structuring of a PPP project, namely interest-rate risk (§11.2), and issues related to inflation (§11.3).

Another possible macroeconomic risk is that of currency exchange-rate movements, but this can only occur if the funding, Service Fees, capex or opex are in different currencies. Although this happens in other project-finance sectors, this is not normally the case in a PPP project. The few exceptions may occur in Concessions where users pay in foreign currencies, *e.g.* port or airport projects, or in cases where there is a high component of imported capital equipment in the project, which is not common in the infrastructure field. Therefore this issue is not dealt with here. (The topic is covered in Chapter 9 of *Principles of Project Finance*.)

Financial hedging may have a direct or indirect affect on the Public Authority, by affecting either the original Service Fees (*cf.* §11.2.13), or the amounts the Public Authority has to pay on termination of the PPP Contract in some circumstances (*cf.* §15.5.1). Review and approval of financial hedging issues can therefore be an important part of the Public Authority's due-diligence process (*cf.* §6.5.3)

§11.2 INTEREST-RATE RISK

A Project Company may need a loan for 20–30 years to finance its PPP project. Although project-finance bonds for PPP projects always carry a fixed-rate coupon (except inflation-indexed bonds—*cf.* §11.3.6), commercial banks do not generally lend for such a long term at a fixed rate, because they cannot fund the loan with matching deposits. Therefore most bank loans have a 'floating' interest rate, whereby the interest rate on the loan is adjusted, say every 6 months, to current market rates for their short-term deposits, with the credit margin (*cf.* §10.4.1) being charged in addition. Examples of such floating rates are 'LIBOR' (the London inter-bank offered rate), in which floating rates are quoted

Table 11.1
Effect of interest-rate fluctuations

Interest rate:		6%	7%	8%
Debt term: 25 years				
Debt outstanding		1,000	1,000	1,000
CADS	[a]	94	94	94
Interest payment		−60	−70	−80
Principal repayment		−18	−18	−18
Total debt service	[b]	−78	−86	−94
Surplus for investors		**16**	**8**	**0**
ADSCR	[a] ÷ [b]	1.20	1.10	1.00

both in domestic £ sterling and a variety of international currencies such as the US$, or its cousin Euribor (the € inter-bank offered rate).

Table 11.1 shows the effect of fluctuations in such floating interest rates. It assumes that a project with 1,000 of debt; at an interest rate of 6% and with annuity repayment over 25 years has a CADS of 94. Thus in year 1 annual debt service is 78 (18 principal and 60 interest), giving an ADSCR of 1.20x. If the interest rate on the debt changes to 7% or 8% the ADSCR reduces to 1.10x and 1.00x respectively, which is bad enough for the lenders but disastrous for the investors, whose return is halved with a 1% rise in the interest rate, and eliminated entirely with a 2% rise. This is an inevitable consequence of the high leverage and tight debt-service cover inherent in project finance—small changes in interest rates make a big difference to the net cash flow.

There is a similar issue with respect to IDC. During the construction period the interest is not paid in cash, but capitalised (*i.e.* added to the loan amount), or paid by making a new drawing on the loan. Thus IDC becomes part of the project's capex budget (*cf.* §10.3.2), and so there is a risk that if the interest rate for the IDC is not fixed, and is eventually higher than originally projected, there will be a construction-cost overrun (*cf.* §14.6). Lenders do not normally allow any general construction-cost contingency to be used to cover this risk, as it is primarily intended to cover overruns in the 'hard' costs (mainly the construction contract), or the effect of a delay causing higher total interest costs.

So in cases where the Project Company has a high leverage, a floating interest rate on its debt is not viable for investors or lenders, nor is it in the interests of the Public Authority for the Project Company to be financially vulnerable to changes in interest rates, which could threaten delivery of the service under the PPP Contract. Financial hedging is therefore required to eliminate this risk.

§11.2.1 HEDGING BY THE PUBLIC AUTHORITY

The simplest (and cheapest) way of hedging the risk would be for the Service Fees to be adjusted for movements in the floating-rate interest on the Project Company's debt. This is not unknown in other sectors of the project-finance market, but is seldom seen with

PPPs, because it is likely to give the Public Authority a balance-sheet problem with PFI-model projects. The effect of such a payment structure is that part of the Service Fees have to be specifically allocated to the Project Company's debt service—this Separability is likely to result in the debt being in the public budget (*cf.* §5.5.4). This approach is also impossible with Concessions, as users would not accept constant changes. This therefore means that the Project Company is likely to have to undertake the hedging instead.

§11.2.2 INTEREST-RATE SWAPS

The most common form of financial hedging used to cover floating interest-rate risk—indeed almost universal in a project-finance context—is the interest-rate swap. Under an interest-rate swap agreement (also known as a 'coupon swap') one party exchanges an obligation to pay interest on a floating-rate basis for an obligation to pay interest on a fixed-rate basis, and the other party does the opposite. Interest-rate swaps are a long-established form of financial derivative (dating back to the late 1970s), and banks in the derivatives markets run large swap books. The market for swaps is far deeper than for other interest-rate derivatives, especially for the long maturities which are characteristic of PPP projects, and hence pricing is more competitive—unless there is no competition (*cf.* §11.2.8).

Under an intrest-rate swap, a Project Company with an obligation to pay interest at a floating rate under its loan agrees to pay its counterpart (a bank or banks—the 'swap provider') the difference between the floating rate and the agreed-upon fixed rate if the floating rate is below this fixed rate, or will be paid by the swap provider if the floating rate is above the fixed rate. These payments take place when the floating interest rate is adjusted, say every 6 months, the dates for payment being known as 'settlement dates'.

For the swap provider, arranging a matching swap in the market is far easier than raising long-term fixed-rate funding and on-lending this to the Project Company, since its own financial market counterparts take a much lower credit risk in providing a swap than making a long-term loan. The swap provider can thus make use of its access to short-term floating-rate funding, making the assumption that this will always be renewed, and then swap this to a fixed rate. Although the swap provider does not have to be the lender, this is usually the case (*cf.* §11.2.8).

The calculation of the net payment amount between the Project Company and the swap provider is based on the 'notional principal amount' for each period (*i.e.* the amount of the loan on which the interest is being calculated), although in a swap agreement neither side lends the other any money, but simply pays over the difference in the two interest rates. Table 11.2 shows how an interest-rate swap between 6-month floating and fixed rates might work in practice, assuming that:

- the Project Company borrows 1,000 (*i.e.* this is the notional principal amount), and repays the loan in one instalment at the end of 2½ years;
- this loan is at a floating interest rate, re-fixed 6-monthly;
- the Project Company swaps its floating interest-rate payment obligation against a fixed rate of 6%;
- the floating-rate interest actually increases from 4% in the first 6-month period to 8% in the fifth 6-month period.

Table 11.2

Interest-rate swap

6-month period:		1	2	3	4	5
(a) Notional principal amount		1000	1000	1000	1000	1000
(b) Floating rate (*p.a*)		4%	5%	6%	7%	8%
(c) Swap fixed rate		6%	6%	6%	6%	6%
(d) Floating-rate interest	[(a) × (b)]	20	25	30	35	40
(e) Fixed-rate interest	[(a) × (c)]	30	30	30	30	30
(f) Difference	[(d) – (e)]	– 10	– 5	0	5	10
Project Company position						
(g) Interest on loan	[=(d)]	20	25	30	35	40
(h) Swap payment/(receipt)	[= – (f)]	10	5	0	– 5	– 10
Net interest cost	[(g) + (h), =(e)]	30	30	30	30	30
Swap provider position						
(i) Interest on notional principal	[=(e)]	30	30	30	30	30
(j) Swap payment/(receipt)	[=(f)]	– 10	– 5	0	5	10
Net interest cost	[(i) + (j), =(d)]	20	25	30	35	40

As can be seen the Project Company has turned its floating-rate interest payments into the equivalent of a fixed rate of 6%, and the swap provider has done the reverse.

§11.2.3 INTEREST-RATE SWAP BREAKAGE RISK AND COST

Although neither side of the swap arrangement is lending the other any money, each side is taking a credit risk on the transaction, if the swap arrangement has to be cancelled, *e.g.* because the Project Company defaults on its debt. In this situation the swap provider will have to terminate the original swap and enter into another swap for the balance of the term (*i.e.* another party effectively takes over the obligations of the Project Company). But if long-term fixed interest rates have gone down since the swap was originally signed, the new counterpart will not be willing to pay the same high rate of fixed interest as the Project Company. The difference between the original fixed-rate and the new fixed rate represents a loss to the original swap provider. This is known as the 'breakage' (or 'unwind') cost. Of course if, when the default takes place, the long-term fixed rate for the remainder of the swap term is higher than the original rate, there is no breakage cost to the swap provider; on the contrary there is a breakage gain which is due to the Project Company.

For example, as shown in Table 11.3, if a swap with a notional principal of 1,000 is provided for 15 years, at a fixed rate of 8%, after 3 years the Project Company defaults, and the swap provider is only able to redeploy the swap at 6%, the swap provider's loss on termination amounts to 20 *p.a.* for the remaining 12 years. The breakage cost is the NPV of these amounts, discounted at 6% (the new swap rate), which can be calculated as 177. This is therefore what would be owed by the Project Company on termination of the swap.

Table 11.3
Calculation of swap-breakage cost

Assumptions:

Notional principal amount	1,000												
Term of loan and swap	15 years												
Original swap fixed rate	8%												
Swap rate on termination	6%												

Year:	3	4	5	6	7	8	9	10	11	12	13	14	15
Fixed-rate payment													
– original amount	80	80	80	80	80	80	80	80	80	80	80	80	80
– revised amount	60	60	60	60	60	60	60	60	60	60	60	60	60
Swap provider's annual loss:	20	20	20	20	20	20	20	20	20	20	20	20	20

NPV of loss (@ 6% discount rate) = 177

Table 11.4 sets out the swap-breakage costs at various points in time for a loan repaid on an annuity basis, calculated semi-annually. Thus if the swap is unwound just after Financial Close, and long-term interest rates have also gone down from 8% to 6% at that time, the loss to the swap provider is 51 (*i.e.* the NPV at 6% of the differences between the 8% and 6% payments). If the swap breakage occurs at the end of period 1 the loss is 42, at the end of period 2, 35, and so on. But if the reinvestment rate is higher than 8%, there will be a gain—which benefits the Project Company—rather than a loss on the breakage. The process of valuing a

Table 11.4
Swap breakage costs over time

Assumptions:

Notional principal amount	1,000
Term of loan and swap	5 years, repaid in 10 semi-annual annuity instalments
Original swap fixed rate	8%
Swap rate on termination	6%

Semi-annual period:	0	1	2	3	4	5	6	7	8	9	10
Notional principal	1,000	917	833	750	667	583	500	417	333	250	167
Interest payment		40	37	33	30	27	23	20	17	13	10
Principal repayment		*83*	*87*	*90*	*93*	*97*	*100*	*103*	*107*	*110*	*113*
Total debt service		*123*	*123*	*123*	*123*	*123*	*123*	*123*	*123*	*123*	*123*
Fixed-rate payment											
– original amount (=interest @ 8%)		40	37	33	30	27	23	20	17	13	10
– revised amount (=interest @ 6%)		30	28	25	23	20	18	15	13	10	8
Difference		10	9	8	8	7	6	5	4	3	3
Breakage cost (=NPV of difference @ 6% discount)	49	42	35	29	23	18	13	9	5	2	

swap against current market rates is known as 'marking to market'; a swap that shows a profit on being unwound is said to be 'in the money', and one which shows a loss is 'out of the money'. The breakage-cost risk is therefore not a fixed figure, but depends on:

- the remaining term of the swap;
- the way market rates have changed, when the default takes place; and
- whether the original swap was at a historically high or low rate (if at a low rate, the likelihood of a breakage cost is less because long-term rates are less likely to go even lower).

The risk of there being a breakage cost is relevant to:

- the swap provider, for whom the breakage cost is the amount they have at risk if the Project Company defaults;
- other lenders, as the swap provider will have a claim *pari passu* with their loan if the Project Company defaults (*cf.* §12.6.1);
- the Project Company, if the original loan is refinanced (*cf.* §16.4); and
- the Public Authority, in cases where the Public Authority pays off the loan, *e.g.* when exercising an option to terminate the PPP Contract (*cf.* §15.6)—which also means paying associated breakage costs.

It should be noted that a floating-rate lender also may have a small breakage cost if the Project Company defaults between the two interest rate-fixing dates.

§11.2.4 How Interest-Rate Swap Rates are Determined

The fixed rate quoted by the swap provider is based on three elements:

Government bond rates. These provide the 'base rate' for the swap; for example a swap in US$ for 7 years would be based on the current yield of a U.S. Treasury bond for the same period.

The swap-market premium. This reflects supply and demand in the swap market and also in the fixed-rate corporate bond market (*cf.* §9.4), since corporate-bond issuers and other market participants can arbitrage between the fixed-rate market and the floating-rate market with a swap. Swap-market rates—*i.e.* the total of the Government bond rate and the swap-market premium—are quoted in the financial press and on dealing screens.

The credit premium. This is the charge for taking the particular credit risk of the Project Company. If the swap provider assumes that the maximum likely level of breakage risk is, say, 10% of the initial notional principal amount, and the credit margin on the loan to the Project Company is, say, 1%, then the credit premium added to the swap rate should be 10% of 1% (*i.e.* 0.10% *p.a*). Note that this is normally a separate figure from the credit margin charged in the underlying loan (*cf.* §10.4.1).

The swap market works on the basis of bullet repayments of notional principal—*i.e.* the type of loan repayment schedule shown in Table 11.2, which assumes none of the notional principal of 1,000 is repaid until the end of the 2½-year schedule. However, a project-finance cash flow is like that set out in Table 11.4, *i.e.* repayment in annuity instalments over a period of time. The way the market deals with this is to quote a weighted average rate for a series of swaps covering each repayment date (known as an 'amortising swap'), and thus on the schedule in Table 11.4 the swap provider would quote a weighted rate for the swap based on the rates for 48 of notional principal repaid after 6 months, 37 after 1 year, 33 after 18 months, and so on.

The swap quotation also has to take into account that the notional principal may not be drawn all at once; most projects have a drawing period of 2–3 years or so during construction, so swap rates are quoted in advance for an increasing notional principal amount during the construction/drawing period (this is known as a 'accreting swap').

§11.2.5 ISDA DOCUMENTATION

Interest-rate swaps are documented in a standard form produced by the International Swap and Derivatives Association ('ISDA'), and on which there is limited room for negotiation. This is necessary because swap dealers want to be able to trade their entire swap book on the basis of standard terms. The specific terms of the swap (nominal amounts, rates, payment dates) are attached as a schedule to the ISDA documentation.

There are currently two standard forms of ISDA documentation being used in the market, those of 1992 and 2002. The most important difference between them in this context relates to the calculation of breakage costs on termination. The 1992 documentation allows the parties to choose between the 'Market Quotation' method (where the breakage is priced in the market) and the 'Loss' method, where it is priced by the swap provider. The latter should be chosen by the Project Company. The 2002 documentation only has one method ('Close-Out Amount'), which uses market quotations except where these are not available.

§11.2.6 THE CREDIT PREMIUM AND BREAKAGE COSTS

As mentioned above, the pricing of a swap includes a credit premium, which in effect equates to the credit margin on a loan. However, when the swap rate is fixed and documented, this credit premium is often just added to the total rate, not dealt with separately. The effect of this is that if the swap is terminated early, the swap provider will get the NPV of all the future credit premiums, which is really the same thing as a lender getting all the future credit margin if a loan is terminated early.

If the swap credit premium is dealt with in this way, it creates a *de facto* termination fee on the swap. Roughly speaking, assuming a 0.10% swap credit premium, this will be of about 1% of the loan outstanding in the early years of the project, declining over time. This is illustrated by Table 11.5, which shows the cost of paying the future credit premium on breakage of a swap during the first five years of a 25-year loan, where there has been no change on the underlying swap rate, and hence there is no inherent loss on breaking the swap.

Table 11.5

Effect of swap credit premium on breakage cost

Assumptions:

Loan amount	100,000					
Loan term	25 years, annual annuity repayments					
[a] Initial swap rate	5.00%					
[b] Swap credit premium	0.10%					
[c] Swap breakage rate	5.00%					

Year:		1	2	3	4	5
Swap payments						
[d] Notional principal O/S		100,000	97,933	95,762	93,479	91,080
Annuity debt service		7,167	7,167	7,167	7,167	7,167
[e] Interest at swap base rate	([d] × [a])	5,000	4,897	4,788	4,674	4,554
[f] Swap credit premium	([d] × [b])	100	98	96	93	91
[g] **Total swap payments**	([e] + [f])	**5,100**	**4,995**	**4,884**	**4,767**	**4,645**
Swap Breakage Cost (at year-end)						
[h] Interest at swap breakage rate		5,000	4,897	4,788	4,674	4,554
NPV of ([g]*, discounted @ 5%)		48,697	46,137	43,560	40,971	38,374
−NPV of ([h]*, discounted @ 5%)		−47,742	−45,233	−42,706	−40,167	−37,622
[j] **Difference** (=breakage cost)		**955**	**905**	**854**	**803**	**752**
Cost of credit premium on breakage		**1.0%**	**0.9%**	**0.9%**	**0.9%**	**0.8%**
as % of loan	([j] ÷ [d])%					

* Calculated for the full remaining term of the swap.

This has various implications for both the Project Company and, potentially, the Public Authority:

- It eats into the benefit of a refinancing (*cf.* §16.4), unless the original swap provider also provides the refinancing.
- It inhibits optional termination of the PPP Contract by the Public Authority, and hence long-term flexibility (*cf.* §15.6).
- In cases where the Public Authority repays debt, including breakage costs, on a 'no fault' termination (*cf.* §15.7) it is clearly inappropriate for this payment to include the lenders' future profits.

There is no good reason for lenders to make a windfall profit on early termination of a swap, when they do not do so on early termination of the loan to which this swap is linked. The credit premium can be separated from the swap, and hence dealt with differently on early termination, in one of two ways:

- It can be documented separately in the ISDA schedule, with a provision that it should not be taken into account in the breakage calculation.
- It can be paid under a separate Swap Premium Agreement, which terminates without any penalty payment if the swap is terminated.

If the loan is refinanced by a different lender, the original swap provider may offer to 'roll over' (*i.e.* transfer) its swap from the Project Company to the new swap provider instead of terminating it. This is helpful insofar as termination of the swap incurs a cost, not taken into account above, reflecting the market bid-offer spread. However, it also means that the original swap provider continues to receive the original credit premium (even though the risk is now the new lender, not the Project Company), while a further credit premium will be charged by the new swap provider.

§11.2.7 SCALE AND TIMING OF INTEREST-RATE HEDGING

In a highly-leveraged financial structure, as has already been seen above, there is little scope for a Project Company to absorb fluctuations in interest rates. However, even in this case there is still a need for some flexibility in the interest-rate hedging programme:

- Some flexibility needs to be left for the drawdown timing, which will depend on the progress of construction (*cf.* §12.2.1).
- It may be possible to delay the swap transaction until shortly after Financial Close, if market rates are felt to be unfavourable.
- If there is a flexible repayment schedule (*cf.* §10.5.5) hedging must allow for this.
- The interest-rate risk on contingent funding (*cf.* §10.5.9), which may never be drawn at all, need not be hedged at the beginning of the construction period.
- If, say, the loan is for 20 years the Project Company might choose to hedge for 15 years if the fixed rate is lower and the risk for the last 5 years is also small. Interest-rate risk obviously diminishes over the life of the project as the loan is repaid and the interest payments reduce as a proportion of the total debt service.
- Alternatively, the hedging may run for only 5 years, because the Project Company intends to refinance the debt then, even though this creates a greater interest-rate risk at that time (*cf.* §10.5.6).

If the Project Company's leverage is lower—*e.g.* the typical 70–80% found in a Concession project—the need for hedging may also be lower, as the Project Company may be more able to absorb changes in interest rates without unduly undermining the lenders' cash-flow cover. It may therefore be easier in such cases for the investors in the Project Company to decide—taking a view on where they think interest rates will be over the project life—to hedge less than the full amount of the debt, or to hedge for less than the full term of the debt.

§11.2.8 COMPETITION IN SWAP PRICING

The simplest way for the Project Company to cover its interest-rate risk through a swap is to have its syndicate of banks providing the floating rate loan also provide the swap *pro rata* to their share of the loan; however, the problems with this are:

- The final syndication of the loan may not be completed until after Financial Close (*cf.* §9.3.6), and swap arrangements have to be concluded at or shortly after Financial Close. (In which case the swap would have to be provided by the Lead Arranger(s).)
- Some of the syndicate banks may be less competitive than others in their swap pricing, and the Project Company may end up having to pay the swap rate of the most expensive bank.

- It leaves the syndicate banks (or the Lead Arranger(s)) with no competition, and therefore the Project Company may not get the best rates for the swap.

Although interest-rate swap rates are quoted and can be checked on trading screens, this is not the case for an interest-rate swap on a project-specific debt-service schedule, for which a 'blended' rate has to be produced, reflecting the drawdown and repayment schedule over the life of the project (*cf.* §11.2.4). While it would not be fair to say that the pricing of such a blended swap, which is done under time pressure at Financial Close, is a complete 'black box', it is difficult for the Project Company to check that the most competitive price has been obtained from its lender. Indeed it is notorious that excess profits on interest-rate swaps form a significant part of project-finance banks' revenues in some PPP sectors.

If there are several banks in the lending syndicate, it may be possible to get them to bid against each other for the whole of the swap business, which is probably the simplest way of achieving a competitive bidding situation, but of course this will not work if syndication has not taken place and there is only one Lead Arranger.

It is not normally possible for the Project Company to go directly to other banks in the market and ask them to quote for the swap, firstly because a bank not already involved in lending is unlikely to want to spend the time bringing in its project-finance department to analyse the risk involved, and secondly because if a swap is provided by a bank which is not also a lender to the Project Company this causes inter-creditor problems (*cf.* §12.6.1).

A structure that gives the Project Company access to the best market rates is for one or more of the banks in the lending syndicate to act as a 'fronting bank'. The Project Company goes into the swap market for quotations, based on the swap provider entering into a swap with the fronting bank; the Project Company then enters into an identical 'back-to-back' swap with the fronting bank. (The fronting bank itself can still quote in competition for the market swap.) The fronting bank charges the credit premium discussed above (or is counter-guaranteed by the syndicate banks and charges a smaller premium reflecting this). This structure also has the advantage of documenting the swap credit premium separately, making it easier to provide for the premium not to be payable on early termination (*cf.* §11.2.6).

§11.2.9 ROLL-OVER RISK

The notional principal schedule used as a basis for the swap is based on estimates of when drawings on the loan will be made during construction, and when loan repayments will be made (beginning when the project is completed). Inevitably these estimates will prove incorrect—*e.g.* a delay in the construction program affects the timing of drawings, or the final completion of the project is delayed, which may also delay the repayment schedule, if this is calculated from the completion date.

If the shift in timing is a relatively short period of a month or so, this does not matter, and the swap can be left to run on the original schedule (assuming that the Project Company will have funds available to make any net payment that is due) since any extra loss in a one-month period is likely to be compensated by a profit in another. If a significant shift in the schedule takes place—say 6 months—because of a delay in completion of the project, it is preferable to 'roll over' the swap (*i.e.* terminate the original swap and enter into a new one on the new schedule). Any breakage cost on termination would be largely matched by the bene-fit of a lower long-term fixed rate, and any profit would compensate for a higher fixed rate.

However the Project Company may face some difficulty with the swap provider:

- The swap provider may no longer wish to provide the swap and try to use the roll-over request as a way of getting out of it.
- If there is no competition on the rate for the roll-over the Project Company could pay too much for it.

If the fronting-bank structure described above has been used, roll-over of the swap should be less of an issue; in other cases it may be possible to agree to a competitive approach in advance. If not the Project Company (and its lenders) may just have to take this risk as one of the inevitable adverse consequences of a delay in completion. A similar issue arises if the loan amount is increased (*e.g.* by drawing on contingent funding because of a delay in completion), and the swap needs to be increased correspondingly. The risk may also flow on to the Public Authority if the delay is its fault (*cf.* §15.2).

§11.2.10 OTHER TYPES OF INTEREST-RATE HEDGING

The interest-rate swap market is the largest and most liquid of the financial derivatives markets in interest rates. (A financial derivative is a contract which produces payments and receipts over a period of time, at prices 'derived' from an underlying market movement, *e.g.* interest rates.) This liquidity is especially evident at the longer maturities required for project-finance cash flows, which is the reason that interest-rate swaps are generally the instrument of choice for this purpose. However, there are some other derivative structures which can be used in a project-finance context.

Interest-rate caps. Under an interest-rate cap, the cap provider agrees to pay the Project Company if floating interest rates go above a certain level (known as the 'strike rate' or 'cap rate'). For example, the current floating rate may be 5%, and the cap rate set at 7%. So long as the floating rate remains below 7% the Project Company just pays the floating rate. If the floating rate goes above 7%, the cap provider pays the Project Company the difference between the two in the same way as in an interest-rate swap. For budget purposes the Project Company can thus assume an interest cost of 7% fixed, and insofar as the floating rate cost comes out below this level, this is a bonus.

Caps are a form of option, and their pricing is based on complex formulae which base the pricing on forward interest rates (*i.e.* market quotations for interest on deposits to be placed in future). Payment for the cap is usually made by way of an up-front premium (unlike an interest-rate swap, where, as seen above, payment if any is made throughout the life of the swap). The amount of the premium will depend on how far the cap is out of the money—*e.g.* if the forward rate is 5% on average, a cap at 6% will cost more than a cap at 7%.

Interest rate caps may provide a short-term solution to interest-rate hedging, for example, if a floating-rate loan during the construction period is to be refinanced by a fixed-rate loan on completion of the project. They have the advantage that the provider does not take a credit risk on the Project Company, because (after payment of the initial premium) payments only ever flow from the provider to the Project Company, and so can be obtained from any provider in the market, but the disadvantage is that the up-front premium adds to the project's development costs. They are therefore seldom used for long-term hedging.

Interest-rate collar. An interest-rate 'collar' combines an interest-rate cap with its reverse, an interest-rate floor (*i.e.* a maximum rate of, say, 6% is fixed with a cap as above, while if the floating rate goes below a floor rate of, say, 4% the Project Company pays the difference to the provider). Interest-rate collars may be obtained at no cost (*i.e.* without an up-front premium) because the cap and the floor have the same cost, and one is being bought and the other sold by the Project Company. However the taker of the floor rate has a credit risk on the Project Company, albeit usually a lower level of risk than that for an interest-rate swap provider. But although a collar offers flexibility, the relative illiquidity of the market at longer maturities makes it difficult to use for long-term hedging of a PPP project.

Swaption. A swaption (or 'contingent swap') is the right to enter into a swap at a future date, which may give some flexibility if the timing of drawings and repayments by the Project Company is not completely fixed. Swaptions are seen in a PPP context, primarily in the situation where construction of part of the project is to go ahead while construction of the rest (and hence the need for funding) is not yet certain, *e.g.* because this latter part is dependent on planning approvals.

Accretion swap. This type of swap (also known as a 'step up swap') achieves the same result as debt accretion (*cf.* §10.5.8); instead of the fixed payments by the Project Company under an interest-rate swap merely hedging its floating-rate payments, part of these payments are shifted to a later time.

§11.2.11 Bond Proceeds Redeposit (GIC)

Although long-term interest-rate hedging is not an issue with a fixed-rate bond, the nature of bond issues does introduce an indirect short-term interest-rate risk which has to be hedged. A bank loan can be drawn by the Project Company as and when needed for the costs of the PPP project during the construction period. A bond issue, on the other hand, has to be drawn in one amount at Financial Close—bond investors will not commit to buy bonds in the future, least of all at a rate fixed today. The result is that the Project Company has to pay interest on the whole of its borrowing from Financial Close, rather than paying interest only on the money as it is drawn. On the other hand the proceeds of the bond issue can be kept on deposit by the Project Company until they are needed, and the interest on this deposit used to offset the extra interest cost on the bond. Under normal market conditions— when short-term rates are lower than long-term rates—there will be a net loss on this offset (*i.e.* the interest on the deposit will be less than the equivalent interest payable on the bond), which has to be taken into account when considering the overall cost of the bond financing.

The redeposit of the bond proceeds also creates an interest-rate risk. The bank taking the deposit will normally only pay interest on a floating-rate basis, and so if interest rates go down the offset against the bond interest costs will be less than expected, which could result in a deficit in the Project Company's construction budget. It is therefore necessary for the Project Company to obtain a fixed rate on the redeposit, which is provided by a bank swapping the floating-rate interest on the deposit for a fixed rate. This is known as a Guaranteed Investment Contract, or 'GIC' (note that this term is also used with wider meanings in the United States, *e.g.* long-term deposits by pension funds with insurance companies).

§11.2.12 BREAKAGE COSTS ON BONDS

A bond investor, or any lender providing a fixed-rate loan, also has a breakage cost if a bond is prepaid early, *e.g.* if the Project Company defaults, for exactly the same reason as the swap provider: if the rate at which the fixed-rate funds can be re-lent has gone down when the Project Company defaults, the bond investor makes a loss. However, the breakage cost on prepayment of a bond issue can be significantly higher than the breakage cost for an interest-rate swap, which magnifies the implications for both the Project Company and the Public Authority discussed above, because:

* The breakage cost is calculated as the NPV of all of the future bond debt service: a low discount rate for this DCF calculation—typically at or near the equivalent government bond rate—substantially increases the amount payable.
* The breakage calculation for a bond may be one way—*i.e.* if interest rates have gone down the bond holder is compensated by the borrower, but if they have gone up the bond holder does not pay over this profit to the Project Company. This is known as a 'par floor'.

The combination of these two requirements is known as a 'make-whole clause' (or the 'Spens clause' in the British bond market, named after the investment banker who imported it into this market). Table 11.6 illustrates how it can work, based on the assumption of a 1,000 bond issue, at a coupon of 6%, with two examples of early termination, one with an increase and

Table 11.6
Bond termination costs

Assumptions:

Bond amount	1,000
Repayment	20 years, annual annuity payments
Interest rate (coupon)	6%

Year:	0	1	2	3	4	5	15	16	17	18	19	20
Interest payment at 6%		60	58	57	55	53	26	22	18	14	10	5
Principal repayment		27	29	31	32	34	61	65	69	73	78	82
Total debt service		87	87	87	87	87	87	87	87	87	87	87
Outstanding amount	1,000	973	944	913	881	847	367	302	233	160	82	0
Termination payments												
Lower rate (4%)	1,185	1,145	1,104	1,061	1,016	969	388	316	242	164	84	
Higher rate (8%)												
– without par floor	856	837	817	795	772	746	348	289	225	155	81	
– with par floor	1,000	973	944	913	881	847	367	302	233	160	82	

the other with a decrease of interest rates at the time of termination. So in year 5, when the outstanding amount is 847, if the termination discount rate has gone down to 4%, a payment of 969 will be due, the extra amount being required to cover the loss on redeploying the funds from 6% to 4%. On the other hand, if the termination discount rate is 8%, a profit is made on redeploying the funds at this higher rate, and taking this into account the payment should be 746, but if a par floor operates the payment will be the outstanding amount of 847 instead.

If the government bond rate is taken as the termination discount rate, this means that the NPV of the whole of the difference between government bond rates and the rate charged to the Project Company—*i.e.* not just the market premium, but the credit margin as well (*cf.* §9.4.2)—has to be paid. This is unreasonable, since the bond investor can easily go out and invest in another corporate bond issue of a similar rating. The discount rate should therefore be somewhere between the government bond rate and the coupon on the Project Company's bond: this is typically a matter of *ad hoc* negotiation. The issue here is similar to that already discussed, of paying the NPV of future credit premiums on a swap break-age (*cf.* §11.2.6) but the potential costs involved are much greater, because the difference between the discount rate and the coupon rate is greater.

The par floor may seem unfair, but it should be borne in mind that the alternative is a capital loss by the bond holder, which may obviously be unattractive because of its effect on accounting results (unless the bond holder marks the value of its bonds to market anyway), and cause tax problems (because the bond holder may not be able to offset the capital loss against tax). It may be possible, in some bond markets, to avoid a make-whole payment by paying a higher coupon for the debt.

In addition to make-whole provisions on the bond, if there is monoline insurance (*cf.* §9.4.4), the insurer may apply its own make-whole provision, either by charging its insurance premium on an up-front basis for the whole life of the bond, and if the bond is terminated early there is no refund, or by charging for the NPV of remaining fees on early termination.

§11.2.13 BID TO FINANCIAL CLOSE

So far this discussion of interest-rate risks and hedging has dealt with the situation at Financial Close, and how interest-rate risk is hedged thereafter. But the bidder for a PPP project has an inherent interest-rate risk from the day of the bid. In order to offer a fixed price for the Service Fees, a cost of debt, including the underlying interest rate, must be assumed. If, by the time Financial Close is reached—perhaps a year or more after the bid—interest rates have gone up, the bidder's return will diminish, and in the worst case the project may become unfinanceable. The greater the leverage, and the longer the period between bid and Financial Close, the more serious the problem becomes. The Sponsors can theoretically deal with this problem in two ways:

- include a safety margin for interest-rate movements in the bid—but of course this may make the bid uncompetitive; or
- hedge the interest rate in advance of Financial Close (perhaps through a swaption—*cf.* §11.2.10), and then transfer the hedge to the Project Company at Financial

Close—but if the Sponsors do not win the bid, or the project does not reach Financial Close, the cost of this hedging would not be recovered if it has gone out of the money; therefore this is a course of action which a bidder would only take very near to Financial Close.

The first alternative is the general course of action in projects with lower leverage (70–80%), especially Concessions, and indeed is the normal procedure in other sectors of the project-finance market besides PPPs. But in cases with high leverage, *e.g.* PFI-Model accommodation projects, it may not offer the Public Authority the best VfM (unless all parties can be confident that the period from bid to Financial Close will be limited) since this implies paying for what may amount to an expensive option to cover the risk of interest-rate movements from the bid to Financial Close—*i.e.* it is part of the process of deciding which particular risks of a PPP Contract it is cost-effective to transfer to the private sector, and which it makes sense for the public sector to retain (*cf.* §14.2). Moreover if the public sector as a whole is undertaking a programme of PPPs, it is reasonable to suppose that losses from interest-rate movements on one project will be offset by gains on another.

If the Public Authority is thus prepared to take the risk of interest-rate movements up to Financial Close the ITT/ITN should specify standard market interest rates (*e.g.* swap rates) to be used by bidders to enable bids to be compared on a like-to-like basis (*cf.* §10.3.1). To give the Public Authority some assurance that it will not be faced with a project which becomes too expensive (unaffordable), these assumed rates should build in a reasonable safety margin over the current market.

The Project Company remains formally responsible for the interest-rate fixing at Financial Close: the rate produced is then used to calculate the final actual level of Service Fees, while maintaining the lenders' Cover Ratios and the investors' Equity IRR at the same levels as those originally bid. However it is self-evident that the Project Company has little interest in getting the best possible rates in this situation. The process therefore has to be supervised by the Public Authority (with its financial advisers), and the Public Authority has to agree to the final terms for the swap. If this procedure is used, the argument for competitive bids for the swap, either by syndicate banks bidding against each other, or through the fronting-bank structure (*cf.* §11.2.8) becomes even stronger.

A further complication is introduced if the Project Company does not hedge its debt for the full term of the loan because the lenders and investors are willing to absorb some level of interest-rate risk based on their view of the financial market (*cf.* §11.2.7). If the Public Authority is adjusting the Service Fees to reflect the rate-fixing at Financial Close, should this be based on the actual rate paid for the shorter swap, or the notional rate that would be charged for the longer swap? In principle it should be the latter, especially if it is a lower rate, but of course this raises difficult questions on how competitive pricing can be achieved.

As far as bond issues are concerned, pricing is more of a 'black box', and introducing competition is difficult (other than for underwriting fees and other ancillary matters such as the GIC rate). The bond underwriter is normally paid a fixed fee, irrespective of the final pricing of the bond, and therefore has a clear incentive to be less than aggressive on the pricing to ensure the bonds are not left on its hands. It is possible to have a more competitive approach for a private placement, but whether the pricing for a publicly-quoted bond is competitive cannot really only be judged by comparing it with other similar quoted bonds already in the market; as the market for project-finance bonds, and their liquidity, is limited, this may be difficult to do.

In general it is not prudent for an Authority to give any advance protection for interest rates before Financial Close, any more than any other part of the PPP Contract arrangements should be activated before everything is signed and effective. However, there is one aspect of interest-rate fixing where this may be necessary. If a very large bond issue is to be placed in the market, the effect may be to push up market rates and so also the Service Fees. The investment bank placing the bond issue may therefore undertake a 'market stabilisation' exercise in advance of the bond issue—in effect hedging against a future rise in rates by selling government bonds forward. If rates for the bond issue do go up, the profit on the forward sale of the government bonds will offset this. A similar exercise can be carried out if a large interest-rate swap is to be placed in the market. In such cases the Public Authority has to underwrite any loss which arises from this exercise, *i.e.* if rates go down, but this stabilisation will still have effectively fixed the price of the bond in advance of its issue.

§11.2.14 SHOULD THE PROJECT COMPANY HAVE TO HEDGE INTEREST RATES?

The interest-rate hedging by the Project Company discussed in this chapter is highly inefficient from the public-sector point of view. It ignores the fact that individual PPP projects are normally part of a larger programme, and hedging them one-by-one is far more expensive than dealing with them on a pool basis. Moreover the hedging of a PPP programme has to be put in the context of the government's economic policy, which determines the very interest rates which may require hedging—in other words the government is hedging itself.

The only reason interest rates cannot be hedged through adjusting the Service Fees (and then hedged on a pooled basis for all PPP projects by the Public Authority or central government) is that, as discussed above (§11.2.1), it is likely to raise balance sheet issues for the public-sector budget. If this is not the case, it makes most sense to adjust the Service Fees for floating-rate interest movements.

It may be possible, however, for the Public Authority to enter into separate interest-rate swap agreements with Project Companies, and then pool the cost of these swaps. The difficulty with it is that the Public Authority then assumes the credit (breakage) risk on the Project Company, but will not be allowed by the lenders to have a *pari passu* claim with them on the Project Company's assets, or to exercise any serious controls on the Project Company to limit the breakage risk (*cf.* §12.6.1). Hence there is a credit issue (which could be covered by the lending banks guaranteeing the swaps).

It is also possible for the Public Authority to enter into a swap or other hedging instrument in advance of Financial Close, to fix its own costs, and then transfer this at Financial Close to the Project Company. However this is quite complex from a legal point of view, and just as prefixing interest rates has dangers for the investors it obviously also involves extra risk for the Public Authority, and may put pressure on the Public Authority to rush the Financial Close.

Another approach to interest-rate hedging—discussed below (*cf.* §17.4.1)—is for fixed-rate funding to be provided by the public sector, but the credit risk to be taken by banks.

§11.3 INFLATION ISSUES

Unfortunately, issues relating to the effect of inflation on PPP Contracts can be far more complex than those relating to interest-rate risk. Because of the cumulative effect of inflation, relatively small annual changes have a substantial effect over the 20–30 years term of a PPP Contract. The Public Authority will also inevitably be far more involved in these issues because Service Fees are usually at least partially indexed against inflation, for which there are several reasons:

- Private-sector bidders are likely to charge heavily for exposure to the risk of inflation on their opex and maintenance costs, which is unlikely to be good VfM from the Public Authority's point of view.
- The Public Authority's own resources, *e.g.* from tax revenues, may themselves be linked to inflation, and therefore it is logical to index Service Fees to match this.
- If the Facility had been procured by the public sector, some costs such as opex and maintenance would have been subject to price inflation anyway; it is therefore logical to index part of the Service Fees against inflation, insofar as these payments relate to similar Project Company costs.

§11.3.1 NOMINAL AND REAL

By way of introduction, the rather confusing terminology of inflation needs to be explained. A 'nominal' cash flow is one that includes the effect, if any, of inflation, and a 'real' cash flow is one that excludes the effect of inflation. Thus a real payment is one in 'money of today' even if at a future date, whereas a nominal payment is the amount actually paid (or expected to be paid) in 'money of the future'. Furthermore, a payment in a PPP cash flow may be described as 'fixed', *i.e.* a nominal payment unaffected by inflation, or 'variable', *i.e.* a real payment subject to inflation. (A 'nominal' interest rate is sometimes referred to, but, to avoid confusion, not in this book. This expression is used where interest is payable less than annually; the nominal rate is the stated annual rate. Thus if the nominal rate is 5%, and payment is made and thus interest is compounded semi-annually, the actual rate of interest—known as the annual effective rate—is 5.06%, because the amount of interest received at the end of one year includes a half-year's interest compounded at 2.5%.)

To give some examples of real and nominal figures in the context of the cash flow for a PPP project:

- Service Fees may be quoted by bidders on a real basis, and then partly or wholly subject to indexation for inflation. So, for example, a real payment of 100 *p.a.*, 50% indexed against inflation, will produce a nominal payment of 102 after one year, assuming inflation of 4% *p.a.* [50 + (50 × 4%)].
- Debt service is normally a fixed series of payments, which are thus on a nominal basis (except for inflation-indexed financing, for which see below). Therefore a debt-service payment of 100 in a year's time, where inflation is 4%, is 96.15 in real terms (*i.e.* 96.15 × 104% = 100), and 100 in nominal terms. (This reduction of a future fixed nominal amount to a real amount is called a deflation calculation.)

- Similarly, bidders usually assess their Equity IRR on a nominal basis.
- Construction Subcontract costs are normally fixed, and hence these costs are nominal payments like debt service, as are most of the other elements of the capex (there may be small exceptions such as the Project Company's staff costs during the construction phase, which will be variable).
- The Project Company's opex is usually projected on a real basis, and then increased for the expected rate of inflation. (Operating Subcontract payments may be payable on a variable basis, *i.e.* indexed for inflation.)

If a DCF calculation is required (*e.g.* for a bid comparison—*cf.* §6.3.6—or to calculate a termination payment—*cf.* §15.5.3), both the cash flow to be discounted and the discount rate itself must be on the same basis, *i.e.* either nominal or real. Therefore if the discount rate, such as the PSDR, is a real rate, and it is to be used to discount nominal cash flows, then either the discount rate has to be converted into a nominal rate, using the 'Fisher formula':

$$n = (1 + r) \times (1 + i) - 1$$

where: n = nominal discount rate, r = real discount rate and i = rate of inflation.

   Thus if the PSDR is 3.5% real, and inflation is projected at 2.5%, the nominal discount rate is

$$n = (1 + 3.5\%) \times (1 + 2.5\%) - 1 = 6.0875\%$$

and not, as might be thought, 6% (3.5% + 2.5%). So if we have 1,060,875 in a year's time, and want to discount this at a rate of 3.5% real plus 2.5% inflation, the discount calculation (*cf.* §4.2) is:

$$\frac{1.060,875}{(1 + 6.0875\%)} = 1,000,000$$

Alternatively, the cash flow can be converted into real figures, and then discounted at the real rate. So to use the same example, 1,060,875 nominal after one year, with inflation of 2.5%, equates to 1,035,000 real (1,060,875 ÷ 1.025), which when discounted at 3.5% is 1,000,000 today.

   It might be thought that if the Service Fees are fully indexed against inflation, it is unnecessary to take account of inflation in the cash flow projections, but this is not likely to be the case, as illustrated by Table 11.7, which shows the effect of mixing nominal and real figures in the calculation. This shows two identical cash flows. (A) ignores the effect of inflation, and produces a level annual cash flow. (B) takes inflation into account, and thus shows nominal figures. But if the nominal figures in (B) are deflated at the rate of inflation in way discussed above, they do not produce the same cash flow as (A). This is because although the revenues and opex figures in (A) are real, the debt-service figures are nominal, and therefore have to be deflated to produce a real cash flow. (A) thus incorrectly mixes up nominal and real cash flows, and the correct nominal and real figures are those in (B).

   To avoid confusion between real and nominal figures, it is thus generally best to prepare financial models with the cash flows calculated on a nominal basis, with any real cash flows adjusted for projected inflation. Another reason for preparing cash-flow figures on a

Table 11.7
Effect of inflation on project cash flow

Assumptions:

Revenues	1,000 *p.a.*, indexed for inflation
Opex	700 *p.a.*, also subject to inflation
Loan	1,000
Repayment	5 years, annuity basis
Interest rate	8%

Year:	1	2	3	4	5	Total
(A)—0% inflation						
Revenues	1,000	1,000	1,000	1,000	1,000	5,000
Opex	−700	−700	−700	−700	−700	−3,500
Debt interest	−80	−66	−52	−36	−19	−253
Debt repayment	−170	−184	−199	−215	−232	−1,000
Net cash flow	**50**	**50**	**50**	**50**	**50**	**250**
(B)—4% inflation						
Revenues	1,000	1,040	1,082	1,125	1,170	5,417
Opex	−700	−728	−757	−787	−819	−3,791
Debt interest	−80	−66	−52	−36	−19	−253
Debt repayment	−170	−184	−199	−215	−232	−1,000
Net cash flow (nominal)	**50**	**62**	**74**	**87**	**101**	**374**
(B) deflated at 4% p.a.	**48**	**57**	**66**	**74**	**83**	**328**
(=real cash flow)						

nominal rather a real basis is that tax calculations are based on nominal cash flows. In the example in Table 11.7, if the cash flow were taxed at 50%, tax actually payable in year 2 would be 31, or 29 in real terms, and it would be wrong to prepare a real cash flow as in (A), showing the tax payable as 25. Moreover tax depreciation (*cf.* §10.8.1) is based on the original nominal cost of the project, and no allowance is normally made for inflation over the years during which this depreciation allowance is offset against tax.

§11.3.2 INFLATION INDICES AND PROJECTIONS

In a PPP project's cash flow, 'inflation' can be on more than one basis:

- If Service Fees are adjusted for inflation, this adjustment will be linked to a specific inflation index (*e.g.* consumer price inflation—'CPI').
- The Project Company's opex under Subcontracts is usually adjusted against the same inflation index (*cf.* §11.3.13).
- Other opex for the Project Company, *e.g.* insurance costs or staff costs, while variable, and hence affected by inflation, will not be linked to any specific inflation index. In fact, changes in costs such as insurance may vary dramatically from general inflation (*cf.* §11.3.13).

The Public Authority has to consider the most appropriate inflation index to use for index-ing the PPP payments; there are two schools of thought on this:

- The index should relate to the business sector in which the Project Company is oper-ating, *e.g.* a construction- or building maintenance-specific index.
- A general consumer-price index such as CPI should be used, on the grounds that the Subcontractors providing the relevant services over the life of the PPP Contract can themselves influence a specific index.

The choice between the two relates to the nature of the costs being indexed: if they consti-tute a long-term and large-scale element of the overall Service Fees there will be more pres-sure for an industry-specific index. The other factor is whether Subcontractors are willing to accept a contract with a non-specific index, as it is generally imprudent for the Project Company to agree with the Public Authority to receive payments indexed on one basis, and then also to agree to make payments to Subcontractors indexed on a different basis (*cf.* §11.3.13). A minor divergence between the two indices can have a very major effect on the cash flow over a period of time, and hence Subcontractors may be reluctant to sign very long-term contracts. A compromise between the two choices, to reduce this risk, is to index at CPI + x%.

However there is an argument for only allowing indexation at 'inflation minus x%', on the grounds that this encourages long-term efficiency savings by the Project Company, because otherwise the PPP Contract 'freezes' the efficiency requirements on day 1 and pre-vents the Public Authority from making such savings in the way it could were it operating the Facility itself (*cf.* §2.9.4). As FM costs generally inflate faster than CPI, using CPI alone as the inflation index for the PPP Contract achieves this result.

§11.3.3 INFLATION FORECASTS

Whether variable costs are specifically indexed against inflation in the PPP Contract or not, an assumption has to be made in the financial model on the projected rate or rates of inflation to be applied against each element of variable costs. The public sector as a whole should have a common approach to inflation assumptions to be used by bidders and in bid evaluation (including the PSC if there is one), but there tends not to be an obvious source for such assumptions. Government inflation projections (as well as those produced by independent sources such as the Organisation for Economic Co-operation and Development (OECD)) may run for no more than five years, whereas a PPP may need assumptions for 25–30 years. If the central bank has an inflation target this can be used for projections, but of course this is a target rather than reality. A long-term inflation rate based on market views can be derived from government inflation-indexed bonds, but for the reasons discussed in §11.3.7 this will be somewhat artificial. In the end the choice of an inflation assumption may be no more than a rough guess, but in making this choice various questions arise, *e.g.*:

- Should this assumption be the same for all the elements of revenues and costs mentioned above?
- Is the prudent assumption a high rate of inflation or a low rate?

Sensitivities should be run on the financial model to show the effect of different approaches on these questions. Bidders and lenders also have to consider these issues, and for the purposes of their own evaluation may take a different view of inflation than that used by the Public Authority.

§11.3.4 EFFECT OF INDEXED SERVICE FEES ON FUNDING STRUCTURE

As discussed in §13.3.2, Service Fees should be level throughout the life of that Contract. However, it is generally accepted that the arguments against a 'back-ended' payment profile do not apply insofar as this is caused by indexing the payments for inflation—*i.e.* inflation-indexed Service Fees are kept level from year to year in real rather than nominal terms.

In the Concession Model, Service Fees are usually fully indexed against inflation; in the PFI Model, as discussed below, payments may also be wholly indexed, or only partly

Table 11.8
Effect of inflation-indexed Service Fees

Assumptions:											
Loan amount	1,000										
Term	25 years										
Interest rate	6.0%										
Inflation	2.5%										
Required ADSCR	1.20										
Year:	**0**	**1**	**2**	**3**	**4**	**10**	**11**	**12**	**24**	**25**	**Total**
Fixed Service Fees											
Opening loan outstanding		1,000	982	962	942	791	760	727	143	74	
Interest		60	59	58	57	47	46	44	9	4	**956**
Loan repayment		18	19	20	22	31	33	35	70	74	
Total debt service		78	78	78	78	78	78	78	78	78	
Service Fees (nominal)	*94*	**94**	**94**	**94**	**94**	**94**	**94**	**94**	**94**	**94**	**2,347**
ADSCR		*1.2*	*1.2*	*1.2*	*1.2*	*1.2*	*1.2*	*1.2*	*1.2*	*1.2*	
Average life of debt	*15 years*										
Service Fees (real)	*94*	**92**	**89**	**87**	**85**	**73**	**72**	**70**	**52**	**51**	**1,730**
Inflation-indexed Service Fees											
Opening loan outstanding		1,000	998	995	990	914	892	866	202	105	
Interest		60	60	60	59	55	54	52	12	6	**1,105**
Loan repayment		2	3	5	7	22	25	29	97	105	
Total debt service		62	63	65	66	77	79	81	109	111	
Service Fees (nominal)	*72*	**74**	**76**	**78**	**80**	**92**	**95**	**97**	**130**	**134**	**2,526**
ADSCR		*1.2*	*1.2*	*1.2*	*1.2*	*1.2*	*1.2*	*1.2*	*1.2*	*1.2*	
Average life of debt	*17 years*										
Service Fees (real)	*72*	**72**	**72**	**72**	**72**	**72**	**72**	**72**	**72**	**72**	**1,800**

indexed. Concentrating for now on the case where payments are fully indexed, this has a significant potential effect on both the funding structure and the Service Fees, as illustrated by Table 11.8. As the table shows, the annual debt service over 25 years for a loan amount of 1,000 at an interest rate of 6%, on an annuity repayment basis, is 78. If the lenders require a minimum ADSCR of 1.20x this means that the annual Service Fees (ignoring the further amounts needed to cover opex, and assuming the Cover Ratio also covers the equity return, for which *cf.* §10.7) have to be 94 (78 × 1.2) in nominal terms, and thus decline over time in real terms.

But if the Service Fees are indexed against inflation, which is assumed in the calculations to be projected at 2.5% *p.a.*, the year 1 Service Fee can be reduced from 94 to 74. The loan repayments can be 'back-ended' to take advantage of the indexed revenues increasing over time, and hence a steady 1.20x Cover Ratio is maintained (although this does increase the average life of the loan), and the Service Fees remain level in real terms. However in total the Service Fees are greater in nominal terms—in year 11 the indexed payments become greater than the fixed ones, and by year 25 the annual indexed payment is 134, compared to the fixed payment of 94. This reflects the fact that the loan is being repaid more slowly, and more interest is thus paid, as can be seen in the totals of the relevant columns.

§11.3.5 SHOULD SERVICE FEES BE FULLY INDEXED?

This therefore suggests that the Public Authority, the Project Company and its lenders should all be quite happy with a fully-indexed stream of PPP Contract. Payments. However, the issues here are quite complex, and the different parties may have differing views on the matter.

Clearly the effect of 'over-indexation' of Service Fees (*i.e.* the indexed proportion being greater than the proportion that inflation-linked costs—mainly opex—bear to the total costs) is that the debt is outstanding for longer. As Table 11.8 shows, the result is that in real terms the PPP Contract becomes more expensive, and thus harder to justify on VfM grounds. Nonetheless, there is obviously a political temptation to get a PPP Facility built at an artificially-reduced cost which may be affordable in year 1, and leave someone else to worry about Affordability in later years.

However, the Public Authority is taking a substantial risk on inflation not being higher than the projected rate. This may or may not be an issue depending on whether the Public Authority's own resources move in step with its liabilities under the PPP Contract, *i.e.* whether it can be confident that these resources will also increase in line with inflation. This is obviously a matter of central government policy. In the PFI Credits system in Britain, for example (*cf.* §3.4.2), the central government makes a fixed stream of payments available to the Public Authority for some or all of the capex of PPP projects, but remaining payments— largely to cover opex—must be paid from the Public Authority's other sources of finance (which are likely to vary with inflation). The result may be that, say, 60% of the Public Authority's resources for the PPP project are fixed and 40% are variable. Clearly lower initial Service Fees can be produced by making them 100% variable against inflation instead of 40%. But this means that the Public Authority is taking the risk of a long-term mismatch in its resources for making the Service Fees—its own resources to be used for the 40% of

Table 11.9

Effect of over-indexation

Year:	1	2	3	4	10	11	12	24	25	Total
Service Fees (nominal)	73	74	74	75	80	80	81	92	93	2,058
Total debt service	62	63	65	66	77	79	81	109	111	
ADSCR	*1.18*	*1.17*	*1.15*	*1.13*	*1.04*	*1.02*	*1.01*	*0.84*	*0.83*	

variable Service Fees have to increase by 2½ times the rate of inflation—which is difficult to justify on policy grounds. This is of course part of the wider issue for the Public Authority, and the central government, of ensuring that the public-sector budget will support a PPP programme in the long-term (*cf.* §2.4). On the other hand in the case of a Concession-model project, as already mentioned, 100% indexation of Service Fees is not uncommon. (To be precise, the Project Company may have the right to index Service Fees up to a cap equal to 100% of inflation, but may choose not to do so.) Assuming the initial Service Fees are acceptable (*cf.* §13.4.1), users would not normally object to them being increased each year by the rate of inflation.

Even if the Public Authority can initially satisfy itself that 100% indexation of the Service Fees is appropriate, this may still raise issues for the Project Company's lenders and investors. The danger of this 'over-indexation' is that a large part of the Project Company's cash flow is required for debt service, which is fixed—if the outturn (actual) inflation is lower than the projections on which the funding structure was based, and hence revenues are lower than projected, there will be problems with this debt service.

This is illustrated by Table 11.9, which assumes that the debt-service schedule in Table 11.8 has been adopted, with inflation projected at 2.5%, but in fact outturn inflation is 1%.

As can be seen, the result is bad from the lenders' point of view, with debt-service coverage disappearing and disastrous for the investors since their return will gradually vanish.

This risk of over-indexation and low inflation is most acute where the leverage is relatively high, and projected inflation is also relatively high. (The latter is always a temptation for the Project Company with indexed Service Fees, as it makes the operating cash flow higher, and hence more debt can be raised.)

§11.3.6 INFLATION-INDEXED LOANS

Just as interest-rate risk can be eliminated by fixed-rate funding or an interest-rate swap, the lenders' and investors' low-inflation risk discussed above can also be eliminated by an inflation-indexed loan (which may be a bond or a loan, the latter usually by a non-banking institution such as an insurance company or pension fund, although the European Investment Bank—*cf.* §17.4.4—also lends on this basis), or an inflation swap (for which *cf.* §11.3.9).

As will be seen, this type of funding may bring other benefits for both the Project Company and the Public Authority, but also carries hidden risks.

The pricing and structure of inflation-indexed loans is based on that for inflation-indexed government bonds—which have a variety of names such as 'Treasury Inflation-Protected Securities (TIPS)' (U.S.A), 'Commonwealth Treasury Indexed Bonds' (Australia), 'real return bonds' (Canada), 'indexed gilts' (U.K.)—in the same way as the pricing for fixed-rate loans is linked to that of fixed-rate government bonds (*cf.* §9.4.2). Such bonds are issued with a real interest-rate coupon, and interest and principal payments under the bond are then indexed against the agreed inflation index. For example, if an inflation-indexed loan of 1,000 is made at a real interest rate of 2%, and inflation for the first year is 2.5%, the amount owing at the end of the first year is:

- principal: $1,000 \times (1 + 2.5\%) = 1,025.0$
- interest: $0 \times (1 + 2.5\%)$ $= 20.5$
- total $= 1,045.5$

This result can be checked using the Fisher formula:

$$n = (1 + 2.0\%) \times (1 + 2.5\%) - 1 = 4.55\%$$

The NPV of 1,045.5 discounted at 4.55% for one year is 1,000. This demonstrates that the lender has received a real return of 2%.

In year 2 the calculation (assuming the same rate of inflation) is:

- principal: $1,025 \times (1 + 2.5\%) = 1,050.6250$
- interest: $0 \times (1 + 2.5\%)^2$ $= 21.0125$
- total $= 1,071.6375$

Note that the interest is still calculated on the real amount of the loan (1,000) not the nominal amount (1,025), but then adjusted for two years' cumulative inflation. The total cash flow is now 20.5 in year 1 and 1071.6375 in year 2. Using the same discount rate of 4.55% to discount this cash flow gives an NPV of 1,000—again confirming that the real return is 2%. It can also be seen from these calculations that the principal amount outstanding under an inflation-indexed loan increases over time, unlike a fixed-rate loan, where the amount outstanding never increases.

The calculations are more complex for a project-finance cash flow, since unlike government bonds, an indexed loan for a project financing is repaid in instalments. A typical calculation for an inflation-indexed loan, repaid on an annuity basis, is set out in Table 11.10, and compared to a fixed-rate loan using the same nominal interest rate. As would be expected, the debt-service payment schedule of the inflation-indexed loan is identical to that of the fixed-rate loan, so that the latter can thus be used to hedge inflation-indexed Service Fees which would otherwise be financed with a 'back-ended' fixed-rate loan similar to that in Table 11.8. But if inflation goes down, reducing the Service Fees, the debt service for the inflation-indexed loan will go down *pro rata*, so maintaining the lenders' Cover Ratios, avoiding the problem set out in Table 11.9. If inflation goes up both the Service Fees and the debt service go up. The real Equity IRR is also maintained at a constant figure thanks to this inflation hedging.

Table 11.10

Inflation-indexed v. fixed-rate loan

Assumptions:

Loan amount	1,000
Loan term	20 years
Inflation-indexed loan:	
Annuity repayment (in real terms)	
Real interest rate	2%
Projected inflation	2.5%
Fixed-rate loan:	
Sculptured repayment = annuity repayment in real terms	
Interest rate	4.55%

Year:	0	1	2	3	4	5	16	17	18	19	20	Total
Inflation-indexed loan												
Real payments												
Interest		20	19	18	17	17	6	5	4	2	1	
Principal repayment		41	42	43	44	45	55	56	58	59	60	
Total debt service		61	61	61	61	61	61	61	61	61	61	
Loan balance	1,000	959	917	874	830	786	233	176	119	60	0	
Nominal payments (= real payments × inflation index)												
Inflation index	1.000	1.025	1.051	1.077	1.104	1.131	1.485	1.522	1.560	1.599	1.639	
Interest		21	20	20	19	19	9	7	6	4	2	250
Principal repayment		42	44	46	48	50	82	86	90	94	98	1,288
Total debt service		**63**	**64**	**66**	**68**	**69**	**91**	**93**	**95**	**98**	**100**	**1,539**
Loan balance	1,000	983	963	941	917	889	346	268	185	96	0	
Fixed-rate loan												
Interest		45	45	44	43	42	19	16	12	8	4	556
Principal repayment		17	20	22	25	27	72	77	83	89	96	983
Total debt service		**63**	**64**	**66**	**68**	**69**	**91**	**93**	**95**	**98**	**100**	**1,539**
Loan balance	1,000	983	963	941	917	889	346	268	185	96	0	

§11.3.7 INFLATION ARBITRAGE

Inflation-indexed loans have another pricing advantage—under normal financial market conditions—as they can produce a lower debt-service cost than equivalent fixed-rate loans. This is because the underlying government inflation-indexed bonds tend to have a lower real yield than equivalent fixed-rate bonds. This is the result of:

- governments issuing limited quantities of indexed bonds, even though there is usually a high demand from institutions such as pension funds; and
- indexed bonds effectively offering 'insurance' against high rates of inflation (which lead to high interest rates, which in their turn erode the value of fixed-rate bonds); this has an inherent value which is also reflected in the lower real yield for indexed bonds.

For example, a fixed-rate government bond may have a nominal yield of 4.5%, whereas an equivalent inflation-indexed bond may have a real yield of 1.5%. The implicit rate of inflation in the inflation-indexed bond is 2.96%—*i.e.* this is the 'break-even' inflation rate which would result in the indexed bond's nominal outturn cost being the same as that for the equivalent fixed-rate bond. (Again using the Fisher formula this is calculated as $[(1 + 1.5\%) \times (1 + 2.96\%) - 1 = 4.5\%]$.) Typically break-even inflation is higher than the real market expectation for inflation, because the yield of the inflation-indexed bonds has been pushed down for the reasons discussed above.

Suppose the Project Company is happy with an inflation projection of 2.5% compared to the implicit rate of 2.96% above: if it raises debt on an inflation-indexed basis, the nominal cost (ignoring the market and credit premiums—*cf.* §9.4.1) will be projected as 4.04% $[(1 + 1.5\%) \times (1 + 2.5\%) - 1]$, compared to 4.5% for fixed-rate debt, thus saving 0.46% *p.a.* In effect the Project Company can arbitrage between the rate of inflation implicit in inflation-indexed bond yields, and its own expectation of inflation. This is another strong motivation, apart from hedging variable Service Fees, for using inflation-indexed debt as this benefit may of course be fed through to the Public Authority by way of lower Service Fees in the original bid.

A bidder can easily mix together the over-indexation and inflation arbitrage points by saying to a Public Authority, 'if you will index $x\%$ of the Service Fees I can take out an inflation-indexed loan and offer you a y reduction in the initial payment'. In such cases the Public Authority has to distinguish between the risks of a higher level of indexation and whether an indexed financing offers a lower real cost than fixed-rate financing, and consider the benefits and drawbacks of each.

§11.3.8 BREAKAGE COSTS

The breakage cost of an inflation-indexed loan is calculated by:

- taking the stream of future real payments;
- inflating these by the implied inflation rate (for the remaining term of the loan) at the time of the breakage;
- discounting them at the current market fixed rate (for the remaining term of the loan) at the time of the breakage.

Table 11.11
Inflation-indexed loan—breakage costs

Year:	0	1	2	3	4	5	16	17	18	19	20
2.5% inflation	1000	983	963	941	917	889	417	346	268	185	0
3.5% inflation	1000	992	982	969	953	933	483	404	317	221	0
Increase in breakage cost	0	10	19	28	36	44	65	58	48	35	0

On the basis of the repayment schedule set out in Table 11.10, the amount that has to be repaid if the inflation-indexed loan is terminated early with no change in any of the assumptions is the balance shown as the nominal loan balance, *e.g.* 889 in year 5, identical to that for the fixed-rate loan.

But if the inflation outturn is above the projected 2.5%, the result can be serious, as illustrated in Table 11.11. This takes the same real debt-service payments as set out in Table 11.10, but increases the outturn inflation from 2.5% to 3.5% from year 1; the discount rate for the breakage calculation is assumed to be derived from the unchanged 2% real interest rate and a 3.5% projected inflation rate, *i.e.* 5.57%. The resulting increases in breakage costs are shown. Note that the effect of any make-whole clause (*cf.* §11.2.12) is ignored in these breakage calculations.

The 2.5% inflation figures produce a similar pattern of breakage costs as a fixed-rate bond (*cf.* Table 11.6). But as can be seen the increased outturn inflation means that breakage of the indexed bond becomes relatively more and more expensive over time. This is because past history is of no relevance for an interest-rate breakage calculation, which is only affected by market rates for the remainder of the loan term at the time of the breakage. However, on an inflation-indexed loan a higher rate of inflation builds up the nominal balance, and the breakage calculation in this case reflects this. A relatively small cumulative annual excess over the projected rate of inflation therefore has a relatively large effect on the breakage costs for an inflation-indexed loan. So although an inflation-indexed loan may bring benefits, it does involve significant extra contingent risks.

§11.3.9 INFLATION SWAPS

As with fixed-rate finance, inflation-indexed loans are primarily provided by the bond market, but the banking market produces the same 'synthetic' result through inflation swaps (known as 'RPI swaps' in the United Kingdom). The inflation-swap rate (the 'strike price') is based on the implicit rate of inflation on an inflation-indexed government bond (*e.g.* 2.96% in the example in §11.3.7), to which is also added a market spread and a credit premium as for an interest-rate swap (*cf.* §11.2.4).

An inflation swap can work in two ways, both of which have the same final effect:

- As with an inflation-indexed loan, the Project Company can swap a stream of fixed payments equal to the debt service for equivalent variable payments. The Project

Table 11.12

Inflation swap

Year:	0	1	2	3	4	5	16	17	18	19	20	Total
PPP Contract receipts												
Real receipts		61	61	61	61	61	61	61	61	61	61	
Inflation Index		1.035	1.071	1.109	1.148	1.188	1.734	1.795	1.857	1.923	1.990	
Nominal receipts		63	66	68	70	73	106	110	114	118	122	**1,727**
Fixed swap payments		63	64	66	68	69	91	93	95	98	100	**1,539**
Net swap payment		1	1	2	3	3	15	17	18	20	21	**188**
Breakage payment	90	94	98	102	105	107	66	53	38	20		

Company is then receiving a variable income from the Service Fees, and paying a variable debt-service stream under the swap, so the two hedge each other.

• Alternatively, the Project Company can swap a stream of variable receipts equal to the Service Fees (or the portion of these which is to be hedged), for a stream of fixed receipts, thus hedging the fixed debt service.

The net result of either in cash-flow terms is identical to an inflation-indexed loan, just as the net result of a fixed-rate loan, and a floating-rate loan with an interest-rate swap, are also identical, assuming of course that the market and credit premiums are the same in each case.

The breakage cost for a inflation swap is the difference between the original fixed payment stream and the variable payment stream, with inflation projected at the then ruling implied inflation rate, discounted at the current-market fixed rate.

Thus if we take the example in Table 11.10, and swap inflation-indexed Service Fees for fixed payments to hedge the fixed-rate loan (N.B. the Cover Ratio on these payments is ignored here), and assume that outturn inflation goes up to 3.5%, the pattern of inflation swap payments and breakage costs is as set out in Table 11.12.

As can be seen the breakage costs do not decline but go up for the first few years, and remain at a high proportion of the nominal loan amount throughout the life of the project. These breakage costs are greater than that shown for the equivalent inflation-indexed loan in Table 11.11, because they do not take account of the gain which will be made on breaking the parallel interest-rate swap (on the assumption that nominal interest rates will go up with inflation, *i.e.* the real rate will remain at 2%). If this is taken into account the net breakage costs should be identical.

§11.3.10 LPI Swap

It should also be mentioned that, just as a collar is an alternative to an interest-rate swap (*cf.* §11.2.10), it is also possible to enter into a limited price inflation ('LPI') swap, whereby there is a floor and a ceiling on inflation increases and decreases. However if the floor is made so high as to eliminate all downward movements in inflation, the pricing will be little different from a simple swap.

§11.3.11 COMBINING AN INTEREST-RATE SWAP AND AN INFLATION SWAP

The argument may be used that an inflation swap is a natural hedge for the risk under an interest-rate swap, since the latter is out-of-the-money when interest rates go down, while the inflation swap is in-the-money, and *vice-versa*. But this is not the case, because the pattern of breakage costs on the two is different, as can be seen by comparing Table 11.4 and Table 11.12. In fact Table 11.11 shows the effect of combining the two, because effectively that is what is done with an inflation-indexed loan, and these calculations show that the benefit of breakage gains on increased interest rates are not offset by breakage losses on increased inflation.

Furthermore, payment of the NPV of the future credit premium on termination of the inflation swap, in the same way as for an interest-rate swap (*cf.* §11.2.6) adds a substantial extra burden on termination, because while the NPV of the credit premium on the interest-rate swap will decline over time, in line with breakage costs on this swap, that for an inflation swap does not, in line with its breakage costs. Of course the same effect (or worse) is found with a 'make-whole' clause under an inflation-indexed bond or loan (*cf.* §11.2.12).

Combining these two swaps also raises some acute issues of ensuring competitive pricing at Financial Close (*cf.* §11.2.8). Although there are two separate swaps, they are circular, because the pricing of one affects the pricing of the other. A change in the fixed interest rate affects the stream of payments which are to be hedged against inflation, which leads to a change in the inflation swap profile and pricing, which changes the stream of payments which are to be hedged against interest-rate movements, and so on. Fixing these two swaps at the same time is therefore complex and difficult to monitor.

§11.3.12 POSITION OF THE PUBLIC AUTHORITY

From the point of view of the Public Authority, inflation hedging, whether by an inflation-indexed loan or an inflation swap, does not in any way hedge its own Service-Fee payments (in the PFI Model). In this respect it is quite different from an interest-rate swap, which can fix Service Fees for the Authority as well as the Project Company and its lenders. In fact, the greater the level of inflation indexation on the Service Fees, the greater the risk on inflation which the Public Authority is taking, whether this is hedged by the Project Company or not. Therefore in principle only if the Public Authority is confident that its resources will in fact rise in line with inflation over the whole life of the PPP Contract (of which it is difficult to be certain), should over-indexation of the Service Fees be considered. The problem is that the Affordability benefit of over-indexation may overwhelm objective consideration of its long-term risks.

If the Service Fees are over-indexed, inflation hedging may offer a saving in the debt-service costs which can feed through to the Service Fees (*cf.* §11.3.7). Even if such a saving is not offered, if the lenders are unhappy about the inflation risk, hedging may be an alternative to the lenders requiring a higher Cover Ratio for inflation-indexed Service Fees, with consequent effects on the level of these. Obviously it is important to ensure that this issue is dealt with when the bidders and their lenders are still competing (or in a Funding Competition—*cf.* §16.2).

If the Public Authority is taking the risk of interest rates at Financial Close (*cf.* §11.2.13), a combined interest-rate and inflation swap is, as discussed above, very difficult to monitor, and therefore any cost benefit may be eroded at this stage. And if the Public Authority shares in any Refinancing Gains (*cf.* §16.4.5), these may be eroded by the doubling-up of the credit premium discussed above. Finally, inflation hedging may significantly increase termination payments (*cf.* §11.3.8, §11.3.9), where the Authority is liable for breakage costs (*cf.* §15.5– §15.8). On balance, therefore, inflation hedging is quite difficult to justify from the Public Authority's point of view, especially in the PFI Model.

So if Service Fees are over-indexed, can the Public Authority discourage inflation hedging by offering something in lieu? One possibility is to offer to take back some of the inflation risk, if this offers better VfM than inflation hedging. This is done by indexing the Service Fees by a fixed amount for inflation—say 2.5% *p.a.*—which means that if inflation goes over 2.5% the Public Authority gains but if it goes below 2.5% it loses. Alternatively, the Public Authority can offer the equivalent of an LPI swap (*cf.* §11.3.10), *i.e.* a floor and ceiling on inflation adjustments in the Service Fees. (A one-way bet—*i.e.* only putting a floor on Service Fees—is obviously undesirable.) These structures avoid the problem of termination payments.

But clearly the simplest and most risk-free way of dealing with inflation is to balance the Service Fees between fixed and variable proportions which broadly match the Project Company's fixed and variable costs. This also reflects the structure of what the Public Authority's own costs would have been had it procured and operated the Facility itself.

§11.3.13 INFLATION-INDEX MISMATCH RISK

It has already been mentioned (*cf.* §11.3.2) that it is not advisable for the Project Company to enter into Subcontracts where the payments are indexed against inflation using a different index to that used for Service Fees. However the Project Company may find it difficult to find Subcontractors, especially for FM services, who are prepared to sign long-term contracts with the pricing only indexed against general rather than industry-specific inflation.

If Soft FM costs (cleaning, catering, security, *etc.*) are included within the scope of the PPP Contract, they are a significant part of the variable opex against which the Service Fees are inflation-indexed, and the Project Company cannot get a Subcontract with the costs indexed against the same inflation index as the Service Fees, there will be concern about a discrepancy between inflation of revenues and costs in this respect. Alternatively, the Soft FM Subcontractor may agree to this matching of indexation on a short-term basis (say for 5 years) but not for the life of the PPP Contract. Lenders may also have concerns about the long-term viability of the FM Subcontract if its commercial basis is eroded through inflation.

Bidders can deal with this risk by adding a large contingency into the initial Soft FM costs, but this is not necessarily the best VfM solution for the Public Authority. An alternative is therefore to allow an adjustment to Service Fees at intervals of, say, five years, whereby the element of costs related to Soft FM is either benchmarked against costs elsewhere, or the Soft FM Subcontract is actually re-tendered (the latter being known as 'market testing'). If the costs have changed by more than an agreed minimum percentage (up or down) the Service Fees are adjusted accordingly (possibly splitting costs and benefits between the

Project Company and the Public Authority). Care obviously has to be taken that this does not fall foul of off balance-sheet rules (*cf.* §5.5), and if the Soft FM services are effectively split out in this way, this raises the question of whether they should be included in the scope of the PPP Contract at all (*cf.* §13.2). Moreover there is a problem of information asymmetry between public and private sector on benchmarking, given the lack of publicly-available data on the pricing of such services, and benchmarking and market testing both encourage short-term under-pricing in bids.

This method of hedging inflation mismatches can also be used for insurance costs (*cf.* §12.4.5), but it is less suitable for maintenance costs because these are partly a function of the original design and therefore something which should be taken into account in the bid (*cf.* §2.8). Benchmarking or market testing the cost of maintenance work destroys this link—if this risk is not left with the Project Company, there will be no incentive to control maintenance requirements through the original design of the Facility.

Chapter 12

Lenders' Cash-Flow Controls, Security and Enforcement

§12.1 INTRODUCTION

This chapter looks at how the financial structuring and hedging issues discussed in the last two chapters feed through to the lenders' documentation, and in particular:

- how the lenders control the Project Company's cash flow (§12.2);
- the nature of the lenders' legal security (§12.3);
- the rôle of insurance (§12.4);
- default procedures (§12.5); and
- relationships between different classes of lenders (§12.6).

These are largely issues between the lenders and the Project Company (and its investors), but the Public Authority will need to review the lenders' documentation to ensure that there are no provisions which weaken or unduly inhibit the Project Company's ability to carry out its responsibilities under the PPP Contract.

§12.2 CONTROL OF CASH FLOW

The Project Company's cash flow is closely controlled by the lenders, both during the construction phase of the project, to ensure that the funds are being spent as planned, and during the operating phase, to ensure cash flow is applied according to the agreed priorities.

During the construction phase, a construction-cost budget (*cf.* §10.3.2) is agreed with the lenders, and any actual or projected excesses over the amounts set out in the major cost categories normally need to be approved by them as they occur or are projected, even if there is still enough overall funding to complete the project. However, lenders should be discouraged from trying to set up too detailed a 'line-item' control of the budget; most of the construction-cost budget is contractually fixed, or represents financing costs, and some flexibility needs to be given to the Project Company to manage remaining minor variations in cost categories, especially if the overall project cost is not significantly affected. Similarly, during the operating phase, the lenders will also exercise some control over the budget for costs under the Project Company's direct control (*i.e.* excluding those costs under Subcontracts).

Apart from these budgetary controls, during the construction phase the lenders control expenditure *via* the Disbursement Account (§12.2.1), and have the ability to stop funding if something goes wrong (§12.2.2). During the operation phase lenders set out priorities for application of cash flow (§12.2.3), require funds to be kept in Reserve Accounts to provide an additional cushion (§12.2.4), and also control Distributions to investors (§12.2.5).

§12.2.1 DISBURSEMENT ACCOUNT

The procedure for drawing on the loan to fund construction usually involves the Project Company presenting a formal drawing request several days in advance of the date on which funds are required (there is usually only one drawing a month). This drawing request:

- attaches a payment request from the Construction Subcontractor, certified by the lenders' T/A;
- summarises the purpose for which other drawings are required (*e.g.* for Project Company costs or debt interest);
- sets out how these costs are to be funded (*i.e.* by equity or debt, and if there are several loans, which one is to be drawn);
- compares the monthly and cumulative project costs with the construction budget;
- demonstrates that enough funds remain available to complete the project;
- demonstrates compliance with any other conditions precedent to drawings.

Both equity investment and loan drawings are paid into a Disbursement Account (also known as a Proceeds Account) in the Project Company's name, one of a number of Project Accounts (also known as 'Control Accounts' or escrow accounts) or they are paid directly to the beneficiaries, *e.g.* the Construction Subcontractor. Although this and other Project Accounts are in the Project Company's name, withdrawal of funds may require the consent of the agent bank or security trustee, and the account balances form part of the lenders' security. (Note that this procedure relates to bank loans—bond proceeds are drawn from the GIC account (*cf.* §11.2.11) as and when required, but the result in terms of budgetary control is similar.)

Lenders may control all payments from the Disbursement Account or allow the Project Company to make the payments for the purposes set out in its drawing requests, only taking control of payments if there is a default. The latter is a more practical procedure—if a drawing-request procedure as set out above is being used, there is no need for lenders to do anything other than monitor payments out of the account.

§12.2.2 DRAWSTOPS

If there is an Event of Default under the loan documentation (*cf.* §12.5), the lenders may refuse to advance further funds for construction of the project until this default is remedied to their satisfaction. This is known as a 'Drawstop'.

§12.2.3 THE CASH-FLOW CASCADE

Once the Project Company has started operating, and earning revenues under the PPP Contract, the lenders control its cash flow through the operation of a cash-flow Cascade (or 'waterfall'), setting out their required order of priorities for the use of this cash. A typical order of priorities is:

1. Payment of opex, including the Subcontractors, and taxes, *i.e.* all the costs the Project Company needs to pay to continue operating the project. (Note that the cash flow at this level is not equal to CADS, as CADS also needs to take account of the items in 5.)
2. Fees and expenses due to the agent bank and security trustee, if any.
3*. Interest on the debt and any swap or other hedging payments.
4*. Debt repayments (to the 'minimum' schedule if there is one—*cf.* §10.5.5—if so, remaining payments to the 'target' schedule come at 6).
5. Payments to Reserve Accounts (*cf.* §12.2.4).
6. Cash Sweep, if any (*cf.* §10.5.7).
7. Distributions to investors (*cf.* §12.2.5).

(* These may be accumulated on a month-by-month basis in a Debt Payment Reserve Account—see below.)

Once all the funds required for the first category have been paid, remaining cash available is moved down to the second, and so on (like water flowing down a series of pools— hence the name for this system of cash-flow allocation). It follows that if there is insufficient cash to pay the first five items, no cash is distributed to the investors. Items 6 and 7 are usually only paid half-yearly, during a limited time window after calculations of the Project Company's results and hence the lenders' Cover Ratios for the previous six months (*cf.* §12.2.5).

Revenues can flow into the Cascade in two ways:

*   Lenders may require the Project Company to segregate funds for the first category of costs in a separate Operating Account under the Project Company's day-to-day control, leaving the other funds in a Revenue Account under the joint control of the agent bank or security trustee and the Project Company until the other Cascade payments need to be made.
*   Alternatively, all revenues may flow into one account, from which the Cascade payments are made by the Project Company when required.

The latter is obviously preferable for the Project Company and generally more practical for day-to-day operations.

§12.2.4 RESERVE ACCOUNTS

Cash is paid out of the Cascade, as necessary, into various Reserve Accounts, which are under lenders' control like the other Project Accounts. These serve to protect the Project Company's liquidity should there be a temporary shortage of revenues or increase in opex, build up funds for particular purposes such as maintenance, or segregate special funds such as insurance proceeds. Although the Public Authority does not have any direct security or control over these accounts, which are for the benefit of the lenders, there is an indirect benefit since they give some assurance of continuity of service while any cash-flow problems are being dealt with. On the other hand, it is in the interest of neither the Public Authority nor the investors in the Project Company for cash to be tied up unnecessarily in Reserve Accounts, since this delays Distributions, so reducing the Equity IRR, and may thus be reflected in higher Service Fees in the original bid than would otherwise have been necessary.

Reserve Accounts may include:

Debt Service Reserve Account ('DSRA'). This account contains sufficient funds to pay the next debt service (principal and interest) instalment, usually six months'-worth of debt service. If the Project Company cannot pay some or all of the debt service from its normal cash flow (or a Debt Payment Reserve Account, if any—see below), funds are taken out of this account to do so. The DSRA has to be established at the beginning of the operating phase. There are two ways of doing this:

- including the DSRA as part of the construction-cost budget for the project, and filling it up at the end of the construction phase;
- funding the DSRA from operating cash flow under the Cascade (which means that it is filled up as cash flow comes in from initial operations, and thus until it is filled up no distributions of can be made to the investors).

The first approach is preferable from the investors' point of view, because most of the funds required for the DSRA are funded by the lenders (*i.e. pro rata* to the debt portion of the debt-equity ratio) rather than out of the equity cash flow. It also has the benefit from the lenders' point of view that they know that the DSRA is funded as soon as the project begins operation. As a halfway house between these two alternative approaches, the Project Company may be allowed to draw funds for the DSRA at the end of the construction phase from any unused or contingency funding not required for any other purpose.

To improve their Equity IRR the Sponsors may provide the lenders with a bank letter of credit ('L/C') or, if acceptable, corporate guarantees, in lieu of a DSRA, which avoids this cash being trapped in the Project Company (but in such cases they cannot have a claim against the Project Company for any drawings on the L/C, as this creates inter-creditor problems—*cf.* §12.6). Another variant on this theme is for the lenders themselves to provide a standby Debt Service Facility in lieu of the DSRA: this can be drawn, and must be paid back, in the same way as drawings on a DSRA.

Some lenders may accept the provision of an Interest Reserve Account only (*i.e.* with a balance equal to the next interest payment due), perhaps coupled with the establishment of a Debt Payment Reserve Account, as below.

Debt Payment Reserve Account. This account may be used to accumulate funds on a month-by-month basis to pay the next instalment of principal and interest, instead of leaving the funds in the Project Company's operating account (usually if the Project Company's revenues flow into one account, instead of being split into Operating and Revenue Accounts as described above). If so, the account is emptied at the end of each payment period to pay the interest and principal instalment then due.

Maintenance Reserve Account ('MRA'). The original purpose of an MRA in project-finance structures was to deal with projects that have a major-maintenance cycle (*e.g.* a power plant that has to be maintained every 5 years, with most of the maintenance costs thus being incurred every 5 years rather than annually); in such cases the MRA smoothes out this maintenance 'spike', and ensures the funds are there when they are needed, by placing one-fifth of the estimated maintenance costs in the MRA every year, and then emptying the account to pay for the maintenance in year 5. This is obviously relevant to PPP projects involving process plant with this kind of maintenance cycle, such as a waste incinerator. It is also relevant to fixed infrastructure projects such as roads, which may have to fund major maintenance such as a resurfacing, say, after 15 years (although in such cases the build-up of the MRA may not be continuous, but begin, say, 5 years before the maintenance work is required), and other projects where lifecycle costs are significant. However, the effect is to add another cost to PPPs compared to public-sector procurement, because in the latter case there would not be a need to accumulate maintenance costs years in advance. There is also a danger that if the Project Company fails it is the lenders who will take the cash in the MRA, so the Public Authority (or users in the case of a Concession) will end up paying twice for the same maintenance; this suggests that the Public Authority should have a prior claim on the MRA in case of default by the Project Company (or its balance should be offset against any Termination Sum).

An MRA is less relevant to accommodation and other projects where Hard FM may fluctuate somewhat from year to year, but does not have the same spike pattern. Some lenders require a 'rolling' MRA in such cases—*e.g.* the MRA should be funded with enough cash to cover the next two years' maintenance (or say 100% of what is required next year, 50% of the following year and 25% of the following year), the amounts required being agreed by the lenders' T/A. This does not remove the long-term risk of such costs being higher than expected (*cf.* §14.8.6) and there is really no reason for cash to be trapped in the Project Company to this extent. The creation of such unnecessary Reserve Accounts reduces the investors' Equity IRR, and so will probably push up the level of the Service Fees.

On the other hand, at the time of a refinancing (*cf.* §16.2), there may be a temptation for the Project Company to persuade new lenders to reduce the balance of the MRA. If the Public Authority has to consent to the refinancing, this is an aspect which should be considered carefully as it may not be in the long-term interests of the project and continuity of service if there is a future maintenance spike.

Tax Reserve Account. If the Project Company incurs a significant tax liability in one year, but does not have to pay the tax until a later year (§10.8.2), a Tax Reserve

Account is normally established to set aside the cash for this purpose. Other 'smoothing' Reserve Accounts of this nature may be established to cover deferred liabilities or irregular costs if they would have a significant effect on the lenders' ADSCR.

Change in Law Reserve Account. The Project Company may have to take the risk of having to fund the cost of certain changes in law (*e.g.* capex to meet new fire-safety requirements); the rôle of a Reserve Account in this situation is discussed in §15.2.5. Again it is preferable not to trap cash in the Project Company for nothing, in the same way as establishing an MRA when there is no maintenance spike.

Insurance Proceeds Account. A separate Reserve Account may be established into which the proceeds of insurance claims are paid, and from which amounts are paid under the lenders' control for restoration of the project or reduction of the debt (*cf.* §12.4.6). Similar accounts may be used for other types of compensation received by the Project Company, such as liquidated damages from the construction contractor (*cf.* §14.7.1). In these accounts, where money has been received for a specific purpose, the cash does not flow through the Cascade, but directly into the account, to be applied on a specifically-agreed basis.

§12.2.5 CONTROLS ON DISTRIBUTIONS TO INVESTORS

The investors come at the bottom of the cash-flow Cascade; once opex, tax, debt-service and Reserve Account requirements have been met, in principle Distributions to investors can be made. If the Project Company cannot immediately pay Distributions over to the investors (*e.g.* because there may be a delay before the annual general meeting can be held and a dividend declared), they are paid into a Shareholder Distribution Account in the name of the Project Company. The lenders may wish to take security over the Distribution Account, along with the other Reserve Accounts, but as the cash in this account is supposed to be out of their control, the case for doing so is not strong. However, this would only make a difference if the Project Company went into default under the loan, at which time the lenders would be able to block payments from the account.

But it is not quite as simple as seeing if there is any cash left at the bottom of the Cascade and just paying it to the investors: there are other hurdles to be jumped. The Project Company obviously has to demonstrate that sufficient cash will remain or be generated in the future to repay debt after the Distributions have been made. This is dealt with by establishing a 'Distribution Block' ratio (also known as a 'Dividend Stop' or 'Lock-Up' ratio); for example if the Base-Case average ADSCR was 1.20:1, Distributions cannot be made if the previous year's actual ADSCR is lower than, say, 1.10:1. The calculation of whether there is sufficient cash to make Distributions is usually carried out on a rolling annual basis once every six months (and hence Distributions can only be made once every six months). If cash flow cannot be distributed because Distribution-Block ratio requirements are not met, any cash available may be used to reduce the debt or held in a special Reserve Account, until the cover-ratio calculations again fall on the right side of the line after allowing for the debt reduction or funds held in the special Reserve Account.

If the Base Case Cover Ratios are low (*e.g.* an ADSCR of 1.15x), and hence close to the Distribution-Block ratio (say an ADSCR of 1.10x), this is quite a dangerous situation for investors. A small drop in cash flow will result in their cash flow being blocked. So while low Cover Ratios are advantageous in winning a bid (*cf.* §10.7), they may not be so advantageous later on.

An issue in calculating the Distribution Block ratio is whether 'forward-looking' ratios (*i.e.* the projected ADSCR for the next year, or the LLCR or average ADSCR as projected for the rest of the loan) should be also used for this purpose. Once the project is operating, the best way of projecting how it will operate in the future is to look at how it has actually operated in the past, so it is the actual ADSCRs achieved that should mainly concern lenders. Especially in a project with a regular assured cash flow under a PPP Contract, it is difficult to conceive why the projections of cash flow for the next year should be much lower than those for the last year (predictable fluctuations, *e.g.* maintenance, should be dealt with using Reserve Accounts). This approach is more relevant to mining or other natural resources projects. Therefore, although beloved by lenders, forward-looking ratios are largely a waste of time in this situation, and doing away with them also eliminates the problem of deciding what assumptions should be used in the financial projections for this purpose. However, if a Project Company is taking usage risk on a Concession, there is more of a case for forward-looking ratios, especially if these are based on future growth in usage.

The Project Company will have to fulfil further requirements before making Distributions, in particular no Event of Default should have occurred under the PPP Contract (*cf.* §15.5) or the financing documentation.

§12.3 SECURITY

Lenders to a Project Company cannot expect to take security over the Facility which is the object of the PPP Contract. Maintenance of the public service has to take priority over any claims by the lenders in this respect—clearly the idea of lenders foreclosing on a public-sector school and selling it would be unacceptable, and selling off a road or a bridge is impossible. Even if they could theoretically be sold, the specialised nature of most PPP assets means that they have little open-market value. And if the Public Authority originally provided an asset to the PPP Contract with a wider market use, such as commercially-zoned land or an office building, this should not form part of the lenders' security unless this can be done without disturbing the Public Authority's own continuing rights.

Therefore lenders in a PPP project-financing can only rely on the cash flow of a successful continuing Project Company for their repayment. However, it remains important for the lenders to hold security to ensure that:

- the lenders are involved at an early stage if the project begins to go wrong;
- the lenders can take over and run the project if necessary;
- third parties (such as unsecured creditors) do not gain any prior or *pari passu* rights over the project assets;
- project assets are not disposed of without the lenders' agreement; and
- lenders can 'encourage' co-operation by the Project Company if it gets into trouble.

The lenders' security normally has four layers:

- control of cash flow, as discussed above;
- security over the Project Company's contracts and financial assets (§12.3.1);
- security over the Project Company's shares (§12.3.2);
- the ability to Step-In to the project under Direct Agreements (§12.3.3).

§12.3.1 SECURITY OVER CONTRACTS AND FINANCIAL ASSETS

In the absence of security over physical assets, lenders will expect a comprehensive package which assigns to them the Project Company's rights over all its major contracts, *e.g.*:

- the PPP Contract;
- Subcontracts, and any bonds or guarantees for these contracts;
- insurances (*cf.* §12.4.5);
- any continuing advisory contracts (*cf.* §7.7).

This implies, *inter alia*, that changes to Project Contracts cannot be made without the lenders' consent. In addition security will be taken over financial assets, *e.g.*:

- pledges over the Project Company's bank accounts, including Reserve Accounts, with dual signatures from the Project Company and the agent bank or security trustee required where lender approval is needed to transfer funds from an account;
- assignment of the Project Company's right to receive payments of equity from the Sponsors;
- assignment of the shareholders' claims under their subordinated loans (*cf.* §7.3.3), if any (to make sure they cannot interfere with enforcement);
- assignment of the Project Company's right to receive any payment due to it if the financial hedging is broken (*cf.* §11.2.3);
- assignment of insurance policies (*cf.* §12.4.5).

Consent to pledges or assignments by the other parties to the relevant agreements will also be necessary, preferably accompanied by Direct Agreements as discussed below.

Depending on the particular legal jurisdiction, there may be problems with security where there are preferential creditors (*e.g.* tax claims with priority over a secured creditor), or high levels of stamp duty or other fees to register security.

§12.3.2 SECURITY OVER THE PROJECT COMPANY'S SHARES

Lenders normally take security over the investors' shares in the Project Company. This is to enable the lenders to take over management of the Project Company more quickly than may be achieved by taking action under contract assignments.

There may be some difficulties with this in some legal jurisdictions where the procedures for enforcing security may be too cumbersome for lenders who want to be able to take over control of the project quickly, especially if lenders are required to sell the assets in a public auction or after a court action rather than take over their control and operation immediately through an administrator or receiver. On the other hand, this may be the only way in which the lenders can take over management of the Project Company in some countries, as local bankruptcy laws (such as, see Chapter 11, in the United States) may prevent them from doing so *via* their security over the Project Company's assets.

An investor's corporate lenders may have imposed 'negative pledge' provisions, under which the investor is not to give security over its assets to any third party, which would prevent a pledge being given over their holding of Project Company's shares. It is preferable for the investor to negotiate a waiver of this provision in the case of its Project Company shares.

It is fairly common for the Project Company to be owned by an intermediary holding company (*cf.* §7.6.1), whose shares are owned by the investors and then pledged to the lenders. Reasons for this include:

- Lenders will wish to ensure that the Project Company is not affected by one of its investors getting into financial difficulties (*i.e.* it is 'bankruptcy remote'). For example, if an investor is made insolvent this should not result in its Project Company subsidiary or affiliate being made insolvent as well, or remove the benefit of a pledge of the Project Company's shares. An intermediary holding company between the investors and the Project Company reduces this risk.
- The holding-company structure may also give the lenders greater control in the case of insolvency of the Project Company itself.
- There may be tax advantages to the structure.
- If the lenders are also investors in the Project Company, they may not wish to have it as a direct subsidiary or affiliate in case there is adverse publicity if something goes wrong with the project.

§12.3.3 DIRECT AGREEMENTS

The Public Authority and other key Project Contract counterparties are all normally required to sign Direct Agreements (also known as Tripartite Deeds) with the lenders (to which the Project Company may also be a party). These are also known as 'acknowledgments and consents', since they acknowledge the position of the lenders, and consent to them taking an assignment of the contracts as security. This may not be strictly necessary in legal systems which allow a contract to have a *stipulatio altri* (provisions for the benefit of a third party), but in view of their complexity it is still probably easier to use a separate agreement.

The PPP Contract Direct Agreement will normally constitute the only legal link between the Public Authority and the lenders, and is therefore probably the most important of these documents. Under this Agreement the Public Authority:

- acknowledges the lenders' security interest in the PPP Contract;
- agrees to make payments to a specific Project Account or as notified by the lenders;
- agrees that amendments will not be made to the PPP Contract without the lenders' consent;
- gives the lenders various rights to intervene if the Project Company is in default (*cf.* §15.4.2);

- may agree that if the lenders enforce their security, the PPP Contract will automatically be terminated, thus ensuring the Termination Sum is paid (*cf.* §15.5). (In return, the Public Authority may also want the right to terminate the Project Agreement immediately if the lenders cease to make funds available for construction of the project.)

The Public Authority may be reluctant to sign such a Direct Agreement, on the grounds that the lenders should not have any extra rights which are not in the PPP Contract. It could be also argued that the practical value to the lenders of many of the provisions of such a Direct Agreement is questionable. In practice, if a project is going wrong all parties have to sit around the table and try to find a solution, whether there is a Direct Agreement or not. However, from the lenders' point of view the PPP Contract is the most important part of their security, and a Direct Agreement may help them to step rapidly into the picture after a Project Company default to preserve the position, and find another party to take over responsibility for the project. Given that protection of the public service must be the first priority for the Public Authority, a Direct Agreement is itself an effective way of helping to ensure this.

Similar Direct Agreements are signed with, for example, the Construction Subcontractor, which will ensure that if the Project Company gets into trouble during the construction phase, the lenders can take over and complete the project on the basis of the original Construction Subcontract.

The lenders may also obtain collateral warranties with respect to construction or operation of the project from, *e.g.* from the Construction Subcontractor, under which direct liability is accepted (to the extent agreed in the relevant contract with the Project Company) *vis-à-vis* the lenders.

§12.4 THE RÔLE OF INSURANCE

As discussed below (*cf.* §15.7), *Force Majeure* risks which can be managed by insurance (*e.g.* natural disasters such as fire or flood) are generally left with the Project Company, and it is up to the latter to arrange insurance cover for these risks. With very limited exceptions, all risks of physical damage (or economic loss arising from this) which cannot be passed to Subcontractors or the Public Authority (*cf.* §15.2.4) should be thus covered by insurance.

Public Authorities often rely on self-insurance rather than commercial insurance. This offers better VfM in cases where the portfolio of assets is large and varied enough to spread the risks widely. In a limited number of cases it may make sense to bring the Project Company under that umbrella, *i.e.* for the Public Authority to take on liabilities for losses which would otherwise be insured, especially where, for whatever reason, obtaining commercial insurance is difficult, but in the overall context of transfer of risks to the private sector, this approach is generally not desirable. However, the Public Authority may give some protection against specified risks becoming uninsurable (*cf.* §12.4.6), and against third-party claims (*cf.* §15.2.4).

As the Project Company has no free resources with which to cover the possibility of an insurable risk interrupting the service under the PPP Contract, the Public Authority will want to ensure that there is adequate insurance to cover any damage to the Facility, and so ensure continuity of service. It is prudent for the Public Authority to specify in the PPP Contract the minimum levels of insurance cover which the Project Company will be required to obtain under the various headings set out below, since these insurances are indirectly for its protection and security. Similarly, some minimum credit standard for the insurers is also desirable.

The insurances are arranged in two phases: first, the insurances covering the whole of the construction phase of the project (§12.4.2), and second, insurances when the project is in operation (§12.4.3), which are usually renewed annually.

In addition, non-project specific insurances required by law, such as employer's liability, vehicle insurances, *etc.,* may also be required.

§12.4.1 INSURANCE BROKERS AND ADVISERS

When bidding for a PPP project's development, the Sponsors need to appoint an insurance broker with specific experience in insurance for project finance to advise on insurance costs, and eventually place the insurance programme for the Project Company. Brokers are often paid a percentage of the insurance premiums, but this is obviously not an incentive to keep premiums down, and it is preferable to negotiate a fixed fee for this work.

The Project Company's broker also plays an important rôle in communicating information about the project to the insurer, which is important in jurisdictions where insurance is an *uberrimæ fidei* ('of the utmost good faith') contract; in such cases, if any material information is not disclosed to the insurer there is no obligation to pay under the policy (*cf.* comments on non-vitiation cover in §12.4.5). The broker must therefore work with the Project Company and the Sponsors to ensure that this does not happen.

Insurances form a key element of the lenders' security, but the Public Authority should not rely on the lenders and their insurance adviser (*cf.* §9.3.4)—the lenders are primarily concerned about protecting their loan, while the Public Authority is primarily concerned about protecting the public service. Therefore the Public Authority will need its own insurance advisers to review and agree the insurance programme (*cf.* §6.7.4). Having said this, however, the lenders' and the Public Authority's objectives are not incompatible, and indeed have much in common.

§12.4.2 CONSTRUCTION-PHASE INSURANCES

In construction contracts that are not being project-financed, it is common for the contractor to arrange the main insurances for the construction phase of the project and to include this as part of the contract price. This is logical, because under a standard construction contract the contractor is at risk of loss from insurable events; if part of the project is destroyed in a fire during construction, the contractor is required to replace it, whether it is insured or not. However, contractor-arranged insurance is not always suitable in project finance for several reasons:

- As will be seen below, lenders require Delay in Start-Up ('DSU') insurance, which cannot easily be obtained by a Construction Subcontractor, who is not at risk of loss

in this respect. If the Project Company takes out a separate insurance for this purpose, there is a risk that the two policies will not match properly.
- It is quite common in project finance to arrange insurance for the first year of operation as part of the package of construction-phase insurances, to ensure that there are no problems of transition between the two phases; again this could not be done in the name of the Construction Subcontractor.
- Lenders wish to exercise a close control on the terms of the insurance and on any claims, working through the Project Company, rather than through the Construction Subcontractor.
- There are a number of specific lender requirements on insurance policies that may be difficult to accommodate if the policy is not in the Project Company's name (*cf.* §12.4.5).
- Lenders normally control application of the insurance proceeds (*cf.* §12.4.6).

Construction Subcontractor-sourced insurance may appear cheaper, but this is usually because the coverage is less comprehensive than that required by lenders. However, the Construction Subcontractor will be a beneficiary of the Project Company's cover.

The main insurances required for the construction phase of a project are:

Contractor's All Risks ('CAR'), also known as 'Builder's All Risks' (or Construction and Erection All Risks ('CEAR') for an EPC Contract). This covers physical loss or damage to works, materials, and equipment at the project site. The level of coverage is normally on a replacement-cost basis. Insured events include most *Force Majeure* risks, such as acts of war, fire, and natural disaster, as well as damage caused by defective design, material, or workmanship.

The main exception for the requirement for replacement-cost coverage is if it is inconceivable that the whole construction site could be destroyed at once (*e.g.* a road or a long pipeline). In such cases 'first loss' cover may be effected—a level of coverage sufficient to cover the largest possible individual loss which could occur.

Third-Party Liability, also known as Public Liability. This is usually bundled up with CAR and covers all those involved in the project from third-party damage claims. As this insurance is relatively inexpensive, the levels of coverage are usually high.

Delay in Start-Up (DSU), also known as Advance Loss of Profits (ALOP). This compensates the Project Company for loss of profit or additional costs (or at least the cost of the debt interest and fixed operating costs, plus any penalties payable for late completion of the project) resulting from a delay in start of operations of the project caused by a loss insured under the CAR policy. The DSU coverage pays an agreed amount per day of delay, for an agreed maximum period of time. The level of coverage should be sufficient to deal with the longest-possible delay caused by loss or damage to a crucial element of the project at the worst-possible time. It has to be issued by the same insurer as the CAR policy, because the losses on the two are linked—*e.g.* the insurer may agree to pay more to have the damage repaired faster (or, say, a spare part flown in instead of being sent by sea), to reduce the payment on the DSU policy.

DSU cover is expensive—roughly speaking it may double the cost of the construction-phase insurances, and may be the most difficult area to agree between the parties. Lenders will want a high level of cover, which the Sponsors may resist on cost grounds.

Theoretically Public Authority does not need to specify DSU as a required insurance under the PPP Contract, since loss of revenue by the Project Company, as opposed to physical restoration of the Facility, is of no relevance from its point of view, but may have to take it into account if inability to obtain insurance, including DSU, is a *Force Majeure* event under the PPP Contract (*cf.* §12.4.8).

Force Majeure. The cover provided by *Force Majeure* insurance (N.B.: not directly-related to the definition of *Force Majeure* under the PPP Contract—*cf.* §15.7) is to enable the Project Company to pay its debt-service obligations if the Facility is completed late or abandoned following *Force Majeure* events that do not cause direct damage to the Facility (which should be covered by DSU) such as:

- natural *Force Majeure* events away from the project site, including damage in transit and at a supplier's premises (to the extent this is not covered under the DSU insurances);
- strikes, *etc.*, but not between the Project Company and its employees;
- any other cause beyond the control of any project participants (*e.g.* damage affecting third party connections), but not including a loss caused by financial default or insolvency.

In effect, *Force Majeure* insurance may be used to cover any significant gaps in the DSU cover.

Insurance may also be available to cover the risk of finding hidden pollution or hazardous waste on the construction site (*cf.* §14.5.4). 'Efficacy' insurance, which covers the Construction Subcontractor's liability to pay LDs for poor performance on completion (*cf.* §14.7.4) may also be taken out.

12.4.3 OPERATION-PHASE INSURANCES

The operation-phase insurance cover is similar in nature to that for the construction phase:

All Risks. Covers the project against physical damage. The level of coverage is normally the replacement cost of the Facility. This coverage may be split into Property (or Material Damage) insurance and Machinery Breakdown (also known as Boiler & Machinery) insurance in the case of process plant.

Third-Party Liability. Similar to the coverage during the construction phase. However this risk may be retained by the Public Authority where it offers better VfM to do so (*cf.* §15.2.4).

Business Interruption ('BI'). This is the equivalent of DSU insurance for the operation phase (and therefore also has to be provided by the same insurer as for the All Risks cover). Again, the scale of coverage should be sufficient to cover losses (or at least interest, any penalties, and fixed operating costs) during the maximum period of interruption that could be caused by having to replace a key physical element of the project. As with the DSU insurance negotiations on the level of cover may be difficult, and the same questions arise as to how far the Public Authority should impose any requirements for, or accept any risk of failure to obtain, BI insurance.

Contingent BI (also known as BI Supplier's or Customer's Extension). This is the equivalent of *Force Majeure* insurance for the operation phase, and covers the Project Company against *Force Majeure* events affecting a third-party's site which have a knock-on effect on the Project Company.

A Public Authority may not consider it necessary or feasible for some PPP projects (*e.g.* road and transportation projects where the Facility is on a large scale) to take out operating insurances for physical damage through the Project Company. In such cases the Public Authority continues to be responsible for any physical damage (but not BI) insurance or for providing the Project Company with compensation for losses from physical damage that would otherwise be insured.

It should be noted that the operation-phase insurances (other than perhaps the first year) cannot be arranged or their premiums fixed in advance; the risks relating to this are discussed below.

§12.4.4 DEDUCTIBLES

All these insurances are subject to deductibles (*i.e.* the loss to be borne by the Project Company before payments are made under the insurance cover). There is a simple trade-off—the higher the deductibles, the lower the cost of the insurance. The Project Company may try to make the deductibles relatively large. The Construction Subcontractor will try to make the CAR deductibles as low as possible, to limit liability for such uninsured losses. The lenders will also try to keep all deductibles low to reduce their risk. Insofar as lower deductibles increase the cost of the insurances, which feeds through to the level of Service Fees, the Public Authority has to strike a balance between increased cost and increased risk, and therefore straddles the positions of the Project Company and the lenders in this respect.

§12.4.5 INSURANCE PREMIUM COST RISK

Insurance costs have increased rapidly in recent years, and some older Project Companies have suffered as a result of premiums being much higher than expected. Insurance premiums may be one of the largest single cost risks left with the Project Company after other risks have been passed down to Subcontractors. If bidders are only prepared to take the risk of large (above-inflation) increases in operation-phase insurance costs by building in large contingencies into their bids, it may be better VfM for this risk to be shared with the Public Authority. If so:

- A band can be set for insurance-cost increases and decreases within which the Project Company bears the risks of increases or receives the benefits of reductions and thereafter these are transferred. However, a sliding scale whereby as the increases (or decreases) in insurance premiums become greater the Public Authority pays (or gets) a larger share is preferable as this incentivises the Project Company to continue controlling costs, *e.g.* by increasing deductibles.

- Any premium cost increases related to the claims record of the Project Company itself should be excluded from any risk-sharing formula.
- These premium risk-sharing arrangements should only relate to insurances for physical damage, and possibly BI. Although the Public Authority does not benefit from the latter, it will make up a significant part of the total insurance premiums, and again a large contingency against BI cost increases may not be good VfM for the Public Authority.

§12.4.6 UNINSURABILITY

It may no longer be possible to obtain one or more of the insurances which the Public Authority agreed were requirements for the Project Company, the cost of such insurances may have become so high that it is no longer viable to pay the premiums, or new restrictions on the terms for, or the scope of, cover may be imposed. The issue may be peculiar to particular sectors—*e.g.* prisons are one type of PPP where there have been temporary problems of this nature—or result from more general problems in the insurance market, *e.g.* unavailability of cover for terrorism.

In such cases the Public Authority may be prepared to indemnify the Project Company from carrying on without the required insurances, *i.e.* primarily those for physical damage and third-party liability (the lenders will press for BI cover as well, but the case for the Public Authority taking on these is not so strong as any benefit it receives is only indirect— the argument here is the same as for the risk of insurance-premium cost increases discussed above). If so, the project can continue on that basis, but if the Public Authority does not wish to do this, the PPP Contract may be terminated for *Force Majeure* (*cf.* §15.7). If the Public Authority does cover the uninsurable risks, there should be a deduction from the Service Fees equivalent to the saving in premiums (measured against the Base Case).

It is quite difficult to define uninsurability exactly—clearly if the insurance is not available at all then a risk is uninsurable, but, for example, does a large increase in deductibles result in the Facility being uninsurable? Or at what point does an increase in premiums become so high that it is no longer viable to insure (especially if there are premium risk-sharing arrangements such as those described above)? The only real way to tell that a risk is uninsurable is if other parties operating similar Facilities have ceased to insure—but these Facilities may be public-sector operated rather than PPPs and thus may self-insure anyway.

Uninsurability provisions transfer the risk back to the Public Authority just at the time when—presumably—the insurance market thinks the risk is very high, and therefore the triggers for them need to be carefully limited.

§12.4.7 CONTROL OF INSURANCE PROCEEDS

The lenders may wish to have the option of using the proceeds of an insurance claim for physical damage to repay their debt rather than restore the Facility—the so-called 'head for the hills' option. This is unlikely to be realistic:

- Even a Facility on one site is unlikely to be a total loss, and it is evident that will not be the case for a Facility on several sites, or a linear project such as a road: in such cases, the insurance claim would normally not be enough to repay all the debt unless it came at a late stage in the project life.

- The insurer may require restoration of the Facility as a condition for paying out under the claim.
- The purpose of DSU/BI insurances is precisely to cover the situation where physical damage has occurred and the Facility is being rebuilt, so it is perverse if lenders ask for DSU/BI cover but still want to walk away.
- The Public Authority will normally also wish to ensure that insurance proceeds are applied to restoration of the Facility, rather than used to reduce debt.

Nonetheless, the lenders may be given this right if it can be shown that the Facility would no longer be economically viable after the restoration works. (The meaning of economic viability may be a matter of much negotiation, but the most obvious test is one relating to the remaining LLCR.) In any case the lenders generally supervise how the insurance proceeds are disbursed (*cf.* §12.2.4), although the Public Authority may also be involved in this process.

In principle any payment covering loss of revenue (*i.e.* claims on DSU or BI policies) is controlled by the lenders in the same way as they control the application of the general revenues of the Project Company, *i.e.* it is fed in to the cash-flow Cascade and the Public Authority has no claim or control over such payments. However, the Public Authority may wish to reinforce the Cascade structure by specifically requiring that these proceeds are used to keep the Facility operating (if this is possible) in priority to debt service, and that Distributions should not be made to investors from these funds. It should also be noted that claims can only be made under these policies if the insurer is satisfied that efforts are actually being made to restart the business: the Public Authority's speed of response to plans for restoration of the Facility is therefore important.

Third-party liability payments are usually paid directly to the claimant; the Public Authority may wish to control the litigation on any third-party liability claim if it could form a precedent for similar claims relating to public facilities which are not in the PPP—this will require negotiation with the insurer, who normally controls such litigation.

§12.4.8 LENDERS' REQUIREMENTS

As the insurance forms an important part of the lenders' security package, the detailed terms of the policies and the insurer's credit standing must be acceptable to them. The Public Authority's requirements for the protection of its interests are similar. There are also a number of specific requirements that lenders require to be included in insurance policies to ensure that they are properly protected (known as 'banker's clauses'):

Additional insured. The lenders' agent bank or security trustee is named as an additional insured (or co-insured) party on the policies. As an additional insured party, the lenders are treated as if they were separately covered under the insurance policy, but have no obligations under the policy (*e.g.* to pay premiums). Other parties with an interest in the project such as the Construction Subcontractor and the Public Authority may also be named as additional insured. If this is not possible, the lenders' interests should be 'noted', on the insurance policy, preferably with a loss-payable clause, as below.

Severability. The policies are stated to operate as providing separate insurances for each of the insured parties.

Changes in and cancellation of the policy. The insurer is required to give the lenders prior notice of any proposed cancellation of, or material change proposed in, the policies, and agrees that the policies cannot be amended without the lenders' consent. (The Public Authority may be given similar rights.)

Non-payment of premiums. The insurer agrees to give the lenders notice of any non-payment of a premium. As additional insured, the lenders have the option, but not the obligation, to pay premiums if these are not paid by the Project Company (and again these rights may apply to the Public Authority).

Loss payee. The lenders' agent bank or security trustee is named as sole loss payee on policies covering loss or damage (or sole loss payee for amounts above an agreed figure, with smaller amounts payable to the Project Company)—this is known as a 'loss-payable' clause. (However, payments for third-party liability are made direct to the affected party.) This may also give the lenders the right to take action directly against the insurer in some jurisdictions, but in any case assignment of the insurance policies forms part of the lenders' security package.

Waiver of subrogation. The insurer waives the right of subrogation against the lenders; in general insurance law an insurer who makes payment under a policy claim may be entitled to any share in a later recovery that is made by the lenders; such a repayment to the insurer is not acceptable to the lenders until the debt is fully repaid.

Non-vitiation. Lenders prefer to have a non-vitiation clause (also known as a 'breach of provision' or 'breach of warranty' clause) included in the insurance policies, which provides that even if another insured party does something to vitiate (*i.e.* invalidate) the insurances (*e.g.* failure to disclose material information), the lenders' coverage will not be affected. This can be a very difficult area to negotiate with the insurer, as it may add to their potential liability in a way that is not usual. In fact, in tighter insurance market conditions, it may not be possible to get the insurer to agree, and in such circumstances—if their insurance adviser advises there is no choice—lenders have to live without it.

It is sometimes possible to obtain separate coverage for this risk, and in some jurisdictions it may be dealt with by naming the lenders as additional insured parties and including a severability clause, thus giving lenders their own direct rights that cannot be affected by the actions of others.

§12.5 EVENTS OF DEFAULT

Project-finance lenders do not want to have wait to take action until the Project Company has run out of funds to service the debt; they therefore create a defined set of triggers which give them the right to take action against the Project Company. These are 'Events of Default'. Once an Event of Default has occurred, the Project Company is no longer able to manage the project without lender involvement. It should be noted that these events do not of themselves put the project in default (*i.e.* bring the financing to an end and allowing the lenders to enforce their security): a positive decision to take this next stage of action has to be made by the lenders after the Event of Default has occurred. The threat of moving to this next stage gives the lenders a lever to ensure that they can sit at the table with the Project Company, Subcontractors and the Public Authority to find a way out of the problem, which either exists already, or is indicated by the trigger events to be on the horizon.

Some of these events (such as failure to pay, insolvency, *etc.*) would apply to any corporate financing, but others are peculiar to project finance, *e.g.*:

- cost overruns, or delays in completing the project (beyond a back stop date);
- failure to complete the project, or any other default under the PPP Contract;
- ADSCR falls below a certain level; thus the initial Base Case average ADSCR might be 1.20:1, the Distribution Block level (*cf.* §12.2.5) 1.10:1, and this 'Default Ratio' level 1.05:1; as with Distribution Blocks, there is the issue of whether forward-looking ratios should be used in this context;
- a similar drop in LLCR, which means that the Project Company's ability to pay the debt off over its remaining life is serious jeopardised.

Various courses of action are open to the lenders after an Event of Default, partly depending on what stage the project has reached:

- to waive (*i.e.* ignore) the Event of Default;
- if the project is still under construction, to impose a Drawstop;
- if the project is in the operating phase, to require that all net cash flow be applied to reduction of debt or held in a separate reserve or escrow account under the lenders' control, rather than distributed to investors; or
- to enforce the lenders' security.

Once the Event of Default has occurred it is entirely within the lenders' discretion which of these actions they choose to take. The Project Company may also ask the lenders to waive or amend a particular term of the financing documentation so it does not fall into default in the first place.

If there is a syndicate of banks or a group of bond holders providing the loan, there has to be a decision-making process, or one rogue lender could pull the house down by taking individual action against the Project Company while the rest are trying to find a solution. (Indeed, it is not unknown for a small lender to blackmail the larger ones by threatening to do this, so that the larger lenders will buy out the smaller lender's loan.) The agent bank or security trustee also needs to have clear instructions from the lenders as a whole on what action is to be taken on their behalf. Voting mechanisms therefore have to be agreed to in advance between lenders; the Project Company also has an interest in these arrangements, to try to ensure that one or two 'hostile' lenders cannot dictate the action taken, against the wishes of the majority.

§12.6 INTERCREDITOR ISSUES

If there is only one lender, or group of lenders in a syndicate, the situation is quite straightforward—these lenders will hold their security and claims on the Project Company through their agent bank (or trustee), take decisions collectively as discussed above, and the Project Company will also deal with them as necessary through their agent or trustee. Between themselves, the lenders have a vote on decisions proportionate to their loan amount. However it is seldom quite as simple as this, and if there are different groups of lenders, or Senior Lenders and lower-ranking lenders, or other parties with financial claims such as swap providers, some complex negotiations may result. Although the Project Company may not be a direct party to these intercreditor arrangements, it has a strong interest in ensuring that they are practical and workable, and should therefore be aware of such issues when considering the basic financial viability of a bid.

Each of the lending groups will have its own loan or other financing documentation with the Project Company, but they also need to establish machinery for working together, or the Project Company will soon find itself like a bone between two dogs, with the project in pieces after being pulled in different directions. This is usually done through a Common Terms Agreement, under which, apart from sharing security, the parties agree on a common approach, *e.g.* to the cash-flow Cascade (*cf.* §12.2.3), and to voting on amendments and waivers to the loan documentation or on agreeing changes to the Project Contracts.

As discussed below, particular classes of financial claim can raise various issues.

§12.6.1 INTEREST-RATE SWAP PROVIDERS

If an interest-rate swap is provided *pro rata* by all the banks in a lending syndicate there is obviously no need for any special intercreditor arrangements to take account of this, but if—as is commonly the case—the swap is being provided by just one or two banks (either for their own account or acting as a fronting bank as discussed in §11.2.8), their voting rights and share in security *vis-à-vis* the rest of the syndicate need to be considered. Because their breakage costs at any one time cannot be predicted (and may be zero if rates move the right way), the extent of their risk—if any—on a default by the Project Company cannot be fixed in advance. Theoretically the swap provider would wish to have a vote in the syndicate equal to whatever proportion the breakage cost at the time of the vote bears to the rest of the debt: this uncertainty is usually not acceptable to the other lenders. The end result is often that:

- the swap provider does not take part in voting on waivers and amendments (the swap provider is usually also a lending bank and thus still has a voice that can be heard in this way);
- the swap provider may only terminate the swap independently if the Project Company is in default under a limited number of categories (such as non-payment and insolvency); and
- once the claim has been crystallised by termination of the swap, the swap provider's vote on enforcement is also fixed *pro rata* to this.

This explains why swap quotations direct from the market are not usually feasible—a swap provider who is not also a lender to the Project Company cannot easily be fitted into the control and security structure—hence another way has to be found to introduce competition for swap pricing (*cf.* §11.2.8).

However the voting rights are structured, the swap provider shares *pro rata* in any enforcement proceeds based on the crystallised breakage cost.

§12.6.2 FIXED-RATE LENDERS

Fixed-rate lenders are in a similar position to interest-swap providers when a default takes place: they may also have a breakage cost. This does not normally give them any extra voting rights, but is taken into account in determining their *pro rata* share of any enforcement proceeds.

A problem may arise, however, if the fixed-rate lender has a make-whole clause (*cf.* §11.2.12), and other floating rate lenders do not. This may lead to a large discrepancy in the relative size of the claim that the different groups of lenders have on a default in relation to their actual loan outstanding.

§12.6.3 INFLATION-INDEXED LOANS OR SWAPS

This problem become more acute if one group of lenders has an indexed-linked loan or inflation swap, and the other does not. The discrepancy between relative loan outstandings and actual claims can become much greater in such cases (*cf.* §11.3.8, §11.3.9), and so it is quite difficult to structure a financing with both inflation-indexed and fixed-rate finance from different groups of lenders.

§12.6.4 MEZZANINE LENDERS

Mezzanine debt may be provided by third parties unconnected with the Sponsors or other investors (*cf.* §9.6), usually secured by a second mortgage or junior position on the Senior Lenders' security. This raises a number of difficult inter-creditor issues:

Drawing priority. Senior Lenders may wish mezzanine loans to be drawn first by the Project Company, in a similar way to equity funding; but if funding is being drawn on a *pro rata* basis, Senior Lenders will want there to be only very limited conditions precedent to the mezzanine lenders' funding, to ensure they cannot exercise an independent Drawstop (*cf.* §12.2.2).

Cashflow Cascade. In principle mezzanine lenders are placed in the cash flow Cascade above Distributions to investors, and so are repaid if sufficient cash flow is available after senior debt service payments have been made. But do the Senior Lenders' DSRA, MRA or other Reserve Accounts have to be filled up before mezzanine lenders can be paid, and can payments to mezzanine lenders be blocked in a similar way to Distributions to investors (*cf.* §12.2.5)?

Default and enforcement. Mezzanine lenders accept that if the financing package as a whole is in default, and enforcement action is taken, they will only be repaid if the Senior Lenders are fully repaid. But Senior Lenders will be concerned about 'Samson in the temple' behaviour by mezzanine lenders—if the project goes wrong and there is only enough money to repay the Senior Lenders, the mezzanine lenders have nothing to lose so they can threaten to pull the whole project to pieces unless the Senior Lenders share some of the value that their loans still have. Therefore

Senior Lenders restrict the rights of mezzanine lenders in a number of ways to try to avoid this happening:

- Senior Lenders want freedom to make amendments to their loan terms, including the repayment schedule and interest rate, and the ability to increase the amount of senior debt if the project gets into trouble. Obviously this may make the mezzanine lenders' position worse: a compromise may be to limit the amount of extra debt or other costs that can be added on to the senior debt at various points in the project life.
- Any amendments to the Project Contracts require Senior Lenders' consent; they normally require freedom to allow such amendments without interference by mezzanine lenders, unless the result is to increase the senior debt amount, as discussed above.
- Mezzanine lenders want to have the right to take enforcement action if they are not paid when due. It is difficult for Senior Lenders to exclude the mezzanine lenders completely from taking action; a common compromise is to require the mezzanine lenders to wait, say, six months after a payment default before they can take action (and of course such action will trigger action by the Senior Lenders, so ensuring that any enforcement proceeds still accrue to them first).

§12.6.5 SUBORDINATED LENDERS

The position of subordinated lenders, *i.e.* on a loan provided by investors as an alternative way of investing their equity into the Project Company (*cf.* §7.3.3), is quite different to that of mezzanine lenders. The investors cannot expect to get any rights which they would not otherwise have had, just because of the form in which they make their investment.

The Senior Lenders will therefore require them to agree that they have no security rights and cannot take any independent enforcement action to recover their debt, or otherwise obstruct the Senior Lenders, until all the Senior Lenders' debt has been fully repaid.

Chapter 13

Service-Fee Mechanism

§13.1 INTRODUCTION

This chapter considers issues relevant to the Service-Fee mechanism:

- scope of services (§13.2);
- Service-Fee payment structure (§13.3);
- structuring Service Fees based on:
  - usage/demand (§13.4);
  - Availability/service (§13.5); or
  - mixed usage and Availability (§13.6);
- dealing with third-party revenues (§13.7).

§13.2 CONTRACT SCOPE

A preliminary issue, before considering various Service Fee mechanisms in more detail, is what should be included within the scope of a PPP Contract anyway? There is a fundamental difference between projects such as roads, where most if not all the services (such as accident recovery, repair and maintenance) are normally included within the scope of a PPP Contract, and projects such as hospitals, where there is a considerable variation in the possible scope of services (for example it obviously makes a substantial difference to the PPP Contract whether or not medical equipment or clinical services are included).

The argument for the 'whole-life' benefit of an integrated approach to a PPP bid has been set out above (*cf.* §2.8), but questions can be raised:

- How does a Public Authority deal with the situation where a bid consortium has strong and weak members, *e.g.* a good Construction Subcontractor, but a poor FM services provider, or a good financial package but a poor Construction Subcontract?

- Should design always be left to the bidders (*cf.* §6.6.1, §14.7.3)? It is arguable that in case of a straightforward project where there is little scope for innovation (*cf.* §2.9.5), the Public Authority is in as good a position as any bidder to prepare the design, which would make the bidding process quicker and cheaper. Bidders can of course suggest improvements. (This approach was adopted, for example, for Chilean toll roads—see Bibliography.)
- Should finance be left to the bidders? Funding.competitions (*cf.* §16.2) effectively separate finance out at the bid stage, and debt finance can even be provided by the public sector and so removed from the bid package completely (*cf.* §17.4)—this again raises the issue of whether the rôle of 'financial facilitators' is helpful to the PPP market (*cf.* §7.2.1).
- Should Soft FM services be included in the scope of the PPP contract?

The most common of these 'unbundling' questions probably relates to Soft FM services. As discussed above, two types of service may be included within the scope of a PPP Contract—Hard FM, *i.e.* routine maintenance of buildings and equipment, and Soft FM, *e.g.* cleaning, catering, security, *etc.* Hard FM is an inherent part of a PPP Contract, since the whole basis of the Contract is the provision of the Facility in 'working order' throughout the terms of the PPP Contract. The provision of Soft FM services is less intrinsically embedded in a PPP Contract. The arguments for including Soft FM are:

- Bidders will take account of Soft FM requirements when bidding for and designing the Facility (*cf.* §2.8).
- It removes the interface risk—*e.g.* the Project Company will not have the excuse that a failure of Availability was actually caused by Soft FM providers not involved in the PPP Contract.
- It gives the Public Authority a one-stop point of contact for all service issues on the Facility.

Balanced against this:

- The level of payment deductions which can be made for poor service (*cf.* §13.5.2) is limited, since the level of fees paid for soft services is such that the Soft FM Subcontractor cannot realistically be expected to take on responsibility for disproportionate financial consequences for failure to perform. For example, penalties may be a maximum of one year's fees under the FM Subcontract.
- It is precisely these Soft FM services which are at the front end of the Facility's interface with the users and general public, and where failure has a disproportionate effect on support for PPP projects in general.
- These services also tend to employ the most staff, and therefore raise the most difficult issues relating to transfers of staff from the public sector (*cf.* §2.13).
- The Public Authority's soft-service requirements may change substantially over the life of a PPP Contract, and therefore a very long-term Soft FM Subcontract is too rigid for this purpose.
- Soft FM service providers are reluctant to sign very long-term Subcontracts because of the difficulty of predicting their own costs.

- If there are provisions for benchmarking or market testing (*cf.* §11.3.13), these really divorce the Soft FM Subcontract from the rest of the PPP Contract and further weaken the case for its inclusion.

Exclusion of Soft FM services from the PPP Contract does not mean they cannot be provided by the private sector, as they can still be provided under an entirely separate contract on an out-sourced basis (*cf.* §1.5). If Soft FM is not included, specifying service quality is likely to be less complex, since it will relate primarily to maintenance. So where a relatively straightfor-ward building project is involved, the case for including Soft FM services within the scope of a PPP Contract is not strong, and a Public Authority will probably benefit from the greater flexibility of dealing separately with these services. However, if the Facility is complex, then there may be benefits in transferring all of the FM interface risk to the private sector.

To take the 'unbundling' argument to its logical conclusion, a Public Authority could set up its own Project Company, and then procure each of the Subcontracting elements and the financing separately, a point discussed in §17.2.2.

§13.3 PAYMENT STRUCTURE

The basis for building up the basic Service Fee schedule, and the levels of the payments, has been discussed in §10.7. In summary, the revenue stream—whatever the type of PPP Contract—must be sufficient to cover:

- opex;
- debt service, plus the lenders' required Cover Ratios; and
- equity return.

This is a function of the PPP Contract term (§13.3.1) and payment profile (§13.3.2). Inflation must also be taken into account, as relevant, when structuring Service-Fee revenues and projecting costs (*cf.* §11.3).

The Service-Fee provisions also have to take into account:

- revenue during construction (§13.3.3);
- the effect of a delay in completion (§13.3.4);
- capex contributions by the Public Authority (§13.3.5);
- capex payments to the Public Authority (§13.3.6); and
- revenue payments to the Public Authority (§13.3.7).

§13.3.1 Contract Term

Arithmetically speaking, the longer a PPP Contract lasts, the lower the level of Service Fees and so if the Public Authority wants to keep the Service Fees as low as possible, the PPP Contract should be signed for as long a term as possible. For example, if a project costing 1,000 is financed at an overall cost of 8% *p.a.* over 15 years, the annual payments to provide this return will be 117, but over 30 years the annual payments will be 89. However, it should be borne in mind that the longer the term of the PPP Contract, the longer the period of the private-sector financing at a comparatively high cost, and therefore any annual 'saving' derived from lengthening the PPP Contract period is an illusion. In the example just given, total (undiscounted) payments over 15 years are 1,752, while over 30 years they are 2,665—*i.e.* the cost of paying for the project over another 15 years is over 50% higher.

The natural limit for a PPP Contract period is the life of the Facility which is the object of the Contract, but a road, for example, really has no natural life, as it is continually being renewed with maintenance, and a building such as a school has no obvious or predictable end to its life. So the effective life of the Facility is often of limited relevance. Conversely, if the Facility has a very short life (*e.g.* because it is technology-related) a PPP is not likely to be appropriate anyway (*cf.* §2.12). Therefore the main factors which need to be taken in to account in considering the appropriate term for a PPP Contract are:

- *Affordability*: if the PPP Contract term is too short the Service Fees may be too high to be affordable either by end-users in the case of a Concession, or by the Public Authority in the case of a PFI-Model project;
- *whole-life benefits*: if the PPP Contract term is too short, the benefits from whole-life design and costing from the initial bids (*cf.* §2.8) will not be achieved;
- *lenders' term*: the length of the repayment term lenders are willing to offer (*cf.* §10.5.1) may set a maximum length on the PPP Contract term, since it is not financially efficient to have a long Tail period after the debt is repaid (*cf.* §10.5.4);
- *the absolute financial benefit from extending the term*: *e.g.* in the example above, extending the term from 15 to 30 years cuts the annual payments from the public budget from 117 to 89, albeit increasing the total amount of the payments; if the term were increased to 35 years the annual payment would be 85—*i.e.* the marginal benefit of each increase in the term, in terms of lower annual payments, gets smaller and smaller;
- *long-term flexibility* (*cf.* §2.12): this is probably the most important limiting factor in setting the term—it makes little sense to make a small annual saving in payments while locking the Public Authority into a PPP Contract which cannot be easily changed if its requirements may have changed substantially;
- *the maintenance cycle for the Facility*: *e.g.* does the Public Authority want to have the Facility returned shortly after a major maintenance, or, say, half-way through the major-maintenance cycle? (*cf.* §15.11)

Especially in the case of Concessions, there may be a case for fixing the Service Fees and then letting bidders propose the term of the PPP Contract as part of their bid (*cf.* §6.3.6).

§13.3.2 PAYMENT PROFILE

The payment profile is also important. There is obviously a temptation for the Public Authority to 'back-end' the payment stream, so making the project cost less today and leaving someone else to worry about making higher payments in 20 years' time (*cf.* §5.4). Such behaviour pushes a PPP project towards being an expensive way of borrowing money. In principle, Service Fees should be level over the life of the Contract. The same public service is being provided by the Project Company over the life of the project, so the payments should be the same. This is a matter of 'inter-generational equity'—we should not expect our children to make disproportionate payments for benefits which we enjoy today.

Conversely, investors will usually prefer to 'front-end' the payments, to increase their Equity IRR, which will mean that their long-term interest in project performance will be reduced. A structure where Service Fees reduce sharply after the debt has been paid off is also unsuitable for these reasons. This general level-payment principle is, however, subject to the effects of inflation (*cf.* §11.3.4).

§13.3.3 REVENUE PAYMENTS DURING CONSTRUCTION

The Public Authority should not make payments for something which is not completed, and hence normally payments should not begin until the Facility has met the required standard of completion. (In the case of a Concession, clearly users will not pay until there is something to pay for.) However, if some form of interim service is being provided by the Project Company during the construction period—perhaps because construction is in phases—then a proportional payment can reasonably be made for this (*cf.* §6.6.5). Interim revenues can also be provided when the Project Company takes over an already-operating Facility, typically a Concession such as a road where tolls are already being paid, and uses these revenues as part-funding for construction. Any such arrangement adds to the construction-phase risks for the Project Company (*cf.* §14.6.5), and raises similar VfM issues for the Public Authority to other types of capex contribution, as discussed below.

§13.3.4 DELAY IN COMPLETION

Subject to this point on interim revenues, the main incentive for the Project Company to ensure that the Facility is completed on time is that Service Fees are not paid until it is complete. Moreover late completion will eat into the operation phase, and thus further reduce the return for investors. However, the Public Authority may itself suffer a loss resulting from the late completion, because it has to make other arrangements for continued provision of the service. If such additional costs can be reasonably anticipated and quantified in advance it is appropriate for there to be delay liquidated damages payments (LDs) under the PPP Contract to cover them. LDs are not intended as a penalty, but a pre-agreed fair estimate of the losses the Public Authority will suffer from the delay; they may be secured by a bank bond (payment guarantee). The maximum amounts payable will normally be capped—*i.e.* there cannot be unlimited delays.

Any LDs will probably be passed on by the Project Company to its Construction Subcontractor (*cf.* §14.7.1), who will take the risk of taking them into account in setting the construction price. Thus LDs have a direct effect on the whole-life VfM of the PPP Contract since this extra cost will have to be covered by extra Service Fees. It may be worth while getting the bidders to bid for the PPP Contract with and without Delay LDs to assess the best VfM position.

There may come a point (sometimes referred to as the 'Sunset Date') where completion of the Facility has been delayed so long that the Public Authority may wish to have the right to terminate the PPP Contract. If the Public Authority is charging Delay LDs, this point would normally come when these LDs run out (or if they are not paid).

In other cases, the longer the delay goes on, the more the financial pressure on the Project Company, its investors and lenders, to sort the matter out. Assuming that the Public Authority would prefer to have the Facility delivered late than not at all, there is no need for a 'hair-trigger' approach to termination for delay, and quite a lot of extra time can be allowed.

§13.3.5 CAPEX CONTRIBUTIONS BY THE PUBLIC AUTHORITY

A financial contribution from the Public Authority towards capex may be used as a way of lowering long-term Service Fees to make a PFI-Model project affordable, or a Concession financially viable; the contribution may be derived from revenue during construction, as discussed above, or the proceeds of sale of surplus land as a result of building the new Facility (*cf.* §14.5.9). However, capex contributions raise some risk-transfer issues (*cf.* §13.4.3).

§13.3.6 CAPITAL PAYMENTS TO THE PUBLIC AUTHORITY

In Concession projects, the project may already have been partly-built with public-sector funding, so that for example a section of a road may already be collecting tolls from users; this already-built road section may be included in the Concession to make the project more viable by providing a stream of existing revenue while the new toll-road section is being built, as discussed above. The value of the toll revenues from the existing road section can obviously be taken into account by the private-sector investors, so reducing the tolls which have to be paid on the new road section. However, the Public Authority may consider that the effect of doing this is that the general taxpayer has paid the cost of constructing the initial road section, and now there are no toll revenues to offset these costs (and perhaps service public-sector debt which was taken on to cover them). Therefore the Public Authority may require bidders to include an initial lump-sum payment in their bids to cover this 'sunk cost'. The economic efficiency of this is open to question, as the end result is that the private-sector investors will have to take on more debt, at a higher cost than any public-sector debt which it is replacing, and feed this extra cost through to the road users' tolls.

Payment for a Franchise to operate an existing Facility is similar in effect (*cf.* §3.5), but the motive is even more likely to be the benefit to the public budget despite any economic inefficiency. A toll road will have a higher value for a Public Authority than it does for a private-sector purchaser if the Public Authority values the stream of revenues by discounting them at the PSDR whereas the purchaser discounts at a higher cost of capital (which of course raises again the issue of whether the PSDR should be different to the private-sector cost of capital—*cf.* §5.3.2). On the other hand if the proceeds of a Franchise sale enable the Public Authority to pay off debt originally raised to pay for the Facility, this may improve its credit rating and thus reduce its overall cost of borrowing.

§13.3.7 REVENUE PAYMENTS TO THE PUBLIC AUTHORITY

A Concession Agreement may also provide for payment of 'Concession fees' to the Public Authority. If these are based on a sliding scale depending on the usage of the

Facility, this is a reasonable way for the Public Authority to share in the success of the project (*cf.* §13.4.4), although this does put the Public Authority in the position of a *de facto* investor without the normal rights which an investor has to control the business.

Payment of a fixed Concession Fee, on the other hand, is open to similar objections as those against payment of an initial capital sum to the Public Authority, discussed above: effectively this is an expensive way of raising revenue for the public sector as it will mean that the Concession term will have to be longer to fund these extra payments.

§13.4 USAGE-BASED PAYMENTS

In general, private-sector investors are willing to take demand risk on a Facility:

- where it has an open-market use, *e.g.* an office building which is provided to the Public Authority under a PPP, but if the Public Authority chooses to leave the building it can be leased to a private-sector user; or
- where there is likely to be a consistent demand, *e.g.* for transportation.

The private sector will generally not take demand risk where usage is dependent on the Public Authority's actions. For example in the early development of PFI in Britain the idea of investors taking demand risk for PPP prisons was tested, but there was no appetite for this.

Having placed the Facility in the category where demand or usage risk might be transferred to the private sector, how is the decision whether to do this finally reached? For example, a road could either be provided under a Concession and thus subject to real tolls, or funded by the Public Authority with Shadow Tolls, or paid for on an Availability basis by the Public Authority. How is the choice made between these alternatives?

- Firstly, the Public Authority will normally examine if the road can be provided through a Concession, possibly with some public-sector financial support.
- Secondly, if the Public Authority wishes to transfer the usage risk, but real tolls are not practical (*e.g.* because of insufficient traffic, complex links with other roads, or because tolls would distort traffic flows too much), a Shadow-Toll structure can be considered.
- Alternatively, if the transfer of usage risk is not considered practical or does not provide VfM for the Public Authority, an Availability- or service-based payment structure can be adopted.

These alternatives are discussed in detail below.

§13.4.1 REQUIREMENTS FOR A CONCESSION

Taking a road as an example, whether a Concession is likely to be viable is a function of:

- traffic projections (*cf.* §14.8.1); as a rough rule of thumb, traffic lower than 10,000–20,000 vehicles per day (vpd) is likely to make it difficult to generate enough toll revenue to fund a stand-alone Concession;
- the level of tolls which could be generated on these assumptions;

- if traffic levels are too low, whether the project would become viable with some level of financial support by the Public Authority (*cf.* §13.4.3);
- even assuming that tolls could be generated, the Public Authority has to consider whether it is suitable for this road to be tolled, taking into account factors such as:
  - how tolling fits within the overall national roads policy;
  - whether there is a free, if slower, alternative road; closure of free roads to force drivers onto the toll road is fairly certain to cause political problems;
  - whether there is a 'willingness to pay' on the part of users—*e.g.* there are usually strong objections if a road which has not previously been tolled is then made subject to tolls unless there are clear new benefits for drivers; and the actual level of the tolls must take into account not only the financial requirements of the project, but also the 'reasonableness' of the toll level as perceived by users;
  - whether traffic not wishing to pay the toll would be diverted onto other less suitable roads, causing obstruction, or increasing environmental problems (*e.g.* from additional pollution);
  - the behaviour of heavy goods vehicles (HGVs), tolls from which are usually a major component of revenues, as there is typically a substantial differential between tolls for cars and tolls for large vehicles; HGVs are much more likely to divert to free roads, so if HGV drivers decide to use alternative routes a toll road is unlikely to be viable;
  - how easy is it to operate a toll system, and how well would this fit with connecting roads; (note that there are two ways of tolling a road—a 'closed' system measures where drivers get on and off the road, and charges are paid for distance, and an 'open' system where there is one fixed payment for using any part of the road);
  - conversely, whether tolling the road would discourage local short-distance use of a road which is intended for long-distance traffic (the biggest problem with any new road which runs past a major conurbation).

If, having been through this exercise, it is clear that a real toll system is not workable (even with support from the Public Authority as discussed below), the Public Authority will then consider PFI-Model alternatives, namely either Shadow Tolls or an Availability-based payment, as discussed below. Similar principles can of course be applied to other Concession-model Contracts.

§13.4.2 Toll Levels

The level of tolls for a Concession road can be set in three possible ways:

- Bidders bid on the basis of fixed initial toll payments, which can then only be increased at, say, the rate of inflation during the Concession period.
- Bidders are given freedom to set tolls at whatever level the traffic will bear.
- The Public Authority sets the tolls, as part of a national road-tolling strategy.

The approach to this is likely to be linked to the extent to which the Public Authority provides any financial support for the Concession.

§13.4.3 FINANCIAL SUPPORT FROM THE PUBLIC AUTHORITY

If the projected usage and Service Fees for a Concession produce insufficient cash flow to make the project financially viable, the Public Authority may use various means to support the project. If the Public Authority is trying to keep the Concession out of the public budget, rules for the amount of support which can be given before it ceases to be off-balance sheet need to be borne in mind (*e.g.* no more than 50% support under Eurostat rules—*cf.* §5.5.1). This public-sector support can be justified by the wider externalities produced by the Concession (*cf.* §5.2.1), although it could also be argued that the very fact that these externalities cannot be priced into tolls suggests that tolling should be used with caution. Support can take a variety of different forms:

- capex contributions;
- revenue guarantees;
- subsidies; or
- debt guarantees.

Alternatively the Public Authority may decide that the Concession Model is not the ideal one, and support is best provided through the PFI Model *via* Shadow Tolls (§13.4.5) or Availability payments (§13.5).

Capex contribution. The Public Authority may provide a capex contribution, *i.e.* funding for part of the capex (*cf.* §13.3.5), through:

- grants or subsidies (non-refundable);
- the proceeds of sale of surplus land no longer required for the Facility (*cf.* §14.5.9);
- a loan—any loan will have to be subordinated to the other lenders (*cf.* §12.6.5), and interest payments and principal repayments may be postponed until net cash flow after the Senior Lenders' debt service has reached a certain level, or surplus cash flow may be divided between payments on the public-sector funding and Distributions to investors;
- equity investment—like the loan, payments of public-sector dividends may only be made after the private-sector investors have secured an agreed level of return.

Capex contributions raise risk-transfer issues. It is obviously inappropriate for the public-sector money to go in first and thus bear the whole initial construction risk on the project—so it should go in last. Indeed the ideal position is that the Project Company should fund construction fully, and then only if completion takes place should any public-sector funding be injected, as otherwise the Public Authority is effectively taking back some of the construction-phase risk. The Project Company should be able to arrange interim funding which would he repaid from the public-sector contribution after completion. An alternative approach is to require the investors in the Project Company to guarantee repayment of any such capex contribution if construction is not completed (or to provide bank guarantees for this).

But even after completion of construction there remain risk-transfer issues with capex contributions. There is a case for suggesting that capex contributions are simply inappropriate as they do not reflect the long-term nature of risk-sharing in a

PPP—if the Project Company defaults a few years into the PPP Contract the Public Authority will probably not receive proper value for any capex contribution, since the Senior Lenders will have first claim on any value which the project has at that point.

On the other hand, if support is provided for revenues, as discussed below, rather than capex, this means that the Project Company has to raise more private-sector funding, with a consequent effect on the Service Fees.

Revenue subsidies. If it is necessary to reduce Service Fees to make the Concession viable, a fixed subsidy towards operating costs can be offered. Clearly this remains a fairly crude approach, which makes it possible for the Project Company to earn windfalls from unexpected traffic growth. A preferable method of subsidy is therefore payments on a sliding scale, reducing as usage increases.

Revenue guarantee. If the issue is not one of reducing the Service Fees, but uncertainty of whether there may be enough revenue although the Base Case gives a reasonable expectation that enough revenue can be generated, then a 'Fare Box Guarantee' (as it is known where passengers are involved, but the same principle applies to other usage guarantees, *e.g.* for a road Concession) may be used, *i.e.* the break-even level of passengers which covers opex and debt service is agreed, and insofar as the level of passengers is below this, the Public Authority pays the equivalent of enough fares to bring the total up again. If the number of passengers is over the guarantee level, the benefit of this is usually split on a sliding-scale basis between the Project Company and the Public Authority. This can be limited to a ramp-up guarantee, whereby minimum usage levels during the first few years of operation are guaranteed, the theory here being that all parties expect the projected usage levels to be reached, and the only doubt is how long it will take to achieve these levels.

In all such cases, the proportion of support needs to be carefully considered: it is obviously unreasonable for the Public Authority to guarantee 100% of the Base Case revenues or passenger usage, as this not only negates any real risk transfer but also removes the incentive on the part of the Project Company to increase the numbers of passengers. Therefore a revenue guarantee should either be for a fixed percentage of projected revenues (*e.g.* 70% as under the Chilean 1991 Concession Law), or a sliding scale of support (as used in South Korea—*cf.* §3.8.1), which takes the ramp-up point discussed above into account: thus 80% usage may be guaranteed for the first 5 years, 70% for the next 5, 60% for the next 5 and nothing thereafter, the effect being to cover opex and some, but not all, of the debt service, leaving equity fully at risk.

However, there is a fairly sorry history in various countries, *e.g.* Mexico in the early 1990s (see Bibliography) and more recently in South Korea (*cf.* §3.8.2), of Concessions being undertaken on the strength of revenue guarantees rather than a proper evaluation of the usage risks, with consequent heavy costs falling on the Public Authority as the guarantees are called in.

Debt guarantee. If the Public Authority and the investors consider that the project is viable as a Concession, but the lenders are not confident on the usage level, another cost-effective way of providing support to enable the project to proceed will be for the Public Authority to guarantee some of the debt (*cf.* §13.5, §15.5.7). As with revenue guarantees, so long as a case can be made that such a guarantee is unlikely to be called upon, this may not have any effect on the public budget.

Concession extension. Rather than providing direct financial support, the Public Authority may agree that if usage falls below a mutually-agreed level, the Concession term can be extended *pro rata*: the additional revenue at the tail-end may thus help to make up any deficit. This is very similar to bids on the basis of lowest NPV of revenues (*cf.* §6.3.6).

§13.4.4 LIMITING REVENUES

The reverse issue, of whether there should be any limit on the revenues which can be earned under Concession Agreements by the Project Company also needs to be considered by the Public Authority. There may come a point in Concessions where the total usage level, and hence the Service-Fee income, is far above what either party to the Contract originally envisaged. It might be said that since the Project Company's investors have taken on the usage risk, they should be entitled to the rewards for doing so, and this may indeed be a fair point of view in a minority of circumstances where development of this usage is derived solely from the Project Company's efforts. But this is seldom entirely the case. If, for example, traffic on a Concession road is well above the original forecasts, this is likely to be partly a product of other public-sector actions such as:

- the public sector having made it attractive to use the Concession road by making other changes to the surrounding road network;
- public policy on issues such as fuel taxes, sales taxes on cars, and road pricing elsewhere;
- general economic growth thanks to the government's economic policies.

Therefore if the levels of traffic are so high that the marginal revenues (net of higher costs caused by greater usage) have become so great as to constitute a 'windfall', it may be reasonable for both the public- and private-sector sides to share in this unexpected benefit. There is also an obvious case for sharing or capping revenues if the Public Authority has given any form of financial support as discussed above. This can be done in a number of ways:

Capping revenues. This approach, and the issues which arise out of this, are similar to the position where the Public Authority pays Shadow Tolls, where revenues are also capped (*cf.* §13.4.5). The problem with a simple cap is that this may give the Project Company perverse incentives to limit traffic growth.

Sharing surplus revenues. This is the most straightforward approach, and especially appropriate where a minimum revenue guarantee has been given. Thus under the Korean PPI Law, where an MRG has been given, when the revenue is 110–140% of Base Case projections, this surplus is divided between the Project Company and the Public Authority.

Concession fee. Payment of a sliding-scale Concession fee (*cf.* §13.3.7), based on the level of revenues, *i.e.* in effect the Public Authority gets a share of excess revenues: again a relatively straightforward approach, and probably gives greater incentive to maximise revenues than a simple revenue cap.

Rate of Return Cap. The Equity IRR which can be earned by the Project Company can be capped at a certain level (obviously well over the Base Case), and surpluses paid over to the Public Authority as they build up. However, this is fraught with difficulties, since it is very difficult to create a 'leak-proof' system which prevents the surplus over the Equity IRR cap being drained off through financial engineering, or manipulation of the Subcontracts (especially where the Project Company's investors are also Subcontractors). Moreover, investors will be reluctant to make interim payments during the life of the Concession, as usage may drop off later on, so reducing their overall project-life Equity IRR below the Base Case—but by then the previous surplus will have been paid over to the Public Authority, so the overall Base Case cannot be preserved. This means that any excess-sharing may have to be kept in a Reserve Account until the end of the Concession.

Alternatively the Concession may be terminated early if the toll revenues have produced a certain level of Equity IRR (obviously above the Base Case) for the Project Company's investors (*cf.* §6.3.6). This is a cleaner approach, but may cause balance-sheet problems for the Public Authority, as it in effect becomes an investor in the residual value of the Concession. It is also again open to financial engineering or other manipulation.

However, in considering either of these alternatives, it may be more appropriate to cap the overall rate of return, *i.e.* the Project IRR, which looks at the financial return without splitting this between debt service and Equity IRR. This at least avoids any distortion from artificial financial structuring as between debt and equity, and is the approach often used in regulation of privatised utilities.

Lowest NPV of revenues. This is a more sophisticated alternative which offers particular merits in balancing risks and rewards from usage-based payments—the Concession is awarded to the bidder who requires the lowest NPV of toll revenues (known as 'LPVR'—least present value of revenue; *cf.* §6.3.6). Once the bidder has received this NPV sum, the Concession terminates. (The NPV calculation 'backdates' the actual revenue flows to the date of signature of the Concession.) Thus the Concession has no specific term, although there is usually a long-stop date by which it must finally terminate whatever the return. The benefits of this are:

- Traffic risk is still transferred, but with less need for any support by the Public Authority. This means that lenders will concentrate on ensuring the project is viable rather than just relying on public-sector support.
- It cuts the cost to the end-user, as bidders should have a lower cost of capital (reflecting the lower risk) and do not have to build in large safety margins in their pricing.
- It gives the Public Authority greater flexibility; a fixed-term Concession has to be compensated for some changes which affect traffic flows (*cf.* §15.2.4), but this may not be necessary in this case.
- It should ensure that the private sector eliminates political 'white elephants', *i.e.* projects which are promoted by the Public Authority for political reasons but which will never recover their costs, and so are not financially viable.
- It eliminates the 'winner's curse' (*cf.* §14.8.1).
- Because it is based on gross revenues not net return, it retains construction- and operating-cost risks with the private sector, and also ensures that costs cannot be manipulated, unlike capping the Equity IRR as discussed above.

However there are some points which need to be borne in mind:

- The choice of the discount rate for the NPV calculation is obviously very important. In this case the discount rate should relate to the private sector's WACC rather than using the PSDR, *i.e.* the rate will be relatively high. If this is not done, bidders will have to build in an unnecessarily large safety margin because if revenues come in slower than expected, this will reduce their return on capital.
- This structure may provide less incentive to improve service and hence demand, *e.g.* through better road maintenance or service at the toll booths.
- It may fail the balance-sheet test, because the Public Authority is taking too much 'risk' on the project.

Purchase option. If the Public Authority has an option to terminate the Concession and then purchase the Facility at a fixed price rather than a current valuation (*cf.* §15.6), this effectively caps the return which can be earned by the investors. However, this is more suitable for a PFI-Model project than a Concession, where such a purchase option could leave the investors seriously at risk if revenues are below projections.

§13.4.5 SHADOW TOLLS

Shadow Tolls on PFI-Model Contracts are usage-based payments paid by the Public Authority rather than users. (They are known in Portugal, which has been a large-scale user of this system, as 'SCUTs', short for '*Sem Combrança ao Utilizador*'—'without payment by the user'.) They are usually structured on a 'banded' basis, *e.g.*:

- *Band A*: a payment of x per vpd or per vehicle-kilometre (vkm) for the first $(a \times 1,000)$ vpd/vkm;
- *Band B*: a payment of y per vpd/vkm for the next $(b \times 1,000)$ of vpd/vkm;
- *Band C*: a payment of z per vpd/vkm for the next $(c \times 1,000)$ of vpd/vkm;
- *Band D*: all higher levels of vpd/vkm—no payment.

Band A represents a conservative view of the likely traffic levels: it will probably be the same or less than the lenders' Base Case; total payments will be calculated to be sufficient to cover opex and debt service. Band B will be the investors' Base Case, and total payments will thus be sufficient to provide the lenders' Cover Ratios and the Base Case Equity IRR. Band C will be an 'upside' case for the investors, which might, say, take their IRR from 15% to 18%. Band D then ensures that the investors can earn no more than an 18% Equity IRR whatever the level of traffic.

It is clearly reasonable to cap the revenues in this case, because the actual risk transfer to the private sector has itself been limited: Band A will be pitched at such a traffic level as to ensure that the lenders are taking little real traffic risk, and Band B is also likely to be at a sufficiently conservative level as to protect the investors as well. In general principle, if usage risk transfer is not complete, there should always be a limit on revenues, as discussed above.

But since the risk transfer to the private sector is so limited, and the Project Company may have little real influence on traffic levels anyway, there is clearly a question whether a Shadow-Toll system is appropriate. In fact it was abandoned in Britain because it became clear that there was so little risk transfer that the early PFI Shadow-Toll projects had to be put back on the public-sector balance sheet (*cf.* §5.5.4). If there is little real risk transfer it is probably better to concentrate on payments for Availability and service, where more risk and responsibility can be properly passed over to the Project Company, as discussed below.

§13.4.6 PENALTIES

The Project Company has an overall incentive to provide the services as required, since failure to do so will probably result in a drop in revenue (although if revenues are guaranteed by the Public Authority the incentive may not be as great). There is thus a natural regulator to this extent, but the monopoly nature of the services to be provided means that failure to reach agreed Availability and service standards must also lead to some penalty payment by the Project Company in a similar way to deductions for Unavailability or poor service quality in the PFI Model, as discussed below.

§13.5 AVAILABILITY-BASED PAYMENTS

Where Service Fees are made on an Availability basis, the process of arriving at the base payment stream is rather simpler than for usage-based Service Fees: it is a product of opex and funding costs, and the investors' required return (*cf.* §10.7), *i.e.* rather than the financing being structured to fit revenues, as in a Concession, it is structured to fit costs. These base payments are then adjusted as set out below.

The essence of Service-Fee payments under the PFI Model is that they are only made when the Facility is 'available' (which means capable of providing the service as required). This concept derives from Availability Charges for process plant, *e.g.* under PPAs (*cf.* §1.4.2), which are quite simple in nature. For a power station to be 'available', it has only to demonstrate its ability to start-up, and produce so many megawatts of power (while adhering to environmental requirements on emissions, *etc.*), subject to an allowance for downtime for routine and major maintenance. Similar fairly limited requirements are all that are needed for other types of process plant. But under the PFI Model, the concept of Availability is usually more complex than this. Availability is relatively easy to measure if a single specific piece of equipment or service is being provided, but such cases form a small minority of PFI-Model projects. It is much more difficult to measure Availability for a public-service building such as a prison, hospital, or school, or a number of buildings such as accommodation units. Moreover quality of service, which is not an issue with a process plant, since it either functions (within specified limits) or it does not, must also be taken into account.

PFI-Model Service-Fee payment structures therefore normally have two main features:

- payment deductions (abatements) are made for any part of the Facility which is unavailable, weighted according to the importance of the unavailable portion (§13.5.1);
- service quality is monitored through performance indicators: failure to meet these also leads to payment deductions (§13.5.2).

Unavailability is crucial to the Facility's operation, and therefore leads to immediate payment deductions; poor service quality does not prevent immediate use of the Facility, but will have an impact over time and hence more time may be given for rectification before payment deductions for poor performance are made.

One issue with this approach is the need to incentivise the Project Company to offer improvements in service, not just to operate to avoid payment deductions: the possibility of bonuses in some circumstances should therefore also be considered where better performance is self-funding in some way, or is sustainable within the Public Authority's budget. For example, in a road project an extra payment can be made for safety standards above the average for the Public Authority's whole road portfolio. Some account may also have to be taken of excess usage leading to higher maintenance costs.

However, it is highly unlikely that Availability and performance deductions will ever substantially erode the Service-Fee stream to the extent of jeopardising debt service and indeed lenders are unlikely to finance a PPP Contract where this is a likely scenario (*i.e.* deductions primarily affect investors not lenders). Once construction of a Facility is complete, the chances of any prolonged period of Unavailability are quite small. Hence in French PPPs the administrative law concept of the '*Cession de Créance*' (loan transfer) can be applied, under which, on satisfactory completion of a PPP Facility, the Public Authority takes direct liability for a pre-agreed proportion of the Project Company's debt. (If deductions exceed the remaining Service Fees, they remain a claim against the Project Company.) Similar provisions can be found in South Africa (*cf.* §15.5.7) and a similar structure was used in some early British PFI contracts, but has now been abandoned. This reflects the reality that even the poorest performance post-completion by the Project Company is unlikely to result in the Service Fees being reduced below this level, so it makes sense to guarantee what is without risk, and to benefit from the lower cost of funding that this attracts. The effect is similar to a minimum revenue guarantee under a Concession (*cf.* §13.4.3).

It should be noted that this deduction régime is the Public Authority's only basis for claims against the Project Company (other than LDs—*cf.* §13.3.4); so the Public Authority cannot make a separate claim for some other consequential loss because the services are not adequately provided. (This provision is known as an 'exclusive remedy' clause.)

§13.5.1 UNAVAILABILITY

When dealing with a road project, it is easy to see that a particular stretch of the road is 'available' if it is open for traffic. But even in this simple case a distinction has to be made between the reasons for Unavailability, and hence the deduction to be made: Unavailability due to unplanned maintenance (which is clearly the Project Company's fault) is different to Unavailability due to heavy snow or a vehicle breakdown, and hence there should be a different level of deduction. Similarly, if the traffic has to slow down for some reason related to management of the road, this should also result in Unavailability deductions, but again on a different basis to the road not being available at all. And the time of day is also relevant: Unavailability is obviously more of an issue during the rush hour than in the middle of the night.

These matters become more complex in an accommodation project. At what point is a building available or unavailable? Obviously if the whole building has to be closed—perhaps because the heating system has stopped working—it is unavailable. But what if only part of the building has to be closed? Calculation of the *pro rata* share of this loss of

Availability is complex (and very project-specific)—and so to determine Unavailability deductions in a building or similar Facility, a detailed weighting scheme for each area or aspect of the Facility has to be worked out in the PPP Contract. For example, in a hospital the floor areas may be divided into three weighting categories:

- *Critical*: accident and emergency, operating theatres, patient services (wards, X-ray rooms, *etc.*);
- *Medium*: clinical support such as physiotherapy, pharmacy, waiting rooms;
- *Normal*: offices and training facilities.

Or each of the parts of a school may be divided into weighting factors such as:

- *1*: storage rooms;
- *2*: staff rooms;
- *4*: standard classrooms;
- *6*: specialised facilities, *e.g.* for laboratories, arts and drama, sports;
- *10*: assembly hall, kitchen, dining hall, IT system.

Thus one classroom is weighted as 4, whereas the kitchen is weighted as 10, so a class-room is said to be worth 4 service units, while the kitchen is 10 service units. (Note that simple floor area is not used as a basis for weighting.) Multiplying the total of the individual areas by their respective service unit weightings gives a total for the service units of the whole school. Suppose these come to 1,000—then if a classroom is out of action for a day, the Unavailability deduction is (the *pro rata* Service Fee for that day $\times$ 4 $\div$ 1,000).

In addition the meaning of Unavailability (which should be objective and clearly measurable) needs to be worked out with respect to each area, *e.g.* it may be decided that a school classroom will be unavailable if the heating is below a certain temperature (even if the pupils could theoretically wrap up warm and use the room). Thus Unavailability may include lack or inadequacy of:

- shelter from wind and rain;
- health and safety arrangements, or compliance with the law in other respects;
- heating, lighting, water or other utilities;
- key equipment, communications or IT infrastructure;
- any other specific element required to keep the area in operation.

There also has to be a reporting and recording system for determining when Unavailability begins, and a remedy period before a payment deduction is made, which may be shorter for a critical area (perhaps less than an hour) than for a normal area (say half a day), although Performance Points (see below) may still accrue during this period. However, if the matter is not remedied in this period, Unavailability will be measured from the beginning of the problem.

It is possible to turn this calculation the other way round—*i.e.* the Project Company is paid for the number of weighted service units available (which is the normal approach in a BOT contract for process plant), rather than having sums deducted from the PPP Contracts for those service units which are unavailable. But this means that there cannot be a system of 'ratcheting' Unavailability deductions over 100%, *i.e.* the payment for the Service Area may be 100, and so the deduction may be 100 for the first period of Unavailability, but then it could increase to say 120, putting more pressure on the Project Company and its FM Subcontractor (to whom these deductions would be passed) to remedy the problem.

However, in process-plant projects such as waste incinerators, payment is usually made based on the volume processed (e.g. a 'Gate Fee' per tonne of waste) on a 'deliver or pay' basis (*i.e.* if the Public Authority does not deliver a minimum volume of say, waste, for processing it must still make a minimum payment similar to an Availability charge).

There may be situations when a space or service is unavailable as defined in the PPP Contract, but the Public Authority still wants to use it. Obviously if this use prevents the Project Company remedying the problem there should not be a full payment deduction; this situation can be dealt with either by a lower rate of Unavailability deduction or by accruing Performance Points instead.

Scheduled maintenance, which should be set out in the PPP Contract, does not make the Facility unavailable. The scheduling should of course fit the Public Authority's routine, *e.g.* a school should be maintained during the holidays or at weekends. However, unscheduled maintenance does make the space unavailable.

It should also be noted that even if particular elements of the Service Fees are separately variable (*cf.* §12.4.5, §15.2.5), these should not be 'ring-fenced' from deductions from the Service Fees as a whole.

§13.5.2 SERVICE QUALITY

Quality of service is not a matter of great concern in a process-plant project: it is a fairly black-and-white issue whether a power plant works or not. If it works badly it will not produce the level of power required, and so this failure will be caught under the capacity/Availability payment provisions. Again this question is more complex in a PFI-Model contract, depending on the nature of the Facility being provided. Broadly speaking, Unavailability deductions relate to critical failures to provide what is intended under the PPP Contract, while all other failures under the PPP Contract will relate to service quality. Also, Availability measures should be objective, whereas some service measures may be subjective.

Service (which in this context includes routine maintenance) is often provided under a separate FM Contract, and FM Contractors are not prepared to suffer deductions or penalties which are out of scale with the (limited) fees which they charge for their work. Thus any deduction régime which penalises poor service quality generally is again likely to be limited, but at the same time there have to be sanctions for persistent poor service.

A typical approach to measurement of service quality is to create a matrix of key performance indicators (KPIs) setting out the requirement for each service. For example, in a road project, performance may be measured, *inter alia*, by the quality of lighting, cleaning of the road surface, replacement of broken signage, *etc.*, or by more fundamental measures such as the speed of the traffic, an indication of how well traffic flow is being managed, and the number of accidents, an indication of how safely the road is being operated. (Indeed, the latter cases may be dealt with under the Availability heading, which illustrates the difficulty of drawing a precise borderline between Availability and service quality.)

KPIs may have to be very detailed—*e.g.* it may not be enough to say a room must be 'clean', the meaning of 'clean' may need to be defined too—and clearly FM Subcontractors will interpret incomplete or ambiguous Project-Contract requirements to their advantage. The problem about this is that the more detailed the specification becomes, the more it becomes an input rather than an output specification, and the more likely it is that some element of the specification will get lost in the detail.

Having established the KPIs, these are again weighted according to the importance of the service. Quality of service may be measured objectively, *e.g.* by speed of traffic, numbers of accidents, or time of response to problems, or more subjectively, *e.g.* by inspection, or feedback from users of the service. Measurement of performance can be complex, and may depend to a considerable extent on records maintained by the Project Company, if there is not to be a substantial extra monitoring cost for the Public Authority. Poor service will incur 'Performance Points' based on the KPI weightings, rather than an immediate deduction from the PPP Contract as for Unavailability. There is often a 'ratcheting' mechanism whereby:

- more Performance Points may be imposed, *pro rata*, the longer the problem persists or the more frequently it occurs;
- accumulation of Performance Points eventually leads to a Service Fee deduction; and
- if this accumulation passes a very high level such that there is a persistent failure of service, the PPP Contract may be terminated (*cf.* §15.5).

The Project Company should not be penalised for Unavailability and then incur Performance Points in relation to the same issue. The primary aim is to ensure Availability and therefore these provisions take precedence.

§13.5.3 REPLACEMENT OF SUBCONTRACTORS

The Project Company (or its lenders) may wish to deal with poor service by replacing the relevant FM Subcontractor (although the number of times such a replacement is allowed should be limited). In such cases it could be argued that there has to be a system for wiping out accumulated Performance Points, as otherwise the new Subcontractor has no room for manoeuvre before running into default. This may be dealt with by creating stricter triggers for termination in the FM Subcontract than in the PPP Contract, but if a large number of Performance Points have accumulated, or there is a limited pool of prospective FM Subcontractors, it may be necessary to reset the clock.

It is not the Public Authority's rôle to intervene with Subcontractors (*cf.* §6.6.7), either to direct how they can improve the service, or to suggest their replacement: this is an inherent part of the Project Company's management rôle; the Public Authority has to rely on the PPP Contract as a basis for enforcing its requirements. However, as the Public Authority would originally have approved the FM Subcontractor (*cf.* §6.5.2), it is reasonable for it to have a right of approving replacements, using similar criteria as to financial and technical capacity to those used at the time of the original procurement.

§13.5.4 OTHER PERFORMANCE MEASUREMENTS

It is possible to go beyond these FM-based measures of performance in some circumstances. For example, in a school project, the quality of the school building and the services provided should have some effect on the educational results which the school can achieve. Therefore a payment deduction could be made if, say, measurable results (such as examination grades) do not improve by a certain percentage. However, it is evident that the Project Company only has a limited ability to influence such matters, and therefore deductions could only relate to a small proportion of the total payments receivable.

§13.6 MIXED USAGE AND AVAILABILITY PAYMENTS

Especially in transport projects, there has been a recent trend towards a mixed base of Service Fees:

- Availability payments which are adequate to cover opex and debt service, and
- A demand fee (or toll), which is linked to usage, and provides the equity return.

As with any case where usage risk is not wholly transferred (*cf.* §13.4.4), there should be a cap on the demand-fee payments under this structure.

§13.7 THIRD-PARTY AND SECONDARY REVENUES

Under some PPP Contracts where payments are based on Availability (*e.g.* accommodation projects), the Project Company may be allowed to earn additional revenues by making the Facility available to third parties—*e.g.* a school hall may be hired out in the evenings for private functions.

Similarly, especially in the Concession Model, the Project Company may be given the right to generate secondary revenues from the PPP, for example the right to develop petrol stations, restaurants and lodging facilities on land adjacent to a Concession road. In such cases investors may be reluctant to return such development to the Public Authority at the end of the Concession, and hence will look for a permanent (or much longer-term) right to exploit secondary developments.

Third-party or secondary revenues may help to reduce the Service Fees, but normally lenders are reluctant to take such revenues into account in financial projections unless there is a high degree of certainty that they will occur, which means that the Public Authority may not in fact get the benefit of third-party revenues in the initial bid pricing. If third-party or secondary revenues are not taken into account in the bid pricing, the best practice is to split them between the Public Authority and the Project Company as and when they occur.

Chapter 14

Risk Evaluation and Transfer

§14.1 INTRODUCTION

Risk in a PPP relates to uncertain outcomes which have a direct effect either on the provision of the services (*e.g.* because the Facility is not built on time), or the financial viability of the project (*e.g.* loss of revenue or increased costs). In either case the result is a loss or cost which has to be borne by someone, and one of the main elements of PPP structuring is to determine where this loss or cost will lie.

This chapter therefore summarises the basic principles which lie behind risk transfer in PPP projects (§14.2), and then reviews the application of these principles in detail, using the 'Risk Matrix' approach (§14.3) used by all parties to identify and evaluate risks at each phase of the project:

- general political risks (§14.4);
- site-related risks (§14.5);
- construction risks (§14.6);
- completion risks (§14.7);
- operation-phase risks (§14.8).

§14.2 PRINCIPLES OF RISK TRANSFER

Risk transfer is at the heart of structuring a PPP project. Although the term 'risk-sharing' is often used in this context, PPPs do not generally involve risk-sharing in the sense of $x\%$ of the risk being taken by the Public Authority and $(100 - x\%)$ by the Project Company; risks are normally transferred fully to one side or the other (although there can be some limited exceptions to this—*cf.* §12.4.5, §15.2.5). There are only a limited number of ways in which any project risks can be handled:

- Risks can be retained by the Public Authority.
- Risks can be transferred to, and retained by the Project Company.

- Risks can be transferred to the Project Company, but then reallocated to third parties by:
  - passing them on a 'back-to-back' basis to Subcontractors;
  - covering them by insurance (*cf.* §12.4); or
  - having them guaranteed by Sponsors (*cf.* §10.9).
- In the case of Concessions, risks can be transferred to end-users through the Project Company having a right to impose higher Service Fees.

The default position, which may be set out in the PPP Contract, is that unless provided otherwise it is the Project Company's obligation to deliver the service as required, and bear or manage (by reallocation or otherwise) all risks accordingly.

Risk transfer is important for the Public Authority, as it is at the heart of the VfM case for a PPP procurement (*cf.* §2.6). Setting aside balance-sheet issues (*cf.* §5.5), the main purpose of risk transfer from the public-sector point of view is to ensure that the Project Company and its investors are appropriately incentivised to provide the service which is the subject of the PPP Contract. But it will not offer the best VfM for a Public Authority to try to transfer risks which are so difficult for the Project Company, its lenders or Subcontractors to limit or control, that if they do take them on they must charge heavily for doing so. The principle is that risks should be transferred to those best able to control them *at the lowest cost.* This also implies that whoever assumes the risk must have the freedom to handle it as they think best. It is therefore appropriate for the Public Authority to retain risks which relate to matters which the private sector cannot control cost-effectively (*i.e.* such a large risk premium would have to be built into the private-sector pricing that it is not VfM), or which the private sector cannot be given freedom to handle (perhaps because of the need to maintain the public service). Nonetheless, in order to take a PPP project out of the public budget, excessive risks cannot be retained by the Public Authority either, so a balance has to be struck. If the Public Authority does retain risks, it should also benefit from any associated 'upside', *i.e.* where possible there should be symmetrical allocation of risks and benefits (*cf.* §13.4.4).

A common mistake by the public-sector side in new PPP programmes is to push bidders to accept too much risk—in particular risks that have to be retained by the Project Company and cannot be reallocated elsewhere—with the result that when the lenders come into the picture the risk arrangements have to be renegotiated. As far as lenders are concerned, a risk which is transferred to and retained by the Project Company means that it effectively becomes the lenders' risk, because the Project Company has limited resources to bear any risks:

- It has a high level of debt, and no reserves of cash or other resources, other than limited Reserve Accounts (*cf.* §12.2.4), and any surplus cash flow from the lenders' Cover Ratio (*cf.* §10.5.8).
- Its investors generally have no obligation to make any further funds available beyond their initial equity investment (*cf.* §10.9).

As far as possible, therefore, the lenders wish the Project Company to be an 'empty box' (*cf.* §7.6.1), with all its risks reallocated elsewhere. The lenders' approach to risk in project finance is summed up by the maxim, 'A banker is a man who lends you an umbrella when it is not raining'. In other words, lenders are very reluctant to accept any but the most limited (and clearly-measurable) risks. This reflects the reality that the return the lenders get is not sufficient to absorb any substantial risk. A typical bank loan may earn a credit margin of less than 1% over cost of funds (*cf.* §10.4.1): this means that if one in a hundred loans fails to repay, the bank has made a loss from its project-finance business. So even a 1/100th risk of failure is too great for a project-finance loan portfolio. The lenders are therefore not 'investors' in the project, although the Sponsors or the Public Authority often like to use this expression in the heat of negotiation. If the lenders were investors they would get an equity rate of return, but they do not—typically in a successful project, the gross rate of return on the equity is at least twice that on the debt (*cf.* §7.3.2), which reflects the different risks taken by investors and lenders. Moreover, lenders have no 'upside'—*i.e.* the lenders' return is fixed, whereas the equity return can be improved by generating more value in the project (*e.g.* by more efficient operation, or financial restructuring—*cf.* §16.4).

Turning this round the other way, lenders are able to offer project-finance loans with low credit margins because the risk is low. This has been proved in connection with the 'Basel II' capital regime for banks which is being introduced from 2007. Basel refers to the Swiss headquarters of the Bank for International Settlements ('BIS'), which hosts the Basel Committee on Banking Supervision, consisting of the representatives of central banks or other banking supervisory bodies from major financial centres, who try to agree a common approach on requirements for bank capitalisation, to ensure banking stability and that banks compete internationally on the same basis. In 1988 the Committee introduced capital-adequacy rules for banks (known as the Basel Capital Accord), which were based, *inter alia*, on the simple measure that banks should hold capital equal to 8% of their commercial loans (including project finance). Basel II is a sophisticated revision of the 1988 Accord, which allows banks to allocate capital based on loan quality (linked to external ratings—*cf.* §9.4.1, §9.4.4—or the historical data on defaults and losses in their portfolio). When the Basel II scheme was first drawn up, project finance was placed in a relatively high-risk category with other structured finance (*cf.* §8.4.2), meaning that banks would have to allocate more capital against such lending, making it less attractive and so diminishing the supply of project-finance credit and increasing its cost to the borrower. The leading project-finance banks commissioned studies of their historical portfolios which showed that in fact the risk of default and consequent loss on project-finance loans was probably lower than on their general corporate-finance business, and as a result the proposed Basel II rules were changed in 2005 to reflect this. Paradoxically, this may not be a good thing for project-finance lenders: the amount of capital required for project-finance loans may actually reduce after Basel II comes into effect, which may be one factor in the reduction in project-finance loan margins in recent times. (The other key factor was probably a high level of liquidity generally, which led to a large number of new banks entering the market—*cf.* §9.3.1).

Risk assessment by lenders is based as much on the financial impact that a particular risk may have on the project's viability as on the likelihood of it actually happening. So a 'low possibility/high impact' risk—*i.e.* one which the Public Authority or the Sponsors feel is highly unlikely—will still be of concern to lenders. This means that the lenders assess risk by a series of 'worst-case' sensitivities (*cf.* §10.3.6), an analysis which is quite different from the weighting of risks which the Public Authority may undertake when considering VfM (*cf.* §5.3).

It is also important to note that any change in the project arrangements which may impact the risk balance—*e.g.* alterations to the Project Contracts—will always be subject to lender control in some way. Similarly, any adverse change in performance under the PPP Contract is likely to trigger lender controls over the Project Company's operations (*cf.* §12.3).

§14.3 THE RISK MATRIX

The project-finance approach to risk allocation means that attention has to be focused on detailed specific risks, rather than relying on any general background guarantee from the Public Authority or Sponsors. A process of due diligence and risk evaluation thus has to be undertaken by Sponsors and lenders throughout the bidding and negotiation phases. It is also necessary for the Public Authority before putting a PPP project out to tender, when evaluating bids, and during negotiations with bidders—this may be part of the decision on balance-sheet treatment (*cf.* §5.5), or when considering VfM (*cf.* §5.3).

A key product of this process is a 'Risk Matrix' (or 'Risk Register') which sets out:

- the nature of each risk;
- the effect (financial or otherwise) of the risk occurring;
- allocation of the risk under the PPP Contract;
- any mitigation of this risk from its being passed down to Subcontractors or covered by insurance;
- the financial impact of any risk which remains with the Project Company (which may be calculated by making use of sensitivity calculations—see above).

Table 14.1 sets out a typical list of topics which might have to be considered in a Risk Matrix; of course there are always project-specific risks, and so this is only a general guide. As shown in the table, project risks can be divided into a few broad categories:

- general political or economic risks;
- risks related to the project site;
- risks related to construction;
- risks related to completion of the Facility;
- revenue during construction;
- operation-phase risks; and
- risks on termination of the PPP Contract.

Within this matrix, risks which are not just passed to the Project Company (and usually mirrored in the relevant Subcontract) may be categorised in the PPP Contract as:

- 'Compensation Events', whereby the Public Authority compensates the Project Company for their effects (*cf.* §15.2); or
- 'Relief Events', whereby the Project Company is not penalised for failure to complete the project or perform the services, but is not paid either (*cf.* §15.3);
- *Force Majeure* (also known as 'Acts of God'), where, though neither party is at fault, the effect of the event is so severe (and cannot be mitigated by insurance, for which see below) that the Project Contract has to be terminated (cf. §15.7).

Table 14.1
Risk Matrix

Risk phase	Risk category	See	Nature of risk	See
General	Political		Political opposition to project	§14.4
			Change in law	§15.2.5
	Economic	Chapter 11	Interest rates	§11.2
			Inflation	§11.3
Construction phase	Site	§14.5	Site acquisition	§14.5.1
			Ground condition	§14.5.2
			Permits	§14.5.3
			Environmental permits & risks	§14.5.4
			Archaeology and fossils	§14.5.5
			Access, rights of way & easements	§14.5.6
			Connections to the site	§14.5.7
			Protesters	§14.5.8
			Disposal of surplus land	§14.5.9
	Construction	§14.6	Construction Subcontract	§2.6.1; §14.6.1
			Construction Subcontractor	§14.6.2
			Price adjustments	§14.6.3
			Changes by the Public Authority	§15.2.3
			Construction Subcontractor's risks	§14.6.4
			Revenue during construction	§14.6.5
	Completion	§14.7	Delay by Construction Subcontractor	§14.7.1
			Other causes of delay	§14.7.2
			Design	§14.7.3
			Performance	§14.7.4
Operation phase	Operation	§14.8	Usage/demand risk	§2.6.2; §14.8.1
			Network	§14.8.2
			Revenue payment	§14.8.3
			Availability and service	§2.6.3; §14.8.4
			Opex	§2.6.4; §14.8.5
			Maintenance	§2.6.4; §14.8.6
	Termination		Project Company default	§2.6.5 / §15.5
			Termination by the Public Authority	§15.6
			Force Majeure	§15.7
			Residual value	§15.11

Where risks are passed from the Public Authority to the Project Company, and then passed on again on a back-to-back basis to Subcontractors, it is important to ensure that the definitions and consequences of these risks in the PPP Contract and the relevant Subcontract are the same. Examples of areas where contract mismatches may arise are:

- differences between the scope of the works under the Construction Subcontract and the requirements of the PPP Contract, or the service required under an FM Subcontract and those required under the PPP Contract;

- a different definition of completion, or a mismatch between the level of Delay LDs under the PPP Contract (*cf.* §13.3.4) and the Construction Subcontract (*cf.* §14.7.1);
- a different procedure for fixing the cost of a variation in the project requested under the PPP Contract by the Public Authority (*cf.* §15.2.1), and for fixing the cost of the same variation in the Construction Subcontract, so that the cost of the variation payable to the Construction Subcontractor may not be fully passed through to the Public Authority;
- a similar issue arises with extra costs caused by a change in law (*cf.* §15.2.5);
- different definitions of Compensation or Relief Events between the Construction Subcontract and the PPP Contract.

The need to ensure this matching can mean that Subcontract negotiations effectively become multi-party, involving—directly or indirectly—the Public Authority (and sometimes also the lenders—*cf.* §16.2.1), the Sponsors and the Subcontractor.

Another related issue arises where one PPP project depends on another. For example, a new Concession road may rely on traffic generated by a new Concession-based bridge, and *vice-versa*. If the completion of the bridge PPP cannot be guaranteed, the road PPP will probably not be able to get financing; conversely if the completion of the road PPP cannot be guaranteed, the bridge PPP will probably not be able to get financing. The lenders to one project will have no interest in taking an extra risk on another project, with different lenders, which they cannot properly assess or control. Financing the two projects as one may be a way out of this impasse, but if they have been procured separately this will probably be impossible. In such cases the Public Authority may have to stand in the middle and guarantee each project's completion for the benefit of the other (which is obviously not ideal in risk-transfer terms). Similarly, where there is a coordinated country-wide programme for developing road Concessions this will probably be procured in stages, as otherwise it would be too big to be financed as a whole: a similar problem may arise with each stage being dependent on the others being built as well.

Finally it is worth remarking that the Public Authority always retains the risk of having specified its requirements incorrectly, and so having to pay for a service which does not properly meet its needs. The requirements can be changed, but this is an expensive and relatively inflexible process (*cf.* §15.2.2).

§14.4 POLITICAL RISKS

Just as developing a PPP programme requires political support (*cf.* §2.13), a PPP project which falls out of political favour is likely to face difficulties. From the Project Company's point of view, having a long-term PPP Contract to which strong political opposition has developed puts it in a vulnerable position. A PPP Contract differs from normal commercial contracts because one party—the Public Authority—may be able to use its power to change the law, or take executive action, to the detriment of the Project Company. So long as actions are taken in a non-discriminatory way, it can be argued that they are just the risk of doing business in a particular country and have to be accepted (*cf.* §15.2.5). But political pressure can take many subtle forms, and it is unlikely to be in the long-term interests of the Project Company or its investors to insist on full performance of the PPP Contract if it has fallen seriously out of political favour. In such cases it will probably be better to find a compromise solution through a negotiated change or termination.

It should be noted that this book does not deal with 'cross-border' political risks, which are typically relevant when investing in a project in a developing country. These risks (discussed in detail in Chapters 10 and 11 of *Principles of Project Finance*) include:

- foreign currency availability and transfer;
- war and civil disturbance;
- expropriation (*i.e.* a government take-over of the Facility without compensation);
- contract repudiation (by the Public Authority).

(Strictly speaking, these risks do not only relate to cross-border investors, but such problems usually arise in a cross-border investment context.)

§14.5 SITE RISKS

A variety of risks related to the project site have to be allocated between the Public Authority, the Project Company and the Construction Subcontractor:

- site acquisition (§14.5.1);
- ground condition (§14.5.2);
- permits (for construction of the project) (§14.5.3);
- environmental permits and risks (§14.5.4);
- archæology and fossils (§14.5.5);
- rights of way (access to the site) and easements (right to use an adjacent site, *e.g.* for water discharge) (§14.5.6);
- connections to the site (§14.5.7);
- protesters (§14.5.8);
- disposal of surplus land (§14.5.9).

The lenders' aim will be to ensure that site risks should either be retained by the Public Authority, or passed on a back-to-back basis to the Construction Subcontractor, but should not be retained by the Project Company.

§14.5.1 SITE ACQUISITION

The title to the project site will usually remain in the hands of the Public Authority (perhaps with a lease to the Project Company for the duration of the PPP Contract), and therefore generally cannot form part of the lenders' security (*cf.* §12.3). It is common for site acquisition to be the responsibility of the Public Authority (if the land is not already in

public ownership), especially if this involves acquiring large areas of land in multiple ownership, for which a Public Authority's compulsory-purchase (eminent domain) powers may
be needed; also if there is any political controversy on the location of the Facility, this is
best dealt with by the Public Authority. Moreover, if bidders have to estimate the cost of
acquiring land (and a possible risk of not being able to acquire it) they will have to include
a contingency in their bids which will probably not be good VfM for the Public Authority,
and bidders' different site acquisition costs could distort evaluation of the bids as a whole.
However, in cases where the Facility does not have to be on a particular site, bidders may
be allowed to propose various different solutions for its location, and to take responsibility
for acquiring the site.

   If the Public Authority has to acquire the land specifically for the Facility, the cost of
doing so may reasonably be included as part of the project costs to be paid by the Project
Company, but if the Facility is to be built on a site already owned by the Public Authority
there is less of a case for any transfer payment being required from bidders if it is to revert
to public-sector ownership at the end of the PPP Contract (cf. §15.11).

   Lenders will not normally lend until the Project Company has a clear right of access to
the project site and any additional land needed during construction. This is most likely to
be a problem in a linear project, for example where land has to be acquired for a road or a
railway line, and acquisition is not complete at the time construction on one part of the
project begins. Indeed land expropriation can be a major cause of delay in transport PPPs,
with consequent cost increases for the Public Authority. If the Public Authority wants the
Project Company to begin construction in advance of acquisition of title to all the land, the
PPP Contract will have to indemnify the Project Company against the results of failure to
acquire the balance of the land.

§14.5.2 GROUND CONDITION

   The risks that the geology of the site is not as expected, and thus that, *e.g.* extra piling
may be required for foundations, or that past usage of the site (*e.g.* for underground mining)
will cause construction problems should preferably be passed from the Public Authority to
the Project Company, and then to the Construction Subcontractor. Site surveys may be
carried out in advance of Financial Close to reduce this risk (if one party is willing to pay
for them—one possibility is that the bidders collectively share the cost, another is that the
Public Authority pays for them).

   However, this is a difficult area of risk transfer. A survey of the site can never provide
100% certainty that there is not a problem that has not been picked up by the survey.
Similarly, a detailed knowledge of the history of the past usage of the site, while helpful,
does not eliminate these risks. The problem is especially acute in:

- linear projects, *i.e.* projects not occupying one site, but being built over a long stretch
  of land where detailed site investigation may be impossible, such as a road;
- 'brownfield' sites where there has been complex past use of the site, or where access
  for surveys may be difficult because there are old buildings sitting on the site (as
  compared to 'greenfield' sites where there have been no major structures on the site).

In such cases there is a stronger case for the Public Authority to take responsibility for ground condition. It may therefore offer the Public Authority better VfM to take this risk on in some projects rather than pay (directly or via the Service Fees) for expensive surveys.

In cases where the Public Authority provides the site, to what extent should the Public Authority be held liable if information it has provided on ground condition proves to be incorrect and the Project Company suffers a loss as a result? This will probably be unavoidable in cases where the Public Authority is the only realistic source of information, and this cannot be independently verified by bidders at a reasonable cost and in a reasonable period of time.

From the lenders' point of view, a possible mitigation of such risks is that problems of this nature should often be apparent at an early stage of construction, when project costs may not yet have exceeded the amount of the equity investment; if so, they can draw stop at that point, with their risk covered by the equity.

§14.5.3 PLANNING AND PERMITS

Lenders will also expect all necessary planning and construction permits to be obtained before they will advance funds. In fact planning problems are one of the commonest reasons for delays in reaching Financial Close on PPP projects (*cf.* §6.3.8). Procedures in this respect vary greatly from country to country. In some cases the Public Authority will have obtained the key planning permits before the bids take place, which is the ideal procedure as it will probably speed up the whole progress of the project. However this may not be a viable approach when each bidder is offering different solutions to the output specification.

Even if outline planning permits are obtained, detailed designs for the Facility may require further permits. If the design work will not be complete until after Financial Close (*cf.* §6.6.1), the risk of such detailed changes of design causing a construction-cost increase will normally fall on the Construction Subcontractor as part of the overall responsibility for design.

§14.5.4 ENVIRONMENTAL IMPACT AND RELATED RISKS

Most major projects require an Environmental Impact Assessment ('EIA') as part of the permitting process. The EIA examines the environmental impact of the project in a variety of ways such as:

- the effect of construction and operation of the project on the surrounding natural environment (plant and animal habitats, landscape, *etc.*);
- the effect of construction on local communities, including noise, dust, other pollution, and construction traffic;
- any emissions into the atmosphere caused by operation of the project;
- water supply and discharge;
- long-term effects of the project on local traffic, transportation, and utilities;
- other long-term effects of the project on local communities or the natural environment.

As with planning and construction permits generally, lenders will require any necessary environmental clearances to be obtained before they advance any funding.

An environmental audit of the project site may also be required; this examines the site for potential pollution or hazardous waste, taking account of its previous uses. If this is discovered, a programme for containing or removing it is required. The Public Authority may have to take responsibility for known problems, but unknown 'site-legacy' risk (*e.g.* on a brownfield site which has been used for industrial processes) may be taken on by the Construction Subcontractor as part of the responsibility for ground condition, discussed above.

If there is known to be significant pollution or hazardous waste on the site this is also likely to be a major issue with lenders, as they may end up with a liability for damage caused by pollution from a site over which they take security; in general lenders feel vulnerable, as the parties with 'deep pockets', to the problem proving more difficult than expected or to long-term damage caused from site pollution. Insurance may be available to mitigate the risk (*cf.* §12.4.2).

§14.5.5 ARCHAEOLOGY AND FOSSILS

Discovery of important archaeology or fossils on the project site may seriously delay construction or even require some revision of the construction plans. If the project is in a location where this is a high risk, the Public Authority normally undertakes site surveys (*e.g.* a geophysical survey and digging test trenches, or even a full-scale archaeological dig) in advance of Financial Close. Thereafter, the Project Company may have to carry the risk of delay, at least to a certain level, which will thus be categorised as a Relief Event both under the PPP Contract and under the Construction Subcontract.

§14.5.6 ACCESS, RIGHTS OF WAY AND EASEMENTS

Site access is not normally a problem, except in cases where the Facility is still being used during the construction phase. This is a particular issue with rail projects, where the Project Company's Subcontractors may only be able to get access for limited time windows during the night or at weekends. Construction risk in such cases becomes considerably greater because of the difficulty of managing this process.

The Project Company may also need to have rights of way (*e.g.* access to the site for construction or operation or to connect to utilities), or easements (*e.g.* a right to discharge water) from parties owning adjacent land, who may have no other connection with the project. Again this is normally a risk which lenders will want to see dealt with before they advance any funding, and may be best dealt with by the Public Authority in advance of Financial Close.

Conversely, the Public Authority may wish to retain rights of way or access for other utilities or public services, which could include the right to enter the Facility to undertake further works on these.

§14.5.7 CONNECTIONS TO THE SITE

The project may be dependent on the provision of connections to the site. For example, a water supply may have to be linked to the site, or a connecting road may be needed to enable traffic to use a toll road or bridge. The party providing the connection may also be dependent on others (*e.g.* for rights of way).

If the connection is to be provided by the Public Authority it must obviously be responsible for the consequences of failing to do so, *e.g.* loss of revenue, but a party providing these connections who is not otherwise involved with the project may have no particular incentive to keep to the project timetable, and the damage to the project caused by late connection may be disproportionate to the cost of the connection. In such cases the Project Company can only assess the degree of risk by looking at the record of the third party in similar situations, and try to control the risk by close coordination with, and monitoring of, the third party. The Construction Subcontractor's relationship and experience with such third parties may also be relevant.

Similarly, projects such as construction of a road need to arrange for diversion or relocation of utilities (*e.g.* a gas, water or sewage pipeline may need to be moved under the road). The utility concerned will probably have control of this procedure, and their cooperation is needed.

The risk that such events could delay progress may be passed to the Construction Subcontractor, as it is a relatively routine requirement in construction, although it may be treated as a Relief Event (*cf.* §15.3).

If the connections are being provided by the Public Authority—a connecting road being a common case—then the Public Authority should clearly be responsible for the consequences of delay or failure to complete the connection, including loss of revenue that the Project Company suffers as a result. The issue becomes more complex where another public authority is providing the connection, since each may be unwilling to cover the other's delay or failure, and yet it is reasonable to expect the public sector as a whole to be responsible.

§14.5.8 PROTESTERS

As a sub-set of political risk (*cf.* §14.4), projects involving the construction of public infrastructure (*e.g.* a road) may also be the subject of public protest, which may seriously affect the construction schedule. In general, the Public Authority should take responsibility for delays of this kind, first by ensuring the provision of appropriate police protection for the Construction Subcontractor to carry out the work, and second by treating delays caused in this way at least as Relief Events, thus exempting the Project Company from penalties for delay in completion, if not compensating the Project Company for loss of revenue.

§14.5.9 DISPOSAL OF SURPLUS LAND

It is often the case that when a new PPP Facility is built the site of an old Facility is surplus and can be sold to help fund the project. This cuts down the long-term level of the

Service Fees, but raises the question of who is to take the risk of the disposal, the Public Authority or the Project Company? Lenders are unwilling to take on this risk, so unless an advance sale can be organised, or one of the Sponsors is willing to take the risk as part of their bid, the Public Authority will most likely have to do so.

Even if the old site is sold in advance, so there is no risk on the sale price, the completion of the sale will be dependent on construction progress on the new site, which enables the Public Authority to move out of the old site. Therefore if there is a delay in construction, the advance sale may be lost because the old site is not available in time. The issue becomes more complex where a Facility is being built in stages; this may involve a complex process of 'decanting', *i.e.* moving users from one old site to the new site (or maybe interim moves between old sites). This is a risk which the Public Authority may expect the Project Company to take on, and to pass to its Construction Subcontractor. However, this may cause difficulties with the latter, depending on the scale of the financial effect of failure to sell the land, and the Sponsors may have to consider giving support in this respect.

But wider risk-transfer issues also arise with using land sales as a form of capex contribution from the Public Authority (*cf.* §13.4.3).

§14.6 CONSTRUCTION RISKS

Construction risks usually translate into an overrun in construction costs against the budget on which the funding structure has been based. This may have various effects:

- There may be insufficient funding available to complete the project, thus forcing the Sponsors to invest funds for which they have made no commitment, to avoid a loss of their investment, or putting them at a severe disadvantage (and therefore liable to higher borrowing costs or other disadvantageous changes in loan terms) by having to ask the lenders to advance further funds or to agree to new financing arrangements.
- Even if additional funding is available, the Project Company's capex, and hence debt service costs, will increase, with no corresponding increase in revenue: therefore, the investors' return will inevitably be reduced. In the worst case, this may lead to them abandoning the project because the increased costs destroy its viability.
- From the lenders' point of view, any increase in debt-service costs reduces their Cover Ratios and thus makes the loan more risky.

Risk analysis before Financial Close, when the capex budget can still be influenced, therefore needs to consider the main cost headings in the budget (*cf.* §10.3.2), how these costs are controlled, and the likelihood of overruns under each cost heading.

The Public Authority is not obliged to do anything to support a Project Company suffering cost overruns, but political pressures for the PPP not to be seen to be 'failing', or to ensure continuity of the public service, may put the Public Authority under pressure to provide some form of extra-contractual support or relief (*cf.* §2.6.5). The Public Authority's due diligence should therefore take account of these risks. After Financial Close the Public Authority is unlikely to have any ability to influence or control what is going on with the Project Company's capex budget, and must rely on the lenders (as well as the Project Company's own prudence) in this respect (*cf.* §12.2.1).

The final protection against construction-cost overruns or a delay in completion is a contingency reserve. However well managed the budget, there is always a risk of unexpected events causing a cost overrun. Therefore a contingency reserve covered by matching funding is often required by lenders (*cf.* §10.5.9). As a rough rule of thumb, a contingency of around 10% of the 'hard' construction cost, or 7–8% of total project costs is prudent. The contingency is also intended to cover the effects of delays in the completion of construction, where Delay LDs are not payable by the Construction Subcontractor (*cf.* §14.7.2). But contingency funding is not intended to cover macroeconomic risks such as interest-rate movements during the construction phase, which must be covered in other ways (*cf.* §11.2). During the operation phase, the Reserve Accounts fulfil a similar function.

'Hard' construction costs are invariably the most important item in the construction-phase budget, and may make up 80% or more of the total; the next-largest cost—IDC—is largely an arithmetical product of drawing funding to meet the construction costs. It is therefore the risks related to the Construction Subcontract which require the closest review. These may be summarised as:

- risks relating to the Construction Subcontract itself (§14.6.1);
- risks related to the Construction Subcontractor (§14.6.2); and
- price-adjustment risks (§14.6.3).

Furthermore, the Construction Subcontractor's own risk analysis has to be borne in mind (§14.6.4), and if there is revenue during construction this raises some further issues (§14.6.5).

§14.6.1 CONSTRUCTION SUBCONTRACT

In the conventional design-bid-build public-procurement procedure for a major project, the Public Authority has architects and consulting engineers draw up the design, based on which a bid for the construction is invited with detailed drawings, bill of quantities, and so on; construction may be split into smaller works packages, and any specific equipment required is procured separately. Alternatively, a consulting engineer may be appointed as construction manager, with the responsibility of handling all aspects of the procurement of the project, against payment of a management fee, which may vary according to the final outcome of the construction costs. Neither of these approaches is usually acceptable to project-finance lenders:

- 'One-stop' or 'turnkey' responsibility for completing the project satisfactorily is necessary, since the Project Company must not be caught in the middle of disputes as to who is responsible for a failure to do part of the work correctly.
- A construction cost which is not fully fixed in advance is not acceptable because of the risk of a cost overrun for which there may not be sufficient funding, or which adds so much to the costs that the project cannot operate economically.
- A guaranteed completion date is also necessary, to match the requirements of the PPP Contract for commencement of the service.

In summary therefore, a turnkey, fixed-price, date-certain Construction Subcontract is required, which should substantially eliminate the risk of construction-cost overruns and delays, since this contract passes these risks on from the Project Company to its Construction Subcontractor. This is clearly likely to be reflected in the Construction Subcontractor building more contingencies into the contract costings, and hence a higher contract price than in design-bid-build procurement (*cf.* §5.3.1).

Two types of Construction Subcontract are seen in PPPs, depending on the nature of the project:

- Design & Build (D&B), used for fixed infrastructure such as accommodation or roads; under this contract the D&B Construction Contractor has responsibility for both the detailed design of the Facility as well as its construction—this means that there is no room for later dispute whether any problems are caused by bad design or bad construction.
- Engineering, Procurement and Construction (EPC), used for process plant and equipment (also known as a design, procurement and construction or DPC Contract), again the turnkey nature of the Contract is important in ensuring 'one-stop' responsibility for it.

§14.6.2 CONSTRUCTION SUBCONTRACTOR

Risk analysis of the Construction Subcontractor takes account of:

- the competence to undertake the work;
- the Construction Subcontractor's overall credit standing;
- conflicts of interest;
- the scale of the Construction Subcontractor's direct involvement in the works.

Technical competence. The Construction Subcontractor's competence should be reviewed carefully by the Public Authority as part of the prequalification process (*cf.* §6.3.3), and will also be reviewed by the lenders' T/A. The Construction Subcontractor should be able to demonstrate experience to build the type of project required successfully—this would include providing references for similar projects already built, including, where appropriate, references for the technology being employed in the project. Similar references may be required for the Construction Subcontractor's own major subcontractors, and the Construction Subcontract should provide the Project Company a list of approved subcontractors, or the right to veto them (and may give some rights of approval over the terms of these Subcontracts, although Subcontract prices are not usually revealed). If the Construction Subcontractor is working overseas, experience in the country of the project, and good relationships with strong local subcontractors, are also relevant. Finally the expertise of the Construction Subcontractor's key personnel who are actually working on the construction should be examined.

Credit risk. Allocating project risk to the Construction Subcontractor is not worthwhile if the company concerned is not creditworthy. If the Construction Subcontractor's wider business gets into financial difficulties, the project is likely to suffer. The credit standing of the Construction Subcontractor therefore also needs to be reviewed as part of the pre-qualification to assess whether it could cause any risk to the project. In cases where the Construction Subcontractor is involved in PPP projects on a large scale, or as a major part of its business, the Public Authority and the lenders will need to consider whether it can adequately handle this work as a whole, especially if its involvement in this sector has grown rapidly.

The Construction Subcontract should also not be excessively large in relation to the Construction Subcontractor's other business, as otherwise there is a risk that if the Project Contract gets into trouble, the Construction Subcontractor may not be able to deal with such problems because of their financial effect on the business as a whole. The scale of the Construction Subcontract should therefore be compared with the Construction Subcontractor's annual turnover; if it is more than, say, 10% of this figure, the Construction Subcontract may be too big for the Construction Subcontractor to handle alone, and a joint-venture approach with a larger contractor may be preferable. If the Construction Subcontractor is part of a larger group of companies, guarantees of its obligations by its ultimate parent company may also be necessary to support the performance and credit risk.

Despite the turnkey nature of the Construction Subcontract, both the Public Authority's and the lenders' due diligence should include a review of the construction management and programme, covering such issues as the critical-path timing for each stage (including, *e.g.* allowances for bad weather during the winter), adequacy of the pricing for the works, *etc.* The right to claim LDs, bonds, and other security provided under the Construction Subcontract (*cf.* §14.7.1), even when strengthened by bank bonding, cannot substitute for the competence of the Construction Subcontractor. Even a termination payment that recovers all the money spent on the Construction Subcontract will not adequately compensate the Project Company for losses if the project is not built, since the Construction Subcontract price is only a part (though a large one) of the total capex. Similarly, the Public Authority wants to get the Facility completed on time and to specification, and not to have to rely on the Project Company's claims against the Construction Subcontractor as a way of doing this.

Conflicts of interest. A Sponsor who is also the Construction Subcontractor has an obvious conflict of interest between this rôle and that of an investor in the Project Company. The risk of inappropriate contractual arrangements, or a less than rigorous supervision of the Construction Subcontract on an arm's length basis, is evident. These risks may be mitigated in several ways:

- Other Sponsors not involved in the construction process may specify the work and negotiate the Construction Subcontract (assuming they have the relevant expertise or external advisers to do so).
- Supervision of the Construction Subcontract may be carried out by Project Company personnel who are not connected with the Construction Subcontractor, with the assistance of an Owner's Engineer (*cf.* §7.7), or a Checker (*cf.* §6.7.3).
- The Construction Subcontractor's directors on the Project Company's board should absent themselves from discussions on the Construction Subcontract, or at least be disbarred from voting on such matters.
- The lenders' T/A is likely to play a more prominent checking rôle.

But if the Construction Subcontractor is a major Sponsor of the project, which is inevitably often the case with PPP projects (*cf.* §7.2.1), realistically there is a limit to the extent that it can be isolated from the Sponsor side of discussions on the Construction Subcontract.

Limited involvement in the Construction Subcontract. A Construction Subcontractor often further subcontracts a significant part of the Construction Subcontract; for example, a main contractor whose primary business is that of equipment supply will normally subcontract the civil works (charging LDs and taking security from its subcontractors that parallel the terms of the main Construction Subcontract). This process, however, can be carried too far if the Construction Subcontractor is not a significant supplier of either equipment or works to the project, but just provides an 'envelope' or 'wrap' for a contract largely carried out by its subcontractors, especially if the Construction Subcontractor has insufficient experienced in-house personnel to supervise the works and so relies too much on its subcontractors.

In such a situation, the risk of poor overall control of the project may be reduced by requiring the Construction Subcontractor to work in joint venture with one or more companies that would otherwise have been its subcontractors.

§14.6.3 PRICE ADJUSTMENTS

But a so-called fixed-price contract is never 100% fixed, and the risk of the Construction Subcontractor making claims for additional payments under various contract provisions has to be considered. These claims come under several categories:

Changes in the project schedule. The start-up of the Construction Subcontract may be delayed, perhaps because of difficulties in raising the finance, other negotiation delays, or satisfying all the lenders' conditions precedent. The Construction Subcontractor cannot be expected to keep the price fixed indefinitely, and therefore a cut-off date for the fixed price is normally set out in the Sponsors' bid. The Construction Subcontractor may be willing to agree to a formula for adjusting the final fixed price against CPI or another index after the cut-off date; this may be manageable within the financing plan. If no formula is agreed to, lenders may be reluctant to continue with work on the financing, as one of the main cost elements is no longer fixed.

Owner's Risks. Apart from making payments under the Construction Subcontract when these fall due, the Project Company (often called the 'owner' in this context) is responsible for 'Owner's Risks' such as:

- making the project site available and ensuring access (*cf.* §14.5.1);
- obtaining outline planning permits (*cf.* §14.5.3);
- in some cases, ground condition (*cf.* §14.5.2) or archaeology and fossil finds (*cf.* §14.5.5);
- again in some cases, latent defects (see below);

- providing access to utilities needed for construction, such as electricity and water and ensuring that third-party contracts (e.g. an access road) are carried out as required (cf. §14.5.7).

As discussed above, some of these risks may be passed on a back-to-back basis to the Public Authority.

> **Unforeseen events.** The Project Company will normally take the risk of changes in law affecting the construction-cost requirements (*e.g.* because of new public-health or safety requirements), which may be covered off by the Public Authority (*cf.* §15.2.5). The arrangements between the Public Authority and the Project Company as to:
>
> - Relief Events (*cf.* §15.3);
> - Compensation Events, including changes in specification by the Public Authority (*cf.* §15.2); and
> - *Force Majeure* (cf. §15.7)—which may be covered by insurance (cf. §12.4);
>
> will normally be reflected on a back-to-back basis in the Construction Subcontract; hence a Compensation Event under the PPP Contract will be an Owner's Risk under the Construction Subcontract. This means that the Public Authority may find itself *de facto* negotiating these points with the Construction Subcontractor, either directly, or indirectly *via* the Project Company.
>
> **Latent defects.** Particular problems arise on projects which do not involve construction on a greenfield site, but refurbishment, repair or maintenance on an existing 'brownfield' Facility, in respect of latent defects (*i.e.* defects which no-one could reasonably have found and whose effect does not appear until later), which may have the effect of making the reconstruction or maintenance of the Facility more expensive than could reasonably have been anticipated. If the Facility has been in the ownership of the Public Authority for many years, and it is difficult to investigate its condition, there is a strong case for the Public Authority to take some responsibility for latent defects—*e.g.* that they will be treated as Compensation Events above a certain limit, with the Project Company (and hence the Construction Subcontractor) taking on the first slice of the risk before the Public Authority's back-stop is triggered.

§14.6.4 THE CONSTRUCTION SUBCONTRACTOR'S RISKS

A Construction Subcontractor might reasonably ask what security is offered that payments will be made by the Project Company. Lenders have first security over the project assets including bank accounts. Neither the Sponsors nor the lenders will normally provide the Construction Subcontractor with guarantees. (Of course, one of the Sponsors may be the Construction Subcontractor.)

Normally the Construction Subcontractor's only security is the existence of the financing arrangements, and the fact that it is seldom in the lenders' interests to cut off funding for construction of the project. Therefore the Construction Subcontractor will not normally begin work until Financial Close has been reached (in respect of other Project Contracts and the financing documentation), and it is clear that financing has been made available by lenders on terms that should ensure that stage payments due under the Construction Subcontract can be made, and that the funding will not be withdrawn by the lenders on an arbitrary basis.

The Construction Subcontractor should also ensure that the Construction Subcontract payment schedule is linked as closely as possible to its own financial exposure to direct costs and payments to its own subcontractors and equipment suppliers, so that if the Project Company does collapse the Construction Subcontractor's own losses can be limited.

§14.6.5 REVENUE DURING CONSTRUCTION

If interim revenues are receivable during the construction phase to fund part of the capex (*cf.* §13.3.3), the risk has to be assessed that such revenues will not be received as expected. Even a fairly small deviation from projections could leave the Project Company with an awkward hole in its funding plan. Therefore projections of interim revenues during construction if anything have to be even more conservative than Base Case projections of revenues during the operating phase, as at least in the latter case there is a Cover Ratio to protect debt service, whereas 100% of the revenue during construction is needed to fund costs.

§14.7 COMPLETION RISKS

A delay in completion of the project may have several consequences:

- Financing costs, in particular IDC, will be higher because the construction debt is outstanding for a longer period: this is, in effect, another form of construction cost overrun.
- Revenues from operating the project will be deferred or lost.
- LDs may be payable to the Public Authority (cf. §13.3.4).

The effect of delays is thus to increase costs, decrease revenues, and hence reduce investors' returns and the lenders' Cover Ratios. However, these consequences may be mitigated for the Project Company if they are the Construction Subcontractor's fault (§14.7.1), and in some other cases (*cf.* §14.7.2).

Project completion, which triggers the Service Availability Date, is a concept that will appear in the PPP Contract (*cf.* §6.6.6), the Construction Subcontract, and as a required milestone date in the financing documentation. It is therefore important to ensure that the definitions of completion between all these different contracts fit together. If the Project Company is subject to penalties for late completion in the PPP Contract it will want the definition of Service Availability in that contract to be as 'loose' as possible so completion can easily be achieved (but possibly impose a higher completion hurdle on the Construction Subcontractor).

There is maybe a concept of 'practical completion'—*i.e.* the construction work has been substantially finished to the required specifications, and the Facility is accepted for use by the Public Authority, but there may still be small elements of the works such as landscaping (known as 'snagging' or the 'punch list') still outstanding.

The Facility may have to fulfil design requirements on completion (§14.7.3); an EPC Contract usually requires the Facility to pass performance tests to achieve completion (§14.7.4).

§14.7.1 DELAY BY THE CONSTRUCTION SUBCONTRACTOR

Insofar as delay in completion results in loss of Service-Fee revenue or LD payments to the Public Authority (*cf.* §13.3.4), the Project Company, will want to ensure that this risk is minimised, and that if it materialises the consequences are passed to the Construction Subcontractor.

The construction programme should contain adequate provision for such reasonably-foreseeable events such as bad weather during the winter, and hence the Construction Subcontractor should not be excused for such delays. A delay in completion is often quite predictable if detailed programming for the project is in place, as it will become evident that critical-path items (*i.e.* aspects of the project which, if delayed, will delay the final completion) are falling behind schedule. The Project Company should supervise progress sufficiently closely to ensure that potential delays in the critical path are spotted, and then assist (or put pressure on) the Construction Subcontractor to catch up. The lenders' T/A also monitors this process.

If delay does occur and is caused by the Construction Subcontractor's fault (*i.e.* one of the justifications for delay discussed below do not apply), the Project Company will need to be compensated for the losses that result. This is covered by the LD provisions of the Construction Subcontract, which are based on agreed formulae that both sides agree are sufficient to cover the Project Company's financial losses resulting from late completion of the project (or, where relevant, failure of the project to perform as specified, for which *cf.* §14.7.4). If specific amounts are not agreed to in this way there would be lengthy disputes about loss in each case: the uncertainty involved in this would not be acceptable to lenders, and the time spent in dispute could be financially disastrous for the Project Company. LDs are not intended as a penalty (indeed, many legal systems make a penalty payment of this type unenforceable), but a fair compensation for the loss suffered. Apart from the LD amounts, the Project Company cannot make claims against the Construction Subcontractor for loss of profits or extra costs, except on termination of the Construction Subcontract (see below). Delay LDs are not payable if the Project Company is receiving insurance payments to compensate for the delay (*cf.* §12.4.2), as this implies the cause of the delay is a *Force Majeure* event outside the Construction Subcontractor's control.

LDs are important for lenders, who tend to require higher levels of LDs than might be found in a construction contract that is not being project-financed. Obviously the Construction Subcontractor takes the risk of providing high levels of LDs into account when proposing a construction schedule and pricing the contract, together with the higher risks inherent in being responsible for all its own subcontractors. Moreover, the profit margin by these subcontractors at each level have to be added in. These additional factors mean that the price for a turnkey construction contract can be up to 20% higher than a design-bid-build approach with separate contractors, a point which needs to be borne in mind when comparing a PPC with private-sector procurement (*cf.* §5.3.1).

Delay LDs are calculated on a daily basis, at a rate that is a matter for negotiation, but should at the minimum be sufficient to cover the Project Company's interest costs and fixed overheads, plus any LDs payable to the Public Authority for late completion—*i.e.* the costs incurred as a result of the delay; ideally they should be high enough to cover the total loss of revenue (less any variable overheads). The total sum payable as Delay LDs is normally capped; lenders normally expect this cap to be at a high enough level to cover at least 6 months of delay in completion. A typical cap for Delay LDs would be 15–20% of the Construction Subcontract value.

Delay LDs should thus be sufficient to keep the Project Company financially whole, at least for some time, and provide an incentive for the Construction Subcontractor to take any necessary action to deal with prospective problems. But if the delay extends beyond 6 months or so, it is likely that Delay LDs will run out, and the pressure then reduces considerably. Therefore once the LD cap has been reached, the Project Company will normally have the right to terminate the Construction Subcontract. The Project Company's loss in getting another contractor to finish the works will then become the liability of the original Construction Subcontractor, although again the amount of this loss may be capped, *e.g.* at 100% of the original contract value.

The Construction Subcontractor normally provides the Project Company with specific security for its obligations in these respects:

Retainage. A percentage (usually around 5–10%) of each contract payment may be retained by the Project Company until satisfactory final completion of the project. This ensures that the Construction Subcontractor will deal expeditiously with snagging items at the end of the contract.

Completion Bond. The Construction Subcontractor is usually required to provide a bond (which may also be referred to as a Construction or Performance Bond) for 10–15% of contract value as security for general performance under the contract, including completion. This also provides further security to cover the obligation to pay LDs, insofar as the retention amount is not sufficient for this purpose.

Advance-Payment Bond. If any payments have been made in advance of the work being done (for example, an initial deposit of say 10%, which is quite common) the Construction Subcontractor provides an Advance-Payment Bond, under which the amounts concerned will be repaid *pro rata* if the contract is terminated before the work is complete.

Maintenance Bond. After completion of construction the retention and completion bonds may be converted into a maintenance bond, covering the cost of remedying latent defects during the defects liability (construction warranty) period, which will normally last for several years.

These obligations (if they are not covered by cash retainage) should be secured by bank letters of credit or insurance-company bonds that enable the Project Company to make an immediate drawing of cash rather than having to go through a dispute procedure or legal action before being paid anything. If this is not the case the Project Company may face a cash crisis if the events being covered by the security arise and payment cannot be obtained immediately. Alternatively, the Project Company may accept a guarantee from the Construction Company's parent company, if it is of a sufficient financial substance.

Although the Public Authority should not get involved in detailed negotiations with the Construction Subcontractor, it should ensure that the Construction Subcontract has appropriate levels of LDs, bonding and liability on termination, as these indirectly serve to protect the Public Authority's own interests (*cf.* §6.5.2).

§14.7.2 OTHER CAUSES OF DELAY

As for construction-cost overruns (*cf.* §14.6), the financial effects of other causes of delays which are not the Construction Subcontractor's fault depends on whether they come into the category of Compensation Events (*cf.* §15.2), Relief Events (*cf.* §15.3), or are covered by insurance (*cf.* §12.4). Failing any of these, delay risks will be left wholly with the Project Company.

§14.7.3 DESIGN RISK

Design risk overlaps the construction and operating phases: on completion the Facility must be designed to meet the PPP Contract specifications, but also during the early years of operations some flaw in design may emerge which, say, increases heating or maintenance costs more than expected. The benefit of a 'whole-life' approach to design of the Facility, and hence the issue of whether the Project Company should be responsible for design, has been discussed above (*cf.* §2.8, §13.2): assuming that this is the case, a back-to-back responsibility for design will be passed down to the Construction Subcontractor (*cf.* §6.6.1), which will also be reflected in design warranties provided by the latter covering at least the first few years of operation, or in the terms of a Hard FM contract. Thereafter, the benefits of whole-life design should emerge over time.

§14.7.4 PERFORMANCE ON COMPLETION

This is an issue which primarily arises where process plant is involved, and is being constructed under an EPC Contract, where equipment problems or inadequate technology may affect the ability of the project to perform as expected on completion. It is interesting to note that (to mid-2006) only four of the 700 or so PFI contracts in Britain had been terminated for default by the Project Company (*cf.* §15.5). All of these defaults related to performance of some form of process plant: a laboratory, a medical-waste incinerator, and two municipal-waste incinerators. Private-sector investors and lenders lost heavily in these cases, all of which involved excessive technology risks, *e.g.* because the technology was untried. From the public-sector point of view, this suggests that where there are high tech-nology risks, or the technology is unproven, the VfM argument for risk transfer to the private sector through a PPP is a strong one (*cf.* §2.6). On the other hand, it could also be said that the Public Authorities concerned should not have chosen bidders who were using unproven technology, since the result was that the Facility was not delivered as required, and public money was thus wasted on the procurement process.

Process-plant performance is measured by a (usually relatively limited) number of per-formance tests, which may measure both the ability to operate as specified and meet emis-sions or other environmental requirements. As with completion generally (*cf.* §6.6.6), the Public Authority or an independent Checker will be involved in this performance testing. If the performance tests are not passed (usually after several iterations to give the EPC Contractor a chance to remedy the problem), Performance LDs will become payable by the EPC Contractor, which should have originally been calculated as sufficient to cover the NPV of the financial loss from this poor performance for the life of the project. Performance LDs are normally used to reduce the debt so as to leave the lenders with the same cash-flow Cover Ratios as they would have had if the project had performed as expected. (Any surplus should be paid as a special distribution to investors to compensate them for their reduced equity return.)

Obviously the performance measurements of the project on completion are only a snap-shot taken over a limited period of time, and there may still be further variations in per-formance as time goes on which will not produce further LDs, but as it is difficult to separate the effect of how the project is operated from its original performance, LDs can really only be paid on this basis. Thus there is also no opportunity (unless claims can be made under warranty) to go back to the EPC Contractor several years after completion if performance gets worse. The Project Company should be aware of the uncertainty of these assumptions and allow a margin for this in negotiating the Performance LD calculations with the EPC Contractor.

There is normally an overall cap for Delay and Performance LDs, typically around 25–30% of the contract value—a figure higher than that usually found in non-project financed EPC Contracts. It is important to note again, therefore, that LDs do not provide compensation for a complete inability by the EPC Contractor to complete the contract: termination of the contract (*cf.* §14.7.1) may provide further remedies in this case.

§14.8 OPERATION-PHASE RISKS

Operation-phase risks may be summarised as:

- usage (§14.8.1);
- network (§14.8.2);
- revenue payment (§14.8.3);
- availability and service quality (§14.8.4);
- operating costs (§14.8.5);
- maintenance (§14.8.6);

as well as the effects of 'unforeseeable' risks such as:

- changes in the project's specification by the Public Authority (*cf.* §15.2.2);
- changes in law, leading to a need for additional capex or opex (*cf.* §15.2.5);
- *Force Majeure* (*cf.* §15.7)—which may be covered by insurance (*cf.* §12.4).

§14.8.1 USAGE

Usage risk depends on the nature of the PPP Contract:

- Concession Model—usage risk is always taken by Project Company.
- PFI Model—usage risk may be taken either by the Project Company or the Public Authority.

PPP Contracts with the Project Company taking usage risk generally relate to transportation projects. Finance can only be raised for such projects where there is a clearly-established demand (*cf.* §13.4.1). For example, a project may consist of building a tolled bridge alongside an existing one to add capacity: the established traffic flows make projections of future toll revenues relatively easy. The risk assessment is more difficult if, for example, a toll road is to be built near to other roads with no toll. In these cases, however, if the current demand is clearly demonstrated by congestion on the roads, and the cost of tolls or fares is reasonable in relation to the cost of existing transport modes, investors and their lenders are willing to consider taking the usage risk.

Usage projections for transportation projects are based on modelling by the Public Authority, the Project Company's traffic consultants, and the lenders' traffic advisers. Modelling of usage is based on projections, which in a road project could take into account factors such as:

- overall population growth, distribution, and movement;
- general and local economic activity;
- land use around the area of the project;
- travel at different times of the day or different seasons;
- distribution of travel (*i.e.* the split between local and long distance travel);
- split between commercial and private traffic;
- split between modes of travel such as bus, car, or train.

These and other factors combine to produce a model of current traffic patterns, which it should be possible to validate by using it to project traffic growth from a date in the past up to the present and comparing the results with the actual growth figures. Future projections of traffic growth for project finance purposes are based on macroeconomic factors such as growth in the national and regional economy leading to growth in private and commercial vehicle ownership, and generally do not take into account extra traffic that may be created by the construction of the project itself.

Having said all this, traffic projections seem to be as much of an art as a science, and the record of failure in such projections is not encouraging. Perhaps around 10% of road

Concessions are financial failures, defining failure as a situation requiring financial support from either the investors and lenders, a renegotiation of the Concession Agreement, or a financial bail-out by the Public Authority. This is a much higher level of failure than found in other types of PPP, reasons for which include:

- the winning bidder taking too optimistic a view of traffic, often influenced by similar optimism from the Public Authority; this is known as the 'winner's curse';
- difficulty of valuing time saved, *i.e.* how much drivers are willing to pay to avoid spending more time on alternate but slower free routes;
- lower than expected usage by trucks, whose tolls usually constitute a major factor in total revenue projections as they are substantially higher than tolls for cars; truck drivers typically take a much more conservative view on the value of time saved than car drivers;
- slower than expected ramp-up (*i.e.* initial growth in traffic);
- unexpected public-sector investment in competing free roads, or failure to invest in anticipated connecting roads (cf. §14.8.2).

In addition to these obvious failures, projects may be undertaken primarily on the strength of revenue guarantees or other financial support from the Public Authority rather than the inherent strength of the project, and end up placing unexpected burdens on the Public Authority because investors' usage projections are not carried out rigorously (*cf.* §13.4.3).

In fact, road Concessions tend to have either so little traffic risk (and a high risk of excess profits as a result) that there seems little value in transferring this risk to the private sector, or so much that it is better not to transfer it to the private sector because there is a high risk of the project collapsing and needing to be bailed out. Similar problems exist with other types of transportation Concessions such as tram and light rail projects, but the problems in such cases can be made worse by competing modes of transport such as buses.

Transfer of usage risk to the Project Company in the PFI Model also occurs primarily in transportation projects, through the use of Shadow Tolls. As discussed in §13.4.5, the risk transfer in such cases is more limited than with real tolls under a Concession-model Contract, and the lenders' risk in particular is very firmly based on existing traffic-flow volumes and patterns. Shadow-toll structures have fallen out of favour because of this limited risk transfer.

Where Service Fees are based on Availability, it is evident that, by default, usage risk is retained by the Public Authority. What this implies is that the Public Authority has signed a long-term PPP Contract to use the Facility, but may find that, some years into the Contract, it no longer fulfils its purpose—e.g. a school has become redundant because of local population changes, and it would be better to move it elsewhere, or advances in technology have rendered a hospital unsuitable for up-to-date medical procedures. As discussed in §2.12, the usage risk for the Public Authority in such cases is much the same as if the Facility had been constructed using public-sector procurement, where the same issues arise, but the PPP structure creates additional financial costs resulting from termination of the PPP Contract, rather than termination of the use of the Facility (*cf.* §15.6).

§14.8.2 NETWORK

Any project involving usage risk also has to take into account the effect of public-sector policies on this usage. Policy changes which are local to a project are known as 'network' risks: these may result from construction of other roads that take traffic from a toll road, changes in local road layout, traffic management, or imposition or removal of tolls or other road-usage fees. It is typically difficult to define all network risks in advance, but insofar as they can be clearly defined investors will normally expect these risks to be borne by the Public Authority (*cf.* §15.2.4), *e.g.* through 'non-compete' provisions in toll-road Concessions, under which the Public Authority must not build competing roads, or compensate for doing so (*cf.* §2.9.1, §3.5). However, if this is the case then the benefit of network changes which improve the Project Company's position (*e.g.* new connecting roads) should accrue to the Public Authority.

The risk of changes in general or national policies which affect the project (*e.g.* an increase in fuel prices that reduces road-traffic volume in general) is generally left with the Project Company.

§14.8.3 REVENUE PAYMENT

Here the issue is not whether there will be sufficient usage to generate revenues, as discussed above, but whether the Project Company can expect to be paid the revenues, *i.e.* the credit-risk aspect of these payments. In relation to Concessions, this is a question of 'willingness to pay', already discussed above (*cf.* §13.4.1).

For PFI-Model projects the credit issue is that of the Public Authority's ability to pay, especially where it is not a central-government department. 'Sub-sovereign' Public Authorities, which would include regional and local governments (municipalities), may have limitations of legal capacity and credit-risk issues which do not apply to the central government. For example, if a PPP intended to be off-balance sheet for such a Public Authority is later reclassified and placed on its balance sheet, its obligations may be outside its legal borrowing powers and hence the PPP Contract could be unenforceable. The credit-risk question arises where the Public Authority is not a tax-raising body, and relies on central or regional funding, or is otherwise restricted in its ability to raise tax revenues. Neither investors nor lenders will find it acceptable to rely on a very long-term stream of payments from the Public Authority if there is any doubt—however theoretical—about the Public Authority's legal or financial capacity to make these payments. This may mean making changes in national laws to give the necessary assurances.

It may also be necessary to give investors and lenders reassurance from independent funding of public-sector payments. This approach has been adopted in the Brazilian PPP Law of 2005; this relates to PFI-Model projects, and provides that the Public Authority's Service-Fee liabilities are backed by a separate fund into which the Public Authority injects assets such as property to support these obligations. Investors and lenders can thus be more certain there will be no later political interference with the payment process. A public-sector fund in Korea fulfils a similar function (*cf.* §3.8.2).

Investors' and lenders' payment risks, especially in developing countries, may also be covered by political-risk insurance: this subject is beyond the scope of this book, but is covered in *Principles of Project Finance* (Chapter 11).

§14.8.4 AVAILABILITY AND SERVICE QUALITY

The consequences under the PPP Contract of the Facility not being available, or of poor quality of service, are set out above in §13.5. As already discussed, the overall level of Availability/performance risk, once a Facility has been completed, is typically very low—*e.g.* none of the 700+ British PFI projects have been terminated so far for Unavailability or poor service.

§14.8.5 OPERATING EXPENSES

The risks of opex being higher than projected have to be considered separately under the various categories of opex. The Project Company may only have a limited direct control over opex, if most of these expenses are covered by FM Subcontracts. In these cases the key to risk management is the matching of payments under these Subcontracts to the Service Fees. Looking in more detail at various possible categories of opex:

Soft FM costs. If there is a Soft FM Subcontractor (*cf.* §10.3.3), the Sponsors will need to persuade this Subcontractor to index payments under the Subcontract on the same basis as those under PPP Contract (*e.g.* against a general CPI index rather than an industry-specific one), but in general Soft FM Subcontractors are reluctant to take a very long-term risk on this basis, which means that a review of the projected pricing may be necessary through benchmarking or market testing (*cf.* §11.3.13); this raises the question of whether Soft FM is a suitable component of a PPP Contract (*cf.* §13.2).

Maintenance costs. See below.

Utilities. Another opex item which may be included within the scope of the PPP Contract, especially for accommodation projects, is utilities, *e.g.* for power and heating. There are two separate issues here:

- *The tariff risk: i.e.* the cost per unit, *e.g.* per kWh of electricity. This is a risk which is beyond the Project Company's control (unless it enters into a long-term purchase contract)—it may well be more efficient for utilities to be purchased by the Public Authority where there are benefits from doing so as part of a bulk-purchase arrangement, and for the Service Fees to be adjusted for the actual tariff on this basis.
- *The usage risk:* even if the Project Company is not taking the usage risk of the Facility, as with maintenance (see below), the level of usage will affect its costs as far as utilities are concerned. Furthermore, if the people working for the Public Authority go round leaving the heating on and the windows open, it is difficult to control this; on the other hand a bidder should be incentivised to design a building which is energy-efficient. There is a difficult balance here: Service Fees can be adjusted after an initial 'bedding down' period to reflect the actual level of utilities usage, but this should not relieve the bidder from responsibility for energy efficiency.

Insurance. This is another large opex item which tends not to move in conjunction with CPI; as discussed in §12.4.5 this risk can also be shared with the Public Authority through adjustments to Service Fees, but once again the Project Company should not be given a complete rescue blanket and should have some incentive to eliminate unnecessary insurance costs.

Project Company's direct costs. Unless the Project Company is running any significant part of its operations itself, instead of delegating to Subcontractors (*cf.* §7.6.3), the Project Company's own direct operating costs will normally be limited in nature and relatively easy to control. Lenders may impose rolling budgetary controls on these costs (*cf.* §12.2).

§14.8.6 MAINTENANCE

Hard FM, lifecycle, or other maintenance, costs, (*cf.* §10.3.3) are the main opex item where real risk transfer from public to private sector should take place. As discussed in §11.3.13, reallocating some of this risk back to the Public Authority through benchmarking or market testing is not appropriate, and bidders should ensure that long-term maintenance requirements are properly taken into account at the time of bidding. There are two aspects to maintenance risk: the effect on Availability of the Facility being out of service for maintenance, and the costs of the maintenance.

A maintenance programme needs to be agreed in the PPP Contract which gives a reasonable allowance for maintenance downtime against Unavailability deductions or other penalties, and sets out a basic schedule for this which ensures the minimum disruption—*e.g.* a school's heating system should be maintained, and its buildings repainted, during the summer holidays. Unscheduled maintenance—*e.g.* because the heating system breaks down—is likely to lead to an Unavailability deduction. The lenders' T/A will therefore want to be satisfied that the regular maintenance programme is managed properly.

The original Construction Subcontractor may have an interest in providing the Hard FM routine maintenance for the Facility: in such cases it can be expected that a Hard FM Subcontract will be signed and routine maintenance risks passed down under this contract. (Typically, a large part of these risks relate to labour costs). If so, failure to perform to the programme may lead to penalties on the Subcontractor, but as with Soft FM services such penalties are likely to be limited by reference to the overall level of income which the Subcontractor can earn. It is much difficult to pass down Lifecycle or other major maintenance risks to a subcontractor, since these are harder to predict.

If this risk is not passed down to a Subcontractor, it will remain significant for the Project Company, even if Service Fees in this respect are indexed against a construction-industry inflation index rather than a general (CPI) index (*cf.* §11.3.2). Quite apart from the indexation issue, these long-term costs are difficult to predict, and constitute the largest risk for investors and lenders. An MRA helps to deal with predictable spikes in lifecycle costs or other major maintenance, but not a steady rise in Hard FM or other routine maintenance costs (*cf.* §12.2.4).

Moreover, even if usage risk has formally been retained by the Public Authority, a high level of usage may result in higher maintenance requirements, and so in this sense the Project Company may be taking an element of usage risk too—*e.g.* higher than expected levels of traffic may result in major road maintenance having to be brought forward and performed more frequently. (*Cf.* the similar case of utilities usage risk discussed above.) In a Concession-model project this higher usage cost would be matched by higher revenues, but this is not the case with a PFI-Model project where Service Fees are not based on usage, or are capped, as with Shadow Tolls (*cf.* §13.4.5).

There may also come a point, in relation to any category of operating risk, whether passed down to a Subcontractor or partially retained by the Project Company, that the cost of provision of the service has become so much larger than anticipated that the Subcontractor's or Project Company's only commercially-sensible action is to default. This is then likely to leave the Public Authority with the choice of terminating the PPP Contract or coming to some arrangement to take back some of this risk (*cf.* §2.6.5). This problem can become acute where the Project Company has taken over responsibility for a large and old building or network, rather than building something new: it is likely to be very difficult to assess the level of maintenance which the system requires, and thus passing this risk to the private sector may be unrealistic (*cf.* §14.6.3).

Chapter 15

Changes in Circumstances and Termination

§15.1 INTRODUCTION

This chapter deals with some of the key changes in circumstances after Financial Close which can affect the rights of either party to the PPP Contract, namely:

- Compensation Events, *i.e.* cases where there is a delay in completion, or increase in capex or opex for which the Public Authority has to compensate the Project Company (§15.2);
- Relief Events (also known as Temporary *Force Majeure*), *i.e.* cases where the Project Company's completion of the Facility is delayed, or its performance after completion does not meet the PPP Contract requirements, but which do not result in the Project Company suffering any penalty or receiving any compensation from the Public Authority (§15.3).

The chapter also deals with the 'Step-In' rights of the lenders and the Public Authority (§15.4), as well as termination of the PPP Contract under various scenarios:

- default by the Project Company (§15.5);
- early termination by the Public Authority, or default by the Public Authority, which is generally treated in the same way (§15.6);
- termination for *Force Majeure*—*i.e.* through no fault of either party, it is impossible to continue with the PPP Contract (§15.7);
- termination for corruption (§15.8);
- scheduled termination and transfer of assets (§15.11).

The position of Subcontractors on early termination (§15.9), and taxation of termination payments (§15.10) are also covered. Along with the Service-Fee mechanism (*cf.* Chapter 13), the topics in this Chapter are the key finance-related aspects of the PPP Contract, *i.e.* the aspects to which lenders pay the most attention. It should be noted that although in common-law countries all these provisions will probably be found in the PPP Contract, in civil-law countries many of them may be automatically implied by Concession or PPP laws, or general public administrative law, and hence not spelt out in the PPP Contract.

§15.2 COMPENSATION EVENTS

Compensation Events, where the Public Authority will have to compensate the Project Company for loss of revenue or additional capex, fall into three main categories:

- change in PPP Contract specifications by the Public Authority ('Changes');
- events not caused by the Public Authority's actions, but for which it takes on liability;
- change in law.

Compensation Event provisions in the PPP Contract may be mirrored in the relevant Subcontract, or to turn it round the other way, the Project Company may push for a particular item to be classified as a Compensation Event under the PPP Contract because the relevant Subcontractor insists on it being considered this way in the Subcontract. As with other aspects of risk transfer, there is a price for anything, and the issue for the Public Authority is therefore whether it is better VfM to cover a particular risk as a Compensation Event, or get the risk transferred to and priced into the relevant Subcontract (either as a Relief Event or with full risk transfer to the Subcontractor) and thus fed through into the Service Fees.

§15.2.1 FINANCIAL BALANCE

The general principle in cases where the Public Authority is responsible for Compensation Events is that of 'Financial Balance'—*i.e.* the level of compensation required to put the Project Company, and its investors and lenders, in a position no worse than they would otherwise have been had the Compensation Event not occurred.

If the Compensation Event only affects opex, the cost of this can be covered by a corresponding increase in the Service Fees. In Concession-model PPPs, the costs may be passed on to end-users; failing which, the Public Authority will have to pay them as they occur. However, the change in opex may also imply some change in the risks involved in the project, which may be more difficult to quantify.

Where capex is involved, the easiest and most economic approach is usually for the capex involved to be funded directly by the Public Authority, but of course there may not be a budget for this. If this is the case, the Public Authority may wish the Project Company to raise finance (which may be a mixture of new equity and debt), against compensation by way of an increase in the Service Fees. However, it is very difficult to impose a requirement to finance the capex on the Project Company: its own financial resources are limited to the existing capex requirements for the Facility, and cannot be used for additional purposes. Existing lenders may agree to increase their loan, but they are also in a monopoly supplier position, compounded by the fact that lenders cannot be forced to admit a new lender to share in their security (*cf.* §12.6). (The one exception to this, and an area in which, unusually, bonds may be more flexible than bank loans, is that variation bonds—*i.e.* undrawn bonds which can be issued at a later date, subject to certain conditions—can be included as part of an initial bond issue, albeit the pricing of these bonds will be affected by market conditions when they are issued.) It is unlikely to be economic to replace the whole of the original loan with an increased loan which both prepays the original loan and covers the new capex, so competitive bidding for financing the new capex is usually not realistic.

If the Project Company does finance the capex, the required increase in the Service Fees is normally calculated using the financial model such that the lenders' Cover Ratios and the Equity IRR remain as in the original Base Case, although there is an argument for the Equity IRR reflecting the current rate of return on an investment of comparable risk, which may be more favourable to the Public Authority as the Equity IRR for a mature project will be lower (*cf.* §7.3.2). But there are some problems with using the financial model for this calculation:

- The financial model was not originally designed for this purpose, and the parties may find it difficult to agree how it should be done (including both changes in assumptions and in the structure of the financial model); this cannot easily be provided for in advance in the PPP Contract.
- Calculations must relate only to the cost increase: it is important to avoid being caught in the trap of calculating adjustments to the Service Fees based on the total cash flow, as opposed to the marginal change, or this underwrites the lenders' risk and investors' return on the whole project.

A simpler approach is for the Public Authority to agree a supplementary Service Fee which relates directly to repayment of financing for the marginal capex—*e.g.* on an annuity basis over the remaining term of the PPP Contract—rather than trying to mix these with the overall financial model, although care must be taken as this may result in Separability of the payment, and hence on-balance sheet treatment.

Yet another alternative is for the PPP Contract term to be extended (this can also apply where there is an increase in opex), which may be more 'painless' if it means that Service Fees do not need to be increased. This can seldom be provided for in advance, however, and would need to be specifically negotiated at the time as an alteration to the PPP Contract.

A Compensation Event during the construction phase may not only involve additional capex, but also delay completion. Obviously the Project Company should not be penalised for this, and moreover compensation will need to be paid by the Public Authority for any loss of revenue.

§15.2.2 Procurement

Where major capex is required as a result of the Compensation Event, this may itself raise procurement issues, and hence require competitive bidding. Even if this is not the case, procurement in such situations is a complex matter, as it is difficult to break away from the monopoly-supplier position of the Project Company and its Subcontractors. The

Public Authority can be given the right to benchmark costs by checking them in the market, if this is possible—but often comparable cost data cannot be obtained, and again there are discrepancies of information between the Public Authority and the Project Company, the latter being much better informed (*cf.* §2.9.9). Similarly, even if the Public Authority has the right to require the Project Company to procure through a competitive bidding procedure, this may not be very easy:

- If the Project Company's main contender for the work is one of its own shareholders, who is an existing Subcontractor, they will have inside knowledge, and an inherent advantage which will mean that other suppliers may be reluctant to bid.
- This reluctance on the part of other bidders will be enhanced if the existing Subcontractor has a 'right to match' any bids received, and get the business in this way.
- It may not be possible for the work to be undertaken by a third party because this would invalidate the liabilities of the existing Subcontractor, *e.g.* the turnkey liability under a Construction Subcontract.

§15.2.3 CHANGES

The Public Authority needs to have some flexibility to make Changes in the specifications for the Facility or the service to be provided under the PPP Contract. It is evident that the Project Company should be properly compensated for such Changes. Funding them is also an issue, since the Project Company will have little, if any, reserve for this purpose.

Small Changes, which have no effect on the service requirements of the PPP Contract, are the most common in occurrence, and should be easily dealt with—an annual and item-size limit can be agreed for such Changes, and the Public Authority can just pay for the extra cost, be it capex or opex, as it occurs. The monopoly-supplier problem, *e.g.* the Project Company over-charging for, say, installing a new light fitment, may be overcome by agreeing general time and cost-plus rates in advance for charging in such cases. Thus it should not be difficult for both sides to agree a quick and simple procedure for these minor Changes. The lenders should have no desire to be involved in *de minimis* items of this type.

More major Changes, however, which require substantial capex or a significant Change in the service provisions or opex, can raise risk issues, as well as the issues on Financial Balance and procurement discussed above. Taken together, these issues can have a serious effect on the long-term flexibility of PPP Contracts (*cf.* §2.12). As to risk, there must be some limitations on the scope of Changes:

- The Changes should not be so great as to alter the fundamental nature of the PPP Contract. For example, a Change which added 50% to the construction cost would obviously be out of scale. Therefore there has to be some overall limitation on Changes: thus under Spanish PPP legislation the Public Authority's '*ius variandi*' ('right to change') is limited to 20% of the project value. Similarly, a Facility cannot be halved in size, or a prison turned into a hospital.
- The Changes cannot increase the risks undertaken by the Project Company under the PPP Contract, *e.g.* by interfering with its ability to provide the services required, or by requiring them to be performed in such a way that operating permits may be invalidated.

In fact, the lenders will generally wish to control the discussion in this respect, as the Project Company will not be able to agree to any Changes in the PPP Contract without their consent.

It is possible that a Change will save money rather than cost more. If so, this can be adjusted through the Service Fees, but the provisos above as to not changing the fundamental nature of the project, or its risks, apply here too. Similarly, there also needs to be a procedure for the Project Company to propose Changes which would be beneficial to the Public Authority, and a basis for splitting the benefits of such Changes between the Public Authority and the Project Company, to ensure that the latter has an incentive to propose beneficial Changes.

Finally, a specific timetable for the Change procedure needs to be set out in the PPP Contract, *e.g.* how much time the Project Company has to respond to a request for a Change, and how long the various stages of dialogue can take thereafter.

§15.2.4 PUBLIC AUTHORITY'S RISKS

As has been seen, the Public Authority may be responsible under the PPP Contract for certain aspects of the project risks during construction, especially related to the site (*cf.* §14.5). If such risks cause delay in completion or additional capex, the Public Authority must compensate for loss of revenue or extra costs, such compensation normally being paid direct by the Public Authority rather than by adjusting the Service Fees or expecting the Project Company to obtain extra funding as for Changes (although if the Project Company is able and willing to fund the costs on the same basis as for a Change, this can be an alternative). Delay LDs (*cf.* §13.3.4) are obviously not payable by the Project Company in such circumstances.

The Public Authority may also have continuing liabilities of this kind during the operating phase, for example relating to damage to the Facility caused by its own staff, or persons for whom it is responsible, such as pupils at a school.

As already mentioned, the dividing line between Compensation Events and Relief Events is not a firm one, and will be affected by the extent to which Subcontractors are willing to take on these risks. A compromise position may be reached, whereby the Project Company, and hence its Subcontractors, take on the first layer of the risk as a Relief Event up to a certain amount, with the balance being treated as a Compensation Event. Insurance may also play a part here.

More complex changes in circumstances can affect some projects, especially where usage-risk transfer is involved—*e.g.* a decision to build a new road which affects an existing Concession, where the Project Company would expect to be compensated for loss of revenue (*cf.* §14.8.2), but of course this loss may be difficult to isolate and measure with certainty. Where the connection is more remote—*e.g.* an increase in fuel taxes reducing traffic in general—it becomes even more difficult to decide what compensation, if any, is reasonable. Where it is agreed that such risks should be covered by the Public Authority, increases in tolls or an extension of the PPP Contract term may be considered as a way of compensating the Project Company for loss, rather than direct compensation payments by the Public Authority, but this usually has to be negotiated on an *ad hoc* basis given the difficulty of providing for all eventualities in advance. This problem of providing for policy changes is another reason why transfer of usage risk to the private sector is often not appropriate (*cf.* §14.8.1).

Another potential area of Public Authority liability relates to that for injury to third parties using the Facility. This can be covered by insurance (*cf.* §12.4.3), but this may not offer the best VfM. In the United States, for example, it is standard practice for the Public Authority to retain third-party liability for transportation projects, rather than pass this to the Project Company.

§15.2.5 CHANGE IN LAW

As a matter of basic public policy, a government generally cannot contractually fetter the right of its successors to change the law, and therefore provisions giving any protection of this kind are unlikely to be found in a PPP Contract. However, a Public Authority can agree in the PPP Contract that if the law is changed in a way which the parties agree is detrimental to the Project Company or its investors, they will be compensated accordingly.

A change in law may be directly-related to the PPP project, *e.g.* by requiring a reduction in emissions from a waste incinerator, and hence additional capex, or a new safety requirement for the Facility, which results in additional opex. Alternatively, the change may be of a more general nature, but still affect the Project Company, *e.g.* a change in corporate tax rates, or in requirements for pension provision for employees. The Project Company may have insufficient cash flow or financial resources available to it to accommodate any such changes in law.

One extreme viewpoint here is that as the Public Authority is part of the public sector, which changes the law, the Public Authority should always compensate for the effect of such a change. The other extreme is that the Project Company is no different from any other company doing business in the country concerned, and should not be shielded from the business risks to which all other companies are subject; moreover the particular Public Authority may have no influence over changes in the law at all. The typical PPP-Contract risk transfer falls between these two extremes:

- Costs resulting from changes in the law which are specific to the type of Facility being provided in the PPP project can either be passed on to end-users, in a Concession-model project, or are covered by the Public Authority, in a PFI-Model project: the argument for this is that if the Facility were being provided in the public sector, the same costs would then apply.
- Costs resulting from changes in law which are specific to PPP Project Companies or PPP-provided Facilities (or indeed the particular Project Company or Facility) should also be covered by the Public Authority, since these are in effect discriminatory against PPPs.
- Other more general changes in law which affect opex should be a Project-Company risk, the argument for this being that these are general costs of doing business, and all investors and lenders face these risks. Inflation indexation of the PPP Contract (*cf.* §11.3) provides some protection against such cost increases; in the case of Concession-model projects, these extra costs may be passed on to the end-users if this is commercially sustainable.

- Changes in the general law which require capex are more difficult, since the Project Company will not have the resources to fund any major costs of this type. Lenders may wish the Project Company to establish a Change in Law Reserve (*cf.* §12.2.4) to build up funds to meet any such change: this is really not an effective use of cash flow given that the change may never occur, and if it does there is likely to be plenty of warning, which gives time to build up funds from regular cash flow. A Public Authority may find it better VfM to agree an overall cap on the effect of a change in law in such cases, above which the risk transfers back to the Public Authority. Alternatively the Public Authority may agree to fund $x\%$ of the capex cost of such a change (perhaps on a sliding scale, where the first $\alpha\%$ of cost is funded 100% by the Project Company, the next $\beta\%$ funded 75%, and so on), which ensures that the Project Company has an incentive to fund this capex at the most economic cost. Apart from VfM, the policy argument for such risk-sharing is that, were the Public Authority to operate the Facility itself, it would face the same capex costs.

§15.3 RELIEF EVENTS

Relief Events are anything other than Compensation Events which affect the Project Company's performance, but which the parties agree are not directly controllable by the Project Company (hence the alternative term 'Temporary *Force Majeure*'). Such events excuse the Project Company from failing to perform under the PPP Contract. This means that no Service Fees are paid if the service is not being provided, and the Project Company must suffer any other increased costs or revenue losses, but on the other hand the Public Authority cannot charge the Project Company with any LDs (*cf.* §13.3.4) or penalties (*cf.* §13.4.6), or terminate the PPP Contract (*cf.* §15.5). The Project Company obviously has to take reasonable steps to deal with the problem to receive the benefit of the Relief Event provisions. In summary, Relief Events give the Project Company 'time' (to sort the problem out), whereas Compensation Events give the Project Company 'time and money', but it should be noted that Relief Events do not normally give an extension of time for the PPP Contract as a whole, *i.e.* its final termination date is not extended.

Examples of Relief Events include:

- insurable events such as fire, explosion, accidental damages, *etc.*;
- civil disturbance;
- strikes applying to an industry as a whole (rather than specific to the project or any of the Subcontractors);
- failure by third parties to carry out or facilitate works (*cf.* §14.5.7);
- failure in utility supplies.

As discussed in §15.2.4 the effects of some types of event (*e.g.* archaeological discoveries) may be split between a Relief Event for the first layer of loss and a Compensation Event thereafter. Although it is not usual to allow any extension of the term of the PPP Contract because of a Relief Event, in some cases this may offer better VfM than making the event concerned a Compensation Event. An event which makes it permanently (rather than temporarily) impossible to continue with the project is dealt with as *Force Majeure* (*cf.* §15.7).

§15.4 STEP-IN AND SUBSTITUTION

§15.4.1 EMERGENCY STEP-IN

From the Public Authority's point of view, the first priority for any PPP project must be the maintenance of the public service. There may be situations where the Public Authority has to 'Step In' to control the Facility for service reasons, because of a health or safety risk, to carry out a legal duty, or for reasons of national security.

If the Project Company is not in default under the PPP Contract, and it cooperates with the Public Authority, the normal Service Fees should continue to be payable. If the Project Company is in default, this will probably imply that the Public Authority has to Step In to rectify this default: in this case the Public Authority's costs should be deducted from Service Fees. However, this should not be used as a way of short-circuiting the normal termination provisions (*cf.* §15.5), *i.e.* the Step In is still only allowable in the specific circumstances mentioned above. The Public Authority also needs to ensure that its Step-In rights are reflected in the Subcontracts (as well as any rights to take over the Subcontracts after termination on default by the Project Company—*cf.* §15.5).

In any case, the Public Authority should have a general right of access to the Facility to monitor performance under the PPP Contract.

§15.4.2 LENDER STEP-IN AND SUBSTITUTION

If the Project Company gets into difficulties, the lenders will wish to take control of the situation; it is in the Public Authority's interests to get these problems sorted out by the lenders rather than terminate the PPP Contract. Although the lenders' general security over the Project Company should give them the ability to intervene, *e.g.* by replacement of Subcontractors (*cf.* §13.5.3), their Direct Agreement with the Public Authority (*cf.* §12.3.3) provides them with time and a framework to deal with the most serious problems without being frustrated by the Public Authority itself taking premature action. Various stages and options for lender action can be set out in the Direct Agreement:

Notification. The Public Authority agrees to notify the lenders if it is considering terminating the PPP Contract because of a default by the Project Company, or if the Project Company has accumulated penalties, payment deductions or Performance Points (*cf.* §13.5.2) beyond a trigger level, and gives the lenders right to join in any discussions with the Public Authority at that time.

Cure Periods. If the Project Company is in default under the PPP Contract (and assuming this default can be remedied, or 'cured'), the Direct Agreement gives the lenders 'Cure Periods' (*i.e.* extra time to take action to remedy the Project Company's default, in addition to that already given to the Project Company) before the PPP Contract is terminated. These Cure Periods are limited in length—perhaps only a week or two—where the Project Company has failed to pay money when due, but substantially longer for non-financial default (*e.g.* failure to operate the project to the required minimum Availability or service level)—usually around 6 months if the lenders are taking active steps to find a solution to the problem.

Step In. The Direct Agreement should also give the lenders the right to Step In to the PPP Contract, which means that they can appoint a nominee to undertake the Project Company's obligations in parallel with the Project Company; the nominee is effectively in charge of the project, but the Project Company remains the Public Authority's formal counter-party under the PPP Contract. Step-In is supposed to be a temporary remedy to allow time to find a longer-term solution to the Project Company's problems, and so the length of time allowed for this may be limited, say to 6 months.

Normal Unavailability and other deductions from Service Fees, and accrual of Performance Points, should continue during a Step-In period but should not give rise to a right to terminate the PPP Contract so long as the lenders are taking active steps to remedy the problems.

Lenders will resist any requirement to guarantee the Project Company's obligations in return for allowing them to Step In, as this leaves the Public Authority in a better position than if the Project Company had not got into trouble at all: the Public Authority, on the other hand, may argue that the lenders should accept this as they are delaying its ability to take control of the situation by terminating the PPP Contract. Even if lenders accept some responsibility for liabilities which cannot be offset against Service Fees, they will not accept long-term liabilities, *e.g.* to bring the maintenance of the Facility to a specified condition before returning it to the Public Authority (*cf.* §15.11), which is reasonable if the Step In is only for a limited period.

Substitution. The lenders normally also have the right to 'Substitution', in other words, appointment of a new obligor in the place of the Project Company, which then ceases to have any further involvement with the project, other than a possible retransfer of the Project Agreement, after the lenders have been repaid, as the Project Company retains the right to any surplus cash-flow from the project after the repayment. In such cases the new obligor must take on any accrued liabilities, but the accrual of Performance Points needs to start from zero or it will difficult for the lenders to find anyone to take over. This is meant to cover sale of the project to a long-term buyer, and is in effect a lender-controlled version of the market sale discussed in §15.5.5. As such, it may raise concerns that an arm's length public-procurement procedure is not being followed.

The technical and financial capacity of the lenders' Step-In nominee or substitute obligor will have to be acceptable to the Public Authority (lenders will prefer specific qualification criteria rather than some basis of 'reasonable opinion' on the Public Authority's part).

The Public Authority may also allow the lenders to exercise their Step-In and Substitution rights when an Event of Default under the financing documentation has occurred, as the lenders may wish to Step In under such circumstances even if the PPP Contract is not in default.

In reality, as discussed in §12.3, the main purpose of these powers is for the lenders to ensure that they are kept fully in the picture if things start going wrong, and that they can force the Project Company to take any remedial action. The existence on paper of Step-In and Substitution rights means that they seldom have to be used.

§15.5 EARLY TERMINATION: DEFAULT BY THE PROJECT COMPANY

Similarly, it is very unusual for the Project Company to be placed in default, and hence for the PPP Contract to be terminated (*cf.* §14.7.4, §14.8.4). It is usually in the lenders' interests for the situation to be sorted out by other means, *e.g.* additional finance to keep the project going (*cf.* §16.4.4) , and to deal with any problems rather than lose control of the situation through a default under the PPP Contract—hence the Step-In provisions just discussed. But of course, the Public Authority needs to have the default gun available to 'encourage' the lenders to take action.

Events of Default by the Project Company that give the Public Authority the right to terminate the PPP Contract should clearly only be of so fundamental a nature that the Facility is really no longer delivering the service required. A short-term failure to perform to the required standard can generally be dealt with by penalties or deductions (*cf.* §13.5.1–§13.5.2) rather than a termination. Events that come under the 'fundamental' heading may include:

- failure to construct the project or to be available for prolonged periods of time ('Abandonment');
- a Drawstop by the lenders: this is to ensure that the Public Authority will have a relatively early seat at the table if the project is going seriously wrong, but may face lender resistance if the lenders want the ability to sort out the problem by themselves;
- the Service Availability Date does not take place by an agreed backstop date (*cf.* §13.3.4);
- non-payment of LDs or penalties;
- Unavailability deductions reach more than a certain percentage of the Service Fees over a period of x months;
- accumulated Performance Points exceed a trigger level (*cf.* §13.5.2);
- other minor breaches (which do not incur Performance Points) keep occurring and the problems have not been rectified despite warning notices from the Public Authority—this is known as 'Persistent Breach' (and is typically very difficult to negotiate);
- insolvency/bankruptcy of the Project Company;
- breach of any other 'fundamental' provisions of the PPP Contract, *e.g.* not taking out insurance, or a major failure to maintain health and safety of the users of the Facility.

If—as is commonly the case—the Public Authority is the legal owner of the Facility, and the Project Company only has contractual rights, the argument could be made that if the Project Company defaults and the PPP Contract is terminated, then the Project Company and its creditors should get nothing. After all, the PPP Contract is about providing a long-term service, and if the service is not provided, surely it is the Public Authority which should be compensated not the Project Company?

In the early British DBFO road projects payment of no 'Termination Sum', as such a default payment is known ('CompOnTerm' = compensation on termination, is also used), was standard; this was based on the view, discussed above, that there would never be a default leading to termination and therefore setting a Termination Sum served no purpose. While there is logic in the argument for no payment, lenders are—not surprisingly—uneasy about this approach, and payment of a Termination Sum is more normal. Clearly a Facility has been built, though perhaps not to the required standard, and it has a value. It would therefore be unreasonable for the Public Authority to have even a theoretical right to get a windfall gain by getting an asset for which it has paid nothing, although if for some reason the Public Authority chose not to take over the Facility (*cf.* §15.11) there would be no reason for a Termination-Sum payment. (Similarly, in private-sector projects such as under a PPA, the offtaker only pays a Termination Sum if it opts to acquire the plant—and it is not obliged to do so.) This is not an aspect of the PPP Contract which concerns investors too much, as the assumption can reasonably be made that if the project goes wrong to the extent of being placed in default, the value of the equity investment will have already been destroyed.

The Public Authority may also object to paying a Termination Sum for the simple reason that there will be no budget for doing so, the whole point of the PPP being to fund outside the public budget. This problem can be dealt with by making the payment in instalments over the remaining life of the PPP Contract (or by the market-sale alternative discussed below). Lenders should not object to payment by instalments, as rather than a high risk on the Project Company they will then have a low risk on the Public Authority—indeed there is a case for interest on the deferred payments being at a lower credit margin than that being paid by the Project Company to reflect this reduction in risk.

There are several possible methods of calculating a default Termination Sum:

- repayment of outstanding debt (§15.5.1);
- cost of assets (§15.5.2);
- NPV of projected cash flows (§15.5.3);
- an adjusted Base Case calculation (§15.5.4); or
- open-market sale of the PPP Contract (§15.5.5)—here the Public Authority does not have to pay the Termination Sum: the buyer of the PPP Contract will do so.

In addition, a different approach may be taken for default during the construction phase (§15.5.6), and a hybrid of the above can also be used (§15.5.7).

In all cases but open-market sale, the value of any Reserve Accounts (*cf.* §12.2.4) or other security held by lenders (*e.g.* Sponsor guarantees or undrawn equity) should also be deducted from the payment. The Public Authority will also wish to deduct its costs in dealing with the termination, including the cost of re-tendering to find a new service provider.

§15.5.1 Repayment of Outstanding Debt

The early Turkish BOT model (*cf.* §1.4.3) guaranteed the debt after completion of construction, and thus paid the lenders in full on default termination, but paid nothing to the investors. This structure was also used in the first Greek PPPs, and had the advantage of making it easier to obtain debt, which might otherwise have been impossible at the time. But obviously the transfer of risk to the private sector is then capped at the amount of the equity and such a structure may leave the project in the public-sector balance sheet under the accounting rules discussed in §5.5. Moreover, it means that the lenders have little incentive to undertake due diligence, monitor the project closely, or sort out any problems.

This method of payment also raises a problem of who controls how much debt is outstanding:

- Should it be the amount of debt that was projected in the Base Case to be outstanding on the termination date?
- Or should it be the amount actually outstanding, which may include repayments deferred because of cash-flow difficulties, or extra amounts of debt added at the time of a refinancing (*cf.* §16.4.3), or because new money was needed to rescue the Project Company from financial difficulties (*i.e.* a Rescue Refinancing—*cf.* §16.4.4)?

The other issue here is breakage costs on any hedging, *e.g.* an interest-rate swap (*cf.* §11.2.3): if the intention is to keep the lenders whole, these have to be paid (though conversely if there is a breakage profit the Public Authority should benefit from this), but of course payment of any future swap credit premium (*cf.* §11.2.6) should not be made as there is no reason to pay the swap provider for loss of future profits.

The issues on controlling debt outstandings and on breakage costs also reoccur in other termination scenarios, as discussed below, where the Public Authority specifically repays the debt. If carried a stage further this structure leads to the Public Authority just repaying the debt (or taking it over) after completion (*cf.* §17.3.2).

§15.5.2 COST OF ASSETS

This approach is used, for example, in the Spanish legislation relating to Concessions and PFI-Model PPPs, which has a concept of '*Responsabilidad Patrimonial de la Administración*', under which the Public Authority must pay on termination for:

- the cost of land acquired by the Project Company;
- construction works, based on the Base Case costs (*i.e.* excluding cost overruns);
- operating equipment.

A deduction is made from this payment for the amount of any accounting depreciation (which should be roughly *pro rata* to the return on the project to date), and for 'damages' suffered by the Public Authority, which presumably includes the cost to bring the Facility up to the standard required by the PPP Contract. There is some uncertainty about how this might apply in practice, as, in Spain as elsewhere, there has been no case of default termination on a PPP.

This approach ignores the cost of replacing the long-term service element and operating costs of the PPP Contract as it deals only with capex, with no reduction in the value of the project because, *e.g.* operating or maintenance costs have proved to be higher than expected. But it reflects a view that PPPs are primarily about capex rather than long-term service provision.

§15.5.3 NPV OF PROJECTED CASH FLOWS

A fair market value ('FMV') calculation projects the future cash flow of the Project Company, taking account of its performance under the PPP Contract to date (and hence likely revenue levels or payment deductions), and the further capex required to remedy any

problem. This cash flow is discounted at a market rate for a project in this situation to produce the Termination Sum. Obviously if the Public Authority is providing any support for the
project's revenues (*cf.* §13.4.3), the value of this should be deducted in calculating the FMV.

While this provides a fair valuation in theory, in practice it may be difficult for the
parties to agree on either the projections or the discount rate, and a third-party arbitrator will
also find this complex. However, as default is so rare, it may be simplest just to keep to this
approach.

§15.5.4 ADJUSTED BASE CASE CALCULATION

Another approach for PFI-Model projects is to calculate the FMV against an adjusted
Base Case. This FMV is the NPV of:

- future Service Fees, assuming no penalties or deductions; less
- future capex and opex under the Base Case; less
- future additional costs (capex or opex) required to bring the Facility or its operation
  up to the standard required by the PPP Contract.

Note that:

- this is a pre-tax calculation;
- nominal figures and a nominal discount rate should be used unless the Service
  Fees are fully indexed, in which case real figures and a real discount rate can be
  used (*cf.* §11.3.1);
- if nominal figures are used an agreed basis is needed for projecting the rate of
  inflation: the lower the assumed rate of inflation the higher the NPV payment by
  the Public Authority (because the fixed portion of the Service Fees, *e.g.* covering
  debt service, is discounted at a lower rate).

This method does not work well for the Concession Model, because realistic rather than
Base-Case revenue projections would be needed, as set out in §15.5.3.

But one difficult aspect of this method is what discount rate should be used. If we
assume that the project goes into default the day after completion, and requires no extra
costs to be spent on it, then the Base Case Project IRR (*cf.* §7.3.1—*i.e.* the IRR before
taking the financing structure into account) is the correct rate, as the NPV amount will be
exactly equally to the equity and debt which has been used to fund the Project Company,
which is also the FMV of the project at that point. However, if the Project IRR—a relatively high rate—is used to discount the third leg of the calculation, *i.e.* the additional
costs, this is quite unfavourable for the Public Authority:

- Suppose the Project IRR is 8%, and the additional costs are 1,000 in a year's time.
- The Public Authority would be paid 926 (1,000 ÷ 1.08).

The Public Authority's rate of return on this money is either:

- the PSDR; or
- the marginal cost to the Public Authority of obtaining funding, for which this
  cash can be used in substitution; or
- the rate at which the Public Authority can place the funds on deposit in a bank.

- In any of these cases the rate of return may easily be below the Project IRR (*e.g.* 6% instead of 8%), which means that in a year's time the Public Authority will have 926 × (say) 1.06 = 981, *i.e.* not enough money to pay the additional costs of 1,000.

There is thus an argument for using a different discount rate—the PSDR or one of the other alternatives set out above—for the future additional costs to remedy the Project Company's default, while retaining the Project IRR as the discount rate for the Base Case cash flows. This reflects the reality that a buyer of the Project Company in the open market would take into account the fact that the project had failed and required extra costs to remedy the position, and hence would apply a higher discount rate to the overall cash flows than that used for the original Base Case: applying a lower discount rate for the additional costs, combined with the Base Case Project IRR for the Base Case costs, has the same net effect. The alternative approach is to decide what would be a reasonable discount rate at the time, and apply this to the whole cash flow, which actually comes to the same thing as the FMV calculation discussed in §15.5.3.

If the Base Case Project IRR is used as the discount rate, however, there is also an argument for adjusting it to reflect current market interest rates, because these would be reflected in a new buyer's calculations. If interest rates have gone down this means that the Public Authority will pay more (because the discount rate will be lower), but on the other hand its cost of funding the Termination Sum will be lower, and *vice-versa*. Similarly, changes in the underlying rate of inflation need to be taken into account. One formula for this adjustment, assuming a nominal discount rate is to be used, is:

$$(1 + PIRR + r^2 - r^1) \times (1 + i) - 1$$

where:
$PIRR$ = real project IRR;
$\quad r^1$ = real government bond rate at Financial Close (for the average life of the debt);
$\quad r^2$ = real government bond rate at the time of default (for the average life of the remaining debt);
$\quad i$ = projected rate of inflation at the time of default.

§15.5.5 OPEN-MARKET SALE

The final alternative is not to terminate the PPP Contract completely, but for the Public Authority to sell the Project Company's rights under this Contract in the open market on an 'as is' basis (*i.e.* bidders will have to spend extra costs on remedying problems, and/or take into account the fact that revenues are below the original Base Case, but no alterations are made to the PPP Contract itself), and pay the proceeds to the Project Company as a Termination Sum (or to the Public Authority who pays them over to the Project Company). The PPP Contract is then transferred to the buyer, or an identical PPP Contract is signed with the buyer. (The lenders can achieve a similar result through Substitution under the Direct Agreement—*cf.* §15.4.2—which has the advantage of putting the procedure under their control rather than the Public Authority's.)

The benefits of this approach (which was first introduced with the British Treasury Task Force's standard contract in 1999) are:

- It establishes the 'true' FMV of the PPP Contract.
- It avoids any windfalls from excess value (admittedly unlikely) being gained by the Public Authority.
- It may offer better continuity of service than a complete termination in the ways described above.

The difficulty is that defaults are so rare that lenders cannot be sure that there will be a real and liquid market for the PPP Contract if the time ever comes; an attempt can be made to define a liquid market—e.g. a certain number of investors willing to bid—but if there are no regular precedents for such an auction it is difficult for lenders to see how it will work in practice. In the worst case, if there is deemed to be a liquid market but nobody bids, the lenders will get nothing. On the other hand if the view is taken, as discussed above, that defaults never happen lenders can probably live with this approach. (As a fall back the British SoPC allows the method set out in §15.5.4 to be used if it can be demonstrated that there is no liquid market.)

§15.5.6 DEFAULT DURING THE CONSTRUCTION PHASE

All the above formulae work for both the construction and operation phases. However, default during construction may be treated differently, on the grounds that this is the most serious type of failure by the Project Company. If so, a standard approach is to pay a Termination Sum equal to the original Base Case construction cost (including 'soft' costs), less the NPV of costs to complete the Facility to the required specifications.

§15.5.7 UNDERPINNED FUNDING

Finally yet another approach is a hybrid of those above: a combination of a partial debt guarantee (cf. §15.5.1), ensuring there will be an agreed minimum payment, but also allowing one of the other methods set out in §15.5.3–§15.5.5 to be used if this would produce a higher figure. Thus in South Africa the standard form of PPP Contract prescribes that lenders will be paid the greater of:

- the open market value, as in §15.5.5;
- the adjusted Base Case, as in §15.5.4, if there is no open market sale; or
- a fixed percentage of the debt, the requirement for which is to be set out in the original bid ('Underpinned Funding').

The effect of the latter is similar to the French *Cession de Créance* (cf. §13.5). Underpinned Funding is based on the assumption that it is highly unlikely that the amount payable to lenders after a Facility has been completed would ever be less than, say, 75% of their debt outstanding. Therefore once the Facility has been completed and has operated for an initial period the Public Authority guarantees 75% of the debt, which should bring down its cost; this can be reflected in the Service Fees. The Public Authority can specify that the guaranteed and unguaranteed debt must be 'stapled', *i.e.* must be held *pro rata* and cannot be split and sold off separately, to ensure that lenders have an incentive to protect both tranches of debt (although it is probably impossible to prevent one of the tranches being *de facto* sold off through a sub-participation or derivative contract). Equity investors of course remain at risk in the normal way. The Public Authority will argue that the debt or associated guarantee liability should not be in the public budget because there is no realistic chance of the guarantee being called upon (*cf.* §5.5), because the open-market value of the project will always be more than 75% of the debt. This may be considered an alternative to guaranteeing a minimum revenue post-completion (*cf.* §13.4.3).

§15.6 OPTIONAL TERMINATION OR DEFAULT BY THE PUBLIC AUTHORITY

Optional termination by the Public Authority (known as Authority Voluntary Termination ('AVT') or termination 'for convenience') and default are usually treated in the same way, as otherwise if default cost the Authority more it would use AVT, and *vice-versa*.

Default by a Public Authority is a rather unlikely event. Action which could cause a default would include:

- non-payment of any sums due to the Project Company, after a reasonable grace period;
- expropriation of the Facility or other assets of the Project Company;
- breach of obligations under the PPP Contract (*cf.* §15.2.4) which make it impossible for the Project Company to complete or operate the Facility—*i.e.* where treating this as a Compensation Event is not sufficient (which it will be in most cases);
- a significant change in the legal status or powers of the Public Authority.

But AVT is a realistic possibility which has to be considered carefully in structuring a PPP Contract. For reasons already discussed (*cf.* §2.12), a Public Authority often cannot be certain that the PPP Contract will serve its originally-designed purpose for its whole life, and there may come a point when such a fundamental change in the assumptions on which the Public Authority entered into the PPP Contract has occurred, that the best thing to do for the public service is to terminate it. It is evident that the Public Authority must make a 'fair' Termination Sum payment to the Project Company in these circumstances, and should not make a windfall gain at the expense of the Project Company's investors, or deprive them of a reasonable return for taking the risks they have taken.

The lenders, of course, would expect to be fully paid off in this situation. Thus there needs to be a reasonable formula to compensate them both. Simple reimbursement of the depreciated cost of the Facility would cover the lenders but is unlikely to provide fair compensation for investors. A formula which values the Project Company as a whole should give fair compensation to both investors and lenders (and the lenders have first claim on this payment), but generally lenders prefer a specific formula to cover their debt outstandings. The issues on defining these debt outstandings are the same as discussed in §15.5.1—whether to cover additional borrowing above the Base Case, and whether the future credit premium or a make-whole payment should be paid as part of the breakage calculations. The case for making such 'extra' payments is clearly strongest in this situation, but their cost may act as an impediment to the Public Authority's long-term flexibility.

The fairest formula for compensation to the investors is one which values their investment at the time of termination, and pays this as the Termination Sum (along with the debt repayment). Methods of calculating this equity valuation are:

- current market value, *i.e.* the NPV of the investors' projected future cash flows, discounted at the rate of return which could then be obtained by selling the investment in the secondary-market (*cf.* §7.2.2);
- to give greater certainty, a fixed formula can be used: the NPV of the original Base Case cash flows from the date of termination, discounted at the Base Case Equity IRR;
- a variation on the last formula: payment of a sum that will bring the Equity IRR up to the date of termination to the Base Case level for the life of the PPP Contract.

Note that all cash flows and discount rates referred to should be calculated on a nominal, post-tax basis, and IRR calculations should take a consistent approach to investment in cash as compared to investors being on-risk (*cf.* §7.3.4).

Under the first formula it may be difficult for the parties to agree on the cash-flow projections and discount rate to be used, and third-party arbitration on these points may be required. This means that the Public Authority will not know how much it will have to pay for termination until the end of this process. The two latter fixed formulae may mean that if the project has been under-performing the investors will receive more than the market value of their investment, and *vice-versa*, which may be a reasonable trade-off for the investors and the Public Authority.

Investors may argue for a 'make-whole' approach whereby they are paid the higher of one of these fixed formulae and the then-current market value. Assuming this is rejected by the Public Authority (as it probably should be), most investors would choose the first (market-value) formula, because the normal reduction in secondary Equity IRR (*cf.* §7.3.2), and hence lower discount rate which would apply, will produce a much higher value for the Project Company. This can be seen in Table 15.1, which takes the project cash-flow assumptions from Table 16.2, and calculates the value of the equity at the Base Case Equity IRR of 15%, compared with an assumed secondary Equity IRR of 8%; it then also shows the effect on the Termination Sum payment if the refinancing set out in Table 16.2 had taken place.

Table 15.1
AVT Termination Sum calculations

Discount rate	Base Case Equity IRR	Market value
Pre-refinancing		
Debt outstanding	870	870
Value of equity (discount rate)	106 (15%)	196 (8%)
	976	**1,066**
Post-refinancing		
Debt outstanding	955	955
Value of equity (discount rate)	76 (15%)	132 (8%)
	1,031	**1,087**

As can be seen, the current (8% discount) market valuation of the equity leaves the investors better off than discounting at the Base Case Equity IRR, and therefore unless they are pessimistic about the prospects for the project (which is hardly likely or they would not be investing) investors should always push for an AVT Termination Sum based on current market value of their equity.

But the calculation also shows that if a refinancing has taken place and the fixed (Base Case Equity IRR) discount rate is used to value the equity, the Public Authority would—obviously wrongly—pay more after a refinancing, because there has been an increase in the amount of the debt but the equity is still valued on the Base-Case cash flow. This therefore suggests that if the Base-Case formula is used, the Termination Sum should cover what the debt outstanding would have been in the original Base Case, not the actual debt outstanding. However, this would be an issue with lenders, as it gives less flexibility to cover a rescue refinancing (*cf.* §16.4.4). A solution to this is for the Public Authority to pay the higher of the Base Case figure of 976, as shown in Table 15.1, and the actual debt outstanding, subject to a cap of 110% of the scheduled debt outstanding (assuming there is a Rescue-Refinancing allowance of 10%, as discussed in §16.4.4). This would give rise to a payment of 957 in this case (870 × 110%). Thus the Base Case payment of 976 would be the higher and would still apply, the lenders would be repaid their post-refinancing outstanding of 955, and 21 would be left for the investors. But this may leave the investors unhappy, as even if the higher discount rate of 15% is applied to their post-refinancing cash flow, to reflect the higher leverage, this still values this equity at 76.

All of this suggests that the fairest and most appropriate approach is not to use any fixed formula, but to repay actual debt outstandings and the then market value of the equity (which will reduce the more debt there is outstanding), despite the uncertainty in the result mentioned above. Common sense suggests this is the fair result in a situation where the Public Authority has complete freedom whether to terminate the PPP Contract or not.

It should be noted that there is no reason to treat share capital and shareholder subordinated debt differently in these calculations, since the split between these is a matter of convenience for the investors and is of no relevance for the Public Authority (*cf.* §7.3.3).

Optional termination is an expensive exercise for the Public Authority, and is thus a serious impediment to long-term flexibility in a PPP Contract (*cf.* §2.12). One way of giving more flexibility in this respect, is to ask bidders to offer fixed prices for a limited number of set termination dates, say one-third and two-thirds of the way through the PPP Contract. All being well, bid competition will ensure these prices are lower than the 'fair value' amount. (The fixed price can cover both debt and equity together, avoiding complexities arising from any refinancings.) This also has the effect of capping investors' returns (*cf.* §13.4.4).

Finally, the value of the Facility will have to be deducted from the Termination Sum if it is being retained by the Project Company (*cf.* §15.11).

§15.7 EARLY TERMINATION: *FORCE MAJEURE*

As already discussed (*cf.* §15.3), a distinction has to be made between *Force Majeure* events which cause a temporary interruption in the provision of services under the PPP Contract, which are dealt with as Relief Events, and those which destroy the project and so make it impossible to continue without major new investment. The latter should generally be covered by insurance, so if the Facility is not rebuilt (*cf.* §12.4.6) such cases can simply be regarded as defaults by the Project Company, and treated accordingly (*cf.* §15.5): obviously the Project Company will receive little if anything as a Termination Sum, but will receive the insurance proceeds.

There may be a very limited range of events which cannot be covered by insurance, *e.g.* acts of war or terrorism which destroy the project—events so unlikely in nature that there seems little point worrying about them (if they do happen getting a Termination Sum will probably be the least of the investors' and lenders' worries). The simple view can therefore be taken that the essence of *Force Majeure* in these cases too is that each party has to suffer whatever loss it incurs.

However, it is also possible that the insurance cover for other *Force Majeure* risks which the parties had expected to be insured becomes unavailable. This is perhaps a more likely event to occur than the *Force Majeure* risks which cannot be covered by insurance at all. If the Public Authority has an option to take on liability for this unavailable insurance (*cf.* §12.4.6), but chooses not to exercise it, the PPP Contract will have to be terminated as the Project Company cannot carry on without insurance. In such cases, if the Public Authority takes over the Facility, it should reasonably expect to make a Termination Sum payment to lenders of at least outstanding debt and breakage costs but no windfalls or future profits in breakage costs. If the equity investment is to be covered by a Termination Sum payment as well, investors cannot expect to be paid back more than their original investment, perhaps after deduction of returns received to the termination date. However, the argument for covering equity is not that strong, since as the *Force Majeure* is nobody's fault there should be some sharing of risk: an alternative to making no payment for equity is to pay the current market value of the Facility (*i.e.* the physical facility not the PPP Contract as for AVT) if this is higher than debt outstanding. If cover is provided in one of these ways by the Public Authority for unavailable insurance, it can logically be extended to the limited list of *Force Majeure* events which cannot be covered by insurance in the first place.

It should also be noted that French administrative law, as well as that of some other civil-law countries, accepts the 'theory of imprevision' (or *rebus sic stantibus*) for public-sector contracts, under which, if the assumptions which both the public- and private-sector sides made when entering into a contract have been fundamentally invalidated, leading to a substantial deterioration of the private-sector party's position, the latter has a right to compensation. This does not relate to *Force Majeure* as defined above, but an event affecting the economics of the contract, for example hyperinflation. In practice this primarily relates to supply of goods and is therefore unlikely to apply to a PPP Contract. Common-law countries have a similar doctrine of frustration of contracts, which gives rise to a right of termination, but without compensation.

§15.8 EARLY TERMINATION: CORRUPTION

Most countries have a provision for voiding public-sector contracts where corruption is involved. It is reasonable for the lenders to expect a Termination Sum payment equal to their debt outstanding (subject to the points already made on what debt outstanding means), but for the investors in the Project Company to lose their investment in these circumstances, since they are responsible for such actions.

§15.9 TERMINATION AND SUBCONTRACTORS

The Subcontractors also suffer if an early termination takes place. Costs will be incurred in demobilising staff and equipment, and there will obviously be a loss of future profits. Whether they should receive any compensation from the Public Authority for this depends on the circumstances of termination.

In the case of AVT it is reasonable for the Public Authority to pay both Subcontractors' costs incurred as a result of the termination, and an element of foregone future profits. The PPP Contract may state this in general terms, leaving the details to be set out in the Subcontracts, but if so the Public Authority will need to review the Subcontracts (*cf.* §6.5.2), and obviously any future changes to these Subcontracts which may affect the termination liability must be subject to the agreement of the Public Authority. However, it should be noted that this does not necessarily mean that the Subcontractors get all their money, since the lenders have first claim on all payments (*cf.* §14.6.4).

In the case of termination for default by the Project Company (where it is quite possible this default may have been caused by a Subcontractor) there is no strong case for giving Subcontractors any special protection. In other termination cases it may be reasonable to protect their demobilisation costs if they are innocent parties, but obviously not their future profits.

§15.10 TAX IMPLICATIONS OF A TERMINATION-SUM PAYMENT

Finally the tax implications of any Termination Sum need to be considered; if the Termination Sum is taxable the amount received by the investors and lenders may be insufficient to compensate them as intended (and at the same time the public sector will have made a Termination Sum payment with one hand and taken some of it back in tax with the other hand). The Termination Sum therefore needs to be 'grossed up' (*i.e.* increased as necessary to produce the net amount required after tax). Obviously this does not apply where the PPP Contract is sold in the open market (*cf.* §15.5.5), or the Termination Sum calculations are on a pre-tax basis (*cf.* §15.5.4).

In cases where part of the Termination Sum payment is specifically designated for debt repayment, it may be preferable for this payment to be made directly from the Public Authority to the lenders, instead of *via* the Project Company, even though the lenders have security over the cash as it flows through the Project Company, as this may avoid raising unnecessary tax issues.

§15.11 FINAL MATURITY, RESIDUAL-VALUE RISK AND HAND-BACK

PPP Contracts can take a variety of legal forms (*cf.* Table 1.1), which may or may not give legal ownership (or other legal title) of the Facility to the Project Company during the term of the PPP Contract. Legal ownership is a matter of policy for the Public Authority and is otherwise of little importance during the term of the PPP Contract, since it is the PPP Contract itself which creates value for investors and security for lenders, not the physical asset (*cf.* §12.3). However, it obviously becomes important at the end of the PPP Contract, and residual ownership of the Facility may also affect balance-sheet treatment (*cf.* §5.5).

Most PPP projects assume there will be no residual value at the end of the PPP Contract, or that the Facility's specialised use makes it inappropriate for it to be transferred away from the public sector, so it simply reverts to the Public Authority's control (assuming it is already under its ownership), or the ownership is transferred for no payment or a nominal sum. In cases where the Facility site has, or may have, a residual value because it has an alternative private-sector use, such as housing or office accommodation, the choice is between:

- giving the Public Authority an option to take over the Facility at nil cost as above, in which case bidders will obviously not take any residual value into account in their pricing;
- leaving the Facility in the hands of the Project Company: this implies that the original bid will have attributed some residual value to the Facility (or the land on which it is built);
- obliging the Public Authority to acquire the Facility for a pre-agreed fixed sum, which will be proposed at the time of the original bid;
- giving the Public Authority an option to acquire the Facility for a pre-agreed fixed sum;
- giving the Public Authority an obligation or an option to acquire the Facility for the then-current market value, perhaps with a cap on the price.

If the Public Authority is obliged to acquire the Facility for a fixed sum bidders can take this into account and thus offer lower Service Fees, but less so if the Public Authority only has an option to purchase at the end of the contract, as the Project Company is then left with the 'downside' risk on the residual value. If the final payment depends on market value (whether through purchase by the Public Authority or sale into the open market) this obviously becomes more speculative and is so far into the future that bidders may attribute little current value to it, and hence it will have little effect on the Service Fees. Obviously the Public Authority should not effectively pay for the full cost of the Facility through the Service Fees and yet leave the residual value with the Project Company. Other than a market-value purchase, any of these options may raise balance-sheet issues for the Public Authority (*cf.* §5.5).

Apart from taking over the Facility at final maturity of the PPP Contract, the Public Authority may have:

- an option to renew the PPP Contract instead of taking over the Facility (on a pricing basis which reflects the fact that its capital cost has been paid off)—this encourages the Project Company to keep the Facility in good condition in case the renewal option is exercised;
- an option to put a new PPP Contract out for a competitive bid (in which the existing Project Company may participate) as a Franchise; the winner of the bid will take over the Facility from the Project Company at no cost.

If the Facility is to be transferred to the Public Authority at the end of the PPP Contract, there is an obvious temptation for the Project Company to neglect maintenance during the final years of operation. By the time of the hand-back, the Project Company may have paid over all its remaining cash to its shareholders, and ceased to have enough financial sub-stance to pay compensation for poor maintenance. The Public Authority can ensure that the maintenance is actually carried out by:

- a requirement to achieve maintenance standards before the end of the PPP Contract term, so that if this is not done, payment deductions can be made;
- alternatively, a requirement that for the last few years of the PPP Contract part of the payments should be paid into an MRA under the control of both the Project Company and the Public Authority to cover the cost of any maintenance to meet the required standard; this fund is used for maintenance as needed, and any final surplus (once all specified maintenance has been carried out) is returned to the Project Company;
- the Project Company may also be required to provide security—a Sponsor guarantee or bank bonding—to ensure that the final maintenance obligations are carried out.
- Provisions are also needed for the transfer of building plans, operating information, manuals, and so on, as relevant.

There is a mirror issue to the above in cases where the Facility is not transferred to the Public Authority at the end of the PPP Contract. If there has been new capex for which the Public Authority is responsible (because it results from a Compensation Event), and so pays for it either through a lump-sum payment or increased Service Fees, and the Facility's assets including those on which this expenditure has been made have a useful life after the end of the PPP Contract, the payments by the Public Authority should take this into account. Thus if, 10 years before the end of the PPP Contract, capex of 100 is incurred, after which the economic life of the Facility is 20 years, the Public Authority's payments should be reduced in proportion: so if payment is to be made through the Service Fees, the cost should be amortised over 20 years instead of 10, with the Public Authority only being responsible for payments covering the first 10 years.

Chapter 16

Funding Competition, Debt Refinancing and Equity Sale

§16.1 INTRODUCTION

This chapter deals with some 'trip-wires' which can be inserted into the PPP process to address concerns about the high cost of funding PPPs or to limit financial windfalls for investors. These issues (which are peculiar to the PPP field, and generally not found elsewhere in the project-finance market) are as much about perception as reality, but a lot of politics is about perception, and a PPP programme depends on political support (*cf.* §2.13, §14.4). The topics covered are:

- Funding Competitions, under which the debt financing is placed separately in the financing market after the appointment of a Preferred Bidder (§16.2);
- equity competition, at the time of Financial Close (§16.3);
- refinancing the debt, and sharing the benefit of this between the investors and the Public Authority (§16.4); and
- the benefit of selling equity once the project is operating, and again how this may be shared between the parties (§16.5).

The first and third items have been developed in some detail in the British PFI programme; the approach on refinancing in particular has been widely imitated elsewhere in the world. The topics relating to equity are more speculative, but address the concern that PPP investors benefit disproportionately to the risks they are taking (*cf.* §7.3.2). Other approaches to lowering the cost of debt have already been considered, namely partial revenue guarantees (*cf.* §13.4.3) or debt guarantees (*cf.* §13.5, §15.5.7).

This chapter thus deals with ways of lowering the cost of capital for a PPP within the framework discussed up to now. The next chapter takes this approach further by examining alternative models.

§16.2 FUNDING COMPETITION

A Funding Competition may be required by the Public Authority after the appointment of the Preferred Bidder, if the terms offered for the financing are felt to be uncompetitive, thus resulting in higher than necessary Service Fees. (Of course the Project Company may decide to hold its own Funding Competition at this point—if so, this will be a matter entirely under its control, without any Public Authority involvement.)

§16.2.1 PURPOSE OF A FUNDING COMPETITION

Although a bidder has every incentive to secure the best terms from lenders at the time of submitting the bid, there may nonetheless be a case for the Public Authority to require a competitive procurement for the financing (known as a 'Funding Competition') after the appointment of the Preferred Bidder, the benefit of which would be reflected in the final Service-Fee pricing. This is because:

- lenders are likely to offer more competitive terms to a Preferred Bidder; and
- lenders are less likely to raise issues on the PPP Contract (or other Project Contracts) if faced with competition from other lenders, which cuts down the risk of deal creep.

A Funding Competition is not all negative from the lenders' point of view, as it means that they know by then that the PPP project should go ahead with the particular Preferred Bidder and they are therefore bidding on a 'real deal'.

It could be argued that a Funding Competition introduces a kind of Separability, and that it is inappropriate to pick on just one of the factors which affects the bidder's pricing and open this up to competition after the bid has been submitted. But there is a substantial difference between the rôle lenders play in a PPP bid and that played by other Subcontractors.

Having said this, however, it is unlikely that a Funding Competition will add much value to a 'standard' deal where there is good competition from bidders, and financial structures and terms are already well-established. This means that it should only be considered in cases where:

- A country is at the early stage of developing a PPP programme, so that market terms are not yet well-established.
- The project involves a new type of PPP, where there may be a considerable variation of view amongst lenders on its financing terms.
- There has been a long period after the appointment of the Preferred Bidder, and hence a greater danger of deal creep.
- The bidder's existing lenders have been raising new issues on the PPP Contract which are not in conformity with the original bid. (Of course a Funding Competition would only be used here if the Public Authority considered that the existing lenders' views would not be shared by others.)

Since the Public Authority will get the benefit of a Funding Competition, as discussed below, it will also have to bear the risks such as:

- Less interest in bidding for PPP projects where finance is not part of the original package because prospective bidders may include financial facilitators who would expect to arrange both equity and debt placement (*cf.* §7.2.1).
- Bids turn out to be more expensive than expected.
- Extra costs for the Public Authority, *e.g.* from its financial advisers having to undertake more work (and reimbursement of extra costs for the bidder, unless these have been built into the bid), which need to be justified by improved terms achieved in the Funding Competition.
- Bidders may employ separate financial advisers rather than just Lead Arrangers (*cf.* §9.3.2), so adding to bid costs and hence the cost of the project.
- Lenders will be less willing to spend time on due diligence at the time of the bid, with the risk that the resulting Project Contracts may prove not to be 'bankable' (*cf.* §2.9.8).

In the end, the threat of a Funding Competition—so long as it is credible—may be enough to keep the bidders' original lenders competitive, and therefore at a minimum the Public Authority can make it a condition in the ITT/ITN that it reserves the right to require one. In any case, it is still prudent to require the bidder to secure lenders' support letters (*cf.* §9.3.3).

§16.2.2 How a Funding Competition Works

The first point to make here is that even if the Public Authority is the driver for holding a Funding Competition, it is the Preferred Bidder who must be responsible for negotiations with lenders. But it is necessary for there to be an agreement between the Project Company and the Preferred Bidder as to procedure, evaluation and costs.

Procedure. The Preferred Bidder negotiates the PPP Contract with the Public Authority, as well as the other Project Contracts. Once they are at a relatively final stage these Project Contracts are reviewed by 'shadow' legal, technical and other advisers appointed on behalf of the prospective lenders by the Preferred Bidder: these advisers will prepare due-diligence reports which form part of an information memorandum package (*cf.* §9.3.6) to be sent to prospective Lead Arrangers. The shadow advisers become direct advisers to the Lead Arrangers in the normal way (*cf.* §9.3.4) once these Lead Arrangers have been mandated. The information package is then sent out to an agreed list of financial institutions.

Evaluation. 'Non-conforming' bids—*i.e.* bids which require changes to the Project Contracts, or to the financing term sheet included in the information memorandum— are excluded from the process (unless the changes are acceptable to both the Preferred Bidder and the Public Authority). Evaluation is thus primarily on financing terms and structure, which could cover:

- lending margins and fees (*cf.* §10.4);
- repayment structure (*cf.* §10.5);
- Cover Ratios and leverage (*cf.* §10.7);

- hedging arrangements (*e.g.* interest-rate swaps—*cf.* §11.2.2);
- Reserve-Account requirements (*cf.* §12.2.4);

in the case of a bank loan, and in the case of a bond issue:

- possibly the coupon (interest rate) in the case of a private placement (*cf.* §9.4.2);
- underwriting and other fees (*cf.* §10.4.6);
- monoline-insurance fees (*cf.* §9.4.4);
- repayment structure;
- Cover Ratios and leverage;
- Reserve-Account requirements;
- the GIC rate (*cf.* §11.2.11);
- prepayment penalties (*cf.* §11.2.12).

The lenders will have to take the Preferred Bidder's Equity IRR requirement (*cf.* §7.3.2) into account, and ensure that their loan proposals are structured in the most cost-effective and financially efficient way to ensure that this equity return is preserved (*cf.* §10.7).

The Public Authority may join meetings with the lenders, and is generally kept informed on progress. The choice of the winning bid is made by the Preferred Bidder (who may wish to take its existing banking relationships into account), but subject to ratification by the Public Authority. The Service Fees are then adjusted to take account of these final financing terms.

If the Preferred Bidder has been using a Lead Arranger as a financial adviser (*cf.* §9.3.2) the latter may be given a 'right to match', *i.e.* if the original Lead Arranger does not win the Funding Competition if it offers the same terms as the winner, it will be allocated 50% of the financing.

Costs. A definition of the marginal costs of the Funding Competition (on top of the Preferred Bidder's other bids costs) should be agreed between the Public Authority and the Preferred Bidder in advance. These marginal costs (*e.g.* additional work by advisers) will have to be funded by the bidders, but offset against the benefit of the Funding Competition when calculating the final Service Fees, unless they were allowed for in the original bid.

At the end of this process the result of the Funding Competition is fed into the financial structure for the project, and hence the final Service Fees. There is no reason why the Public Authority should not get 100% of the benefit of the Funding Competition, but perhaps as an incentive to creativity for the bidder, if the Service Fees can be reduced by more than an agreed level, part of this extra benefit can be left for the Project Company (in the form of a reduction in Service Fees of less than 100% of the benefit).

§16.2.3 REFINANCING

From the Public Authority's point of view, a Funding Competition can perhaps be more widely applied to ensure that the best available terms are obtained from a refinancing, as discussed below, although it must be recognised that the incumbent lenders always have an advantage in this situation.

§16.3 EQUITY COMPETITION

A further refinement in the process of separating finance from the rest of the bidding process, is to hold a competition for part of the equity. This helps to address the issue of excessive primary Equity IRRs (*cf.* §7.3.2). For example, the original bidders may underwrite half of the equity required for the project, and sell the other half at Financial Close to the best bidder. (Competition for all of the equity could be considered, but this is likely to lead to problems of who will bid in the fist place.) Bidders at Financial Close will offer a premium over the Equity IRR required by the original bidders (*cf.* §7.3.2), and this premium can be split between the Public Authority and the original bidders. This helps to alleviate the problem of investors, especially financial investors, earning what appear to be excessive equity returns.

Table 16.1 illustrates how this could work. 50% of the equity is put up for auction just before Financial Close (the bidder keeps the rest), and as can be seen, whereas the original bidder had an Equity IRR of 14.6%, various assumptions are made about the Equity IRR required by the buyer at Financial Close, ranging from 14.6% to 8%. This results in a profit on the equity auction of between 0% and 3% of the total project cost, depending on the buyer's Equity IRR requirement. The original bidder may offer to underwrite the sale of this 50% (for which buyers would most likely be PPP equity funds), and may also underwrite the price, *e.g.* assuming the highest yield at which the equity would be sold would be say 12%. If so, 100% of the benefit of the sale at 12% would go to the Public Authority, and any further benefit from selling at a lower yield could be split, say 50:50 between the parties, which means that the original bidder's Equity IRR improves accordingly, as shown in the table.

Table 16.1
Equity competition

Assumptions:					
Project cost	1,000,000				
Debt-equity ratio	90:10				
Distributions	1,500 *p.a* for 26 years				
Original bidder's Equity IRR	14.6%				
[a] Buyer's Equity IRR requirement		14.6%	12%	10%	8%
[b] Value of 50% of equity					
(= NPV of Distributions discounted at [a])		50,000	59,219	68,707	81,075
[c] Profit on equity auction ([b] − 50,000)		0	9,217	18,707	31,075
[d] Profit as % of capex ([c] ÷ 1,000,000)		0	0.9%	1.9%	3.1%
Share of profit retained by original bidder		0	0	50%	50%
Original bidder's Equity IRR after auction		14.6%	14.6%	16.2%	17.5%

Obviously this approach can only be used where there is an established market of financial investors in PPP equity. It could be argued that the original bidder is at risk of ending up with an unacceptable partner on the project, but given the ease with which PPP Project Companies' equity is traded (*cf.* §7.2.3), this should not be a major issue (and a pre-qualification procedure can be agreed with the Public Authority).

§16.4 DEBT REFINANCING

Having looked in Chapter 9 at the initial financial structuring for a Project Company, it is worth considering what is likely to happen to this financial structure if the project proceeds as expected, *i.e.* construction is completed on-time and on-budget, and the Project Company begins to generate revenues, also as originally projected. Once the project has entered into this new phase, many of the main risks have been eliminated (*cf.* Chapter 14), which opens up new possibilities for its investors—either a refinancing of the debt, or a sale of their equity interests (§16.5).

Apart from the financial benefits discussed below, a refinancing may give the Project Company greater flexibility because some of the more restrictive provisions of the original loan documentations may be negotiated away. It may also offer the investors an opportunity to structure the financing for their PPP business as a whole more efficiently, by combining the financing for several completed and operating projects.

Debt refinancing may be of interest to the Public Authority because:

- It may have an effect on the Project Company's ability to continue delivering the services under the PPP Contract (*e.g.* if its financial position is destabilised by taking on too much new debt).
- It may increase the Public Authority's Termination Sum liabilities in some scenarios (*cf.* §15.5.1, §15.6).
- If the original Sponsors have been able to accelerate the return on their investment they may only have a much-reduced long-term financial interest in the success of the Project Company (*cf.* §7.2.3).
- It may create large 'windfall gains' which suggest that the original PPP Contract was not good VfM for the public sector; this may create political problems which reduce general public support for a PPP programme (*cf.* §2.13).

§16.4.1 WHAT IS A REFINANCING?

Debt refinancing can take various forms:

- reducing the interest cost;
- increasing the debt amount;
- extending the debt repayment term (*i.e.* reducing the Tail);
- otherwise improving loan terms (*e.g.* by reducing Reserve-Account requirements).

The refinancing may be undertaken by the original lenders, or the original debt may be prepaid, and new debt raised on improved terms.

Determining whether a 'gain' has been made by the investors from a refinancing, and if so how much this gain is, is a more complex process than might be supposed at first sight, as can be seen by considering each of the above elements of a refinancing:

Reduced interest costs. It might be thought that if market interest rates have gone down, refinancing the original debt at a lower rate will be a profitable exercise, but this is generally not the case. Although there will be a benefit from the lower cost of the new debt, at the same time there will be a balancing breakage cost from prepaying the fixed-rate finance or interest-rate swap on the original debt (*cf.* §11.2). Therefore only a reduction in the credit margin (*cf.* §10.4.1), not the underlying interest rate, is beneficial.

Increasing the debt amount. If a PPP project requires 1,000 of funding, which has been provided as 900 by debt and 100 by equity, and on a refinancing the debt is increased to 950, it might be thought that the increase of 50 represents the 'gain' on the refinancing. But we do not make ourselves richer by borrowing more money, and in fact the debt-service payments will increase over the remaining term of the debt (as there is more interest to pay on a higher level of debt, and more debt to repay).

Extended debt-repayment term. Similarly, extending the debt repayment schedule by a year or so at the end of the project, reducing the cash-flow Tail, does not create an obvious 'gain'. Debt-service payments do reduce year-by-year, but over the life of the project interest payments will increase, and hence the investors' Distributions after the refinancing will decrease.

Reductions in Reserve Accounts. Reductions in Reserve Accounts (*cf.* §12.2.4) only accelerate a process which happens over the life of the project anyway—by the end of the loan term the Reserve Accounts will be reduced to zero. So again the 'gain' is not the amount of the free cash released by the refinancing.

It is evident, therefore, that the benefit of undertaking a refinancing of a Project Company's debt is more complex than at first appears.

§16.4.2 BENEFIT OF A REFINANCING TO INVESTORS

To understand the real benefit which investors receive from a refinancing, it is necessary to look at a typical cash flow, as set out in Table 16.2. As shown:

• The annual pre-refinancing cash flow, after the construction period, consists of 89 of CADS, less 74 of debt service, leaving 15 of surplus cash flow to be paid out as Distributions to the investors in the Project Company.
• Before the refinancing the projected Base Case Equity IRR was 15%.
• The refinancing takes place at the end of year 4, *i.e.* 2 years from completion of construction.
• It is based on reducing the lenders' initial 1.20x Cover Ratio to 1.15x, and extending the debt term by 2 years (*i.e.* leaving a 1-year Tail); there is no change in the debt interest rate.
• The refinancing raises 85 of new debt, which is paid out straight to the investors (*e.g.* by way of prepayment of their subordinated debt (*cf.* §7.3.3).

Table 16.2

Effect of refinancing

Initial assumptions:

Project cost	1,000
Construction period	2 years
Term of PPP Contract	28 years
Annual CADS	89
Initial debt:equity ratio	91:9
Debt interest rate	6%
ADSCR/LLCR	1.20x
Initial debt term	25 years from signing
Repayments	Annual, annuity basis, beginning one year from end of construction

Refinancing (year 4)—as above, except:

Debt term	27 years, annuity repayment of increased debt from year 4
ADSCR / LLCR	1.15
Debt amount in year 4	Increased by 85

Year:	0	1	2	3	4	5	24	25	26	27	28	Total
Pre-refinancing												
Project cost	−333	−333	−333									−1000
CADS				89	89	89	89	89	89	89	89	2314
Interest payments				−55	−53	−52	−8	−4				−791
Principal repayments				−19	−21	−22	−66	−70				−910
Total debt service	303	303	303	−74	−74	−74	−74	−74				−791
Equity cash flow	**−30**	**−30**	**−30**	**15**	**15**	**15**	**15**	**15**	**89**	**89**	**89**	**523**
Year-end debt	300	607	910	891	870	848	70	0				
Post-refinancing												
Project cost	−333	−333	−333									−1000
CADS				89	89	89	89	89	89	89	89	2314
Additional debt					85							85
Interest payments				−55	−53	−57	−16	−12	−9	−4		−938
Principal repayments				−19	−21	−20	−61	−65	−69	−73		−995
Total debt service	303	303	303	−74	−74	−78	−78	−78	−78	−78		−938
Equity cash flow	**−30**	**−30**	**−30**	**15**	**100**	**11**	**11**	**11**	**11**	**11**	**89**	**376**
Year-end debt	300	607	910	891	955	935	208	142	73	0		

Ratios and returns	Pre-refinancing	Post-refinancing
ADSCR	1.20	1.15
LLCR	1.20	1.15
PLCR	1.27	1.17
Equity IRR	15%	23%

- The investors' original investment was 100, and after the refinancing they have received back 15 in the first year of operation, and 100 in the second year.
- After the refinancing the investors' annual cash flow diminishes from 15 to 11 (with a greater reduction in the Tail years), so that the total equity cash flow over the project life goes down from 506 to 369.
- However, the effect of the refinancing is to increase the Equity IRR (over the project life) from 15% to 23%.

This clearly illustrates that the benefit of the refinancing for the investors is based on an improvement to the Equity IRR, not an increase in their revenue over the remaining project life; which actually decreases. The IRR improves because the refinancing has brought the cash flow payments sharply forward, and the IRR calculation gives a much greater weight to this early cash (*cf.* §4.4.3). Of course the result is also a sharp improvement in the investors' reported profits for year 4. This example also illustrates that refinancing in the PPP project-finance context is not primarily about reducing the interest cost, but about increasing the debt amount through lowering Cover Ratios and (where possible) lengthening its term.

§16.4.3 SHOULD REFINANCINGS BE SUBJECT TO THE PUBLIC AUTHORITY'S CONSENT?

A debt refinancing may well require some form of cooperation from the Public Authority, even though it is not a party to any loan documentation, because the Public Authority may have a general right to approve any increases to the debt amount, or the PPP Contract may cap the Public Authority's Termination Sum liability to pay off the debt in some scenarios (*cf.* §15.6–§15.8) based on the original debt schedule, which effectively gives it a similar approval right.

In 2002, the British Treasury went further, and introduced into its standard form of PFI contract (*cf.* §3.4.1) an unrestricted right for the Public Authority to give its consent to (and hence control) a refinancing so long as this gave rise to a gain. But other than a restriction on the level of debt, which can be dealt with separately, why would the Public Authority want to exercise this complete control? The most important reason is that increasing the debt may destabilise the Project Company, and hence jeopardise delivery of the service under the PPP Contract. Therefore a simpler and less restrictive approach may be to set out a specific debt limit above which Public Authority consent for the refinancing is required—*e.g.* if the debt becomes more than 100% of the cost of the project—while retaining the right not to cover any such increased debt on termination unless the Authority specifically agrees to this.

§16.4.4 RESCUE REFINANCINGS

This issue is made more complex by having to deal with 'Rescue Refinancings', where the Project Company has got into financial difficulty and needs to raise more funding for this reason, *i.e.* a 'bad' refinancing rather than a 'good' refinancing (*cf.* §15.5.1). Lenders will claim that if they are willing to take on the risk of injecting more funding than they originally committed to save the project, the Public Authority should not interfere with the process, but the Public Authority's response may well be that if it is to be in any way responsible on termination for more debt than was originally scheduled to be outstanding, it must always have the right to agree to this additional debt. Even if the Public Authority is willing to accommodate Rescue Refinancings the problem here is distinguishing them from a 'good' refinancing. There are several possible answers to this:

- The British approach mentioned above, namely that consent for refinancing is only needed if it produces a gain; a Rescue Refinancing should not do so and so would not require consent.
- A specific cap of, say, 10% extra on the debt outstandings, which in principle is only available for Rescue Refinancings, but without trying to define this too closely (if there is no general cap as suggested above). In fact, this is what now applies in Britain, the 2002 solution having proved unacceptable to the lending market.
- To define the circumstances in which additional debt for a rescue refinancing will be covered—for example the LLCR for the project has dropped below a default level (*cf.* §12.5). The Public Authority may be concerned that any such scenario could be manipulated by the Project Company and the lenders, but it is difficult to see how this could be done in reality.

§16.4.5 SHOULD THE PUBLIC AUTHORITY SHARE IN THE BENEFIT?

If the Public Authority can control increases in debt through having to agree any potential increase in termination liabilities, it is clearly in a good position to negotiate a share of any benefit ('Refinancing Gain') which the investors will receive in return. In 2002 the British Treasury also introduced into its standard form of PFI contract a specific requirement for the Public Authority to share 50% of the benefit of a refinancing. (On a 'voluntary' basis, a 30% share was also applied retrospectively to all PFI contracts already signed, where a refinancing took place thereafter.) The arguments put forward for sharing in the Refinancing Gain—to which there was little objection by the investment market, the main concern being that the right of consent discussed above should not be used as a lever to increase the Public Authority's share over 50%—were:

- The 'value' in the Project Company which provides a basis for the refinancing is the revenues which the public sector provides (on the PFI Model), or facilitates (on the Concession Model).
- The fact that better terms are available is partly the consequence of the public sector having continued to develop its PPP programme since the original PPP Contract was signed, creating greater interest in loans to this sector.
- Public support for the PPP programme will be reduced if investors are seen to be making 'windfall' profits only a short time after making what is supposed to be a long-term investment in a Project Company. (This was the primary motive for introducing the concept into the British PFI market of sharing 50% of Refinancing Gains, as there had been adverse publicity about such large gains from projects signed early in the PFI programme—*cf.* §2.13.)

The Treasury accepted that private-sector investors in a Project Company were entitled to keep the benefits of a refinancing which arose because the risk of the project had reduced (because construction was complete and it was operating profitably), or because the cash flow had increased above initial projections because of efficiency gains on the part of the management of the Project Company. But it is very difficult to isolate the effects of these factors from the others set out above, and thus a 50:50 sharing mechanism was introduced as an approximate basis which took these factors into account. (Provision was, however, made to ensure that if the project had been operating poorly at some stage before the refinancing, such that the original investors were no longer projected to achieve their required Equity IRR over the life of the project, any sharing of Refinancing Gain with the Public Authority would only take place after allowing for the projected Equity IRR to increase back to the Base Case level.)

This approach has been widely adopted in other PPP programmes involving project finance. Countries which have adopted the British standard form of PFI contract (*e.g.* South Africa) have taken over its refinancing provisions. Others have negotiated for a share of refinancing benefits on an *ad hoc* basis (*e.g.* Portugal). PPP legislation may also cover this issue—Korea's 2005 amendment of the PPI Act (*cf.* §3.8.1) included a provision for 50:50 sharing of Refinancing Gains.

The arguments for sharing in Refinancing Gains are not so strong where Concessions are concerned, although similar provisions are to be found in some Concession Agreements (*e.g.* the Texas Department of Transportation's Concession Agreement for SH130—*cf.* §3.5). In a PFI-Model project revenues are largely fixed, and the scope for increasing cash flow through operating efficiencies is also likely to be limited, but in a Concession there is much greater risk on revenues, and lenders will inevitably be more conservative until these are established (*cf.* §10.6.2). A Refinancing Gain is therefore much more the product of project-specific factors than in a PFI-Model project. Probably the better approach on Concessions is for the Public Authority to take a share of windfall revenues (*cf.* §13.4.4).

§16.4.6 CALCULATING THE REFINANCING GAIN

But even if the principle of sharing the Refinancing Gain, say, 50:50 between the Public Authority and the Project Company's investors is agreed, a method has to be found to do this. There is no Refinancing 'Gain'—*i.e.* just one amount of money—which can be split 50:50. So how can it be calculated?

- The reduction in credit margin?—But even if there is such a reduction, as Table 16.2 illustrates the total interest payments increase, not decrease (as the debt has increased).
- The increased loan amount (*i.e.* the extra amount the shareholders take out at the time of the refinancing)?—But this does not take account of the later reductions in return to investors.
- The difference between the pre- and post-refinancing cash flows?—But if this is a negative number it cannot be a gain.
- The increase in (short-term) reported profits?—May be a motive for the refinancing, but will be again be offset by later decreases.

As can be seen, this is a complex question. The answer devised in Britain was that the Refinancing Gain was the NPV of the change in the cash flow, pre- and post-refinancing. Note that the pre-refinancing cash flow is adjusted from the Base Case to reflect the current performance of the project, so that insofar as the project is performing above Base Case, the investors get the benefit of this rather than the Public Authority (albeit if there is a higher CADS than in the Base Case this also increases the Project Company's borrowing capacity, which is another reason for the rough 50:50 split).

The Refinancing Gain calculation is set out in Table 16.3, which uses the results from Table 16.2. An immediately obvious question is, what is the discount rate to be used for the NPV calculation, since it is clear that this will have a major impact on the answer, and hence the size of any share of the Refinancing Gain to be paid out to the Public Authority? As Table 16.3 shows, the higher the discount rate the higher the NPV, and hence the higher the Refinancing Gain on which the Public Authority's 50% share is calculated. This is counter-intuitive, as a higher discount rate normally creates a lower NPV, but in this case the changes in the cash flow after the refinancing has taken place are negative, and so a higher discount rate reduces this negative effect.

Table 16.3 shows that the effect of different discount rates is substantial—dropping from a gain of 55 with a 15% discount rate, to 11 at a 7% discount rate. In fact if the discount rate were further reduced to 6% in this case, the Refinancing Gain would disappear entirely. A high discount rate is thus generally in the interests of the Public Authority, and a low rate in the interests of the investors in the Project Company. (But this is not the case if the only refinancing change is a reduction in loan margin, as in that case all the future pre- and post-refinancing cash-flow differences are positive not negative.) Even with a high discount rate, however, the Refinancing Gain, calculated as the NPV of the changes in cash flow, is significantly less than the extra cash immediately produced from the refinancing (*i.e.* the increase in debt).

Table 16.3

Refinancing-Gain calculation

Year:	4	5	25	26	27	28	Total
Equity cash flow							
– post-refinancing	100.0	11.4	11.4	11.4	11.4	89.0	450.5
– pre-refinancing	15.0	15.0	89.0	89.0	89.0	89.0	597.8
– annual difference	85.0	−3.7	−3.7	−77.6	−77.6	0.0	−147.3
Discount rate = 15%							
Discount factor		1.150	18.822	21.645	24.891	—	
NPV of annual differences	85.0	−3.2	−0.2	−3.6	−3.1	0.0	**55.1**
Discount rate = 7%							
Discount factor		1.070	4.141	4.430	4.741	—	
NPV of annual differences	85.0	−3.4	−0.9	−17.5	−16.4	0.0	**11.4**

So what is the correct discount rate to use? One argument might be that it should be the PSDR (see above), but this is a 'risk free' rate which is not appropriate in this context. An equity risk-related discount seems to be more appropriate, and in fact in the British case the rate chosen for this purpose is the Base-Case (post-tax) Equity IRR, a relatively high rate. It could be argued that a more appropriate rate would be not the primary Equity IRR, but the (lower) secondary Equity IRR, *i.e.* the rate of return a new investor would expect when coming into the project at the time of the refinancing—with its lower risk profile (*cf.* §7.3.2). The difficulty about this is that the original Equity IRR is clear from the Base-Case financial model, in which it is calculated, whereas determining what the market would consider a fair secondary Equity IRR is more difficult. In the example in Table 16.3, and using the 15% discount rate which was the Base Case Equity IRR (*cf.* Table 16.2), the effect of paying out half of the Refinancing Gain (55.1 ÷ 2) to the Public Authority is to reduce the post-refinancing Equity IRR from 23% to 19%.

The end result of this calculation is virtually the same as saying that the Refinancing Gain is the sum of money today which equates to half of the increase in the Base Case Equity IRR as a result of the refinancing. So in the case set out in Table 16.2, where the Equity IRR has increased from 15% to 23%, after payment of the Public Authority's share of the Refinancing Gain, the projected Equity IRR should increase by half of the difference between 15% and 23%, *i.e.* to 19%. A payment of (55.1 ÷ 2) achieves this result. (Of course if this formula is adopted by the Public Authority instead of the NPV calculation used in Table 16.3, a 'base' rate lower than the Base Case Equity IRR is beneficial.)

§16.4.7 SHARING THE REFINANCING GAIN

But calculating the Refinancing Gain to fix the amount to be shared between the Public Authority and the investors in the Project Company is still not the end of this rather tortuous story. In the example in Table 16.3 (with a 15% discount rate), the Refinancing Gain is 55; if this were to be split 50:50, this implies a payment of 27.5 to each party. In this case there is 85 of extra cash available from the refinancing, so it is not difficult for the Public Authority to be paid its 27.5, and for all the rest of the surplus cash (57.5) to be paid to the investors in the Project Company—the extra amount of payment compared to the Public Authority thus compensating them for the reductions in Distributions which occur afterwards.

There may, however, be cases where the Public Authority's share of the gain needs to be paid over the remaining life of the PPP Contract, rather than in an initial lump sum as described above:

- The public-budgeting system may mean that such lump-sum receipts are taken off the Public Authority's other budget allocations, so giving the Public Authority no incentive to agree to a refinancing unless another way can be found of paying its share of the Refinancing Gain.
- There may not be a lump sum of money immediately available, from which the Public Authority's share of the Refinancing Gain can be paid, *e.g.* because there has only been a rescheduling of debt service payments over a longer period, rather than an immediate increase in the debt amount.

In such cases an alternative method is needed for spreading the payment of the Public Authority's share of the Refinancing Gain over time. There are two possible approaches here:

- Assuming that the cash-flow changes after the refinancing are all positive (as they would be with an interest-rate reduction) the Public Authority and the Project Company's investors can just 'split the difference'. But this means having one system in one case and another in other types of refinancing, which is not ideal.
- The second approach is to calculate the Refinancing Gain on an NPV basis as above, agree an interest rate to be credited on its deferred payment, and spread the payments out evenly over the remaining PPP Contract. The interest rate which should be charged should take account of the risk involved in the deferral from the Public Authority's point of view.

This risk is a function of where the deferred payment comes in the cash-flow 'Cascade' (*cf.* §12.2.3). If the payments to the Public Authority are made *pari passu* with payments to the investors in the Project Company, *i.e.* from surplus cash flow after opex and debt service, this leaves the Public Authority in the *de facto* position of being an equity investor, but without the control over the Project Company's business which its other investors have. A more suitable approach, therefore, is to make these payments by way of reductions in the Service Fees. If this approach is adopted, the risk of non-receipt is limited, and it would be appropriate to use a lower interest rate on the deferred payments than that used for the original discount rate when calculating the Refinancing Gain—*e.g.* instead of, say, a 15% rate it should be something closer to the PSDR (risk-free rate).

However, deferred payment should not be the preferred route for a Public Authority if the lump-sum option is available, as this in effect means that the Public Authority lends the money that it would otherwise take as the lump sum to the Project Company, and will be paid back from increased PPP payments. This is both economically inefficient, and allows the Project Company's investors to take this extra amount out of the Project Company at the time of the refinancing, and so further accelerating their return (and reducing their financial incentive to ensure the Project Company meets the requirements of the PPP Contract).

§16.4.8 REFINANCING AND CONTRACT EXTENSIONS

Yet another refinement of the debate on refinancing arises if the Project Company offers the Public Authority a 'package deal' of an extension to the PPP Contract term, and a reduction in annual Service Fees, along with a payment for Refinancing Gain-sharing similar to what would have been paid normally.

This may seem like a 'win-win' for the Public Authority, but of course the lower annual payments are achieved by lengthening the debt term. Effectively the Public Authority is borrowing money (the Refinancing-Gain payment and the annual reductions in Service Fees), and paying it back from the additional annual payments made during the extension period. This extra borrowing is at the Project Company's relatively high borrowing rate, not the lower rate at which the Public Authority could borrow in its own name. So the justification for a Public Authority agreeing to an extension in the PPP Contract term is not any saving in cost (because this is illusory), but that this is a way to use to PPP to raise additional funds for the Public Authority outside the public budget. (This situation is thus similar in nature to selling off a Franchise to the private sector—*cf.* §13.3.6.)

§16.4.9 SHOULD REFINANCING GAIN-SHARING APPLY IN ALL CASES?

The whole issue of sharing Refinancing Gains between the public and private sectors is thus very complex, and the question must be asked whether the issue is sufficiently import-ant to deserve attention. It has received a great deal of attention in Britain, but this was because the early PFI projects were financed on much less attractive terms than the later generations of such projects, especially as to the term of the debt, where Tail periods of 5 years were not unusual. This left a lot of scope for subsequent Refinancing Gains. The pace of refinancings subsequently slowed down substantially, because:

- Later projects were financed on more competitive terms, so reducing the room for any Refinancing Gains.
- Having to pay away half of the Refinancing Gain to the Public Authority obviously reduces the incentive to refinance, especially since sale of the equity shareholding provides an alternative way of making a early gain (*cf.* §16.5).
- Also, some refinancings have been done 'behind the curtain' to avoid paying out any Refinancing Gain, *e.g.* by portfolio refinancing though holding companies, leaving the original lenders of record in place, rather than an individual refinancing through the Project Company.
- Some refinancings ran into tax problems as to the treatment of the Refinancing Gain payment received by the investors. Also borrowing more money just to pay it straight out to shareholders may not be tax-deductible for the Project Company, since this new debt has not been raised for the purposes of the business.
- Refinancings involve a lot of management time on the part of investors which could be more profitably spent on bidding for new PPP projects; this is especially the case for smaller projects, where the relative costs (legal and financial) of a refinancing are high in relation to the likely level of benefits.

'Excess' or 'windfall' Refinancing Gains are therefore really only likely to be an issue:

- When a PPP programme is in an early stage of development, and there is likely to be a rapid improvement in financing terms offered by the market.
- For a 'non-standard' project, where financial market perception of its risks may change substantially.
- When there has been deal creep on a project, and no Funding Competition (*cf.* §16.2), so that the debt-financing terms are out of line with the general market.

Even then, it can be argued that insofar as refinancings accelerate revenue or produce a genuine profit for private-sector investors this will be subject to tax, and the public sector will benefit in this way.

It is also very difficult for a Public Authority to define a refinancing in a PPP Contract in such a way as to catch all possible ways of investors restructuring the debt, directly or indirectly, so as to accelerate withdrawal of equity cash flow out of the Project Company.

Apart from the Project Company simply borrowing more money, drafting has to cover matters such as:

- refinancings which were already taken into account in the bid, and hence the Service Fees: if bidders take the risk of refinancing in this way they should not be expected to share the benefit;
- refinancings which do not involve lending new money, such as:
  - lengthening the repayment schedule;
  - reducing the loan margin;
  - reducing requirements for Reserve Accounts (*cf.* §12.2.4);
- Refinancing Gains are calculated based on changes in Distributions to investors, not just dividends (*cf.* §7.3.3); however there may be other movements of cash which are not obviously Distributions, but which should still be caught, *e.g.* extra payments under the Subcontracts where Subcontractors are linked to the investors in the Project Company, this may be an alternative way of getting money out of the Project Company without sharing any Refinancing Gain;
- refinancings through holding companies, as discussed above;
- syndication of the loan (*cf.* §9.3.6) or placement of bonds (*cf.* §9.4.1);
- normal day-to-day waivers and amendments of loan documentation, which should not be caught in the definition of a refinancing (even if they produce a notional Refinancing Gain);
- raising new debt to fund PPP Contract variations (*cf.* §15.2.1);
- Rescue Refinancings (*cf.* §16.4.4);
- sale of equity (discussed below).

There must also come a point where any Refinancing Gain is so *de minimis* that the original policy reasons for paying a share to the Public Authority, or for the Public Authority having any control over the matter, have really disappeared. Investors and lenders will not wish refinancing provisions in a PPP Contract to be used by the Public Authority to control the normal business activities of the Project Company.

In a fully competitive market, the benefits which can be achieved by a refinancing should be factored into the initial bids for a PPP project, and therefore if a sharing of Refinancing Gains is imposed, it may well result in bidders increasing the Service Fees they would otherwise have proposed, which leaves the Public Authority in a worse position, as the 'bird in the hand' of lower Service Fees is clearly better than the 'bird in the bush' of a prospect of a share in any Refinancing Gain.

If windfall gains of whatever nature (*i.e.* on debt, or on equity as considered below) are considered likely, the simplest way for a Public Authority to share in these may be to take a substantial minority shareholding in a Joint-venture PPP (*cf.* §17.5), rather than try to catch these through provisions in the PPP Contract.

§16.5 EQUITY SALE

While refinancing may involve the investors in the Project Company in complex negotiations with the Public Authority, and result in a significant share of its benefit being paid away to the Public Authority in return for permission to go ahead, sale of the equity share-holding (along with any shareholder-provided subordinated debt) is usually subject to less control by the Public Authority. There may be an initial period during which the original Sponsors cannot sell their shares, but thereafter the Public Authority's right to object to equity disposals is likely to be limited (cf. §7.2.3).

Sale of equity is a highly-likely scenario, as it is based on the substantial difference between the Equity IRR required by an original bidder for a PPP project, and that required by a secondary purchaser who comes in after the initial construction risks of the project have passed (cf. §7.3.2). Table 16.4 illustrates the benefit of this from the point of view of the original investors, using the same assumptions as Table 16.2 for this purpose.

In this example the buyer of the equity is a secondary investor willing to accept an Equity IRR of 8% on a 'mature' investment such as a completed and operating PPP. Therefore, using the same cash flow as in Table 16.2, such an investor would pay 200 at the end of year 4, in return for the Project Company's cash flow from year 5 onwards. The seller of the equity is the original primary investor, who funds the original investment and receives the cash flow until the end of year 4, and then the lump-sum payment of 200 from the buyer. In absolute terms, the original investor has made a profit of 140 (230–90) on an original investment of 90 over a 4-year period.

As can easily be seen by comparing these results with Table 16.3, in terms of immediate gain sale of the equity may be much more attractive than a refinancing from the original investor's point of view especially if this gain does not have to be shared with the Public Authority (although the remaining revenue from the Project Company over the life of the project is then lost). It should be noted that a refinancing reduces the future cash flow of the project, and thus its value to another equity purchaser, so it may not be beneficial for the original investor to refinance the debt if the intention is to sell the equity.

It is also apparent from these figures that the political embarrassment for a PPP programme of such equity-sale profits is potentially just as great, if not greater, than from

Table 16.4

Equity sale

Year:		0	1	2	3	4	5	24	25	26	27	28
Buyer												
Purchase						−250						
Project cash flow							15	15	15	89	89	89
Total cash flow						−200	15	15	15	89	89	89
Equity IRR	= 8%											
Seller												
Project cash flow		−30	−30	−30	15	15						
Sale						200						
Total cash flow		−30	−30	−30	15	215						
Original investment = 90												
Profit on investment = 140												
Equity IRR	= 36%											

Refinancing Gains, which therefore raises the question whether the Public Authority should seek to share in such profits as well as Refinancing Gains. It is possible to construct a 'super profit' formula, whereby all cash flow received by investors, whether by way of refinancing or equity sale, are measured, and if the resulting IRR exceeds a threshold level (obviously higher than the Base Case Equity IRR) part of this excess is shared with the Public Authority. But problems of definition and legal drafting, already complex enough with Refinancing Gain-sharing, become far worse with a structure of this type. Moreover it could again be argued that a profit on the sale of the equity is taxable, so the public sector will benefit in this way instead. The simpler approach, where equity windfalls are likely to be an issue, is again for the Public Authority to take a minority shareholding in the Project Company, and thus benefit to that extent by the primary/secondary equity IRR difference through selling this shareholding when the Facility is operating (*cf.* §17.5). But *cf.* §16.3, where an easier method of sharing in equity gains at the bid stage is described.

If there is an especially high level of equity-sale profits, the most important reason for this is likely to be a discrepancy between primary- and secondary-market equity yields, discussed above (*cf.* §7.3.2): the figures used, of 15% and 8%, are not out of line with those seen in recent years in some mature PPP markets such as the United Kingdom and Australia. It is evident that if the gap between primary and secondary yields were lower, large profits on equity sales would disappear. But as has been seen (*cf.* §10.7), if the leverage is high, it is the lenders' Cover Ratio which really determines the Equity IRR. So the issue of equity-sale profits is linked to wider issues of financial structuring for PPPs.

Chapter 17

Alternative Models

§17.1 INTRODUCTION

This final chapter looks at some alternatives to the PPP model discussed in the rest of this book, *i.e.* a model which assumes:

- a PPP Contract integrating finance, construction and operation of the Facility;
- carried out by a Project Company with most of the project risks transferred to Subcontractors;
- with debt financing from commercial banks or the bond market; and
- equity investment by private-sector Sponsors and other investors.

The alternative routes all involve 'unbundling'—*i.e.* the Public Authority procuring one or more of the PPP building blocks (*cf.* §8.3) separately instead in one bundle within the PPP Contract. This has already been discussed in relation to:

- Funding—a funding competition allows finance to be procured separately instead of in an integrated bid (*cf.* §16.2).
- Soft FM services—there is a case for excluding Soft FM services from the PPP Contract (*cf.* §13.2); even if the Public Authority wants to use a private-sector Soft FM contractor, this can be done independently of the PPP Contract (although interface issues with the Project Company need to be well-managed).

However, more radical approaches to unbundling, including removal of some elements of the standard PPP package, can be considered:

Public-sector procurement (§17.2). Public-sector procurement may be adapted to achieve the main benefits of a PPP structure, without some of the drawbacks of cost and inflexibility. However, this will probably involve funding wholly provided by (or at the risk of) the public sector, with the budgetary disadvantages that this entails.

Post-construction take-out (§17.3). As the highest-risk phase for a PPP is usually during construction, a post-construction take-out (or assumption of risk) by the Public Authority cuts out the 'higher' cost of private-sector funding thereafter in return for taking operation-phase risks. This also at least allows the Facility to be kept off the public-sector balance sheet during the construction phase.

Public-sector debt funding (§17.4). Using public-sector funding for the Project Company's debt may be proposed as a way of reducing its capital-cost disadvantages, while leaving the rest of the standard PPP structure in place. However, the absolute benefit from this is limited if any financing risks are retained in the private sector.

Joint-Venture PPPs (§17.5). In a Joint-Venture PPP the Public Authority becomes an equity shareholder, the idea of this being to ensure that the public sector shares in equity returns and any funding windfalls. However this is liable to lead to a conflict of interest which may not be in the Public Authority's best interests.

Not-for-profit structures (§17.6). Another approach to reducing the cost of capital for PPP projects is to eliminate the equity return which goes to the private sector, or retain it for the benefit of the public sector. Paradoxically, however, this may result in higher initial Service Fees.

The menu of alternatives is a complex one, and while these approaches may all be worth consideration, as can be seen from this summary, they have disadvantages which may outweigh their benefits.

§17.2 PUBLIC-SECTOR PROCUREMENT

Ignoring the question of whether public-sector funding is really 'cheaper' (*cf.* §2.5), it is possible to adapt public-sector procurement so that it takes advantages of some of the benefits inherent in a PPP structure without a 'fully-fledged' PPP structure.

§17.2.1 DESIGN-BUILD-OPERATE (DBO)

As already discussed, a turnkey D&B or EPC Contract eliminates the construction risk without the need for the full panoply of a PPP structure, but may lose the benefit of the 'whole-life' approach to operation and maintenance (*cf.* §2.6, §2.8). A DBO Contract is an extension of the D&B structure which tries to alleviate this problem. It takes the 'F' out of DBFO, and just requires an integrated bid for construction of the Facility, together with provision of long-term FM services. (An alternative term is 'Design Construct and Maintain' (DCM).)

Under a DBO Contract the Public Authority pays for both construction and FM costs as they are incurred, in the same way as a Project Company pays for these in the standard PPP structure. If felt necessary, a private-sector project-management company can supervise and manage these contracts on behalf of the Public Authority, in a similar way to a PPP Project

Company. Clearly since financing will come from the public sector, its cost will be lower, and there will be greater long-term flexibility to make changes in the DBO contract because it is not bundled up with the financing. Moreover the DBO structure is less complex (fewer parties are involved) and so should be quicker to complete and inherently reduce costs.

However, there must be some question whether the same long-term risk transfer can be achieved as in the conventional PPP structure, especially as to maintenance risk (*cf.* §14.8.6). What happens if the DBO contractor fails to maintain the Facility? Clearly there will be penalties, but can these ever be as significant as the potential loss of capital (equity and debt) which arises when a PPP Contract is terminated for failure to perform (*cf.* §2.9.7)? If not, the apparent transfer of risk in this structure may be illusory, because it may be cheaper for the DBO contractor to walk away than to deal with a long-term problem with maintenance costs.

In any case a DBO requires public-sector funding, which may not fit with the primary objective for a PPP programme (*cf.* §2.3).

§17.2.2 PUBLIC–PUBLIC PARTNERSHIPS

Another approach makes use of the organisational benefits of a Project Company to manage the construction and operation of the Facility, using Subcontractors for construction and operating services in the same way as a PPP, but with all the funding being either provided or guaranteed by the Public Authority. This is a fairly common structure. It was used, for example, to fund the construction of the Öresund Bridge between Sweden and Denmark (completed in 2000): a publicly-owned SPV was granted a concession to operate the bridge and collect tolls and railway usage fees. The SPV was funded by loans and bonds guaranteed by the Danish and Swedish governments, and entered into various Subcontracts including that for construction.

A similar approach was used in financing construction of the first motorways in France (*cf.* §3.5): the main motive for this at the time was that the funding was outside the state budget, but this is likely to be more difficult to achieve now.

However, a publicly-run Project Company may be less effective than a private-sector Project Company's Sponsors in negotiating with Subcontractors, especially if these Sponsors are not themselves Subcontractors (and hence have no conflict about squeezing Subcontract costs); and because the debt funding is public-sector provided or guaranteed, lender discipline over the process is lost. Thus a Public–Public Partnership's lower financing costs may be offset by higher Subcontract costs. Again there is no risk capital in this structure, and if the objective is to introduce private-sector funding which is outside the public-sector budget this structure will probably not achieve this.

§17.3 POST-CONSTRUCTION TAKE-OUT

The idea here is to leave the construction risk with the private sector, but for the Public Authority to take over responsibility either for the project as a whole, or for its debt at least, thereafter. This reflects the fact that even if a Facility might be considered to be procured under a finance lease, and hence on the public-sector balance sheet, this need not apply when it is still under construction, when construction and completion risks remain with the private sector (*cf.* §5.5.2). As the construction period may last several years, this postpones any budgetary problem.

§17.3.1 DESIGN-BUILD-GUARANTEE-OPERATE (DBGO)

This is a development of the DBO approach discussed above: the key extension is that commercial banks or other private-sector financial institutions guarantee construction funding provided by the Public Authority, the guarantee being released on completion of the Facility. DBGO has the advantage of bringing lender discipline back into the picture during the highest period of risk.

§17.3.2 CONSTRUCTION FUNDING WITH A TAKE-OUT

A further development of the DBGO model is to require an SPV to raise private-sector funding for construction of the Facility, which will be repaid when it is completed. 'Equity' may be provided by the construction contractor, but in effect this is nothing more than a deferral of their profit on the construction and is also paid off on completion.

This structure has been used in Italy, for example, under the 2001 *Legge Obiettivo* ('Target Law'), intended to fund major infrastructure projects. The Law provides for DBFO structures, but alternatively for financing by the construction contractor during the construction period, with a take-out by the public sector on completion. A further variant has been used in Germany—construction is funded by the contractor, but on completion the Public Authority takes over responsibility for the debt and pays it off over the term of the PPP Contract. Obviously the post-completion debt pricing reflects the transfer from project risk to government risk.

In risk terms, the result is similar to the lenders' debt being fully guaranteed by the Public Authority once the Facility is completed (*cf.* §15.5.1).

§17.4 PUBLIC-SECTOR DEBT FUNDING

Another approach which is easier to fit within the requirement to keep the PPP out of the public budget, is to leave the PPP structure and risk transfer in place, but to source the underlying debt funding from the public sector on an arm's length basis. This is aimed at producing a lower cost of funding, hence narrowing the financing-cost gap between public-sector procurement and PPPs. However, it does not eliminate this gap, firstly because it only reduces the cost of debt and an equity return is still required, and secondly because any retention of risk in the private sector still has a cost (*cf.* §2.5).

Such public-sector debt can be provided in a number of ways:

- direct public-sector lending with private-sector bank or insurance-company guarantees (§17.4.1);
- using public-sector development banks to fund PPP projects (§17.4.2);
- using international financing institutions (§17.4.3), an important example of this being the European Investment Bank (§17.4.4).

§17.4.1 DIRECT LENDING WITH GUARANTEES

Under this structure, the government lends to the Project Company, on similar terms as to repayment profile, Cover Ratios, security, *etc.*, to private-sector lenders, but obviously at a lower cost because the loan is at or near to the cost of government bonds. Equity is provided by private-sector investors in the usual way. The debt is guaranteed by private-sector commercial banks or has an insurance-company 'wrap' (*cf.* §9.4.4). Thus risk remains with the private-sector investors as in a standard PPP, but funding is provided by the public sector. Some pilot projects using this scheme have been undertaken by the British Treasury, who give it the name Credit Guarantee Finance ('CGF').

The lower cost of funding is of course reflected in lower Service Fees, but the absolute benefit will be limited. Commercial banks will charge the same guarantee fee as the credit margin they would have charged had they lent direct, and the monoline guarantors also charge the same guarantee fee as they would have charged for a bond issue. The benefits are therefore limited to the difference between the base cost of funds for the public sector and that for the lenders, *i.e.* in the case of a bank loan the interest-rate swap market and credit premiums (*cf.* §11.2.4)—perhaps around 0.7% *p.a.* in total—plus the unmeasurable benefit of a competitive rate for the underlying funding (*cf.* §11.2.8). However, there is also a political benefit as it takes the sting out of the argument that public-sector funding is 'cheaper'.

But a bank or monoline-insurer guarantee does not mean that risk has been entirely eliminated for the public-sector lender: there is still a risk on the guarantor. If the public sector is too restrictive on which institutions qualify as acceptable guarantors, this can easily turn a few private-sector financial institutions into monopoly suppliers, with obvious cost results (and also result in an excessive build up in exposure to these institutions). An over-liberal approach could result in guarantees of limited or diminishing value from poor credits. And of course the guarantee has to last for 25–30 years, which could easily mean that an institution which appeared acceptable at Financial Close ceases to be so some years in the future. In fact it is bad practice to rely only on a guarantee, without any review or monitoring of the underlying credit of the Project Company. There is a parallel here with the practice of rating agencies when rating PPP bond issues which are wrapped by monoline insurers: the agencies look at both the credit of the monoline insurer and the credit of the underlying project (*cf.* §9.4.4).

The public-sector lender therefore has to put systems in place to:

- monitor and review policy on exposure to guarantors;
- review financing and other documentation to ensure it follows required principles;
- manage loan disbursements and administration;
- deal with changes in the project which have an effect on financing (*cf.* §15.2);
- monitor and control the credit standing of its guarantors; and
- be prepared, in the worst case, take direct control of the underlying loan because the guarantor is no longer acceptable, and is unable to provide alternative security, such as cash collateralisation, or a new guarantor to take its place.

A government department is not well equipped to manage such issues, and the better approach for public-sector funding, discussed below, is to use public-sector development-banking institutions which have developed the necessary specialised expertise to evaluate and take on project risks.

CGF is also biased against commercial bank finance:

- Syndication of guarantees will require the approval of the public-sector lender (since the effect is to change the guarantor), which reduces the attraction of the structure for banks compared to a direct loan (*cf.* §9.3.6).
- Banks lose their swap profits (*cf.* §11.2.8), and so may have to increase credit pricing to compensate for this.
- Monoline insurers charge less for their guarantees than the credit margins required by banks (*cf.* §9.4.4), which means that if banks are to be brought in as guarantors projects have to be 'ring-fenced' for them, to avoid the public sector being over-exposed to a limited number of monoline guarantors, and to make it worthwhile for the banks to bid for the business.

So it is not surprising that the CGF structure has yet to make any impact in the PPP market.

§17.4.2 PUBLIC-SECTOR DEVELOPMENT- OR INFRASTRUCTURE-BANK FUNDING

Making a 25-year loan to a PPP Project Company has very limited appeal to a commercial bank in many countries, if banks prefer to concentrate on much shorter-term consumer or commercial lending at rates which may be equal to or better than those for a PPP loan. This is especially the case in developing or newly-industrialised countries, but is also true in the United States (*cf.* §9.4.3, §10.5.6). Therefore, unless funding can be raised from the bond market, or a multilateral source as discussed below, the government will be forced to use public-sector debt funding if a PPP programme is to be developed. This may sound paradoxical if the main purpose of a PPP programme is avoid using the public budget to fund infrastructure, but although a public-sector development or infrastructure bank will require some capital investment by the public sector, it should be able to raise most of the funding required for loans to PPPs and similar projects from the private sector on a stand-alone basis, *i.e.* outside the public budget.

A typical example of using an established public-sector development bank for PPPs is the rôle of the state-owned Korea Development Bank (KDB) in the growth of the Korean PPI programme (*cf.* §3.8.2). Similarly, it is expected that the National Economic Development Bank (BNDE) of Brazil will play the largest initial part in funding Brazil's new PPP programme.

Public-sector banks specifically aimed at financing infrastructure are a newer development. State Infrastructure Banks (SIBs) are to be found, for example, in a number of the U.S. states; these can be capitalised with federal funding, raise debt funding in the private-sector markets, and use these resources, *inter alia*, for lending to PPP projects. However, for the reasons discussed in §3.5 progress on PPPs in the United States has been slow, and the SIBs have been little used in this respect. In Europe, in 2003 Italy established Infrastructure S.p.A. (ISPA), which has been used for funding PPP projects to a limited extent (but its primary use has been for public-sector projects). Similarly the Irish National Development

Finance Agency (*cf.* §3.2) can provide direct funding for PPP projects. In general, however, public-sector infrastructure banks have yet to make a great impact in the PPP market, because of some ambiguity in their rôles, and because they are usually run with small numbers of staff.

The inherent problem with public-sector funding of this type is that due diligence may be at less than arm's-length. Typically the assumption will be made that the Public Authority will ensure that the lender will not suffer a loss if things go wrong. Even worse, the lender may be forced to lend because of political pressure. This means that there is a risk of badly-structured projects being put together, and any cost-saving in funding may therefore be wiped out by the effects of poor due diligence.

§17.4.3 INTERNATIONAL FINANCING INSTITUTIONS (IFIs)

IFIs are described in detail in Chapter 11 of *Principles of Project Finance*—to summarise, these are institutions set up by international treaties to provide development funding. The most important in the PPP context are:

- International Finance Corporation (IFC), part of the World Bank Group;
- Inter-American Development Bank (IADB);
- Asian Development Bank (ADB);
- European Bank for Reconstruction and Development (EBRD)
- European Investment Bank (EIB)— this is different in nature and of particular import-ance for PPPs, and is therefore discussed separately below.

As IFIs are independent of an individual country's budget, and are used to financing public-sector infrastructure, it is a natural step for them to deal with PPPs. However, their business is confined to developing countries, and has to be 'additional' to lending by commercial banks and other private-sector sources, *i.e.* if funding is available on reasonable terms from the latter the IFI must step out of the picture. (Note that this is nothing to do with 'additionality' of PPPs, for which *cf.* §2.4.) IFIs are generally required to lend on arm's-length commercial terms, which also ensures that their lending is additional, for there would be no reason to borrow from them if the same terms could be obtained elsewhere. And as has already been seen (*cf.* §8.4.1), the developing countries to which IFIs lend tend not use PPP structures anyway.

The net result of this is that although IFIs do lend to PPPs their advisory rôle tends to be more important: the World Bank, for example, produces a great deal of literature on private-sector infrastructure, as can be seen from the Bibliography.

§17.4.4 EUROPEAN INVESTMENT BANK

The European Investment Bank (EIB) is the conspicuous exception to the above, and probably the most important public-sector institution lending in the PPP field. EIB's new loans to PPPs amounted to €772 million in 2005, and its cumulative lending to some €20 billion (for 89 projects) making it a larger lender to PPPs than any individual private-sector bank. About a quarter of these loans to PPPs have been in the United Kingdom; other countries in which EIB has a large PPP portfolio include Portugal, Spain and Greece, with the remainder of the portfolio quite diversified. It is therefore worth considering EIB's activities in detail, as these provide a interesting model for public-sector funding.

Structure. Under the 1958 Treaty of Rome, which established what is now the European Union (EU), EIB was created as an autonomous body within the EU to finance investment furthering European integration. Its equity shares are owned by the member countries of the EU, but only 7.5% of these are paid in, the rest being available if required. EIB raises its funding on the capital markets (*i.e.* primarily through public and private placements of bond issues), and thanks to its ownership and capital structure it benefits from an AAA rating. Apart from governments, EIB is probably the largest bond issuer in the European markets.

When originally established, EIB was modelled on other IFIs such as the World Bank (as well as the German state development bank Kreditanstalt für Wiederaufbau). Its activities were intended to be confined to financing public-sector projects (indeed its original purpose was actually to raise funding on the credit of Germany and to funnel this to Italy). Under Art. 267 of the Treaty of Rome EIB is required to operate on a non-profit making basis, providing financing, *inter alia*, for projects in less-developed regions of the EU, and projects of common interest of such a size that they cannot be financed by individual member states. The Statute of the EIB, annexed to the Treaty of Rome, provides (in Art. 18) that the EIB should make loans under Art. 267 'to the extent that funds are not available from other sources on reasonable terms,' *i.e.* the standard additionality requirement discussed above. The public-sector nature of EIB's mission is set out in the same Article, which provides that 'When granting a loan to an undertaking or to a body other than a Member State, the Bank shall make the loan conditional either on a guarantee from the Member State in whose territory the project will be carried out or on other adequate guarantees'. The convenience of EIB as source of funding for PPPs and other purposes has meant that the Bank's Board (all government-appointed) has long since disregarded the intention of these provisions. However EIB does adhere to the further provision in this Article that "As far as possible, loans shall be granted only on condition that other sources of finance are also used", and normally provides a maximum of 50% of a project's cost.

Cost of finance. Finance can be provided both in Euros and other major currencies, on a fixed or floating-rate interest basis (*cf.* §11.2). EIB's public-sector ownership and high credit rating enables the Bank to raise its own funding on terms only slightly worse than European governments, which, combined with the fact that it only has to cover its costs rather than lend on commercial terms or make a return on its capital, means that it is able to lend to projects at a cost significantly lower than the commercial-banking or bond markets. This advantage, and the lack of any additionality restraint, have meant that EIB's lending has expanded substantially compared to other IFIs: in 2005 the Bank approved €51 billion in new loans (of which €45 billion was inside the EU), whereas the World Bank's loan commitments that year were US$14 billion.

Although lower cost is the main reason for the use of EIB funding in PPP projects, where there are problems of capacity in the private-sector financing markets, either because of the size of the project (*e.g.* the large London Underground projects in the United Kingdom), or because the local financing market is not adequately developed (as was the case in Portugal and Greece), the EIB can offer true additionality of funding, as well as act as a catalyst for other funding.

Eligible projects. As required by the Treaty of Rome, broadly speaking the EIB finances social infrastructure projects in less-developed regions, and economic infrastructure projects where these improve links between EU member countries. The most important projects in the latter field relate to the 'TENs' (Trans-European Networks) programmes of the European Commission, which are aimed at upgrading major transport routes (road, rail and maritime) and energy transmission throughout the EU. In 2005, EIB lent €7.4 billion for transport TENs and €900 million for energy TENs (some of which would be included in the figure for PPP lending mentioned above).

All EIB loans have to be approved by the government of the relevant country, as well as the relevant Directorate of the European Commission—where (rare) objections arise from the latter they usually relate to the environmental aspects of a project. The EIB operates unofficial and unpublished quotas for balancing its lending between EU member countries; its allocation of loans within countries is agreed with the government concerned, subject to the general requirements that they should be to less-developed regions or for projects of 'common interest', as mentioned above. Public Authorities generally welcome EIB funding for PPPs because, apart from the saving in cost, they feel the Bank is more 'on their side' than commercial lenders.

EIB carries out due diligence on the technical and financial viability of PPP projects in much the same way as a commercial bank (*cf.* §9.3.4). It is also required to consider their wider economic benefits (*cf.* §5.2), but in reality if the country concerned has decided to undertake a PPP (or it is part of a TENs programme), EIB is unlikely to challenge this on economic grounds. Projects have to meet EU environmental standards, and to follow EU procurement rules (*cf.* §6.3.1).

Guaranteed and unguaranteed lending. As has been seen above, the EIB's Statute requires that it obtains government guarantees or 'other adequate guarantees' for its loans. Despite this EIB has long since lent on a 'single signature' basis—*i.e.* loans are made to private-sector borrowers of high credit quality without any guarantee. In the first major stage of its PPP lending, EIB (following precedents established in lending against PPAs in Britain) did not assume construction risks, and therefore generally required bank guarantees during the construction phase. Even during the operation phase, these guarantees were generally only released on a fairly conservative basis: for example in a road Concession EIB might assume 50% of the operating and revenue risks after year 8 and the rest after year 15, and require the loan to be guaranteed until it takes on these risks. However, with PFI-Model accommodation projects such as schools where there is little operating risk, the bank guarantee would be released shortly after completion. Guarantees from monoline insurers (*cf.* §9.4.4) have also been accepted. Guarantee release is usually triggered by meeting minimum Cover Ratio requirements (*cf.* §10.6).

The amount of these guarantees covers not only the loan outstanding, but also 6 months' interest and an allowance for the breakage cost, including a par floor (*cf.* §11.2.12) if EIB's loan is repaid early. Guarantees must be issued by 'qualifying banks', usually based on minimum credit ratings; if a bank's credit rating is lowered, EIB may require the guarantee to be cash collateralised. In principle, so long as the guarantor is 'on risk', it should take decisions relating to the loan (other than, *e.g.* amending its repayment schedule or interest rate). But clearly if there is a significant deterioration in the guarantor's credit quality EIB has to be ready to take direct responsibility for controlling the loan. This means that the bank still monitors loans even when it is guaranteed.

Switching from a guaranteed loan during construction to an unguaranteed loan during operation obviously raises questions of transition between the two. The bank guarantors should be allowed to take decisions and manage their own risk during the construction phase, but what if a decision they take at that time affects EIB's risk after completion of the project? This is dealt with quite simply by the EIB allowing the guarantors to take their own decisions, but if the EIB does not agree with them the guarantee is not released when the time comes. This could lead to unfair results for the guarantors, but EIB's record in this respect is a fair one.

Once the guarantees have been dropped, EIB is likely to be the biggest single lender to the Project Company, on the assumption that it generally provides 50% of the project's cost; commercial bank lenders lending in parallel may lend about the same amount in total as the EIB, but in much smaller individual shares if they syndicate the loan (*cf.* §9.3.6). As there have to be intercreditor arrangements (*cf.* §12.6), this generally means that EIB has the largest vote, and usually a veto over most actions by the lenders as a whole.

Despite the extra cost implied by requiring bank guarantees, EIB funding for PPPs was initially competitive with commercial banks because of its lower underlying cost of funds. However, increasing competition from commercial banks has led to a greater assumption of risk by EIB, and hence less requirement for bank guarantees, in particular during the construction phase of PFI-Model projects. Some of this additional risk assumption has taken place under EIB's Structured Finance Facility (SFF), established in 2001, under which it takes a variety of project risks through providing:

- senior loans and guarantees under which it will assume pre-completion and early operating risks;
- mezzanine finance and guarantees ranking ahead of shareholder equity or subordinated debt;
- project-related derivatives (hedging).

Total reserves of €750 million were initially set aside for this purpose; in 2006 the SFF programme was increased to €3.75 billion. The SFF has been extensively used for PPP projects, especially in the accommodation sector. The aim of the SFF was stated to be to 'add value for priority projects by complementing commercial banks and capital markets'. In reality little of this lending in the PPP field has been additional to the private sector.

It should be noted that EIB provides a limited amount of lending outside the EU, basically as a component of the EU's aid programme. In such cases it usually requires its loans to be fully bank- or government-guaranteed. Here too the Bank can serve as a catalyst for PPPs in less-developed local financial markets (as has been the case in South Africa).

Does lending additionality matter? It is interesting to contrast the EIB's approach to lending additionality with that of the EBRD, another IFI whose remit overlaps with that of EIB, as it was established to provide financing for the former Soviet Union and its satellites in Eastern Europe. The most important market initially for EBRD was in the central European countries such as Poland, Hungary and the Czech Republic. But as private-sector finance has come into these countries EBRD has withdrawn, and moved its operations further east where it is still needed. EIB on the other hand continues to increase its activities in these countries, as they are now members of the EU.

The reaction of private-sector lenders to the EIB effectively removing a large part of their market is varied: some cannot see the logic of EIB being involved if the private-sector market can provide all the necessary funding, but if cheaper EIB funding is necessary to ensure that their client wins a PPP bid, they have no objection to it. Others object more strongly in principle to losing business to EIB's non-additional lending.

But setting aside the question of whether such lending by EIB is in conformity with the intent of the Treaty of Rome (which it clearly is not) it is not difficult to justify it as far as PPP projects are concerned. In effect, as an EU public-sector body, EIB provides low-cost public-sector finance for such projects, while these still retain the benefits of private-sector management and control. So long as the benefit of this lower cost feeds through to the Service Fees (and is not just diverted to improve investors' returns), EIB's involvement in PPPs is financially beneficial to the Public Authority. This is usually ensured by making EIB funding available on equal terms to all private-sector bidders for a PPP project which is eligible for EIB funding; so long as this availability is made known at the time of the ITT/ITN, bidders can take it into account in their pricing. This means, however, that the EIB has to be brought into a PPP project at an earlier stage than a commercial bank, which has not always been the case, as it was not uncommon for EIB to come into projects after a bidder had been chosen and the Service Fees had already been fixed, and so EIB added little value to the project. EIB is now more conscious of this issue and tries to avoid this situation.

Moreover, EIB provides the same kind of third-party due-diligence benefit as can be obtained from private-sector banks (*cf.* §8.5.2). This distinguishes EIB lending from lending by development banks controlled by individual governments, where the same care may not be taken on due diligence (*cf.* §17.4.2).

Other activities. EIB set up the European Investment Fund (EIF) in 1994 in partnership with private-sector financial institutions. The objectives of EIF were originally to provide guarantees for EIB's loans, including PPPs, but as these largely became unnecessary (or duplicated those provided by commercial banks), EIB bought out its partners in 2000, and EIF is no longer involved in the PPP field.

EIB has obviously developed a lot of in-house expertise on PPPs, and apart from bankers also has a large department of engineers and economists involved in this sector. Nevertheless the Bank does not formally act as a financial adviser, even to Public

Authorities, although a lot of informal advice is given freely, and other support is also given, such as seconding staff to member governments. However in 2006 EIB set up a European PPP Expertise Centre, which is intended to provide support and training for EU member countries' PPP Units (*cf.* §3.2).

§17.5 JOINT-VENTURE PPPS

Joint-Venture PPPs (also known as Institutional PPPs) are Project Companies jointly-owned by public- and private-sector parties; this structure is more common with Franchises for utilities such as water, with joint ventures between municipalities and utility companies, but is also found in PPPs for new Facilities (usually in Concessions). Joint-Venture PPPs reduce the problems arising from windfall profits being earned by the private sector because of better access to information: in a joint venture the Public Authority should have access to much the same information, and benefit from unexpected increases in value in proportion to its shareholding.

However, some significant questions arise relating to the choice of the private-sector partner, and maintenance of an arm's-length relationship between the Joint-Venture PPP and the Public Authority. These issues occur at various stages:

- procurement:
  - should there be a two-stage procedure, first for choosing a partner and then for the PPP Contract itself?
  - should a Joint-Venture PPP have to bid in competition for the PPP Contract against other wholly private-sector owned bidders? If not how can VfM be demonstrated?
  - what procedure is appropriate if the Public Authority first sets up a Public-Public Partnership (*cf.* §17.2.2) and then sells a shareholding in the Project Company to private-sector investors?
- PPP Contract negotiations—how can the Public Authority be on both sides of the table?
- long-term management of the PPP Contract;
- what happens in the project gets into difficulty—will the Public Authority be forced to rescue it to protect its own shareholding?

So while a Joint-Venture PPP has obvious political attraction, this is a structure which the Public Authority has to handle with considerable care to ensure that the wrong decisions are not taken because of its dual rôle.

§17.6 NOT-FOR-PROFIT STRUCTURES

Even if some form of public-sector debt funding is provided as discussed above, the marginal difference compared to private-sector loans is relatively limited. The highest return is of course made by the equity investors in the Project Company, and it is this equity return which can be a key factor in making PPPs politically unacceptable. 'Not-for-profit' structures, also known as non profit-distributing organisations ('NPDOs'), are a way of dealing with this issue. Such structures should also ensure that insofar as there are unexpected financial windfalls from a project, these will accrue to the public sector. Two not-for-profit models are discussed below:

- 'pinpoint equity' or 'debt-only' structures (§17.6.1);
- public trusts (§17.6.2).

§17.6.1 'PINPOINT EQUITY' STRUCTURES

As it is the high equity return which is most vulnerable to any political opposition, and indeed does seem to be higher in many cases than it should be (*cf.* §7.3.2), a 'debt-only' structure has an obvious attraction. In a typical debt-only structure, the Project Company's shares continue to be owned by private-sector investors, but the actual share capital is negligible in size (hence the term 'pinpoint equity'), and no Distributions are made. (Other corporate forms can be used for this purpose, such as the English 'company limited by guarantee', instead of by shares.) Such structures can be used where there is a very secure cash flow, *e.g.* a road Concession which expands the capacity of an existing road bridge by building another in parallel (and hence the traffic and toll-revenue flows are already well-established), which was the case in the early British projects for the Dartford and Severn bridges, and the Portuguese Tagus bridge.

The immediate objection to such structures is that they are inevitably more expensive in Service-Fee terms. This is because the debt must still have a Cover Ratio; the result of this can be seen in Table 17.1, which compares a standard PPP financing with 90% debt with one financed with 100% debt.

The figures at (A) set out the 'standard' structure: calculating in a similar way to Table 10.5, the Service Fees required to cover the Senior Debt service, provide the required Cover Ratio, and a 15% Equity IRR amount to 84.1 *p.a.* (B) then assumes that the project is financed with 100% Senior Debt, on the same terms. The debt service is 76.9 *p.a.*, which means that with a Cover Ratio of 1.2 the Service Fees have to go up to 92.3. Therefore (B) is immediately more expensive for the Public Authority—however (B) is also producing a surplus of 15.4 *p.a.* which cannot be used to provide an equity return but has to go somewhere. (C) therefore assumes that all surplus cash flow after debt interest payments is devoted to principal repayments, and the PPP Contract is terminated when the debt has been paid off; as can be seen, this occurs in year 19, instead of year 28 in the standard structure. (The result is similar to the LPVR model—*cf.* §13.4.4.) This structure has the further advantage that if subsidies have to be paid to make it viable, and too much is handed over in subsidies, these do not benefit equity investors. It can also be combined with partial revenue or debt guarantees by the Public Authority. However, although the cost is much lower over the life of the project, the higher initial Service Fees may raise an Affordability problem. Nonetheless this structure—*i.e.* once the debt is paid off the Facility is toll-free—has commonly been used in Public–Public Partnerships, and was also used in the road bridge PPPs in Britain and Portugal mentioned above.

Assuming that this debt-only structure is a Concession, it should not be on balance-sheet for the public sector, but it is more difficult to use this structure for PFI-Model projects and achieve the same result, as the real level of risk transfer to the private sector becomes very limited.

Table 17.1

100% debt financing

Assumptions:

Project cost	1,000
Senior Debt interest rate	6%
Senior Debt ADSCR	1.20x
Senior Debt term	26 years
PPP Contract term	28 years

Year:	1	2	3	18	19	20	26	27	28
(A) Standard structure									
Debt:equity ratio 90:10									
Annuity debt service	69.2	69.2	69.2	69.2	69.2	69.2	69.2		
Equity return (15% Equity IRR)	14.9	14.9	14.9	14.9	14.9	14.9	14.9	84.1	84.1
Total Service Fees	**84.1**	**84.1**	**84.1**	**84.1**	**84.1**	**84.1**	**84.1**	**84.1**	**84.1**
Senior debt ADSCR	1.2	1.2	1.2	1.2	1.2	1.2	1.2		
(B) 100% Senior Debt									
Opening loan balance	1000.0	983.1	965.2	523.1	477.6	429.3	72.6		
Loan interest	60.0	59.0	57.9	31.4	28.7	25.8	4.4		
Principal repayments	16.9	17.9	19.0	45.5	48.3	51.1	72.6		
Total debt service [a]	76.9	76.9	76.9	76.9	76.9	76.9	76.9		
Closing loan balance	983.1	965.2	946.2	477.6	429.3	378.2	0.0		
Cash flow for Cover Ratio [b] (=Service Fees)	**92.3**	**92.3**	**92.3**	**92.3**	**92.3**	**92.3**	**92.3**	**92.3**	**92.3**
Surplus ([b]—[a])	15.4	15.4	15.4	15.4	15.4	15.4	15.4	92.3	92.3
(C) Surplus used for debt service									
Opening loan balance	1000.0	967.7	933.5	89.1	2.2				
Service Fees (= [b])	92.3	92.3	92.3	92.3	92.3				
Loan interest [c]	60.0	58.1	56.0	5.3	0.1				
Principal repayments ([b]—[c])	32.3	34.2	36.3	86.9	92.2				
Closing loan balance	**967.7**	**933.5**	**897.2**	**2.2**	**−89.9**				

But if structure (C) is used someone has got to own and run the Project Company. There is a danger that the Construction Subcontractor is the only person who has an interest in doing this, but there an obvious conflict of interest here during the construction phase and little or no involvement during the operation phase. The Senior Lenders, on the other hand, have an incentive to ensure that the Facility is built on time and to budget, and operated as required, to ensure their debt is repaid, so the Project Company can be owned by them (assuming this does not cause them any balance-sheet or other regulatory problems).

In fact a more likely structure is for there to be two layers of debt—senior and mezzanine (*cf.* §9.6)—with the mezzanine lenders, who may include the Subcontractors, controlling the Project Company. This may have the effect of lowering the initial Service Fees, because the mezzanine debt, although more expensive than the Senior Debt, should require lower Cover Ratios.

Care still needs to be taken, however, with the governance of the Project Company: the lenders have no incentive to pay their loan off quickly (or to refinance it on better terms), and could be tempted to use the cash-flow surplus for other purposes (*e.g.* to pay themselves a higher credit margin), and if the Construction Subcontractor is a mezzanine lender the conflict of interest remains. Therefore such governance controls need to be imposed *via* the PPP Contract. This position is likely to be less than ideal, which is why the public-trust route, discussed below, may be preferable. Indeed the incentive issue is wider than this, since although the lenders have loan capital at risk, the greater risk/return incentive from equity at risk (*cf.* §2.9.6) has been lost.

§17.6.2 PUBLIC TRUSTS

The concept of a not-for-profit PPP owned by its lenders, although shown to be viable by the projects already mentioned, is still inherently a bit strange. The alternative is for the Project Company to be, or to be owned by, a public trust. The term 'trust' as used here is not a legal term of art, but means an entity which is:

* independent of the Public Authority;
* not owned or controlled by private-sector investors; and
* not-for-profit.

We have come round in a large circle to get to this point, because an 18th-century school or hospital owned by a charity, or a turnpike road operated by a turnpike trust (*cf.* §1.4.1), both fit into this definition. ('Is there any thing whereof it may be said, See this is new? it hath been already of old time, which was before us.'—*Ecclesiastes* I, 10). And interestingly enough the first specific project which the author has found officially described (by President Eisenhower) as a 'public–private partnership' (in *Time* magazine, 14 November 1955) was the construction, with part-financing from federal funds, of the Priest Rapids and Wanapum Dams on the Columbia River, Washington State, by the Grant County Public Utility District, a public trust providing electricity. (However, this was not a PPP as defined in this book, as the federal funding was just a subsidy with no long-term contractual relationship.)

Since a public trust is another debt-only model, it faces the Cover Ratio problem discussed above. In this case, a Cover Ratio can be created in one of two ways:

* provide an existing cash flow to the trust as a 'starter'; using the example in Table 17.1, if the trust has an existing cash flow of 15.4 *p.a.*, it will be able to raise funding for the new investment; this works well if the trust is formed to, say, upgrade an existing toll road;
* higher Service Fees, as shown in Table 17.1.

In either case, the trust will of course have a running cash-flow surplus: this can be used to retire debt early as in Table 17.1, subsidise Service Fees, or spend on other related public services. A 'snowball' effect can develop—as new infrastructure produces increasing cash flows, the surpluses from these can be used to back new borrowing and further investment. Public trusts are quite common in the United States, and were used for some of the first modern toll roads, the Pocahontas Freeway in Virginia and the Southern Connector in South Carolina (*cf.* §3.5). Similarly, public trusts (housing associations) are now the main providers of social housing in Britain: these may begin their activities with transfers of social housing from the public sector, and are then able to raise funding for further investment based on this existing cash flow, with all their surplus cash flow being ploughed back into further investment. The public-trust approach thus works well under the Concession Model.

It is also easier to use a public-trust than pinpoint-equity approach for funding social infrastructure under the PFI Model, because something has to be done with the surplus. As said above the surplus cannot just be used for debt reduction (or paid back to the Public Authority) as this would most probably put the Facility on the public-sector budget. But a Project Company owned by a public trust can develop, say, a school PPP project, with the public trust devoting the surplus cash flow which arises from the lenders' Cover Ratios to related educational purposes. From the Public Authority's point of view this may offer good VfM compared to the standard PPP structure if this application of the surplus by the public trust can be used within the Public Authority's own VfM calculations: *e.g.* if the surplus is applied by the public trust within the geographical area for which the Public Authority is responsible. (There may be further tax benefits from the public trust being a charity, or the Project Company making tax-deductible donations of its cash-flow surplus to a similar charity.)

However, the Public Authority may still struggle to demonstrate that this structure provides VfM compared to the standard PPP structure. The easiest way to compare the two is to take the NPV of the Service Fees under the standard structure, and compare this with the NPV of the Service Fees under the public-trust *minus* the NPV of the running surplus. But, assuming the discount rate for the Service Fees is the PSDR, the same rate should not be used to discount the surpluses: the risk here is quite different, because the surpluses are only paid at the bottom of the cash-flow Cascade, and are thus much more uncertain. A discount rate similar to a private-sector Equity IRR is therefore more appropriate. Taking the examples in Table 17.1, and assuming a PSDR of 6% and a discount rate for the surplus of 15% (the same as the private-sector Equity IRR), the results are as follows:

- Case (A): Standard PPP structure: NPV of Service Fees = 1,127
- Case (B): Debt-only structure: NPV of Service Fees   = 1,237
  - Less: NPV of surplus cash flow   = (104)
  - Net NPV cost   = 1,133

So using these assumptions Case (A) actually offers better VfM for the Public Authority. The results are highly sensitive to the discount rates used, especially for the cash-flow surplus; a lower discount rate for the latter will turn the result around: *e.g.* 12% produces an NPV cost of 1,108, so making Case (B) apparently the better choice. Similar issues arise in the pinpoint-equity structure.

There are also governance problems involved in using a public-trust structure: lenders may be concerned that the lack of a commercial imperative means that the Project Company will not be managed effectively, *i.e.* the benefit of private-sector project management and other skills (*cf.* §2.9) will be lost. This may be avoided by the Project Company being owned by lenders as discussed in §17.6.1, and donating its surplus to a public trust (or charity), but this brings back the governance problems discussed in relation to the pinpoint-equity model.

In summary, therefore, although the real financial benefit of eliminating private-sector equity from PPPs may be more limited than might at first be thought, this may be balanced by not-for-profit structures being more politically acceptable, and avoiding the transfer of later financial windfalls to the private sector.

It could also be argued that PPP contractual structures—however adapted—are too rigid for dealing with long-term public-infrastructure requirements, and so if such infrastructure is to be financed by the private sector this may be better done through a regulatory régime. Under such a régime, investors' long-term service standards and investment returns are controlled by independent regulators rather than set out in contracts, in a similar way to privatised utilities (*cf.* §1.5). This has yet to be adopted outside the utilities sector (other than—partially—in the London Underground PPPs (*cf.* §3.4.2)), but could have a rôle to play in Concessions, and possibly PFI-Model projects. It may have the advantage of eliminating windfalls by capping total investment returns, however derived, while allowing for changes in capex, opex and capital structure over time. It would probably also make it easier for the Public Authority to introduce changes into the scope and nature of the service being provided. However such an approach is outside the scope of this book.

Bibliography

The following bibliography provides a selective list of useful publications on various countries' PPP programmes and related issues. All of these are available at the time of writing from the relevant websites (for links to which see www.yescombe.com), except for books marked*.

GENERAL

Patrick Boeuf, 'Public-private partnerships for transport infrastructure projects', paper at *Transport Infrastructure Development for a Wider Europe* (European Union/UNECE/European Investment Bank joint seminar, 2003).

Franck Bousquet and Alain Fayard, *Road Infrastructure Concession Practice in Europe* (Policy Research Working Paper 2675, World Bank, Washington DC, 2001).

Mathias Dewatripont and Patrick Legros, 'Public-private partnerships: contract design and risk transfer', *EIB Papers*, Vol. 10, No. 1 (European Investment Bank, Luxemburg, 2005), p. 120.

Eduardo Engel, Ronald Fischer and Alexander Galetovic, 'A New Approach to Private Roads', *Regulation* (Cato Institute, Washington DC, Fall 2002), p. 18.

Darrin Grimsey and Mervyn K. Lewis, *The Economics of Public Private Partnerships* (Edward Elgar, Cheltenham, 2005*)—a useful collection of reprints of academic articles.

Paul A. Grout, 'Value-for-money measurement in public-private partnerships', *EIB Papers*, Vol. 10, No. 2 (European Investment Bank, Luxemburg, 2005), p. 32.

Timothy Irwin, *et al.* (eds), *Dealing with Public Risk in Private Infrastructure* (World Bank, Washington DC, 1997*).

Michael Klein, *Risk, Taxpayers, and the Role of Government in Project Finance* (Policy Research Working Paper 1688, World Bank, Washington DC, 1996).

James Leighland, 'Is the public sector comparator right for developing countries?', *Gridlines Note No. 4* (Public-Private Infrastructure Advisory Facility, Washington DC, 2006).

Jarkko Murtaoro, *Public-Private Partnership: A Study on the Economics and Financing Alternatives of Transport Infrastructure Production* (Report 2006/3, Helsinki University of Technology Laboratory of Industrial Management, Espoo, 2006).

Armin Riess, 'Is the PPP model applicable across sectors?', *EIB Papers*, Vol. 10, No. 2 (European Investment Bank, Luxemburg, 2005), p. 10.

Jan Rommel, Johan Christiaens and Carl Devos, *Rhetorics of Reform: The Case of New Public Management as a Paradigm Shift* (Faculteit Economie en Bedrijfskunde Working Paper, University of Ghent, 2005).

Marco Sorge, "The Nature of Credit Risk in Project Finance", *BIS Quarterly Review* (Bank for International Settlements, Basel, December 2004), p. 91.

Timo Välilä, 'How expensive are cost savings? On the economics of public-private partnerships', *EIB Papers*, Vol. 10, No. 1 (European Investment Bank, Luxemburg, 2005), p. 94.

E.R. Yescombe, *Principles of Project Finance* (Academic Press/Elsevier, San Diego CA, 2002).

Hugo Zarco-Jasso, *Public-Private Partnerships: A Multidimensional Model for Contracting* (Public-Private Center Working Paper 584, IESE Business School, University of Navarra, 2005).

MULTILATERAL ORGANISATIONS AND AGENCIES—GUIDANCE AND DATA

Eurostat / IMF / OECD / UN / World Bank, *System of Bational Accounts 1993* (Brussels, Luxemburg, New York, Paris, Washington DC, 1993).

International Monetary Fund (Fiscal Affairs Department), *Public–Private Partnerships* (Washington DC, 2004).

International Organisation of Supreme Audit Institutions, *Guidelines on Best Practice for the Audit of Risk in Public/Private Partnership (PPP)* (INTOSAI, 2004).

Michael Kerf, *Concessions for infrastructure: a guide to their design and award* (Technical Paper 399, World Bank, Washington DC, 1998).

Public–Private Infrastructure Advisory Facility, *Toolkit: A Guide for Hiring and Managing Advisors for Private Participation in Infrastructure* (World Bank, Washington DC, 1999).

United Nations Commission on International Trade Law, *UNCITRAL Legislative Guide on Privately Financed Infrastructure Projects* (United Nations, New York, 2001).

— *UNCITRAL Model Legislative Provisions on Privately Financed Infrastructure Projects* (United Nations, New York, 2004).

World Trade Organisation, *General Agreement on Tariffs and Trade 1994*, Annex 4(b): 'Agreement on Government Procurement' (Geneva, 1994).

The World Bank maintains a Private Participation in Infrastructure (PPI) Project Database, covering PPPs and privatisation projects in developing countries. *Cf.* the annual survey of this data in Ada Karina Izaguirre, *Private Infrastructure: Emerging Market Sponsors Dominate Private Flows* (Public Policy for the Private Sector Note No. 299, World Bank, Washington DC, 2005).

AUSTRALIA

The Australian Council for Infrastructure Development, *Delivering for Australia: A Review of BOOs, BOOTs, Privatisations and Public-Private Partnerships, 1988 to 2004* (AusCID, Sydney, 2005).

Bureau of Transport and Communications Economics, *Benefits of Private Sector Involvement in Road Provision: A Look at the Evidence (Working Paper 33)* (Australian Government Publishing Service, Canberra, 1996).

— *Risk in Cost–Benefit Analysis (Report 110)* (Canberra, 2005).

Department of Finance and Administration, *Commonwealth Policy Principles for the Use of Private Financing* (Canberra, 2002).

New South Wales Government, *Working with Government: Guidelines for Privately Financed Projects* (Sydney, 2001).

Partnerships Victoria, *Guidance Material (2001): Overview/Practitioners' Guide/Risk Allocation and Contractual Issues/Public Sector Comparator* (Department of Treasury and Finance, Melbourne, 2001).

— *Contract Management Guide* (Department of Treasury and Finance, Melbourne, 2003).

— *Technical Notes (2003): Public Sector Comparator Supplementary Technical Note/ Use of Discount Rates in the Partnerships Victoria Process* (Department of Treasury and Finance, Melbourne, 2003).

— *Guidance Material (2005): Standard Commercial Principles/Managing Interest Rate Risk/Determining the General Inflation Rate for Use in Partnerships Victoria Projects* (Department of Treasury and Finance, Melbourne, 2005).

Peter Fitzgerald, *Review of Partnerships Victoria Provided Infrastructure* (Report to the Victoria Treasury, Melbourne, 2004).

Richard Webb and Bernard Pulle, *Public Private Partnerships: An Introduction* (Parliamentary Library Research Paper No. 1, Canberra, 2002).

Victoria Department of Treasury and Finance, *Partnerships Victoria* (Melbourne, 2002).

CANADA

Industry Canada, *Public-Private Partnerships: A Canadian Guide* (Ottawa, 2001).

— *The Public Sector Comparator: A Canadian Best Practices Guide* (Ottawa, 2003).

CHILE

Carlos Cruz Lorenzen and María Elena Barrientos, *Toll Road Concessions: The Chilean Experience* (Private Finance Group Discussion Paper 124, World Bank, Washington DC, n.d.).

Andres Gómez-Lobo and Sergio Hinojosa, *Broad Roads in a Thin Country: Infrastructure Concessions in Chile* (Policy Research Working Paper 2279, World Bank, Washington DC, 2000).

EUROPEAN UNION

European Commission, *Guidelines for Successful Public–Private Partnerships* (DG Regional Policy, Brussels, 2003).
— *Resource Book on PPP Case Studies* (DG Regional Policy, Brussels, 2004).
— *Green Paper on Public-Private Partnerships and Community Law on Public Contracts and Concessions* (COM/2004/327, Brussels 2004).
— *Communication on . . . Public–Private Partnerships and Community Law on Public Procurement and Concessions* (COM/2005/0569, Brussels, 2005).
European Investment Bank, *The EIB's role in Public–Private Partnerships (PPPs)* (Luxemburg, 2004).
— *Evaluation of PPP projects financed by the EIB* (Luxemburg, 2005)—the author acted as external consultant to the EIB's Evaluation Department for this study.
Eurostat, *ESA95 Manual on Government Deficit and Debt* (Office for Official Publications of the European Communities, Luxemburg, 2002 (2nd edition)).
— *Long Term Contracts between Government Units and Non-Government Partners (Public–Private-Partnerships)*, ESA 2004 Edition Part IV, §4.2 (Office for Official Publications of the European Communities, Luxemburg, 2004).

FRANCE

Jean-Yves Perrot and Gautier Chatelis (eds), *Financing of major infrastructure and public service projects: Public–Private Partnership—Lessons from French experience throughout the world* (École Nationale des Ponts et Chaussées, Paris, 2000*).
Ministère de l'Économie, des Finances et de l'Industrie, *Les Contrats de Partenariat: Principes et méthodes* (MINEFI, Paris, n.d.).

IRELAND

Department of Finance, *Framework for Public–Private Partnerships* (Dublin, 2001).
— *Interim Guidelines for the Provision of Infrastructure and Capital Investments through Public Private Partnerships: Procedures for the Assessment, Approval, Audit and Procurement of Projects* (Dublin, n.d.).
— *Guidelines for the Appraisal and Management of Capital Expenditure Proposals in the Public Sector* (Dublin, 2005).
— *Discount Rate Principles for Public Private Partnership Capital Investment Projects* (Dublin, 2006).

KOREA

Fumiyo Harada, *Legal Framework for Private Participation in Infrastructure in the Selected East Asian Countries; Comparative Study on Japan, Korea, and the Philippines* (Development Bank of Japan, Tokyo, 2002).

Ministry of Planning and Budget, *Korean PPI System* (Seoul, 2006).
Paul Noumba Um and Severine Dinghem, *Private Participation in Infrastructure Projects in the Republic of Korea* (Policy Research Working Paper 3689, World Bank, Washington DC, 2005).

MEXICO

Jeff Ruster, 'A Retrospective on the Mexican Toll Road Program (1989–94)', *Public Policy for the Private Sector*, No. 125 (World Bank, Washington DC, 1997).

NETHERLANDS

PPP Knowledge Centre, *PPP and Public Procurement Guide* (Ministry of Finance, Amsterdam, 2001).
— *Public Sector Comparator* (Ministry of Finance, Amsterdam, 2002).
— *Public Private Comparator* (Ministry of Finance, Amsterdam, 2002).

NORWAY

'Norwegian Road Projects are now Profitable—the Government Reduces the Discount Rate', *Nordic Road and Transport Research*, No. 2/3 (VTI, Stockholm, 2005).

PORTUGAL

Rui Sousa Monteiro, 'Public-private partnerships: some lessons from Portugal', *EIB Papers*, Vol. 10, No. 2 (European Investment Bank, Luxemburg, 2005), p. 72.

SINGAPORE

Ministry of Finance, *Public Private Partnership Handbook* (Singapore, 2004).

SOUTH AFRICA

Peter Farlam, *Working Together: Assessing Public–Private Partnerships in Africa (Nepad Policy Focus Report No. 2)* (The South African Institute of International Affairs, Braamfontein, 2005).
National Treasury, *Project Finance: Introductory Manual on Project Finance for Managers of PPP Projects* (Pretoria, 2001).
— *Standardised PPP Provisions* (Pretoria, 2004).

UNITED KINGDOM

Grahame Allen, *The Private Finance Initiative (PFI)* (Research Paper 01/117, House of Commons Library, London, 2001).

Arthur Andersen and Enterprise LSE, *Value for Money Drivers in the Private Finance Initiative* (Report for Treasury Task Force, London, 2000).

Cambridge Economic Policy Associates, *Contract Issues and Financing in PPP/PFI (Do We Need the 'F' in DBFO projects?)* (Report for Institute for Public Policy Research, London, 2000).

— *Public Private Partnerships in Scotland: Evaluation of Performance* (Report for the Scottish Executive, Edinburgh, 2005).

Adrian Chesson and Fenella Maitland-Smith, *Including Finance Lease Liabilities in Public Sector Net Debt: PFI & Other* (Office for National Statistics, London, 2006).

Denise Chevin (ed.), *Public Sector Procurement and the Public Interest* (The Smith Institute, London, 2005).

Pam Edwards, Jean Shaoul, Anne Stafford and Lorna Arblaster, *Evaluating the Operation of PFI in Roads and Hospitals* (ACCA Research Report No. 83) (Certified Accountants Educational Trust, London, 2004).

European Commission, *State Aid No N264/2002—United Kingdom: London Underground Public Private Partnership* (Brussels, 2002).

Bent Flyvbjerg (with COWI A/S), *Procedures for dealing with Optimism Bias in Transport Planning* (Report for Department of Transport, London, 2004).

Institute for Public Policy Research, *Commission on Public Private Partnerships: Building Better Partnerships* (IPPR, London , 2001*).

Mott Macdonald, *Review of Large Public Procurement in the UK* (Report for HM Treasury, London, 2002).

Paul van den Noord, *Managing Public Expenditure: The UK Approach* (Economics Department Working Papers No. 341, Organisation for Economic Co-operation and Development, Paris, 2002).

Partnerships UK, *Report on Operational PFI Projects* (Report for HM Treasury, London, 2006).

Allyson Pollock, Jean Shaoul, David Rowland and Stewart Player, *Public Services and the Private Sector: A Response to the IPPR* (Catalyst Trust, London, 2001).

Allyson Pollock, David Price and Stewart Player, *Public risk for private gain? The public audit implications of risk transfer and private finance* (UNISON, London, 2004).

Philippa Roe and Alistair Craig, *Reforming the Private Finance Initiative* (Centre for Policy Studies, London, 2004*).

PricewaterhouseCoopers (with Julian Franks), *Study into Rates of Return Bid on PFI Projects* (Report for Office of Government Commerce, London, 2002).

Treasury Task Force, *Technical Note No. 1: How to Account For PFI Transactions* (HM Treasury, London 1998).

— *Technical Note No. 3: How to Appoint and Manage Advisers to PFI Projects* (HM Treasury, London, n.d.).

— Technical Note No.4; How to Appoint and Work with a Preferred Bidder (HM Treasury, London, n.d.)

HM Treasury, *Public Private Partnerships: The Government's Approach* (HM Stationery Office, London, 2000).
— *The Green Book: Appraisal and Evaluation in Central Government* (HM Stationery Office, London, 2003 (3rd edition)).
— *PFI: Meeting the Investment Challenge* (HM Stationery Office, London, 2003).
— *Standardisation of PFI Contracts* (HM Stationery Office, London, 2004 (3rd edition)).
— *Value for Money Assessment Guidance* (HM Stationery Office, London, 2006 (2nd edition)).
— *PFI: Strengthening Long-Term Partnerships* (HM Stationery Office, London, 2006).
Private Finance Panel publications (up to 1997) are not listed here. A number of other PFI technical guidance notes have been published by HM Treasury, Office of Government Commerce, individual government departments, 4Ps and the Scottish Executive.
The National Audit Office has produced over 40 published reports on individual PFI projects or more general aspects of PFI; most of these have been the subject of hearings by the House of Commons Public Accounts Committee, which then also publishes reports on these topics.

UNITED STATES

Department of Transportation, *Report to Congress on Public–Private Partnerships* (Washington DC, 2004).
Federal Highway Administration, *Innovative Finance Primer* (Washington DC, 2002).
— *Manual for Using Public–Private Partnerships on Highway Projects* (Washington DC, 2005).
General Accounting Office, *Report to Congressional Requesters—Highways and Transit: Private Sector Sponsorship of and Investment in Major Projects Has Been Limited* (GAO-04-419, Washington DC, 2004).
KCI Technologies Inc., *Current Practices in Public–Private Partnerships for Highways* (Report for Maryland Transportation Authority, Maryland Department of Transport and Maryland State Highway Administration, Hunt Valley MD, 2005).
Office of Management and Budget, *Guidelines and Discount Rates for Benefit-Cost Analysis of Federal Programs* (Circular A-94, Washington DC, 1992).

Glossary and Abbreviations

Technical terms used in this book that are mainly peculiar to PPPs or project finance are capitalised, and briefly explained in this Glossary, with cross-references to the places in the main text where a fuller explanation can be found; other financial terms used in the book are also explained and cross-referenced, as are the various abbreviations used.

Abandonment Failure by the Project Company to construct or operate the Facility for a prolonged period of time. *See* §15.5

ABN Model *See* financial facilitator.

acceptance Confirmation by the Public Authority or the Checker that conditions for the Service Availability Date have been met. *See* §6.6.6

accommodation projects PPP projects involving the provision of buildings such as schools, hospitals and prisons. *See* §1.6.2

accreting swap An interest-rate swap drawn in instalments to match drawing of the notional principal amount. *See* §11.2.4

accretion swap An interest-rate swap which allows part of the fixed-rate interest payment to be deferred to a later date (*cf.* debt accretion). *See* §11.2,1.0

Acts of God *See* Force Majeure.

ADB Asian Development Bank, a regional IFI. *See* §17.4.3

additionality The question whether PPPs result in additional or faster investment in public infrastructure than relying only on public-sector procurement. *See* §2.4

additionality The requirement for IFIs only to lend if funding cannot be provided by the private-sector markets. *See* §17.4.3; §17.4.4

ADSCR Annual Debt-Service Cover Ratio, the ratio between CADS and debt service over any one year of the project. *See* §10.6.2

Advance-Payment Bond Security provided by the Construction Subcontractor for amounts paid in advance under the Construction Subcontract by the Project Company. *See* §14.7.1

Affermage *See* Franchise. *See* §1.4.1; §3.7

Affordability The ability of the Public Authority to pay the Service Fees from its budgetary resources over the life of a PFI-Model PPP Contract; *cf.* willingness to pay in relation to a Concession. *See* §5.4

agent bank The bank liaising between the Project Company and its lenders. *See* §9.3.7; §10.4.5

All Risks insurance Insurance against physical damage to the Facility during operation. *See* §12.4.3

ALOP insurance Advance Loss of Profits insurance; *see* DSU insurance.

amortising swap An interest-rate swap reduced in instalments to match reductions in the notional principal amount. *See* §11.2.4

annuity repayment A debt repayment schedule that produces level debt-service payments. *See* §10.5.2

assumptions book The source data for the financial model. *See* §10.3

Authority *See* Public Authority.

Availability The period when the Facility (or the relevant part thereof) is able to provide the service as required under the PPP Contract. *See* §1.6; §13.5; §14.8.4

Availability Charge The fixed-charge element of a Tariff, payable whether or not the product or service is required, intended to cover debt service and equity return; not normally a separate element in Service Fees; *cf.* Usage Charge, Unitary Charge, Gate Fee. *See* §1.4.2; §5.5.4

average life The average period that the loan principal is outstanding. *See* §10.5.3

AVT Authority voluntary termination, or termination of the PPP Contract at the option of the Public Authority. *See* §15.6

BAFO Best and Final Offer, a second-stage bid in a public procurement. *See* §6.3.1

balloon repayment A large final principal repayment of a loan (after a series of smaller payments); *cf.* bullet repayment, mini-perm. *See* §10.5.6

banker's clauses Additional lender requirements on insurances. *See* §12.4.5

Banking Case *See* Base Case.

Base Case The lenders' projections of project cash flow at or shortly before Financial Close. *See* §10.3.8

Basel II The revised capital requirements for international banks, effective from 2007. *See* §9.4.4, §14.2

benchmarking Adjustment to the Service Fees based on market costs for Soft FM services. *See* §11.3.13

BI insurance Business Interruption insurance, *i.e.* insurance against the loss of revenue after damage to the project. *See* §12.4.3

BIS Bank for International Settlements, which hosts the Basel Committee on Banking Supervision. *See* §14.2

Blended Equity IRR The investors' IRR based on Distributions; *cf.* Equity IRR. *See* §7.3.3

BLOT Build-Lease-Operate-Transfer. *See* §1.5

BLT Build-Lease-Transfer. *See* §1.5

bond A tradable debt instrument. *See* §9.4

bonding Security provided by bidders, the Project Company or Subcontractors. *See* §6.4.4; §13.3.4; §14.7.1

BOO Build-Own-Operate. *See* §1.4.3; §1.5

BOOT Build-Own-Operate-Transfer. *See* §1.5

BOT Build-Operate-Transfer. *See* §1.4.3; §1.5

breach of provision clause *See* non-vitiation clause.

breach of warranty clause *See* non-vitiation clause.

breakage cost The cost of early termination of a swap, bond or other fixed-rate or inflation-indexed loan. *See* §11.2.3; §11.2.6; §11.2.12; §11.3.8; §12.6.1–§12.6.3

brownfield project Project involving refurbishment of an existing Facility, or building on a site where there have previously been major structures; *cf.* greenfield project. *See* §14.5.2; §14.6.3

BTL Build-Transfer-Lease; in Korea refers to PFI-Model projects. *See* §1.5; §3.8.1

BTO Build-Transfer-Operate. *See* §1.4.3; §1.5

Builder's all risks insurance *See* CAR insurance.

bullet repayment Repayment of a loan in one final instalment rather than a series of principal repayments; *cf.* balloon repayment. *See* §10.4.6; §11.2.4

Business Case   The formal presentation of the project for approval within the Public Authority and to other branches of government. *See* §6.1; §6.2.2

CADS   Cash flow available for debt service. *See* §10.3.3; §10.6.1

Capacity Charge   *See* Availability Charge.

capex   Capital expenditure; usually the initial costs of constructing the Facility; *cf.* opex. *See* §10.3.2

Capital accretion bonds   *See* debt accretion.

CAPM   Capital asset pricing model, method of measuring the cost of equity. *See* §7.3.1

CAR insurance   Contractor's All Risks insurance. *See* §12.4.2

Cascade   The order of priorities under the financing documentation for the application of the Project Company's cash flow. *See* §12.2.3

Cash Sweep   Dedication of surplus cash flow to debt prepayment. *See* §10.5.7

CEAR insurance   Construction and Erection All Risks insurance; *see* CAR insurance.

Certifier   *See* Checker.

Cession de Créance   Concept in French administrative law which enables the Public Authority to take over direct responsibility for part of the Project Company's debt; *cf.* Underpinned Funding. *See* §13.5

CGF   Credit Guarantee Finance, the British Treasury's scheme for public-sector funding of PPP Project Companies, with private-sector debt guarantees. *See* §17.4.1

change in law   A change in the law affecting the Project Company or the project, resulting in additional capex or opex. *See* §15.2.5

Changes   Change in PPP-Contract specifications by the Public Authority. *See* §14.6.3; §15.2.3

Checker   An engineering firm not linked to any party to the Project Contracts, who confirms that project construction has been carried out as required by the PPP Contract and Construction Subcontract. *See* §6.7.3

claw-back   Requirement for investors to repay Distributions if the Project Company is later short of cash. *See* §10.9

collateral warranties   Agreements under which Subcontractors accept liability to the lenders for the performance of their Subcontracts. *See* §12.3.3

commercial banks   Private-sector banks, the main suppliers of debt to PPP projects. *See* §9.3

Commercial Close   Signature of the Project Contracts subject to completion of the financing. *See* §6.5.4

commitment fee   Percentage fee charged on the available but undrawn portion of a bank loan. *See* §10.4.4

Common Terms Agreement   Common lending conditions agreed between different groups of lenders. *See* §12.6

Compensation Events   Events for which the Public Authority is required to compensate the Project Company for its increased costs or loss of revenue; *cf.* Relief Events, Force Majeure. *See* §14.3; §15.2

Competitive Dialogue   A more flexible version of the Negotiated Procedure. *See* §6.3.1

Completion Bond   Security provided by the Construction Subcontractor for performance under and completion of Construction Subcontract. *See* §14.7.1

completion risks   Risks relating to the completion of construction of the Facility and its initial ability to provide the services required by the PPP Contract. *See* §14.7

CompOnTerm   *See* Termination Sum.

Concession   A PPP in which the general public pays Service Fees in the form of tolls, fares or other charges for using the Facility; *cf.* PFI Model. *See* §1.4.1

Concession Agreement   A PPP Contract relating to a Concession.

Concessionaire   The private-sector party to a Concession Agreement.

conditions precedent   Conditions to be fulfilled by the Project Company before drawing on the debt, or before Project Contracts become effective. *See* §6.5.4

Construction bond   *See* Completion bond.

construction phase   The period from Financial Close to the Service Availability Date. *See* §6.1

construction risks   Risks relating to the construction of the Facility. *See* §14.6

Construction Subcontract   A D&B or EPC Contract (*q.v.*). *See* §14.6.1

Construction Subcontractor   The Subcontractor responsible for the Construction Subcontract. *See* §14.6.2

construction-phase risks   Risks relating to the construction phase, which may affect the Project Company's capex or ability to operate the Facility; *cf.* site risks, construction risks, completion risks. *See* §14.5–§14.7

contingency   Unallocated reserve in the capex budget, covered by contingent or standby funding. *See* §10.3.2; §10.5.9

Contract Administrator   *See* Checker.

contract debtor   A system of taxation and accounting in the United kingdom under which the NPV of the capex portion of the Service Fees is shown as a financial claim in the Project Company's accounts, rather than showing the Facility as a fixed asset. *See* §10.8.1

Contracting Authority   *See* Public Authority.

Contractual Close   *See* Commercial Close.

Control Accounts   *See* Project Accounts.

corporate loan   A loan against a company's balance sheet and existing business. *See* §8.3; §8.5.3

cost–benefit analysis   The ratio of the NPV of the benefits of a project to the NPV of its costs (from the public-sector point of view). *See* §4.4.1; §5.2.2

cost-effectiveness analysis   A comparison of the costs of different solutions to procurement of a project. *See* §5.2.2

coupon   The interest rate payable on a bond. *See* §9.4.2

coupon swap   *See* interest-rate swap.

Cover Ratio(s)   Ratio(s) of the cash flows from the project against debt service, *i.e.* ADSCR, LLCR, or PLCR. *See* §10.6

CPI   Consumer Price Index, a measure of inflation.

credit margin   The margin over cost of funds charged by a lender to cover its credit risk and provide a return on capital. *See* §10.4.1

credit premium   The margin over the market swap rate charged by a swap provider to cover its credit risk and provide a return on capital. *See* §11.2.4; §11.2.6

cross-border risks   Risks which arise when a loan or investment is made from one country to a project in another. *See* §14.4

Cure Period   A period of time allowed for lenders to remedy a default under a Project Contract. *See* §15.4.2

D&B Contract   Design and Build Contract, a fixed-price, date-certain, turnkey contract for design and construction of infrastructure and buildings. *See* §14.6.1

DBFM   Design-Build-Finance-Maintain; *see* DBFO.

DBFO   Design-Build-Finance-Operate. *See* §1.4.3; §1.5

DBGO   Design-Build-Guarantee-Operate, a contract similar to a DBO contract, but with completion of the Facility guaranteed by private sector banks or other financial institutions. *See* §17.3.1

DBO   Design-Build-Operate, a form of long-term contract for construction and operation of a Facility, in which funding is provided by the Public Authority. *See* §17.2.1

DCF   Discounted cash flow, a calculation of the value today (NPV) of a future cash flow. *See* §4.2

DCM   Design Construct and Maintain; *see* DBO.

DCMF   Design-Construct-Manage-Finance; *see* DBFO.

deal creep   Gradual deterioration in the terms of the Project Agreement compared to the original bid during subsequent negotiations, usually caused by the project requirements not being initially specified in enough detail by the Public Authority, or by changes in requirements. *See* §6.3.8; §16.2.1

debt   Finance provided by the lenders. *See* Chapter 9

debt:equity ratio   Ratio of debt to equity; *cf.* leverage. *See* §8.5; §10.7

debt accretion   Increasing the debt amount during the operation phase of a very long-term concession; *cf.* accretion swap; *See* §10.5.8

debt service   Payment of interest and debt-principal instalments. *See* §1.4.2; §10.5.2

decanting   Moving the Facility (or parts of it) from an old site to a the new site during the process of construction. *See* §14.5.9

deductibles   Initial loss amount which has to be borne before insurance claims are paid. *See* §12.4.4

deductions   Sums deducted from Service-Fee payments for failure to meet Availability or service requirements of a PFI-Model contract; *cf.* penalties. *See* §13.5

Default Ratio   Minimum Cover Ratio(s) below which an Event of Default occurs under the loan documentation. *See* §12.5

deflation calculation   Reduction of a future nominal sum to a real sum. *See* §11.3.1

Delay LDs   LDs payable by the Project Company for failure to complete the Facility by the agreed date, the cost of which may be borne by the Construction Subcontractor. *See* §13.3.4; §14.7.1

depreciation   Writing-down the capex incurred on the Facility for tax or accounting purposes.

derivative   A contract which produces payments and receipts over a period of time, at prices 'derived' from an underlying financial-market movement, *e.g.* an interest-rate swap. *See* §11.2.10

design-bid-build   A standard method of public-sector procurement whereby the Public Authority designs the facility and then calls for bids to construct it. *See* §1.3.2; §2.6.1

Development Agreement   An agreement between Sponsors relating to bidding for and development of the project. *See* §7.5

development costs   Costs incurred by the Sponsors before Financial Close. *See* §10.3.2

Direct Agreement(s)   Agreement(s) between the lenders and the Public Authority or Subcontractors, protecting the lenders' interests under the Project Contracts. *See* §12.3.3; §15.4.2

Disbursement Account   The Project Company's bank account into which equity and debt advances are paid, and from which payments are made for the Facility's construction costs and other capex. *See* §12.2.1

discount rate   The percentage rate used to reduce a future cash flow to a current value, and so calculate its NPV. *See* §4.2

Distribution Block   Cover Ratio(s) below which the lenders prevent payment of Distributions. *See* §12.2.5

Distributions   The Project Company's net cash flow paid to investors as dividends, subordinated-debt interest or principal, or repayment of equity. *See* §1.4.2; §7.3.3; §12.2.5

Dividend Stop   *See* Distribution Block.

dividend trap   Inability of the Project Company to pay dividends, despite having cash available to do so, because of accounting losses. *See* §10.8.3

DPC Contract Design, Procurement and Construction Contract; *see* EPC Contract.

drawing request The formal procedure for drawings on the debt by the Project Company. *See* §12.2.1

Drawstop Suspension of loan advances by the lenders after an Event of Default. *See* §12.2.2; §12.5

DSRA Debt Service Reserve Account, a Reserve Account with a cash balance sufficient to cover the next scheduled debt service payment. *See* §12.2.4

DSU insurance Delay in Start-up insurance, insurance against the loss of revenue or extra costs caused by a delay in completion after damage to the project. *See* §12.4.2

due diligence Review and evaluation of Project Contracts and their related risks, carried out by both the Public Authority and the lenders. *See* §6.5; §8.5.2; §9.3.4

easement A right to use adjacent land, *e.g.* for discharge of water. *See* §14.5.6

EBRD European Bank for Reconstruction and Development, an IFI covering Central and Eastern Europe, and the former Soviet Union. *See* §17.4.3

economic infrastructure Public infrastructure required for day-to-day economic activity, such as transportation and utilities; *cf.* social infrastructure. *See* §1.2

Effective Date *See* Financial Close.

Efficacy insurance Insurance which covers the Construction Subcontractor's liability to pay LDs for delay or poor performance. *See* §12.4.2; §14.7.1

EIA Environmental Impact Assessment, a study of the effect of the construction and operation of the project on the natural and human environment. *See* §14.5.4

EIB European Investment Bank, the long-term lending institution of the European Union. *See* §17.4.4

Emergency Step-In The right of the Public Authority to take over operation of the Facility for reasons of safety, public security, *etc. See* §15.4.1

environmental risks Risks relating to the environmental effect of the construction or operation of the Facility. *See* §14.5.4

EoI Expressions of Interest (call for); *see* RFQ.

EPC Contract Engineering, Procurement and Construction Contract, a fixed-price, date-certain, turnkey contract design and engineering, equipment procurement or manufacture, and construction and erection of process or other plant. *See* §14.6.1

equity The portion of the project's capex contributed by the investors to the Project Company, either as share capital or subordinated debt. *See* §7.3

Equity Bridge loan Finance provided by lenders during the construction period for the amount of the equity investment. *See* §7.3.4

Equity IRR The IRR on the equity paid in by the investors, derived from dividends; *cf.* Blended Equity IRR. *See* §7.3.2

ERR Economic rate of return, a method for the public sector to measure the net benefits of a project; *cf.* FIRR. *See* §5.2.4

escrow account A bank account under the joint control of two parties; *see* Project Accounts.

EU European Union.

Eurostat The Statistical Office of the European Communities, which harmonises public-sector accounting for members of the EU. *See* §5.5

Events of Default Events that give parties to Project Contracts the right to terminate them after due notice, or the lenders the right to Drawstop or terminate the financing. *See* §12.5; §15.5

exchange-rate risks Macroeconomic risks resulting from changes in currency exchange rates. *See* §11.1

external economies/diseconomies *See* externalities.

externalities   Economic, social, environmental or other effects of a project, the benefit or cost of which cannot be charged to users of the Facility. *See* §1.2; §5.2; §13.4.3

Facility   The public infrastructure provided under the PPP Contract. *See* §1.3.1

Fare-Box Guarantee   Guarantee by the Public Authority of a minimum level of usage or toll payments in a transportation PPP. *See* §13.4.3

finance lease   A lease in which economic ownership of the asset passes to the lessee, on whose balance sheet it is therefore treated as a loan; if a PPP is classified as a finance lease the capex element of the Service Fees will be deemed to be public-sector debt. *See* §5.5.2

financial adviser   The Public Authority's adviser on financial aspects of procuring the PPP, or the Sponsors' (separate) adviser on arranging finance for the Project Company. *See* §6.7.1; §9.2

Financial Balance   A mechanism to put the Project Company, and its investors and lenders, in a position no worse than they would otherwise have been had a Compensation Event not occurred. *See* §15.2.1

Financial Close   The date at which all Project Contracts and financing documentation have been signed, and conditions precedent to initial drawing of the debt have been fulfilled. *See* §6.1; §6.5.4

financial facilitator   An investment bank, PPP fund or similar institution which acts as the primary Sponsor. *See* §7.2.1

financial model   The financial model(s) used by the Public Authority, investors and lenders to review and monitor the project. *See* §10.2

FIRR   Financial rate of return, the cash-flow benefit of a project from the point of view of the public-sector (as opposed to its economic benefit—*cf.* ERR), or an investor in the project. *See* §5.2.4

Fisher formula   A formula for adjusting cash flows for inflation. *See* §11.3.1

floating interest rate   An interest rate revised at regular intervals to the current market rate; *cf.* LIBOR. *See* §11.2

FM   Facilities management (for a building); *see* Hard FM, Soft FM.

FM Subcontracts   Subcontracts for the provision of Hard FM or Soft FM.

FMV   Fair market value, a method of calculating the Termination Sum. *See* §15.5.3; §15.5.4

Force Majeure   A event which is not the fault of either party to the PPP Contract, which makes it impossible to continue with the PPP Contract; *cf.* Relief Events. *See* §14.3; §15.7

Force Majeure insurance   Insurance against third-party *Force Majeure* events affecting the Construction Subcontractor. *See* §12.4.2

Franchise   The right to operate existing public infrastructure and receive user payments; differs from a PPP because no substantial new investment is required by the private sector. *See* §1.4.1; §1.5; §3.5; §13.3.6

Franchisee   The private-sector party to a Franchise.

fronting bank   A bank acting as a channel for competitive interest-rate swap quotations. *See* §11.2.8; §11.2.13

Funding Competition   A competitive bidding procedure to provide the debt financing, which takes place after the appointment of a Preferred Bidder. *See* §6.5.3; §13.2; §16.2

Gate Fee   Payment method used in process-plant projects such as waste incinerators, in   lieu of Service Fees; *cf.* Availability charge. *See* §13.5.1

gearing   *See* leverage.

GIC   Guaranteed Investment Contract, a fixed rate of interest paid by a depository bank on the proceeds of a bond issue until these are required to pay construction costs. *See* §11.2.11

Government Procuring Entity *See* Public Authority.

GPA Agreement on Government Procurement, the framework for public procurement under the WTO. *See* §6.3

greenfield project Project involving constructing a completely new Facility, or building on a site where there have previously been no major structures; *cf.* brownfield project. *See* §14.5.2; §14.6.3

hand-back Return of the Facility to the Public Authority at the end of the PPP Contract. *See* §6.6.8; §15.11

Hard FM Routine maintenance of the Facility; *cf.* Lifecycle costs. *See* §13.2; §14.8.6

hard infrastructure Buildings and other physical Facilities. *See* §1.2

hedging An arrangement in the financial markets to protect the Project Company against adverse movements in interest rates or inflation. *See* Chapter 11

hurdle rate The discount rate or minimum IRR used to determine if an investment produces the minimum required return. *See* §4.2; §4.3; §4.5.2

IADB Inter-American Development Bank, a regional IFI. *See* §17.4.3

ICD Invitation to Competitive Dialogue, an invitation to bid in a public procurement using the Competitive Dialogue procedure. *See* §6.3.1

IDC Interest during construction, which is capitalised and forms part of the capex budget. *See* §10.3.2; §11.2

IFC International Finance Corporation, an affiliate of the World Bank dealing with the private sector. *See* §17.4.3

IFI International financing institution. *See* §17.3.1.

IMF International Monetary Fund.

inflation risks Risks to the Project Company's capex or opex resulting from changes in the rate of price inflation. *See* §11.3.4

inflation swap A hedging contract to convert a cash flow subject to inflation adjustment to a fixed cash flow (or *vice-versa*). *See* §11.3.9

inflation-indexed loan A loan whose debt service is indexed against inflation. *See* §11.3.6

innovative finance A term used in the United States for alternative methods of funding public infrastructure. *See* §2.2; §3.5

Institution *See* Public Authority.

Institutional PPP *See* Joint-Venture PPP.

insurance Cover against the effects of *Force Majeure* on construction or operation of the Facility. *See* §12.4

intercreditor Relationship between different groups of lenders. *See* §12.6

interest-rate cap A hedging contract that sets a maximum interest rate. *See* §11.2.10

interest-rate collar A hedging contract that sets a floor (minimum) and ceiling (maximum) interest rate. *See* §11.2.10

interest-rate risks Risks to the Project Company's capex or opex resulting from changes in interest rates. *See* §11.2

interest-rate swap A hedging contract to convert a floating interest rate into a fixed-rate. *See* §11.2.2

investment bank A bank which organises PPP investment funds, or arranges but does not provide debt. *See* §9.2; §9.4.2

investment-grade rating A credit rating of BBB-/Baa3 or above. *See* §9.4.1

investors Sponsors and other parties investing equity into the Project Company. *See* §7.2.1

IRR Internal rate of return, the rate of return on an investment calculated from its future cash flows. *See* §4.3

ISDA International Swap and Derivatives Association, which produces standard form documentation for hedging contracts. *See* §11.2.5

IT   information technology.

ITB   Invitation to Bid; *see* ITT.

ITN   Invitation to Negotiate, an invitation to bid in a public procurement using the Negotiated Procedure. *See* §6.3.4

ITT   Invitation to Tender, an invitation to bid in a public procurement using the Restricted Procedure. *See* §6.3.4

Joint-Venture PPP   A PPP in which the Public Authority is a shareholder in the Project Company, along with private-sector investors. *See* §17.5

KICGF   Korea Infrastructure Credit Guarantee Fund, a public-sector fund providing partial revenue or debt guarantees for Korean PPI projects. *See* §3.8.2

km   Kilometre.

KPIs   Key performance indicators, measuring service standards under the PPP Contract; failure to attain these leads to deductions of Performance Points. *See* §13.5.2

L/C   Letter of credit, a form of on-demand guarantee issued by a bank.

latent defects   Defects in the Facility which no-one could reasonably have found and whose effect does not appear until a later date. *See* §14.6.3; §14.7.1

LDs   Liquidated damages, the agreed level of loss when a party does not perform under a contract. *See* §13.3.4; §14.7.1

Lead Arranger(s)   Bank(s) arranging and underwriting the Project Company's debt. *See* §9.3.2

Lead Manager   *See* Lead Arranger.

lease   A form of debt in which the asset being financed is owned by the lessor; also used (but not in this book) to refer to the right to use a Facility or other property for a specified period of time, and a Franchise (*q.v.*); *cf.* finance lease. *See* §1.4.1; §1.5; §5.5.2; §8.4.2

lease-purchase analysis   A procedure similar to a PSC required by the U.S. Office of Management and Budget. *See* §5.3

lenders   Banks or bond investors.

lenders' advisers   External advisors employed by the lenders. *See* §9.3.4

lessee   The obligor under a lease (equivalent to a borrower). *See* §5.5.2; §8.4.2

lessor   The provider of finance under a lease (equivalent to a lender). *See* §5.5.2; §8.4.2

leverage   The debt:equity ratio (*q.v.*).

LIBOR   London inter-bank offered rate, a floating interest rate. *See* §11.2

lifecycle costs   The costs of major renewals of equipment over the term of the PPP Contract. *See* §10.3.3; §12.2.4; §14.8.6

limited-recourse   Finance with limited guarantees from the Sponsors. *See* §10.9

linear project   A project involving construction of a Facility over a long stretch of land, *e.g.* for a road. *See* §12.4.7; §14.5.1; §14.5.2

LLCR   Loan Life Cover Ratio, the ratio of the NPV of CADS during the remaining term of the debt to the debt principal amount. *See* §10.6.3

Lock Up   *See* Distribution Block.

LPI swap   Limited price inflation swap, whereby there is a floor and a ceiling on inflation increases and decreases. *See* §11.3.10

LPVR   Least present value of revenue; an LPVR Concession is one without a fixed term, which terminates when the NPV of a set revenue level has been achieved. *See* §6.3.6; §13.4.4

macroeconomic risks   Risks to the Project Company's capex or opex related to inflation, interest rates, or currency exchange rates. *See* §11.1

maintenance bond   Security for the Construction Subcontractor's obligations during the warranty period. *See* §14.7.1

Maître d'Oeuvre   *See* Checker.

make-whole clause   A provision in a bond financing, whereby on prepayment of the bond the amount payable includes the NPV of the foregone profit margin, and must not be less than the par value of the bond. *See* §11.2.12

market flex A pricing arrangement which gives banks the right to change pricing before Syndication of a large loan to reflect market changes. *See* §9.3.6

market stabilisation A hedging exercise in advance of placement of a large bond or swap, to ensure that the placement itself does not move market rates. *See* §11.2.13

mark-to-market Calculating the breakage cost, and hence the current value of a loan or hedging contract. *See* §11.2.3

merit goods Infrastructure and services which the public sector needs to provide to ensure availability for all, *e.g.* schools. *See* §1.2

mezzanine debt Subordinated debt provided by third parties other than the investors. *See* §9.6

mini-perm A loan for the construction period and first few years of operation of a project, to be refinanced in due course by longer-term debt; *cf.* balloon repayment. *See* §10.5.6

MIRR Modified IRR, an IRR calculation with a reduced reinvestment rate for cash taken out of the project. *See* §4.4.3

MLAs Minimum liquid asset requirements; *see* MLR.

MLRs The cost of banks' minimum liquidity ratio requirements, if any. *See* §10.4.2

Model Auditor An independent firm of accountants or financial-modelling company that reviews and certifies the financial model. *See* §10.3.7

monoline insurance Insurance of an individual financial risk (rather than general casualty insurance). *See* §9.4.4

MRA Maintenance Reserve Account, a Reserve Account used to set aside cash for the maintenance of the Facility. *See* §12.2.4; §14.8.6

MRG Minimum Revenue Guarantee, the Korean system of support for revenue risks on Concessions. *See* §3.8.1; §13.4.4

NDFA National Development Finance Agency, an Irish government PPP Unit. *See* §3.2

negative arbitrage The loss of interest caused by having to draw the whole of a bond financing at Financial Close and then redeposit the funds until required; *cf.* GIC. *See* §9.5; §11.2.11

negative equity A cumulative accounting loss exceeding the amount of the Project Company's share capital. *See* §10.8.3

negative pledge An agreement by a borrower with its lender not to give security over its assets to any third party. *See* §12.3.2

Negotiated Procedure A public-procurement procedure whereby negotiations take place with bidders to clarify their bids. *See* §6.3.1

network risk The risks for the project resulting from connections outside the project. *See* §14.8.2

nominal cash flow/return The cash flow or return on an investment including inflation, if any—*i.e.* 'money of the future' (*cf.* real cash flow/return). *See* §11.3.1

nonconforming bid A bid which offers an alternative solution for the project to that in the Public Authority's bid requirements. *See* §6.4.2

non-recourse Finance with no guarantee from the Sponsors; *cf.* limited-recourse. *See* §10.9

non-vitiation clause Provision in an insurance policy that the rights of lenders will not be affected by action by the Project Company that invalidates the insurance. *See* §12.4.8

not-for-profit A form of ownership which eliminates private-sector Distributions from a PPP project. *See* §17.6

notional principal amount   The amount of debt which is the subject of an interest-rate or inflation swap. *See* §11.2.2; §11.3.9

NPC   Net present cost; the NPV of the cost of a PPP to the Public Authority. *See* §5.3

NPDO   Non profit-distributing organisation; *see* not-for-profit.

NPM   New Public Management, one of the theoretical bases for PPPs. *See* §2.2

NPV   Net Present Value, the discounted present value of a stream of future cash flows, offsetting benefits against costs. *See* §4.2

O&M   Operation and maintenance. *See* §1.4.2

OECD   Organisation for Economic Co-operation and Development.

operation phase   The period between the Service Acceptance Date and the end of the PPP-Contract term. *See* §5.1; §6.6.7

operation-phase risks   Risks relating to the operation phase which may affect the Project Company's revenues or opex. *See* §14.8

opex   Operating costs; *cf.* capex. *See* §1.4.4: §10.3.3

optimism bias   The tendency for the public sector to underestimate project costs, which needs to be taken into account in considering project risks. *See* §5.2.3; §5.3.3

outputs   Service requirements under a PPP, defined on the basis of the Public Authority's requirements rather than how these requirements are to be delivered. *See* §1.3.2; §2.2; §5.5.4

outsourcing   Provision of soft infrastructure by the private sector under contract to a Public Authority; not considered a PPP as it does not involve substantial provision of fixed assets. *See* §1.3.1; §1.5

over-indexation   Inflation indexation of the Service Fees by a proportion greater than the Project Company's variable costs. *See* §11.3.5; §11.3.7; §11.3.12

Owner's Engineer   The adviser supervising the Construction Subcontract on behalf of the Project Company. *See* §7.7

Owner's Risks   The responsibilities of the Project Company under the Construction Subcontract. *See* §14.6.3

p.a.   Per annum, yearly.

P3   *See* PPP. *See* §1.3.3

PABs   Private-activity bonds: tax exempt bonds which can be issued to fund PPP projects under SAFETEA-LU (*q.v.*). *See* §3.5

par floor   A provision in a bond financing, whereby the pre-payment amount cannot be less than its par value. *See* §11.2.12

pari passu   Equal and *pro rata*; relates to security shared by different lenders, or payments to other claimants.

Partnerships Victoria   The PPP Unit in Victoria, Australia. *See* §3.6

payback period   The period of time in which Distributions to investors equal their original investment. *See* §4.4.3

paying agent   A company distributing debt-service payments from the Project Company to bond investors. *See* §9.4.2

penalties   Payments by the Project Company for failure to meet service requirements under a Concession; *cf.* deductions. *See* §13.4.6

Performance Bond   *See* Completion Bond.

Performance LDs   LDs payable by an EPC Contractor if the Facility is unable to perform as specified on completion (usually relates to process plant); *cf.* Delay LDs. *See* §14.7.4

Performance Points   Penalties for failure to meet KPIs, accumulation of which results in deductions from the Service Fees and may eventually lead to termination of the PPP Contract. *See* §13.5.2

Permits   Planning or other permissions required to construct and operate the Facility. *See* §14.5.3

Persistent Breach   Consistent failure by the Project Company to observe any provisions of the PPP Contract which are not covered by penalties or deductions, or otherwise an Event of Default. *See* §15.5

PFI Private Finance Initiative, the United Kingdom's PPP programme. *See* §1.4.5; §3.4

PFI Credits The British system of central-government funding for PFI-project Service Fees. *See* §3.4.2; §11.3.5

PFI Model A PPP in which the Service Fees are paid by the Public Authority; *cf.* Concession. *See* §1.4.5

PFP Privately-Financed Projects; *see* PPP. *See* §1.3.3

PFP Private Financing Predictor, a 'shadow' financial model prepared for the Public Authority to assess the initial financial feasibility of a PPP. *See* §10.2

PFU Private Finance Unit; *see* PPP Unit.

PIM Preliminary Information Memorandum, the information memorandum on the project used as a basis for obtaining financing bids from prospective Lead Managers. *See* §9.3.6

PIMAC Public and Private Infrastructure Investment Management Center, the Korean PPP Unit. *See* §3.8.1

pinpoint equity A not-for-profit structure which can be used for a PPP. *See* §17.6.1

PLCR Project Life Cover Ratio, the ratio of the NPV of CADS during the remaining life of the PPP Contract and the outstanding debt amount. *See* §10.6.4

political risks Risks related to government action affecting the Project Company or its operations. *See* §14.4

P-P Partnership *See* PPP. *See* §1.3.3

PPA Power Purchase Agreement. *See* §1.4.2

PPI Private Participation in Infrastructure; used in Korea to refer to Concessions; *see* PPP. *See* §1.3.3; §3.8.1

PPP Public–private partnership, a contract under which a private-sector party invests in a Facility to provide a public service to or on behalf of the public sector. *See* §1.3

PPP Contract The contract between the Public Authority and the Project Company for design, construction, finance and operation of the Facility; this may be a Concession Agreement or a Project Agreement. *See* §1.3; §3.3

PPP Unit A specialised centre of PPP expertise in the public sector. *See* §3.2

Preferred Bidder A bidder with whom the Public Authority pursues detailed negotiations under the Negotiated Procedure. *See* §6.3.1

prepayment Early repayment of a loan or bond.

pre-qualification The first stage of a public-procurement process. *See* §6.3.3

primary investors The original investors in the Project Company, including the Sponsors; *cf.* secondary investors. *See* §7.2.1; §7.3.2

principal-agent problem In the context of a PPP, asymmetry of information between the Public Authority and the Project Company. *See* §2.9.9

Private Party *See* Project Company.

private placement Bonds not quoted on a stock exchange. *See* §9.4.2

privatisation Full transfer of former public infrastructure to the private sector, as compared to PPPs, where it remains in the public sector. *See* §2.2

Proceeds Account *See* Disbursement Account.

project The design, construction, finance and operation of the Facility.

Project Agreement A PPP Contract relating to a PFI-Model project.

Project Company The SPV which is the Public Authority's counterparty under the PPP Contract. *See* §1.3.1; §7.6

Project Company costs Costs of running the Project Company itself, excluding Subcontract costs. *See* §7.6.3; §10.3.2; §10.3.3

Project Contracts The PPP Contract and the Subcontracts.

project finance A method of raising long-term debt financing for major projects through 'financial engineering', based on lending against the cash flow generated by the project alone; it depends on a detailed evaluation of a project's construction, operating and revenue risks, and their allocation between investors, lenders and other parties through contractual and other arrangements. *See* §8.1

Project IRR   The IRR of CADS against the original capex. *See* §4.5.2; §7.3.1

Promoter   *See* Public Authority.

Promoters   *See* Sponsors.

PSB   Public-sector benchmark; *see* PSC.

PSC   Public-sector comparator, a theoretical measurement of the cost of public procurement of a Facility, which is compared against the cost of the PPP. *See* §5.3

PSDR   Public-sector discount rate, the discount rate used by Public Authorities when evaluating an investment in public infrastructure. *See* §5.2.3

PSP   Private-Sector Participation; *see* PPP. *See* §1.3.3

Public Authority   The public-sector counterparty under the PPP Contract. *See* §1.3.1

Public Entity   *See* Public Authority.

public goods   Public infrastructure which has to be freely available for all, and for which it is difficult to charge users, *e.g.* street lighting. *See* §1.2

public infrastructure   *See* economic infrastructure, social infrastructure, hard infrastructure, soft infrastructure. *See* §1.2

Public Liability insurance   *See* Third Party Liability insurance.

Public Party   *See* Public Authority.

public procurement   The process of competitive bidding for a contract with the public sector. *See* §6.3

public trust   A not-for-profit structure which can be used for a PPP. *See* §17.6.2

Public–public partnership   A structure substantially similar to a PPP, but with the Project Company owned and funded by the public sector. *See* §5.5; §17.2.2

public-sector balance sheet   Expenditure in the public budget; in the context of a PPP, the issue whether the Facility or its related debt (or the NPV of the capital element of the Service Fees) are recorded in the public-sector budget. *See* §2.3; §5.5

public-sector procurement   Direct procurement of public infrastructure by the Public Authority instead of through a PPP Contract. *See* §1.3.2

PUK   Partnerships UK, a British government PPP Unit (but majority private-sector owned). *See* §3.4.1

QIB   Qualified Institutional Buyer, an institutional investor to whom Rule 144a bonds can be sold. *See* §9.4.3

ramp-up   The early years after completion of a project, when usage is still building up (*e.g.* for a Concession road). *See* §7.3.2; §10.5.2; §10.5.5; §13.4.3; §14.8.1

rating agency   A company providing an independent view on the creditworthiness of the Project Company. *See* §9.4.1

real cash flow/return   The cash flow or return on an investment excluding inflation, if any—i.e. 'money of today'; *cf.* nominal cash flow/return. *See* §11.3.1

real tolls   Tolls paid in cash by the users of the Facility; *cf.* Shadow Tolls. *See* §13.4

refinancing   Prepayment of the debt and substitution of new debt on more attractive terms (*e.g.* lower cost or Cover Ratios, or longer maturity). *See* §16.4

Refinancing Gain   The benefit of a refinancing of the Project Company's debt. *See* §16.4.5; §16.4.6

Relief Events   Temporary *Force Majeure* preventing the completion or continuous operation of the Facility, for which the Project Company is not penalised but receives no compensation from the Public Authority; *cf.* Compensation Events. *See* §14.3; §15.3

Rescue Refinancing   A restructuring of the Project Company's debt made necessary by the project being in financial difficulty. *See* §15.5.1; §15.6; §16.4.4

Reserve Accounts Accounts controlled by the lenders (or their trustee or escrow agent) in which part of the Project Company's cash flow is set aside to provide security for the debt or to cover future costs; *cf.* DSRA, MRA. *See* §12.2.4

Restricted Procedure A public-procurement procedure whereby no negotiation takes places after bids have been made. *See* §6.3.1

retainage The proportion of each payment under the Construction Subcontract retained by the Project Company as security until the Service Availability Date. *See* §14.7.1

RFP Request for Proposals; *see* ITT.

RFQ Request for qualifications, the first stage of a public-procurement process. *See* §6.3.3

right of way A right of access to the Facility through adjacent land. *See* §14.5.6

Risk Matrix Schedule of risk allocation and mitigation. *See* §14.3

Risk Register *See* Risk Matrix.

roll-over risk The risk that an interest-rate swap contract may not be amended on acceptable terms if the amount of debt or repayment schedule changes. *See* §11.2.9

RPI swap *See* inflation swap.

Rule 144a SEC provisions that allow trading in bond private placements with QIBs. *See* §9.4.3

SAFETEA-LU The U.S. Safe, Accountable, Flexible, Efficient Transportation Equity Act: A Legacy for Users of 2005, which extended the support offered by TIFIA (*q.v.*) for PPP projects. *See* §3.5

SCUT *Sem Cobrança ao Utilizador* ('without payment by the user'), the Portuguese system of Shadow Tolls. *See* §2.3; §2.7; §13.4.5

SEC Securities and Exchange Commission (of the United States), which regulates the investment markets. *See* §9.4.3

secondary investors Investors who invest in the Project Company after Financial Close (usually in the early years of the operation phase), purchasing their shares from the primary investors. *See* §7.2.2

Senior Lenders Lenders whose debt service comes before debt service on mezzanine or subordinated debt, or Distributions, and who are repaid first in a liquidation of the Project Company. *See* §9.6; §12.6

sensitivities Variations on the Base Case assuming a worse than expected outcome for the project. *See* §10.3.6

Separability The question whether the Service Fees for a PFI-Model project are identifiably split between capital and operating costs for the project; if so the PPP may have to be shown on the public-sector balance sheet. *See* §5.5.4

Service Availability Date The date on which construction of the Facility is complete and it meets the requirements to begin providing the services under the PPP Contract. *See* §6.1

Service Commencement Date *See* Service Availability Date.

service concession The term used in European Union law for a Franchise.

Service Fees Payments under the PPP Contract, *i.e.* tolls or other user payments (for a Concession) or payments by the Public Authority (for the PFI Model). *See* Chapter 13

SFF EIB's Structured Finance Facility, under which it assumes various additional project risks. *See* §17.4.4

Shadow Tolls Tolls based on usage of the Facility, but payable by the Public Authority rather than users (*cf.* real tolls). *See* §13.4.5

Shareholder Agreement An agreement between Sponsors relating to their investment in and management of the Project Company. *See* §7.6.2

SIBs   State Infrastructure Banks, established in the United States, *inter alia* to support PPP projects. *See* §3.5; §17.4.2

site risks   Risks related to the acquisition or condition of the project site. *See* §14.5; §15.2.4

site-legacy risk   The risk of pre-existing contamination on the project site. *See* §14.5.4

SOC   Social Overhead Capital, the Korean term for public infrastructure. *See* §3.8.1

social infrastructure   Public infrastructure required to sustain society, such as schools, hospitals and prisons; *cf.* economic infrastructure. *See* §1.2

Soft FM   Services connected with the Facility such as cleaning, catering and security. *See* §13.2; §14.8.5

soft infrastructure   Provision of public services such as street cleaning or social services. *See* §1.2

SoPC   *Standardisation of PFI Contracts*, the British standard form contract for PPPs. *See* §3.4.1

SPE   Special-purpose entity; *see* SPV.

Spens clause   The British term for a make-whole clause (*q.v.*).

Sponsors   The investors who bid for, develop and lead the project through their investment in the Project Company. *See* §7.2.1

SPV   Special-Purpose Vehicle, a legal entity with no activity other than those connected with its borrowing. *See* §7.6.1

State Aid   EU rules against public subsidies which distort competition. *See* §5.2.1

Step-In   The right, under the Direct Agreement with the Public Authority, for the lenders to take over management of the Project Company to protect their security; *cf.* Emergency Step-In, Substitution. *See* §15.4.2

STPR   Social time preference rate, the rate which private investors expect to receive

for foregoing present consumption in favour of future consumption, which may be used as the PSDR. *See* §5.2.3

Subcontract   A contract between the Project Company and a third party, providing for performance of part of the Project Company's obligations under the PPP Contract; *cf.* Construction Subcontract; FM Subcontracts. *See* §1.4.2; §6.5.2; §14.2

Subcontractor   The party signing a Subcontract with the Project Company.

subordinated debt   Debt provided by investors whose debt service is paid after amounts due to Senior Lenders, but before payment of dividends; *cf.* mezzanine debt. *See* §7.3.3

subrogation   Right of an insurer or guarantor to take over an asset on which an insurance claim or guarantee has been paid. *See* §12.4.8

sub-sovereign risk   Risk specific to a Public Authority other than the central government. *See* §14.8.3

Substitution   The right, under the Direct Agreement with the Public Authority, for the lenders to substitute a new entity to take over the Project Company's rights and obligations under the PPP Contract. *See* §15.4.2

sukuk bond   A bond based on Islamic principles, with the return based on the underlying business of the borrower rather than interest payment. *See* §9.4.3

swap provider   A bank providing an interest-rate or inflation swap to the Project Company. *See* §11.2.2; §12.6.1

syndication   The process by which the Lead Arrangers reduce their underwriting by placing part of the loan with other banks. *See* §9.3.6

T/A   The lenders' Technical Adviser. *See* §9.3.4

Tail   The period between the scheduled final repayment of the debt and the end of the PPP Contract. *See* §10.5.4

target repayments   A flexible repayment structure to allow for temporary cash-flow deficiencies. *See* §10.5.5

Tariff   Payments under a PPA, or similar contract, consisting of an Availability Charge and a Usage Charge. *See* §1.4.2

TENs   Trans-European Networks, the EU's programme for improving infrastructure between member countries. *See* §17.4.4

term   Duration of the PPP Contract, or the period until the final repayment date of the debt.

term sheet   Heads of terms for the project-finance debt. *See* §9.3.5

Termination Sum   The compensation payable by Public Authority for the early termination of the PPP Contract. *See* §15.5–§15.10

Third-Party Liability insurance Insurance against damage or injury caused to third parties by construction or operation of the Facility. *See* §12.4.2; §12.4.3; §15.2.4

third-party revenues   The ability for the Project Company to generate revenues other than those from users or the Public Authority. *See* §2.9.6; §13.7

TIFIA   The U.S. Transportation Infrastructure Finance and Innovation Act of 1998, which offers federal co-financing for PPP projects. *See* §3.5

Tripartite Deed   *See* Direct Agreement.

turnkey contract   A contract with single-point responsibility for design, engineering, procurement of any equipment, and construction. *See* §2.6.1; §2.9.3; §14.6.1

Unavailability   A period when the Facility is not Available.

Underpinned Funding   Guaranteed repayment by the Public Authority of a minimum proportion of the Project Company's debt; *cf. Cession de Créance. See* §15.5.7

Unitary Charge   A term for Service Fees under a PFI-Model PPP Contract. *See* §5.5.4

Unitary Payment   *See* Unitary Charge.

unsolicited proposals   Proposals for a PPP made without any tender request from the Public Authority. *See* §6.4.7

unwind cost   *See* breakage cost.

Usage Charge   The variable-charge element of a Tariff, payable when a plant is used, *e.g.* for power generation, intended to cover costs which vary with usage such as fuel; not normally a separate element in Service Fees; *cf.* Availability Charge, Unitary Charge. *See* §1.4.2

Variable Charge   *See* Usage Charge.

variable costs   Project Company costs subject to inflation. *See* §11.3.1

variation bonds   Additional bonds which can be issued after Financial Close, to fund future capex, subject to certain conditions. *See* §9.5; §15.2.1

VAT   Value-Added Tax. *See* §10.3.2

VfM   Value for money, the combination of risk transfer, whole-life cost and service provided by the Facility, as a basis for deciding what offers the best value to the Public Authority. *See* §2.6; §5.3

vpd   Vehicles per day.

WACC   Weighted average cost of capital, the weighted average of the costs of a company's equity and debt funding. *See* §7.3.1

warranty period   The period after the Service Availability Date during which the Construction Subcontractor continues to be liable for defects in construction. *See* §14.7.1

Waterfall   *See* Cascade.

willingness to pay   The willingness and ability of users of a Concession to pay the tolls or other usage fees required by the Concessionaire; *cf.* Affordability. *See* §13.4.1

windfall gains   Politically-sensitive profits made by investors in PPPs from high returns on investment, debt refinancing or sale of their investment. *See* §2.13; §7.3.2; §16.2–§16.5

winner's curse   The winning bidder taking too optimistic a view of traffic or other usage risks for a Concession. *See* §13.4.3; §14.8.1

withholding tax   Taxes deducted before paying interest or dividends to overseas investors or lenders. *See* §7.6.1; §10.4.2

working capital   The amount of funding required for operating and financing costs incurred before receipt of revenues. *See* §10.3.2

works concession   The term used in EU law for a Concession.

World Bank   International Bank for Reconstruction and Development, an IFI providing finance to governments (or to the private sector *via* IFC). *See* §17.4.3

wrapped bonds   Bonds guaranteed by a monoline-insurance company. *See* §9.4.4

WTO   World Trade Organisation.